ABERDEEN'S GOLDEN ERA

KEVIN STIRLING

ABERDEEN'S GOLDEN ERA

The Sir Alex Ferguson Years

pitch

First published by Pitch Publishing, 2024

Pitch Publishing
9 Donnington Park,
85 Birdham Road,
Chichester, West Sussex,
PO20 7AJ
www.pitchpublishing.co.uk
info@pitchpublishing.co.uk

A CIP catalogue record is available for this book from the British Library.

ISBN 978 1 80150 756 1

FSC www.fsc.org MIX Paper | Supporting responsible forestry FSC® C013056

Printed and bound in the UK on FSC® certified paper in line with our continuing commitment to ethical business practices, sustainability and the environment.

Typesetting and origination by Pitch Publishing
Printed and bound in Great Britain by TJ Books, Padstow

Contents

To my family; my wife of 39 years, Bernadette, my son Kevin and his partner Ciara. To Joanne and partner Gordon who have made me a proud Papa with the brilliant Jacob and Olivia, our two beautiful grandchildren.

Foreword by Willie Garner

FIRSTLY, I was both delighted and honoured to have been asked by Kevin to contribute the foreword for his sixth book, *Aberdeen's Golden Era*. I've known Kevin for many years, and have shared stories and experiences, in a small way, to several of his previous publications, so to now be asked to contribute to a book that captures our club's finest decade, I am 'chuffed'.

Looking back to Sir Alex's time as manager, I was lucky enough to have been involved in many of the successes – as a player when we won the league in 1980, and as his assistant manager in the mid-80s.

Putting these words down on paper has certainly brought back some memories of great games, trophies won and fantastic team-mates, who have gone on to be legends of Aberdeen Football Club. I am sure, in reading Kevin's work, with his attention to detail, this book will resonate with Dons supporters old and new.

Our club created so many memories during the '80s, and Kevin has managed to capture them through his excellent research and knowledge of 'his team' and also through the words of the former players and people involved with Aberdeen FC and the fans at that time.

Winning league titles, Scottish Cups, the League Cup (which was Sir Alex's one and only success in that particular tournament) and of course 1983, when Aberdeen were 'champions of Europe', created so much excitement for Dons fans, and Kevin has captured the feelings from many legends who were involved.

Only last year, the club and the city celebrated 40 years since the Dons were crowned 'champions of Europe', and the stories from those heady days have been brilliantly captured by Kevin.

The '80s also included many talented local youngsters, along with a core of top senior players who were all integral to the success of that marvellous period. Capturing their feelings of excitement, pride and success will have taken them back to those glory days. It is a period that remains so important to the club and support.

Since 2002, when his first book, *A Centenary History*, was published, Kevin has meticulously documented and charted through the history of Aberdeen FC for many years, and I am sure, with his latest publication, you will enjoy, like myself, reminiscing and once again celebrating Aberdeen's golden era.

Willie Garner
August 2024

Introduction

ABERDEEN FOOTBALL Club has been defined by what the club achieved in the '80s. It was a period in Scottish football that brought change, some enforced, some self-inflicted. The decade began with a new force in the domestic game. Aberdeen, against the odds, won the Premier League. It was a success that was not only welcomed in the north-east of Scotland but for neutrals and fair-minded observers; any side winning the title outside of Glasgow was only seen as good for the game. It had been 15 years since Kilmarnock stunned Hearts in 1965 to win the league on the final day of the season. While the Aberdeen success in 1980 was not as dramatic, it was as stunning. Defeating Celtic in Glasgow twice in the closing weeks of the season then dismantling Hibernian in Edinburgh brought a first championship since 1955. While that triumph highlighted all that was good in the Scottish game, a week later at Hampden Park, the riots that followed the conclusion of the Scottish Cup Final were a stark reminder of the toxic state of football in Glasgow. With Celtic and Rangers bringing shame to the country, the repercussions were long-lasting. Reputational damage apart, the financial implications affected all Scottish clubs.

For Aberdeen it was an opportunity. With the Glasgow clubs failing to rise above mediocrity and their unsavoury obsession with each other, the time was right for a new, dynamic force in Scotland. Free from any sectarian baggage, Aberdeen were better-placed than any other at that time. With several experienced international players established at Pittodrie, they were supplemented by a clutch of the finest youngsters who ever came through the ranks at the club. The spark that ignited Aberdeen was Alex Ferguson, not that many thought that at the time. After being dismissed by St Mirren, Ferguson was appointed in the summer of 1978 and so a remarkable period in Aberdeen FC history began.

It was perhaps ironic that the Aberdeen success story was, in part, made in Glasgow. Celtic's greatest captain, Billy McNeill, laid the foundations in 1977/78 before his great rival – and former Rangers forward – Ferguson took over. There was little to suggest that Ferguson was on the cusp of great success after a difficult and troubled first season. Ferguson was in managerial terms still very young and inexperienced at the top level in Scottish football. What he did have in abundance was a burning desire to succeed, motivated perhaps by his playing career and his acrimonious departure from St Mirren. As a player he failed to land a major honour despite being a prolific scorer for St Johnstone and Dunfermline. His playing days with Rangers effectively ended after he was blamed for not picking up Billy McNeill in the 1969 Scottish Cup Final, as the Gers were demolished by Celtic. There was also the controversial sectarian policy adopted by the Ibrox club whereby they would refuse to sign Catholics. That discrimination, and his experience at St Mirren, fuelled Alex Ferguson to succeed at Pittodrie. The perfect storm.

Before the Dons' Premier League success in 1980, there was pain, and plenty of it. Two League Cup Final defeats in 1979 were hard to take. Losing to Rangers in March in controversial circumstances when Doug Rougvie was sent off after Derek Johnstone had feigned injury further soured relations between the clubs. In December that year, after another change in the format, Aberdeen lost out to Dundee United. After dominating the Hampden final, the Dons were beaten in a Dens Park replay. It was an experience that Ferguson and his players did not want to go through again. The manager told his players there would be no repeat. Aberdeen never lost another final under Ferguson.

In 1983, of course, Aberdeen became the third and last Scottish club to win a European trophy, and the first to win two European titles. That unforgettable night in Gothenburg is without doubt the pinnacle of the club's achievements. In European terms, the name Real Madrid has that magic; perennial winners in the formative years of the European Cup, the Spanish side were, and still are, European royalty. It is well documented that Madrid have not suffered defeat in a knockout European competition final since that fateful night in Sweden. That occasion was the classic David and Goliath clash. Aberdeen had only progressed past the second round in European competition for the first time in 1981. Two years later they were facing six-time European Cup winners Real Madrid in their first European final. What was more remarkable to many was that Aberdeen fully deserved to win. Those opinions were not shared within Pittodrie. Once Alex Ferguson had seen Real Madrid in their semi-final, he was convinced his Aberdeen side had an outstanding opportunity.

In the rain-lashed Ullevi stadium, Aberdeen mastered Madrid, followed by the 15,000-strong Red Army and the thousands watching the game back home. It is a success that has been rightly revered by the club and supporters over the decades, much to the chagrin of opponents. Make no mistake, that victory 'sticks in the craw' of opposition fans. We knew it at the time and over many years it has proved an achievement that other clubs of similar standing in Scotland can only dream of.

European football for Scottish clubs is the yardstick for success. For some context, Aberdeen have played 158 European ties, ahead of Dundee United and Hibernian who have managed just over 100 each. It was during the Ferguson era that the Dons played no fewer than 47 European ties, more than Dundee, Kilmarnock, Motherwell, St Johnstone and St Mirren have played in their entire history. For those clubs, competing in Europe is a bonus; for Aberdeen it is essential. Anything less is seen as a failure at Pittodrie.

The Ferguson era brought a period in Aberdeen FC history that will never be forgotten by those lucky enough to have experienced it. A generation later, the stories and memories of the older Dons fans can be recalled as they wax lyrical on a team and manager that came together to not only dominate the game in Scotland but conquer Europe. That seven-year period encapsulated all that is good about Scottish football. A team, outside of the Glasgow establishment, had the audacity to not only get the better of them, but to rub their collective noses in it. Never before or since has such a prolonged period of success had such a profound effect on the game in Scotland. Who knows what social media would have made of Aberdeen in 1983? Certainly, it would have caused a meltdown in the west. We will never know, but on 11 May in every passing year dozens of 'Gothenburg Day' tweets and posts appear, just to make sure that wonderful success will never be forgotten. As it should be.

Kevin Stirling
July 2024

1

All Roads Lead to Pittodrie

THERE IS no doubt that the Aberdeen job remains one of the more sought after and prestigious managerial positions in Scotland. Certainly, in the '70s Aberdeen had attracted Ally MacLeod, Billy McNeill and Alex Ferguson. MacLeod was only in charge for 18 months before the SFA came calling and asked him to take over as Scotland manager in June 1977. McNeill's reign was shorter; just one season before he was tempted back to Celtic, where he had been their most successful captain in their history.

The Aberdeen board of directors had remained unchanged for several years. The promotion of coach Jim Bonthrone to manager in 1971 on the eve of the season as Eddie Turnbull joined Hibernian had failed. The former East Fife player had excelled as a coach on the training field, but he was always at his best under the more streetwise Turnbull, whose hardline approach had brought success to Aberdeen with the Scottish Cup coming north in April 1970. Bonthrone was a more genial character and ultimately that 'soft' approach was to cost him his job. Aberdeen were known at that time for rarely parting company with managers. Previously only Tommy Pearson was essentially shown the door after a succession of poor results. That trend alone made the role a highly desirable position. While Bonthrone may have been the first Aberdeen manager who had 'lost the dressing room', for Pearson his fate was sealed when he lost the confidence of the directors.

The official statement from the club on Bonthrone confirmed it was a mutual agreement, but the reality was very different. Aberdeen were near the foot of the new Premier League and player unrest was rife. Proof of that came on 13 September 1975 in a home clash with Dundee United. Centre-half Willie Young was no shrinking violet and not one for holding anything back. When he was substituted in the second half, he took his shirt off and threw it towards the home dugout before walking towards the changing room. Young never played for the club again and was sold to Tottenham Hotspur in a £125,000 deal some weeks later. Bonthrone became the first Aberdeen manager to be removed by the club. It was clear the directors looked at the team's position in what was now a cut-throat elite Premier League. The Scottish leagues went through the most radical changes in 1974. The 18-team First Division would be replaced by the top-ten Premier League, with two further divisions being formed; the First and Second. The thinking was that it would end meaningless fixtures towards the end of a season. That was most certainly achieved but perhaps, initially at the expense of better-quality football.

What had been overlooked in those changes was that the top division would still see two of the ten clubs being automatically relegated. That casualty rate was never going to endure but clubs were mindful that any demotion could be financially catastrophic. Aberdeen were no different and as the club had never been relegated in their history the directors were keen to maintain that proud record.

The board had been keen to appoint a younger, hungry manager with potential. That was probably down to the success of Eddie Turnbull. The former Hibernian icon was cutting his coaching teeth with Queen's Park when Aberdeen brought him north in March 1965. Turnbull totally changed the mindset at Pittodrie, 'Once I had cleared the whisky bottles from the boardroom,' he famously said some years later. His acumen in the transfer market had brought the club into profit and silverware followed. The Turnbull blueprint was one that fitted well with the directors. Chairman Dick Donald was always keen to balance the books and was loath to put the club in the red. His prudence may have infuriated supporters at times but on reflection his legacy was one of stability and ultimate success at home and in Europe.

Aberdeen turned to Ally MacLeod in November 1975 as he joined from fellow Premier League strugglers Ayr United. MacLeod had been a success at Somerset Park since joining Ayr in 1966. He guided them back to the top flight and reached the semi-finals of both domestic cup competitions. That relative success with a smaller club was noted at Pittodrie and his knowledge of the lower leagues was important given that Aberdeen were quite frugal when it came to paying out transfer fees. Knowledge of the Scottish game would have been all over the MacLeod CV and his infectious character was, at that time, exactly what Aberdeen needed. MacLeod recalled his move to Pittodrie, which was certainly reflective of the Scottish game back in the '70s:

'The Aberdeen chairman, Dick Donald, did not beat about the bush about the Aberdeen job and what I would be taking on. "We have a terrible team, but there is £100,000 and more available if you want to buy players." That was the kind of ambitious talk I could never hear at Ayr. Quite apart from the substantial amount of cash available, I was excited by the setup in Aberdeen. It was not a part of the country I knew well, but I immediately took to the people and realised the potential of the club. The region had a huge catchment area with supporters' clubs all over the north and east. The area was also caught up in the prosperous North Sea oil boom. Everything seemed to be in place for a successful football team.'

However, the MacLeod era was almost derailed at the end of the 1975/76 season. He took a gamble on his team seeing out what had been a disappointing inaugural Premier League campaign. There was some merit in that risk; although Aberdeen had been in and around the lower reaches of the new setup, they did defeat both Celtic and Rangers in a week. While those results were welcome, they also disguised a side that was fragile in confidence and lacking quality. MacLeod decided to wait to strengthen his squad until after the end-of-March deadline – his frugal habits at Ayr were hard to forget. Back then there were no transfer windows; players could be bought and sold at any stage of the season. However, if any signing was made after 31 March of any season, they would not be able to play in any senior competitive game for the remainder of the campaign. MacLeod gambled on his side being able to retain their status in the top division and then have a real go at it the following year. He was mindful that players bought after the transfer deadline would be obtained at better value. His only signing who was eligible to play was Ian Fleming, a £15,000 capture from Kilmarnock. As the Dons' struggle for survival went down to the final day (only a nerve-wracking 3-0 win over Hibernian confirmed their status), sitting in the Main Stand were Joe Harper and Dom Sullivan, both signed but ineligible to play.

While Bonthrone was the more reserved manager, MacLeod was the opposite – boldly claiming that he would bring silverware to Aberdeen within 18 months. Given the club's plight at the time that seemed ambitious at best, almost to the point of ridicule from some of the national press. MacLeod was of course to endure more prolonged, brutal scrutiny when he managed Scotland, but true to his word he did bring success to Aberdeen when the Dons defeated Celtic to win the League Cup in 1976. The MacLeod era, brief as it was, certainly caught the imagination of the supporters and brought a vibrancy and enthusiasm in contrast to the end of the Bonthrone reign.

With Turnbull and MacLeod both winning silverware and helping balance the books, it was no surprise that Aberdeen turned to Billy McNeill when MacLeod accepted the Scotland role. McNeill had been a legend with his beloved Celtic, captaining them through the most successful period in their history. His retirement after the 1975 Scottish Cup Final surprised many observers as he was only 35 years old. After coaching the Celtic youngsters, he was appointed Clyde manager in April 1977. His time at Shawfield was brief, barely two months and 11 games when he was approached to take over at Pittodrie.

McNeill was appointed on 14 June 1977, promising to give the job everything, telling the *Evening Express* on his first day, 'I will give the supporters excitement, entertainment and success. I will take my time to get to know the players that are here.' McNeill was keen to be a 'tracksuit manager' and form a close relationship with the players. On his appointment he was making all the right noises in terms of gaining favour with the support: 'Every player will get the chance to prove themselves.' With training due to start on 11 July and friendly games to arrange, McNeill had little time to waste and with European football to look forward to it was a challenge that the new boss was relishing: 'Playing in Europe is very important and it is a real bonus for me to be with a club that is in Europe. I have experience of European football and I am looking forward to getting back into that level of competition.'

The general belief in Scottish football was that McNeill would see the Aberdeen job as a prelude for his eventual return to Celtic.

Aberdeen captain Willie Miller recalled the appointment of McNeill, 'When we first met, he was clearly a man to respect. However, I felt I had to prove myself all over again and prove I was worthy of retaining the club captaincy. Billy had his doubts, with my distinct dislike for training creating a real problem. He felt that as captain I should throw myself 100 per cent into running around the park and into the dreaded press-ups. That was never going to happen. As for the training he was aghast that the players scattered after training and did not eat together at the club. Billy, quite rightly, thought it better we eat together and arranged for a local hotelier to deliver food each day after training. We sat down together over our meal and would discuss all things football. It was an important, yet simple, step towards improving eating habits and it developed camaraderie.'

One aspect that McNeill did find daunting was to follow the public relations expertise of Ally MacLeod. Both were ideally suited to management in the new Premier League era and while McNeill carried the stature of being one of Scotland's greatest ever players, he did not have the charisma of MacLeod, whose tenure at Pittodrie was a roller coaster of emotions. McNeill was mindful of the MacLeod influence on the club, 'I am aware of what Ally brought to Aberdeen, but I am my own man. I will be very happy to meet the fans and to get involved in the city. Supporters are the lifeblood of this club and they will always get my full support.' Looking ahead, McNeill was in full agreement with the changes in Scottish football and the implementation of the new Premier League. 'We needed change, but it would have been lucky if the changes were all ideal. I feel that ten clubs are still a bit too small, with little room for error. We need to encourage attacking football, but I suspect the new setup will see clubs becoming more cautious.'

McNeill carried a presence and dignity that commanded respect. His playing career was highly successful, from becoming the first British captain to lift the European Cup to leading his Celtic side to consecutive league titles. While MacLeod had to earn respect, for McNeill his stature in the game ensured his switch to a bigger club was relatively seamless.

There were no bold claims from McNeill ahead of what was ultimately his one season at Pittodrie. There was little doubt that the basis of a very good side was already in place. Keeper Bobby Clark was the senior statesman having been at Pittodrie since 1965, and was the Dons' most-capped player. In defence Stuart Kennedy and Willie Miller were both Scotland internationals with their better days ahead of them. Kennedy had been a MacLeod signing, the right-back joining from Falkirk in a £25,000 deal in 1976. Miller was emerging as a player of great ability, having been at Aberdeen since 1971, and was one of the best 'sweepers' in British football. The experience of Joe Harper and Drew Jarvie was vital for McNeill, who was also keen to add to his squad.

Any doubts about McNeill's commitment to Aberdeen were dispelled on the opening day of the 1977/78 season. A new-look, expensively assembled Rangers side visited Pittodrie and were humbled by Aberdeen in a 3-1 defeat. McNeill took the opportunity to endear himself to the Pittodrie faithful by appearing before kick-off, resplendent in a red shirt as he applauded the supporters. For any Aberdeen manager, any win over bitter rivals Rangers would bring plaudits, and time.

McNeill was left furious after the Dons went out of the UEFA Cup when they were defeated at Pittodrie by RWD Molenbeek. After a 0-0 draw in Belgium, hopes were high of progress but in what was a classic European away performance the Dons were beaten 2-1. They never looked like breaking down a tough, organised defence who hit on the break to great effect. It was after that exit that McNeill persuaded the board to open the purse strings. McNeill identified a flame-haired young midfielder at Dundee as his prime target. A certain Gordon Strachan was no stranger to Aberdeen fans; he was the influence that helped Dundee shock the Dons in a Scottish Cup replay at Pittodrie the previous season. Strachan was one of the most sought-after players in the country, but Dundee were reluctant to let him go. The Dens Park outfit, however, had been one of the bigger clubs that had suffered financially when they were relegated from the first Premier League in 1976. A deal was finally agreed as Aberdeen paid Dundee £40,000 for Strachan. As part of the deal Jim Shirra, another MacLeod signing, went the other way.

In an era when there were no transfer windows, McNeill strengthened his attacking options by going back to Clyde to take Steve Archibald to Pittodrie in January 1978. The former car mechanic had emerged as a midfielder at Shawfield, but McNeill saw his future as a striker and he soon developed a prolific partnership with Joe Harper.

For Aberdeen and McNeill, season 1977/78 will go down as a period of bitter disappointment and frustration. The Dons were the only side to make sure the title race was no formality as they pushed Rangers all the way, taking the outcome of the Premier League until the final week. There was controversy along the way. There was little doubt that the Dons' pressure on Rangers was beginning to see cracks in the Ibrox armoury, and 25 February proved a significant turning point. Rangers' visit to Motherwell saw the home side, resurrected under new boss Roger Hynd, cruise into a two-goal lead. With Aberdeen defeating Hibernian 3-0 at Pittodrie the stage seemed set for a title showdown between the sides at Ibrox the following week.

However, the away fans that day had other ideas. Not for the first time, a sizeable travelling support began to chant, 'There's going to be a riot.' True to their word, several hundred visiting fans spilled on to the pitch and surrounded the Motherwell players and officials. After a lengthy delay the intrusion clearly affected the home players and Rangers went on to rescue the game. Rangers supporters had prior indiscretions; like Newcastle and Barcelona in previous visits. The SFA felt it appropriate to take a stand on their behaviour and recommended that the game be replayed. The Scottish League refused that plea and instead issued a paltry £2,000 fine on the Ibrox club. The outrage from Aberdeen and other Scottish clubs was palpable. The general feeling of any fairness was lost as a replayed game was the favoured outcome by most observers. As it turned out the cost of a Premier League title was cheap at the price; Rangers went on to win the league by two points.

As runners-up in the league, what proved to be McNeill's final game was the Scottish Cup Final against bitter rivals Rangers. Aberdeen went into the Hampden clash on the back of a 23-match unbeaten run which came to a halt in the Hampden sun in a game that will be remembered as the day the Dons froze. Failing to come close to their previous heights they went down 2-1, their goal summing up their afternoon perfectly. A freak mishit from defender Steve Ritchie deceived Rangers keeper Peter McCloy in the closing minutes to offer a glimmer of hope. It was not to be and on reflection it was a huge opportunity missed. Earlier in the season Aberdeen had beaten Rangers 3-1, 4-0 and 3-0 in the league. A crestfallen McNeill ended his short spell at Pittodrie without a trophy.

With Celtic struggling to make any impact in the league and the domestic cups, the Parkhead club were in turmoil and under pressure from their critical support, they turned to McNeill to resurrect their fortunes. For the fourth time in the 1970s Aberdeen were looking for a new manager.

Dick Donald took a call on the morning of 26 May from Celtic, who intimated that they were going to offer McNeill the opportunity to take over from Jock Stein at Parkhead.

McNeill later stated the decision to leave was far from straightforward. The Celtic legend declared the job of managing Aberdeen and watching his family settle in the area made the decision to go more difficult. Aberdeen as a club and city was far removed from the west, still steeped in political and religious differences. McNeill touched on how life in Aberdeen was very different from what he had been familiar with in his playing career.

With so many managerial changes at the club in the 1970s, it was no surprise the playing staff had evolved in a relatively short period. By the time McNeill left, however, the nucleus of the Aberdeen side that was to prevail in the next decade was beginning to emerge. The experienced Bobby Clark was highly thought of within the game and commanded respect. In reserve, young keepers Jim Leighton and John Gardiner were embarking on their senior professional careers. Leighton had been called up in 1976 and was farmed out to Highland League side Deveronvale. Several clubs had been keen to sign him, none more so than Celtic, but it was Aberdeen scout Bobby Calder who once again brought some of the best young players from the west of Scotland to Pittodrie. Leighton recalled signing for the Dons and the good feeling he had about it, 'It had been my experience that you know very quickly whether you are going to enjoy being at any club. I had that feeling from the moment I first walked through the door at Pittodrie and it never wore off.'

In defence, Willie Miller was the leader and captain and after being capped for Scotland in 1976 for the first time he was established as one of the best defenders in Britain. Stuart Kennedy at right-back was another Scotland international; he, Miller, Clark and Joe Harper were all included in the Scotland World Cup squad that went to Argentina in 1978. Willie Garner and Doug Rougvie had been at Pittodrie for several years, both before the arrival of Ally MacLeod. Alex McLeish arrived at Pittodrie in 1976. Signed from Glasgow United by MacLeod, McLeish was farmed out to Lewis United, a local Aberdeen Junior side, in his early career. It was under McNeill that McLeish made a surprise debut against Dundee United in the new year fixture at Pittodrie. Regular centre-half Garner and left-back Bobby Glennie broke a festive club curfew and were dropped ahead of the game.

John McMaster had been at Pittodrie since 1972 but was still to command a regular place in the side; perhaps it was McLeish's versatility that delayed his progress. The former Port Glasgow player had been tried in a variety of roles from full-back to midfield and even as a left-winger by McNeill following Arthur Graham's departure to Leeds United in 1977.

McNeill had signed Gordon Strachan, Steve Archibald, Ian Scanlon and Steve Ritchie and gave debuts to youngsters Andy Watson, Alex McLeish and Bobby Glennie. Strachan and Archibald were to prove outstanding signings and would play a major part in the Aberdeen success. McLeish was still an emerging talent but even at this early stage of his career he was being touted as a future Scotland captain. It can be argued that only Ritchie, a £15,000 buy from Hereford, was a moderate signing at best and his Pittodrie career can best be parcelled up in that crazy last-minute goal in the 1978 Scottish Cup Final. On a day that Aberdeen would like to forget, it was Ritchie's mis-hit 'lob' that dropped into the net with Rangers keeper McCloy hanging on to the crossbar. On a comedy level it was right up there. For Aberdeen supporters though, it was no laughing matter.

While Archibald was set for a great future in the game, the Dons still had the striking pair of Drew Jarvie and Joe Harper. Both were club record signings in 1969 (Harper £40,000 from Morton and Jarvie £72,000 from Airdrie). Dave Robb had been at Pittodrie since 1965 and was another forward whose best years were behind him. It was clear that the squad McNeill left was strong and experienced. However, there would have to be changes made; its average age had to be reduced. Of the 27 players who made appearances in 1977/78, 14 of them would soon find their futures away from Pittodrie. Those decisions would be taken by the new manager.

Before Ally MacLeod left the club in 1977 to take over as Scotland coach, his recommendation to the directors was to go for Alex Ferguson who was a young, aspiring manager with St Mirren. The Paisley club had been in the doldrums in recent years but under Ferguson they were back in the top division after winning the First Division title in 1977. Ferguson remembered the call from MacLeod, 'Ally phoned me before he joined up with the Scotland squad to see if I fancied being his successor at Pittodrie. Like an idiot, I replied that I wanted to build St Mirren into an Aberdeen and therefore must turn down the offer with sincere thanks. Later I would understand that there are fundamental distinctions of scale that apply to football clubs.'

With McNeill leaving, the directors were again left frustrated that another promising manager was tempted away from Pittodrie. Eddie Turnbull left on the eve of the 1971/72 season to go back to Hibernian, where he was part of their legendary 'Famous Five' forward line of the 1950s. The departure of Jim Bonthrone in 1975 was just as disappointing but necessary. It was the loss of MacLeod and McNeill, however, after their brief spells that had at one stage suggested the board would head in another direction. It was perhaps the fact that Alex Ferguson was now available, and any appointment would be relatively straightforward to negotiate.

It was on 4 May 1978 that St Mirren held a private board meeting away from their ground at the Excelsior Hotel near Glasgow Airport. It was at that meeting that the Paisley club's directors decided to sack Ferguson. The decision to announce his departure was delayed until the end of May to allow a fifth board member to return from holiday. The decision stunned the St Mirren support and Scottish football. Ferguson had always been very much a 'hands-on' manager, involved in just about every aspect of running a club. There was no doubt that St Mirren as a club were happy with what he had achieved with the team and getting the club back to a healthy position in the Premier League. As so often happens, the rumour mill in Scottish football was in full flow.

Why would they dispense with a manager who had achieved so much? There had to be compelling reasons and due to the silence from both manager and club there was no shortage of colourful reasons for his departure. There were some claims of financial impropriety. Payments to trialists and possible missing tax payments were mentioned at the time, without foundation. The most likely reason was the toxic relationship Alex Ferguson had with St Mirren chairman Willie Todd. Ever since local businessman Todd arrived at Love Street, Ferguson had never taken to him. As the 1977/78 season was ending Ferguson and Todd were no longer speaking. Todd announced he was becoming a full-time chairman, which made Ferguson more concerned. Those concerns came to fruition with a series of interventions on football matters from Todd. For someone who had adopted such a hands-on approach to the club, there was a clear issue between the chairman and manager.

For a manager who had revived St Mirren's fortunes in such a relatively short space of time, it was hard on Ferguson. When he arrived at Paisley, gates were low, averaging 1,500 each week with the club languishing at the foot of the old Second Division. The St Mirren board were desperate to improve their position with the new three-league setup coming into being in 1975. They had to avoid dropping down to the third tier and told Ferguson to achieve that with little or no playing budget. Ferguson had no option but to turn to youth and history will tell you he was a master at developing younger players. St Mirren were fortunate enough to bring through the likes of Frank McGarvey and Billy Stark and the most money Ferguson paid out was £10,000 for Dundee United defender Jackie Copland. His toughest task was to release no fewer than 18 of the 32-man squad at Love Street in his first season.

When it was announced that Ferguson had been dismissed by the Buddies, there was genuine anger among the Paisley support. While it hurt at the time, looking back it was perhaps inevitable that Ferguson would move on. Having taken St Mirren back to a respectable position in the Premier League and with the Paisley fans now backing their club in greater numbers, it was clear that he had taken St Mirren as far as he could. With his relationship with Todd now toxic, something had to give. With Todd now full-time in his role of chairman, Ferguson accepted that his days at Love Street were coming to an end. When Ferguson was called in to a board meeting, he was shocked to learn of a list of items that Todd had put together, all claiming that he had breached the terms of his contract. Ferguson's initial reaction was to laugh it off as some of the claims were, in his view, ridiculous.

Ferguson later recalled some of the dialogue at the meeting: 'By the time the whole list was read out, I could not hold my laughter. Todd was thoroughly annoyed and asked me to stop laughing. I told him I couldn't and that I thought there was only one reason to sack a manager and that was he wasn't good at his job. I went through to my office, cleared my desk and went home. When my thoughts had settled, I was of course angry, but I had learned the lesson that my attitude to management could make me vulnerable. Even if you hated your chairman you had to find a way of getting on with it. My single-mindedness meant that I was always ready to argue my corner with Todd, but in a power struggle I had no chance. The weird experience in the St Mirren boardroom opened the way for my move to Aberdeen and for that I was always grateful.'

Ferguson was contacted by Jim Rodger of the *Daily Mirror*, one of the few journalists he trusted implicitly. Later claims about Ferguson being 'tapped' by Aberdeen emanated from the St Mirren boardroom but in the days when agents were only seen in spy films, the use of a 'third party' was a way around things. On this occasion it was Rodger who alerted Ferguson to the fact that Aberdeen were keen to speak to him. Ferguson recalled his initial contact with the Dons, 'Once I took the call there was no way I was turning the job down. Soon I was chatting on the telephone to the man who symbolised Aberdeen Football Club and who did so much for me since that day, Dick Donald. He immediately invited me to become manager at Pittodrie and invited me to come up the next day. I accepted both offers immediately.'

Aberdeen were keen to appoint a manager who would find it hard to leave. Vice-chairman Chris Anderson later recalled, 'Many people thought we were crazy to appoint Alex Ferguson. But we didn't need someone with a great record as a player; we needed a manager with a wide knowledge of the game; a top coach. That man with all the warts about him was Alex Ferguson. We had watched his progress with St Mirren, observed his huge vitality and realised that although he had ended up fighting a messy industrial tribunal with the club after he was sacked, in fact, his energy and commitment had overwhelmed them.' Anderson later explained the club's thinking on the appointment. In the '70s there were so many changes to the game in Scotland with the new Premier Division and football becoming more businesslike. Aberdeen as a city was also evolving from a rural fish and farming community to become the 'Oil Capital of Europe'. It was a seismic change and the football club was keen to play its part in the undoubted economic boom that was to follow.

Within hours of accepting the job, Alex Ferguson was making the 150-mile drive north to Aberdeen. That journey gave Ferguson the opportunity to look ahead to his new challenge, 'My thoughts were all about the club and their history. Under Eddie Turnbull they had won the Scottish Cup in 1970. Then Jimmy Bonthrone took over and what a wonderful person he was. He once told me when I was a player at Falkirk, he wanted to offer me the position of assistant manager – until I was sent off at Pittodrie after a clash with their centre-half Willie Young. That as well as my role as a radical chairman of the Players' Union managed to dissuade him. Then Ally MacLeod came and turned the whole place upside down. Ally had won the League Cup. Then a brief spell under my old adversary Billy McNeill followed.'

The appointment of Ferguson was swift. With no contracts to buy out and Ferguson agreeing terms quickly, his arrival at Pittodrie suited both the club and him. After ten minutes with

Dick Donald the deal was signed. Following that there was a lunch with Chris Anderson and within hours the new Aberdeen manager was announced in the press. A brief photo call was arranged and his first interview in the job took place as he spoke to the *Evening Express*, 'This is a club with great traditions and are respected in the game. I will take my time to assess the squad and plan a way ahead. There have been many changes at Aberdeen in recent years, so some stability is needed. Aberdeen has great potential and I will be working hard to make this club one to be not only respected but feared.'

One aspect that Ferguson touched on later in his career was the contrast in his relationship with the board from his experience with St Mirren. It was an unusual, almost unique setup. Aberdeen were run by only three directors, which in itself was rare. They were also all ex-Aberdeen players. Dick Donald, Charles Forbes and Chris Anderson were all Dons in their younger days and their connection with the club was as solid as the city granite. Ferguson would be on a far better salary than he was at St Mirren – his basic starting wage was £12,000 a year. He also received a new car worth £7,000 and an £18,000 interest-free loan to buy a new house. There were also bonus schemes worth £6,000 if Aberdeen won the Premier League and similar cash bonuses for winning the domestic cup competitions and progression in Europe.

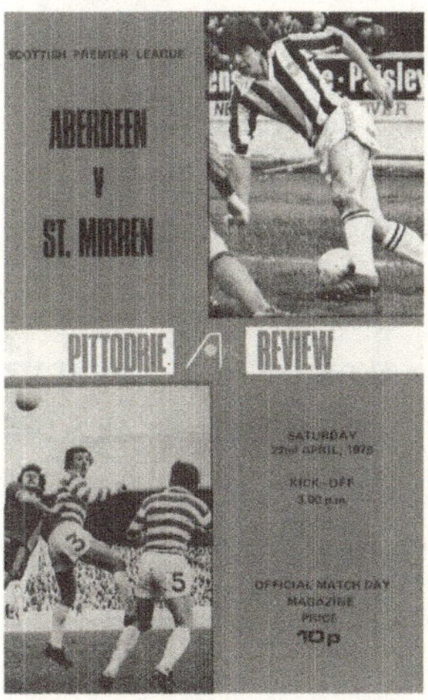

Within days Ferguson was accompanying Chris Anderson on a fact-finding trip to the USA; a three-week visit to study the commercial activities associated with the North American Soccer League. On his return a family holiday to Malta was interrupted by Ferguson watching Scotland imploding at the World Cup in Argentina and his thoughts turned to appointing an assistant at Pittodrie. His first inclination was to take Davie Provan with him from St Mirren. On reflection he thought that his and Provan's Rangers connection might be a problem, so he turned to Walter Smith at Dundee United. Smith was still only 30 and part of the United team. Ferguson had identified that Smith was an emerging coach at Tannadice under Jim McLean. His efforts to prise Smith away from McLean proved impossible so he turned to former Hibernian legend Pat Stanton. After an impressive playing career, Stanton retired and was keen to cut his teeth in coaching. Before Stanton arrived, Ferguson got familiar with Teddy Scott at Pittodrie. Scott had been a constant at the club, serving in a variety of roles. Ferguson immediately identified how important Scott was; a lifelong friendship and respect began to evolve.

Ferguson was joining Aberdeen at a time when the club were marking 75 years since their formation in 1903. The new boss was acutely aware of the history of the Dons and was desperate to make his mark. The club organised a rally at the Capitol Cinema house on Union Street to mark the occasion. On the night the arena was sold out with 2,000 turning up to see some of the greats who had graced Pittodrie down the years. Aberdeen legends from the 1920s through to the current squad were in attendance as a night of nostalgia did not go unnoticed by Ferguson. He had barely got his toes wet in his new role, so he adopted a very low-key approach to the evening, staying on the periphery of events but introducing himself to some of the Dons' finest.

As one era at Pittodrie was ending, a new chapter was just beginning.

2

Teething Troubles

THERE WAS still an air of frustration around Pittodrie following season 1977/78 when Aberdeen had gone so close to a Premier League and Scottish Cup double. Losing out to Rangers made it more difficult to accept. The almost overwhelming disappointment was parcelled up in their final 90 minutes of the season. The Scottish Cup Final defeat at Hampden was hard to bear as the Dons effectively failed to turn up on the big occasion. It was a claim that had been aimed at the club following three Scottish Cup Final defeats in the 1950s, and with only one success since then in 1970, claims of Aberdeen losing their 'bottle' gained more attention. Earlier that season in the two most recent meetings the Dons had beaten Rangers 4-0 at Pittodrie and 3-0 at Ibrox, and they went into the Hampden showdown on the back of an unbeaten run that stretched to 23 games. The final will be remembered as the day they froze. Most experts predicted a close encounter between the two best sides in Scotland at that time, but for reasons unknown the Dons as a team came nowhere near what was expected. They were backed in large numbers in the days when Hampden could house crowds in excess of 70,000, but the supporters were bitterly disappointed on what was a day to forget.

During the close-season there was substantial work carried out on the south side of Pittodrie. The bench-style seating was installed across the last part of the ground that remained uncovered. The decision to put seats in before any covering was in hindsight an error. Pittodrie by its location is regarded as one of the coldest stadiums in the country. Exposure to the elements was always better faced standing than seated. Nevertheless, the club pressed ahead and proudly announced ahead of the new season that Pittodrie had become the first major all-seated ground in Britain. This was ten years before the Taylor Report in England revolutionised stadia down south. Pittodrie was, at that stage, years ahead of its time. Ted Croker, the English FA secretary, declared, 'While Aberdeen look to have their ground all seated and all covered in the next year or two, stadiums in England are nowhere near that stage. I don't expect that to change for several years.'

On 11 July the draws for the opening rounds of European competition were made and news came through that Aberdeen would face little-known Marek Stanke Dimitrov of Bulgaria in the first round of the European Cup Winners' Cup.

Alex Ferguson was delighted with the draw as he spoke to the *Press & Journal*, 'I regard it as an ideal draw and although I do not know much about Marek yet, we will be treating them with respect. You have got to adopt a different approach when it comes to European competitions.' The tie in Bulgaria was the start of a long and memorable European experience for Ferguson. Although he was a novice in European management, he still showed enough to suggest he would learn quickly: 'It is important that we get them watched before we play them; ideally on their own patch. You can watch umpteen videos and view scouting reports, but nothing compares to watching opponents.'

Ferguson met his new players for the first time when the squad returned for pre-season training on Monday, 17 July. The training commenced at Seaton Park, a public park close to Pittodrie. The manager said, 'I was giving them their first team talk when I realised that this was the third time they had to listen to the same kind of thing in as many years. Nevertheless, we got down to work with a couple of runs around Seaton Park, to get the legs going again. I have drawn up a physical programme to suit every player and they might not be familiar with that.' After that first session Ferguson spoke to the *Press & Journal* on his hopes, 'I like ambitious people and I want ambitious players at Pittodrie. This is a club that should match ambitions of players, and if it doesn't then there is something wrong with the club. I know there is a lot of talent here, but there is a lot of work to be done. It is early days yet, but I will be using our visit to Gordonstoun to get a close look at my players.'

The private school in the north was often used by the club as part of any pre-season conditioning. On this occasion the squad would be based there and take in two friendlies against Highland League opposition. Elgin City and Buckie would face the Dons' first team as Ferguson got a first look at his squad in action. The first tests for Ferguson would come against Tottenham Hotspur and Middlesbrough, English opposition lined up for Pittodrie friendlies. Vice-chairman Chris Anderson was keen to showcase Pittodrie to a wider audience and bringing top-flight English opponents north was a common theme back then. Aberdeen had faced several English sides at Pittodrie down the years and the added 'Auld Enemy' factor always ensured that these games were anything but friendly. With the opening Premier League fixture coming against newly promoted Hearts at Tynecastle, the two matches against English opponents were crucial for Ferguson as he got a first serious look at his squad in action.

Tottenham headed north without their Argentine World Cup stars, Osvaldo Ardiles and Ricky Villa. The two major signings captured the imagination, but their clearance did not come through in time for them to make their first appearances in British football at Pittodrie. Tottenham could have done with them as Aberdeen ran out deserved 3-1 winners. An impressive start for Ferguson but he then faced his first problem after Scotland keeper Bobby Clark broke a knuckle and would be out for several weeks. Without a recognised deputy the new boss had to look to rookies Jim Leighton and John Gardiner. For the visit of Middlesbrough on 7 August, the Dons gave a half each to both young keepers. Ferguson could not make up his mind after the 3-2 win and it was after Leighton impressed more in training that the man who had been farmed out to Deveronvale in the Highland League would start for Aberdeen in their league opener in Edinburgh. Ferguson recalled, 'It was a wet day with bad conditions for goalkeepers. The ball was greasy and shooting off the surface. Leighton had an excellent game and gave a superb display of handling. He also proved to be brave and strong and after the match there was no doubt this was a goalkeeper of the future.'

Despite losing an early goal the Dons showed their class by taming an energetic if frantic home side, buoyed by their recent promotion. As Leighton inspired at the other end, Hearts keeper Dunlop let a tame effort from Steve Archibald slip past him. It set the tone for a good afternoon for Aberdeen and the opening-day win that Ferguson craved.

Expectations were high at Pittodrie. It was something that the new boss was acutely aware of and getting off to a positive start was vital. If Aberdeen under Alex Ferguson were to improve on the previous season, then a major success would need to be secured. The immediate concern was to fully assess the squad and the boss adopted a patient approach. One glaring issue was that at 37 years old, he was not that much older than some of the more experienced players at Pittodrie. Bobby Clark was the oldest at 33, while Drew Jarvie and Joe Harper were both in their 30s.

After a promising start to the season with Aberdeen remaining undefeated after seven games, progress was also made in the League Cup at the expense of lowly Meadowbank. The Scottish League had tinkered with the format of the competition for years but having the likes of Aberdeen playing lower-league opposition over two legs was not one for the purists. It demeaned the League Cup and perceptions as to the stature of the cup had suffered over the years. It was also the first competition that Ferguson began to field a weakened starting 11 in, although he was several seasons away from that in 1978. He was gradually getting to grips with the task in hand and the realisation that so many have since discovered who have walked through the doors at Pittodrie, how unique Aberdeen FC are as a club. In his match programme notes in the *Pittodrie Review* edition for the visit of Meadowbank, Ferguson was just realising the potential at Aberdeen, 'The one thing that has annoyed me all of my life is the acceptance that Celtic and Rangers must win, that everything is geared around them, that nobody but nobody is expected to beat them. I played for Rangers and believe me they were not any better than the players at most clubs. They just believed they were better and this to me is the greatest challenge. I look at everything around me and success is staring me in the face. The one thing that is inside heads is the total belief. We have it in the Beach End and that is where we must build and develop from, right through the corridors of Pittodrie and into the dressing room.' For context the Beach End at Pittodrie was the area where the younger, more vibrant Dons supporters would congregate. Ferguson likened that area to the Kop at Liverpool, albeit on a much smaller scale. However, his recognition of the potential at Aberdeen and Pittodrie was something that he was desperate to realise.

By tradition, Aberdeen adopted the more modern-day practice of honouring their more loyal players with testimonial matches. Up until the early '70s the club had paid a loyalty bonus after five years' service. In an era before players held the power, it was commonplace for them to stick around a certain club for most of their careers. It was a policy that chairman Dick Donald was keen to continue from his playing days. Before the war the club arranged 'benefit' matches with gate money going to their more loyal servants. That changed in 1978 when Bobby Clark was awarded a testimonial. Clark had been at Pittodrie since 1965 and at that time was the Dons' most-capped player with 17 appearances for Scotland. Of those caps he played against ten countries, including an appearance in the Maracanã in Rio against Brazil. Clark had played under five managers at Pittodrie: Eddie Turnbull, Jim Bonthrone, Ally MacLeod, Billy McNeill and Alex Ferguson. In his 14 seasons at Pittodrie, Clark shared the number one spot with no fewer than eight other keepers; John Ogston, Ernie McGarr, Andy Geoghegan, Gordon Marshall, Jim George, Ally MacLean, Jim Leighton and John Gardiner.

It was on 3 September that a sell-out capacity crowd of 21,000 filled Pittodrie for what was on reflection a glorified training match between Aberdeen and a 'Former Dons Select' that included the likes of Celtic captain Danny McGrain and winger Jimmy Johnstone. Clark appeared before kick-off and took his bow as he was injured at the time and had to watch from the stands after the game kicked off. The carnival atmosphere was not lost on Ferguson, who was coming to terms with what Aberdeen as a club was all about. The Dons 'family' was something that was embedded in the club for generations. Ferguson identified that and was keen to embrace it.

One issue that Ferguson had observed was the style and approach his players had been used to. He thought that Aberdeen played far too deep in possession and were not brave enough on the ball. His belief was that with the likes of Willie Miller in defence this was the strongest element of the team and that by defending so deep they would give little away. This was nothing new in an Aberdeen side. Back in 1970 under Eddie Turnbull the Dons went 12 league games without conceding a single goal. The use of Martin Buchan in what was a continental 'sweeper' role was a new and successful concept in Scottish football. Ferguson had other views. He wanted his team to be more positive, and fearless. He readily admitted that he was aware of the weaknesses in his squad but due to his personal circumstances, and the Dons' positive start to the season, he decided to let those flaws pass in the meantime. Those personal issues were his father's failing health and his upcoming industrial tribunal case against his former club following his dismissal from St Mirren. Ferguson later declared that his initial season at Pittodrie was a traumatic one and a period where he was keen just to get through relatively unscathed so he could build from there.

The situation with St Mirren was, on reflection, a feud that Ferguson could have done without. There was still a sense of unfairness over the way his departure came about. His desire to have his day in court was derived from a sense of unfairness. Perhaps it was his trade union background that convinced him to take his case through a tribunal. There was also a concern that his tribunal would have a detrimental effect on the day job. Considering the pressure was on Ferguson the day he set foot in Pittodrie, this was no time for any lengthy distractions. To compound matters there appeared to be a growing rift between manager and senior players.

Ferguson admitted some years later that he underestimated the squad he had taken over. The statistics would confirm this. Aberdeen's record in recent years was infinitely superior to what Ferguson had left behind in Paisley. That Aberdeen side also contained 11 past, current and future Scotland international players: Steve Archibald, Bobby Clark, Joe Harper, Drew Jarvie, Stuart Kennedy, Jim Leighton, Alex McLeish, Willie Miller, Doug Rougvie, Neil Simpson and Gordon Strachan. It was reported in training that Ferguson had used his former defender at St Mirren, Jackie Copland as an 'example' to follow. This clearly irked some of the senior players, none more than captain Willie Miller. Just back from the World Cup with Scotland and the current sports writers' player of the year in Scotland, Miller took being compared to Copland personally, a journeyman defender for whom Ferguson paid Dundee United £10,000 in 1976 during his time with St Mirren. Miller recalled, 'He wanted me to play like him. Jackie was a great player in his day and deserved respect, but I was captain of Aberdeen and every time his name was mentioned in training it got to me. I had confidence in my own ability, and I did not feel I should be compared to a player from another club. I resolved to bring matters to a head and confront the gaffer. In a frank discussion I assured him I was totally committed to the club and he listened to me. He did not apologise, but the name Jackie Copland was never mentioned again.'

The Dons' first setbacks under Ferguson came in September in a hectic seven-game schedule. As Aberdeen travelled to Bulgaria to take on Marek Stanke Dimitrov it was a step into the unknown. Ferguson would in time become a master tactician in the European arena, but this trip was a first European tie for him as a manager. Marek were modest opponents but on their own patch they were always going to be tough. A noisy, hostile crowd in excess of 20,000 made it an uncomfortable night for the Dons. Heavy rain throughout made conditions difficult and it took a scrambled goal in the final minute to give Marek a 3-2 first-leg lead. Although Jim Leighton was clearly impeded, the Belgian referee ignored the Dons' appeals. To compound a miserable night, centre-half Willie Garner broke a leg in a horrendous incident on 57 minutes. Ferguson was not that concerned that his side would need to overcome a deficit at Pittodrie, 'We did well on the night and probably deserved to come away with a more positive result. We will be better prepared for the return leg and I am delighted we scored two over here. Conditions were terrible and the injury to Willie was a huge blow.'

Three days later a 1-1 draw at Ibrox with an equaliser in the last minute would usually have been a good result but it was before, during and after that game that Ferguson learned a lot about some of his players' mentality. He had made it clear when the squad gathered at Gordonstoun before the season that his plan was to not only match the Glasgow monopoly, but to crush it. Such bravado would be almost unheard of back then, but Ferguson took the view that for Aberdeen to be successful they would have to beat both Celtic and Rangers in Glasgow on a regular basis. It was in the Ibrox dressing room after Dom Sullivan's late equaliser that Ferguson realised he had to change things: 'Before the game I had been listening to some of the players in the dressing room. They were talking about slowing the game down, taking time at throw-ins and free kicks so that the notoriously fickle Rangers support would turn against their own team. I just could not understand that philosophy. I wanted to go to Ibrox and beat them. Let them worry about us. It was an attitude that disappointed me and I mentally pencilled that in as something that would need to be sorted out.'

By tradition, Aberdeen had a decent record in Glasgow through the years. Certainly, in comparison to other aspiring Scottish clubs, the Dons' record against Celtic and Rangers stood up against any other. That was clearly not good enough for Ferguson, who was determined to set a high bar for Aberdeen. He wanted success and he knew that to achieve anything in Scottish football then both Glasgow clubs would need to be defeated regularly on their own turf.

With Aberdeen hitting a sticky patch in September, they suffered their first league defeat of the season – a 2-1 loss against Hibernian at Easter Road. Despite the encouraging start to the season there was unrest among the support and more importantly, within factions of the squad. The new manager was relatively inexperienced; certainly the Aberdeen job was by far the biggest he had managed in his early years in the dugout. There was also the problem with Ferguson's family still staying in the Glasgow area as relocation was delayed until his personal problems were seen to. As often happened in those early weeks Ferguson would stay over in the west when Aberdeen were playing away from home.

The long coach journeys to Aberdeen after away matches provided the opportunity for players to talk and mull over things without the boss on board. That scenario opened all sorts of issues and it was something that Ferguson was initially oblivious to. It was following the defeat at Easter Road that things came to a head after some of the players were resentful of the tactics deployed. Ferguson had been made aware of the unrest and summoned the players to Pittodrie, where they gathered on the pitch for training. It was declared as a 'clear-the-air' meeting where players could openly share their thoughts. On reflection it was either a masterstroke or sheer folly from Ferguson to invite such clarity. The outcome was that some of the players openly questioned his tactics. Joe Harper, the Dons' record scorer, was and still is a hero and legend at Aberdeen FC. Joe was an experienced striker and was in his second spell at Pittodrie having first joined the club in 1969. He had the utmost respect for Eddie Turnbull, Jim Bonthrone, Ally MacLeod and Billy McNeill, the managers he had played under at Pittodrie, but not so for Alex Ferguson. Other dissenters included Dom Sullivan and Ian Fleming who were latterly known as the 'Westhill Mafia', who stayed in the area, an emerging wealthy suburb of Aberdeen, built on the back of the affluent oil industry. The dissent spread to the local press. The *Evening Express* was the local paper and, in an era when a good relationship with the local football club was vital for both club and paper, the *Express* ran with a story of discontent at Pittodrie as fans were invited to give their opinion. Considering the season was barely two months old, patience was in short supply. It was an acid test for Ferguson and the timing could not have been worse for him.

With a return deficit to overcome in their European Cup Winners' Cup tie, this was the first real test for Ferguson. Fortunately, Marek Stanke Dimitrov were not the strongest of opponents and certainly not the best away from home. With the tie still in the balance after a first-half stalemate the Dons came good with three second-half goals to progress to the second round.

The first clash with Celtic that season came at home on 7 October and it gave the manager a real taste of the potential at Pittodrie. An all-ticket capacity crowd responded to back their team to the hilt in an impressive 4-1 win. With Celtic managed by Billy McNeill, it gave Ferguson a huge boost to get one over him. Having been fierce rivals as players, in management, Ferguson was determined to gain the upper hand. It was not often that the two Glasgow clubs were so outclassed and getting it 'large' from the home support. The atmosphere was ferocious, almost feral on occasion. This was the Pittodrie that Ferguson wanted to see and the hammering of Celtic was a glimpse of what was to come. Those days would have to wait, however, as Aberdeen lost four games in succession, including a damaging 3-0 defeat against Fortuna Düsseldorf in Germany in the next round of the Cup Winners' Cup. It was a hard lesson for the Dons as they barely laid a glove on the Bundesliga side. After the game several players went out and ended up in a nightclub before returning to Scotland the day after. It was another lesson for Ferguson as he ruefully reflected on losing at home to Hearts at Pittodrie three days later. Such time off after games was something that would never be allowed again. Although Aberdeen made a real fist of it in the return leg against Düsseldorf, a 2-0 win was not enough. It did suggest though that this team evolving under Ferguson was moving in the right direction. Fortuna coach Dieter Tippenhauer was just delighted to get through, 'German clubs always fear playing in Scotland ... Aberdeen were strong, aggressive and never gave up. The Aberdeen team is young. I will be looking at their fortunes with interest in the future. Their day will come in European football.' Ferguson was disappointed but proud of his players, 'They gave it everything and could not be faulted. I'm sorry for them and the fans as they did not get the result they deserved. We should have been awarded a penalty in the first half after a blatant handball. Had we scored in the opening period I am convinced we would have gone on to win the tie.'

As the winter months approached, the Dons recovered from their European exit with another unbeaten run which did include some drawn games that continued to frustrate. Progress was also made in the League Cup. At Dens Park in Dundee, an extra-time goal from Stuart Kennedy put Aberdeen through to the League Cup Final after the narrow 1-0 win over Hibernian. On a night when the Dons pummelled the Hibernian goal, it took a piece of good fortune to book a Hampden date with Rangers in March. Kennedy's deep cross from near the touchline flew over Hibernian keeper Mike McDonald to the delight of the sizeable Aberdeen support.

With Aberdeen having now booked another cup final place, and league form improving, it could be assumed that any dissension internally or from the terraces would have alleviated. With Joe Harper once again doing what he did best by scoring goals, there was no doubt that there was more harmony in the squad. Experienced goalkeeper Bobby Clark had an influence. The Scotland international had been around Pittodrie long enough to realise this Aberdeen squad was as good as any he had played in: 'Some of the older lads had been McNeill's boys. I remember grabbing some of the guys and telling them, "Billy's not coming back so why are you doing this? Let's get this going again because you are just taking money out of your own pockets here, you're self-destructing and handing the league over to Celtic." In time people began to realise that Ferguson was a very good manager.'

Premier League table at 23 November 1978

	P	*W*	*D*	*L*	*F*	*A*	*Pts*
Dundee United	15	6	6	3	19	14	18
Aberdeen	**15**	**6**	**5**	**4**	**28**	**16**	**17**
Celtic	15	7	3	5	25	19	17
Partick Thistle	15	7	3	5	16	14	17

It was after the Dons' European Cup Winners' Cup exit that Alex Ferguson's industrial tribunal commenced. The *Evening Express* went with the front-page headline 'Ferguson Cheated on Expenses'. Sensationalist as it was, the claim was made by St Mirren chairman Willie Todd, who clearly retained animosity towards his former manager. Ferguson raised the action after he was dismissed from his £14,000-a-year job with the Paisley club. St Mirren defended the action by declaring no fewer than 12 breaches which led to Ferguson being dismissed. They included swearing at a club secretary, doubling the players' £30-per-point bonus without permission from the board, and even travelling to London for the European Cup Final without permission from the club. The final claim was for a £40 bill the chairman received to cover end-of-season drinks for the players. Ferguson, through his legal counsel, defended these claims vigorously and the counterclaim that Todd had a personal vendetta against him formed the basis of his defence. After two weeks the tribunal declared there was enough in two of the claims and agreed that St Mirren were within their rights to dismiss Ferguson. It is virtually unheard of a for football manager to take their former employers through a tribunal. Looking back on the whole case, it was clear that so much private information being made public served nobody. The whole episode was embarrassing for both St Mirren and Ferguson, who reflected some years later, 'I would not like to go through that again. It took me away from the players at Aberdeen for three weeks. I was strong enough to take it.'

It was at that low point that Ferguson circled the wagons and looked to Dick Donald and Chris Anderson for support. Fortunately, the board were fully supportive and took the view that it was nothing to do with Aberdeen and they were standing by their manager and would back him to the hilt. That loyalty was something Ferguson never did forget and made a lasting impression on him. There was no doubt this period was the worst of times for Ferguson and to compound matters, his father was gravely ill. Having been a huge influence on his career as a player, Alex senior was admitted to Southern General Hospital in Glasgow just before Christmas. It was during a bad-tempered clash at St Mirren of all places that Alex senior passed away on 24 February 1979. The manager was told after the game by a friend at the Paisley club. The match itself was perhaps a reflection of the turmoil that was around. In what was the Dons' first visit to St Mirren following the tribunal, they were coasting and two goals ahead after an hour. Previously Ferguson breached SFA rules by remonstrating with the referee at half-time, clearly annoyed at some of the treatment his players were on the receiving end of and were getting no protection. The second half was carnage; Ian Scanlon and Willie Miller were sent off and St Mirren clawed their way back to rescue a 2-2 draw. Ferguson was livid and was convinced his interference at the break ended with the referee looking to impose his authority. With news of his father's passing, this was personally and professionally as bad as it got for Ferguson.

Aberdeen were making progress in the Scottish Cup and keeping in touch near the top of the league. After comfortable wins in the opening two rounds against lower-league Hamilton and Ayr United, the Dons were drawn at home to Celtic in the quarter-final. Pittodrie was gradually becoming one of the most difficult of venues for visiting teams and the chance to knock Celtic out before the semi-finals was a challenge to relish for Aberdeen. It was clear there was a fierce rivalry between Aberdeen and Celtic and that had been apparent ever since the Dons beat the Glasgow club in the 1970 Scottish Cup Final. Aberdeen had been the team that came so close to breaking Celtic's nine-in-a-row league success and with the Dons also beating the Parkhead side in the 1976 League Cup Final, there was no love lost between the clubs.

A tense affair resulted in a 1-1 draw which was a fair reflection of a tie that saw five bookings. The highlight was Joe Harper's equaliser, a minute after Celtic had taken a 25th-minute lead. Harper latched on to a Stuart Kennedy lob and turned to fire a fierce volley from 25 yards. It was later described by Ferguson as the best goal he had ever seen at Pittodrie. Nevertheless, Celtic were favourites to progress as the tie moved to Glasgow. The Dons had shown on occasion that they could defend in depth and hit teams on the break. It was not a tactic that Ferguson was overly keen on. His preference was an 'early defence' approach. In the modern day it is the 'press'. Perhaps it was an indication of how forward-thinking Ferguson was that he was adopting these tactics back in the late '70s. Aberdeen got off to a great start and stunned the home crowd by going two goals up after only 13 minutes. Celtic did pull a goal back and amid the chaos the home crowd threw bottles and cans on to the pitch as their side were exiting the competition. The Dons held on to go through to the last four. The game was played in a toxic atmosphere, fuelled by the behaviour of the home support. There were clashes in the tunnel between players and officials as the teams left the field. That disappointed Ferguson, 'There were a lot of incidents inside the tunnel, with players exchanging blows and officials arguing over each other. Quite frankly, Celtic took it badly. It detracted attention from what was a marvellous victory.'

The first acid test for the Dons that season came in the League Cup Final. Aberdeen were annoyed that they had to play Motherwell in a rearranged league game on the Monday before the final, so much so they set about the Fir Park side with a then record

8-0 win. Played in dreadful conditions, it was a night to forget for Motherwell manager Ally MacLeod, who returned to Pittodrie as an opposing manager following his eventful time as Scotland coach.

The Hampden clash with Rangers was the first national final Ferguson had faced as a manager. It was also the opportunity for him to gain more favour with the Aberdeen support. Although the Dons were confident they could win the League Cup, that was certainly not shared among the press in Glasgow. It was something that Ferguson and his players would have to deal with in the years ahead. When it came to timing, doubts as to Aberdeen's chances were cast, usually in the days building up to any big game in Glasgow. The modern term for the Glasgow press among the Aberdeen support is the collective 'Weegia', a derogatory term derived from Glaswegians being known as 'Weegies' and their media being complicit in questioning the merits of any team who dared to challenge the Glasgow clubs. In 1979 though there was some merit in their claims. The Dons had effectively frozen when they lost the Scottish Cup Final a year earlier so on this occasion they were easy pickings for the Glasgow media to feast on.

The *Glasgow Herald* was first up, 'Aberdeen must beat the Hampden freeze. That is not an amateur weather forecast but a question to doubt Pittodrie temperaments at the national stadium. They have players of undoubted class, they have also beaten Rangers in lesser matches, but they still have to prove that when it really matters.'

The 1979 League Cup Final ended with Rangers defeating Aberdeen 2-1. That is what the records will reveal. However, the circumstances behind this game triggered one of the most fierce and bitter rivalries in Scottish football. It is well enough known that Glasgow is a divided city, in sport, culture and politics. The sectarian differences between Celtic and Rangers have long been a stain on Scottish football. The rivalry that was spawned between Aberdeen and Rangers after that final was to follow Ferguson during his Pittodrie tenure.

Aberdeen were missing Dom Sullivan through injury and Ferguson was dealt a blow on the eve of the final when his replacement Ian Scanlon told his manager that he was not in the right frame of mind to play. Hard as that was to believe, Ferguson drafted in Duncan Davidson to play alongside Steve Archibald and Joe Harper in attack. In the opening minute Archibald was brutally tackled from behind by Rangers' Derek Johnstone. In Scottish football such treatment was not unheard of and was later outlawed in the game. Archibald never recovered and effectively limped his way through the game. Such a tackle would have drawn a red card on an even playing field. Unfortunately for Aberdeen, as so often happened back then, the cards were stacked against them. Ferguson firmly believed that no Rangers player would be sent off in the first minute of a major final, no matter what.

In what was an even cup final the Dons took the lead just before the hour when Rangers keeper Peter McCloy allowed a weak Duncan Davidson shot to elude him. At that stage it looked as though the cup was going north. Rangers had toiled for long stages and rarely threatened to score but that changed in the closing minutes when Johnstone was again involved. This time he challenged Bobby Clark, causing a neck spasm that spread to his arm. With Clark struggling and kneeling in pain, Rangers equalised when an Alex MacDonald shot was deflected past the ailing keeper. Had Clark stayed down and got treatment it could have been so very different. Minutes later the Dons were furious after centre-half Doug Rougvie was sent off. Once again it was Johnstone, who had been moved upfield and feigned an injury in an off-the-ball clash with Rougvie. Johnstone went down and referee Ian Foote took the view that Rougvie had elbowed the Rangers player. Foote later declared he saw the incident, but television footage proved otherwise. Ferguson was convinced Johnstone was making the most of it and had clearly conned the referee: 'To begin with his back was being treated, then it was his neck. He lay there for fully five minutes. This cost Rougvie his place in the game. To be sent off in a cup final is a terrible blow for any player, particularly when it was unjustified. I did not see the incident but neither did the referee.'

With the injury time being played due to the stoppage with Johnstone, it was a bitter irony for the Dons that Colin Jackson, an Aberdonian by birth, headed the winning goal with Clark still suffering from injury. In the immediate aftermath any doubts Ferguson had over Rougvie's part in the clash were dispelled by the distraught player himself and his Aberdeen team-mates, who rallied round and to a man declared that Johnstone feigned injury. Feelings ran high to such an extent that Ferguson asked assistant Pat Stanton to keep an eye on Rougvie, 'If he goes out there and finds Johnstone, god help him.'

It was a harsh lesson for Aberdeen and Ferguson, who now knew just what it was going to take to conquer the Glasgow clubs. In the *Evening Express,* some days later, Rougvie had his say, 'I am absolutely disgusted with what happened at Hampden. Derek Johnstone backed into me and then dropped to the ground. I was left standing there and looked astonished. I was being conned and there was nothing I could do about it. I never touched Johnstone. I am disgusted that a fellow professional could behave like that. The injustice shattered me.'

Although losing the League Cup Final was a huge blow for all concerned, it did harden Ferguson's resolve and he was now acutely aware of what would be needed if Aberdeen were going to be successful. It had always been accepted that any provincial club would need to go above and beyond to prevail. For generations the two Glasgow clubs, ably backed up by the Glasgow press, would cast doubts on the qualities and nerve of teams coming to the city for the big matches.

The bitter disappointment felt after the 1979 final would be used by Ferguson to motivate his players going forward. Another factor was that most of the Aberdeen squad hailed from the west of Scotland and knew exactly how difficult it was to break the Celtic and Rangers monopoly. Glasgow-born Dons captain Willie Miller recalled the aftermath of the defeat at Hampden, 'Whatever the rights and wrongs of the incident with Doug, it was that match that made all of the players of Aberdeen FC realise that we had to be that much better than Celtic and Rangers to have any chance of winning in Glasgow. The referees were influenced by the home crowds, which Fergie mentioned to us time and time again, and it was something I firmly believed. Do not give me that nonsense that they are not swayed by the support. They were and coming to terms with that was a significant pointer for us to accept.

'It got to the stage, after that League Cup Final defeat, that we would travel to Glasgow almost hoping against hope that the officials would turn out to be fair. Celtic and Rangers fans in that era simply could not accept that we were developing into a better team, and they had to find a scapegoat; off the park it was manager Alex Ferguson, on the park it was Willie Miller. Because officials were influenced by their support, we had to be not just better than Celtic and Rangers, but much, much better. After that final defeat we aimed at being capable of travelling to Glasgow carrying a bit of arrogance; they hated that but that was what was needed to win the big matches. We wanted to build things under Alex Ferguson to the point where both Glasgow clubs would be frightened to play us, and they could not handle our style.'

Ferguson was determined to change how his team would approach these games. Following that defeat to Rangers, he set about the task; one that would see his team never lose to Celtic or Rangers in a Hampden final for the rest of his Pittodrie tenure.

Four days after their Hampden horror the Dons were on their travels again, this time to face Morton at Cappielow. A narrow win was welcome as was the debut of Mark McGhee. The Greenock-born forward was Ferguson's first major signing for the club, a £70,000 transfer from Newcastle United.

Aberdeen made a return to Hampden on 11 April to face Hibernian in the semi-final of the Scottish Cup. Following on from their efforts to get past Celtic in the quarter-final, the Hampden clash was another huge disappointment as the Edinburgh side exacted revenge for the Dons' League Cup success at the same stage earlier in the season. The Hibernian clash was in stark contrast to their most recent visit as a poor attendance of 9,900 made for an almost eerie atmosphere in the national stadium. A semi-final played in Glasgow in midweek with two sides from the east did little to capture the imagination. For Aberdeen supporters it was perhaps a game too many; raw emotions from the League Cup Final were a factor. For Hibernian it was a poor turnout, considering the proximity to Hampden from Edinburgh, but it did call into question the merits of the SFA using the stadium as a neutral venue for a semi-final. A 2-1 defeat did little to raise morale as Aberdeen looked at another season without silverware. They still had an outside chance of the league title, but their more realistic target of European qualification was achieved with games to spare. The Dons did manage to defeat Rangers 2-1 at Pittodrie on 25 April, a result that allowed Celtic the opportunity to win the Premier League from their own efforts which they gleefully accepted to the detriment of their Glasgow rivals.

Aberdeen finished in fourth place, a point behind Dundee United and eight away from Celtic. It was no secret that Ferguson welcomed the conclusion of that first season. From a personal and professional point of view it had been a period that he was gglad to see the back of, 'The season could not come to an end quickly enough. I was desperate to go and rethink and analyse, to assess myself, where I was going and how I should go about it. I knew what I wanted, there was no doubt about that. Going away to rethink. Coming back into next season after a summer break was important after what had been a difficult time.'

The summer break offered Ferguson the time to reflect and properly assess his squad. There were the initial concerns over some of the dissenters at Pittodrie but on reflection he realised he had the foundations of a great side. Ferguson had the utmost respect for Bobby Clark, who was now entering the latter stages of his career. Although he had clear differences with Joe Harper, the Dons' record scorer still netted 33 goals that season. With the likes of Stuart Kennedy, Willie Miller, Gordon Strachan and Steve Archibald around, the basis of the side was there. The manager was also keen on overhauling the youth setup at the club, which he had deemed unsuitable on arrival. Jim Leighton, Alex McLeish, Neil Simpson and John Hewitt were emerging from the youth ranks, with more to follow.

For the Aberdeen support it was another season of frustration. The Dons had lost their last two major finals to bitter rivals Rangers. In terms of Ferguson, the jury was still out, but as with most north-east folk patience was the key. The foundations of a great squad were in place. They just needed a manager to bring out the best in them. The stage was set for Alex Ferguson to make his mark.

3

Premier League Champions

'I NEVER want our players and supporters to go through that again. I will make sure of that.' The determined words of manager Alex Ferguson after his side had been beaten in a League Cup Final replay at Dens Park against Dundee United in December 1979. It had been a bitterly disappointing period for Aberdeen. Following their Scottish Cup Final defeat in May 1978, the Dons lost two League Cup finals in 1979; in March against Rangers and against Dundee United some nine months later as the format of the competition was changed. Ferguson used that pain as motivation for himself and his players to great effect. Under his guidance Aberdeen would not lose another major final while he was at Pittodrie.

There was no disguising that Ferguson's first season in charge was disappointing. The frustration was clear. After the 1978 Scottish Cup Final defeat under Billy McNeill, that was followed by the controversial League Cup Final in March 1979 as Aberdeen again lost out to the Ibrox club. A fourth-placed finish in the league guaranteed European football but little else.

Considering this was Ferguson's second season in charge, the lack of new faces was a surprise with free transfer Doug Bell the only new addition to the club. Bell recalled his switch to Pittodrie,

'A year on from my first-team debut for St Mirren I hadn't had any chances to build on my breakthrough. Things got worse for me when at the end of the season [Saints manager] Jim Clunie let me go on a free transfer. His explanation was that I was too skilful for the type of game he wanted to play. I could not get my head around that. Fortunately, later that day I got a call from Falkirk who wanted to sign me. Before I got to Falkirk the phone rang again. Alex Ferguson called me the next morning and told me to pack a bag and get myself up to Aberdeen, where he would sign me. The thought of joining in with what I heard was happening at Pittodrie with a manager I knew, made my decision easy and I immediately made my way to Aberdeen.'

Aberdeen began their pre-season with a gruelling spell at Gordonstoun. The private facility in the north of Scotland provided spartan surroundings as the players went through some tough conditioning work. The Dons then embarked on a week-long trip to Randers in Denmark and three friendlies against local opposition. Ferguson was always keen on such trips as team bonding was essential, 'The visit to Denmark was a great success and the players showed a great attitude in training.' The other new face at the club was Roland Arnott, the new physio to replace Brian Scott, who joined Billy McNeill at Celtic in the close-season. Arnott was English by birth and as such the subject of some high jinks within the squad. His introduction to the players came when he was asked to say grace at the table during their visit to Gordonstoun; a proper introduction to his new surroundings. Arnott, however, was a first-class physio and in his previous roles he worked with some of the world's greatest tennis players during Wimbledon.

Almost unnoticed the club changed kit suppliers in the summer as a new deal was signed with adidas. Admiral, the previous supplier, had been associated with Aberdeen since 1976. The new adidas strip was also the first to include the Dons' club motif, the 'A' style goal frame logo. The first-team kit was the classic all-red strip with the traditional three stripes of adidas on the sleeve. The change strip was all white with red flashings. Previously Admiral had introduced an all-yellow second strip with black stripes as a tribute to the club's heritage and their prewar black and gold strip, but it never really captured the fans' imagination.

The Dons' first domestic challenge came against Kilmarnock at Rugby Park in the Drybrough Cup. The pre-season competition was introduced in 1971 and was competed for by the four top-scoring teams from both divisions from the previous season. Aberdeen had been the winners in the inaugural competition, which was ideal preparation for the new campaign with a trophy also up for grabs.

As so often happens a former player comes back to haunt their previous employers, and on this occasion it was Bobby Street who scored the only goal of the game for Kilmarnock. There was a question mark over Aberdeen's preparations for the season being somewhat disjointed. Three matches in five days in Denmark were followed by their Drybrough Cup exit. Two friendlies in the Highland League preceded a friendly against Coventry City, which was won 4-1 at Pittodrie.

There was little to suggest that Aberdeen would go on to become serious challengers for silverware that season. The honours list from 1978/79 had an all-too-familiar look to it with Celtic and Rangers sharing the domestic titles. Not since 1965 had a team outside of Glasgow won the championship. It was a depressing statistic for the likes of Aberdeen, Hearts and Hibernian, who all tasted league success in the '50s and remained the clubs most likely to break that monopoly. With both Edinburgh clubs often struggling to even stay in the top division, the pressure was on Aberdeen to launch a credible challenge for the title.

The Dons' opening Premier League game was against Partick Thistle at Firhill. The side from Maryhill in Glasgow had traditionally never really posed too many problems for Aberdeen in recent years. With Willie Miller missing the Dons seemed far from their best and with several decisions going against them the game was decided in the final minute when the home side were awarded a controversial penalty. Manager Ferguson was understandably incredulous at the decision as Alex McLeish unintentionally handled the ball in the box to allow Partick to take both points, but he added, 'Do not laugh but I have a scent as to how things are going to go this season.' What was soon to become apparent was that Ferguson was learning his craft and how to handle the Scottish press. In an era before the internet, the printed press was vital for any club to be portrayed in a positive way. Ferguson identified that and after his experience in Paisley he was acutely aware of how a poor relationship with the press could be damaging.

Aberdeen opened their League Cup campaign with a comfortable win over Arbroath at Pittodrie. With the competition's early rounds being played on a two-legged basis with the top clubs seeded, to reach the final a team would need to play nine games. Progress was made at the expense of Meadowbank in the next round, Ferguson resisting the temptation to rest many of his first-team players for the Pittodrie return despite winning 5-0 in Edinburgh. The minnows shocked Aberdeen and held the Dons to a 2-2 draw in what was a meaningless second leg in terms of the result, but Ferguson was far from happy: 'Despite the game being treated like a friendly, I hated that approach and my players were left in no doubt that any slacking would not be acceptable. Fortunately, the result did not have any bearing on the outcome, but it gave the players a reminder that we never let our standards slip.'

In the opening weeks of their league campaign the Dons made an encouraging start. John McMaster excelled when they defeated Hibernian 3-0 at Pittodrie before an excellent 3-1 win over Dundee United at Tannadice on 25 August. The home side included England keeper Peter Bonetti; the 37-year-old was remembered north of the border for his part in England's ill-fated defence of the World Cup at the 1970 finals in Mexico. Bonetti was at fault for the Dons' second goal when he fumbled a cross that allowed Joe Harper to score, much to the delight of the sizeable travelling support.

Aberdeen suffered a second league defeat when they went down by the odd goal against Morton at Cappielow. The general belief around that time and in subsequent seasons was that the Greenock ground had become a bit of a bogey for Aberdeen. While Morton did achieve some decent results against the Dons, the statistics suggest otherwise. What Morton did have in their armoury back then was a dreadful pitch, an unwelcoming town, and Andy Ritchie. It remains one of the anomalies in Scottish football that Ritchie did not go on to achieve better things. A languid, almost lazy-looking player with a physique to match, Ritchie was a natural, with incredible ability. He started out at Celtic but was sold to Morton in 1976. A modern-day maverick, Ritchie only ever made one appearance for the Scotland under-21 side as an over-age player. He later scouted for several clubs including Manchester City and Aberdeen. Reflecting on the Dons' average record against Morton, it was perhaps the environment more than anything else. Greenock was a dour place to visit with relics of a once-proud shipbuilding industry dominating the skyline. Cappielow Park was also a ground that had not aged well and had remained almost untouched since the war. Most players hated the venue and the often-heavy ground conditions.

Eintracht Frankfurt, the Dons' UEFA Cup opponents, sent over a delegation to watch Aberdeen when Rangers came north on 15 September. When the new season's fixtures came out the first visit of the Ibrox club would have been high on the most-anticipated list for the Aberdeen support. Still harbouring a grievance from the League Cup Final in March, there was also the potential reunion of Doug Rougvie and Derek Johnstone to contend with. An all-ticket capacity crowd gathered in vengeful mood; the atmosphere was fevered at best, toxic at worst. With Frankfurt due at Pittodrie in midweek the Dons changed their starting line-up and Rougvie would have to cool his heels with a seat on the bench. Both sides exchanged goals in a frantic first half. With the game delicately poised, the biggest roar of the afternoon came when Rougvie entered the fray after the hour. The defender came on like a gladiator ready for battle. Encouraged by the supporters, big Doug

...immer am Ball HERTIE
FRANKFURT Eintracht Wald-stadion
FC ABERDEEN
Mittwoch, 3. 10. 1979 Anstoß 20.00 Uhr
Stehplatz Erwachsene DM 8,00
BLOCK K
№ 1145
UEFA-Cup 1. Runde
I

did not disappoint when his first act was to send Johnstone spinning in the air. That incident seemed to inspire the Dons, who set about Rangers with renewed vigour. Incessant pressure eventually bore fruit when Aberdeen were awarded an overdue penalty in 75 minutes; Gordon Strachan scored to the delight of the home support. At that stage Rangers were ragged and the stage was then set for Rougvie to exorcise his demons. After a set-piece move from the Dons the defender scored from close range as he and the ball ended up in the net. Pittodrie had not seen anything quite like this. A game played in a real hostile atmosphere; almost tribal. When the dust settled, between Aberdeen and Rangers the gloves were off.

A week later, after the clash with Frankfurt, it was the turn of Celtic to visit Pittodrie. On this occasion the Dons would suffer their one and only defeat to their Parkhead rivals that season. A nasty, bad-tempered game ensued, and as the football was somehow lost in the mayhem, on reflection it did not help Aberdeen. Despite going ahead early through Strachan, the home players were subjected to a series of brutal challenges, the worst of which came when Strachan was on the end of a shocking tackle from Tommy Burns, who was immediately sent off.

Aberdeen would go on to play Celtic on six occasions in 1979/80, winning four of them. Three of those victories were at Parkhead. The Dons would face Rangers on seven occasions that season, winning the first five. In the 13 clashes against the Glasgow clubs, Aberdeen prevailed on nine occasions, drawing twice and losing twice.

It seemed the 'Ferguson effect' was working. If Aberdeen could find a level of consistency, then surely a league challenge was possible. The one lasting criticism of Aberdeen teams in the past was their inability to get the better of the Glasgow clubs over any given season. In recent years the only occasion Aberdeen had mounted a serious challenge for the title was in 1970/71 when they eventually ran out of steam, slipping up in drawn games against mid-table teams. Could they find the right balance in 1980? It seemed a long shot as Aberdeen were not even mentioned in the press at any stage as potential champions, such was the gap that runaway leaders Celtic had created by the turn of the year. Surprise early runners Morton were struggling to maintain that form as the Glasgow bookmakers refused to take any new bets on Celtic retaining the Premier League.

Premier League table at 15 December 1979

	P	*W*	*D*	*L*	*F*	*A*	*Pts*
Celtic	16	10	3	3	34	15	23
Morton	16	10	3	3	34	18	23
Rangers	18	8	3	7	26	23	19
Aberdeen	**15**	**7**	**3**	**5**	**27**	**18**	**17**
St Mirren	17	6	5	6	24	29	17

Before any league business the Dons' attention turned to their League Cup campaign. Aberdeen had beaten Celtic and Rangers along the way and were rightly installed as favourites. After a pulsating 3-2 first-leg win over Celtic at Pittodrie on 24 November, a new Aberdeen star was emerging. Steve Archibald had been working as a mechanic, playing part-time for Clyde in 1977 when Billy McNeill signed him for the Dons. Archibald had learned quickly and was thriving in a front partnership with Mark McGhee and Joe Harper. His hat-trick against Celtic brought him nationwide attention, but not the match ball. The age-old accepted ritual that any player scoring three goals in a game would take the ball home did not find favour with Alex Ferguson. On learning from Teddy Scott that Archibald had indeed taken the ball with him, Ferguson demanded that Archibald return it. Such was Ferguson's involvement in just about every aspect of the club, careful management of club property was important. Archibald was never one for being slow at saying his piece but he did return the ball the next morning by blasting it into Fergie's office followed by a few choice expletives. Far from being annoyed, it was something Ferguson admired. Archibald was no shrinking violet and his approach often mirrored what Ferguson was like in his playing days.

As one Aberdeen striker was evolving into one of the best front players in Europe, another legend was winding down a fantastic career. Although the Dons defeated Celtic at Parkhead in the League Cup return leg, a bad knee injury to Joe Harper effectively brought a premature end to his playing career. With Harper being stretchered off in the Parkhead cauldron, his season was over. His replacement, Mark McGhee, came off the bench and scored the only goal of the game.

Harper had been an icon at Pittodrie and retains his legendary status to the present day; a popular figure in the Pittodrie lounges on a matchday. His two spells ended with him becoming the club's record scorer and winner of a complete set of domestic winners' medals. Despite his popularity with the Aberdeen support, Alex Ferguson was not convinced that Harper would fit into his team ethic. With his career coming to a close, McGhee was just beginning to show his true potential despite a disappointing spell with Newcastle.

The format of the League Cup, which was played on a home and away basis until the semi-final stage, was rightly criticised. It was an open tournament by the quarter-final stage with Rangers and both Edinburgh clubs already eliminated, then the Dons' defeat of Celtic saw themselves, Dundee United, Morton and Hamilton Accies reach the last four. For the sponsors Bell's it was a nightmare. For the purists it was ideal; confirming the first final since 1962 without Celtic or Rangers involved. Of the four clubs left only Aberdeen were able to command a sizeable support. However, with Hampden once again chosen as a neutral venue for the Dons' clash with Morton, there was never any prospect of this game attracting a good attendance. Morton were expected to give Aberdeen a tough time of it, and with the enigmatic Andy Ritchie in the form of his life, the last-four clashes was no easy task. Aberdeen made the ideal start when former Morton striker McGhee scored in 14 minutes. The Dons looked to have booked their place in the final when Gordon Strachan converted a penalty just before half-time. With nothing to lose the Greenock side had the better of the second half and when

Ritchie converted a late penalty the Dons were left hanging on in the closing minutes. A crowd below 12,000 was disappointing and another reason for moving such games to a more suitable venue.

Aberdeen qualified the hard way and had every expectation that they could lift the trophy. In stark contrast, opponents Dundee United had enjoyed the easiest of paths to Hampden, having not faced Premier League opposition at any stage. The Tannadice club had been emerging as a force outside of the two Glasgow sides. Alex Ferguson's close friend Jim McLean had gradually built a competent team in Dundee but until 1979 they had never won a major trophy. In the Hampden final the Dons, playing in their white change strip, dominated and missed numerous chances. Backed by most of the crowd, Aberdeen looked to have scored when Willie Garner headed past Hamish McAlpine, but the ball stuck in the Hampden mud on the goal line and United defender Paul Hegarty cleared. The poor weather conditions made for a frustrating day for Aberdeen and their support. For some it seemed they had missed their opportunity. That proved to be correct.

Both clubs requested the Scottish League move the replay to Dens Park in Dundee; common sense prevailed. It would be advantage United as the game was played in their home city. For Aberdeen, travelling the 70 miles south was more appealing than another long trek to Glasgow, but it was a night to forget and a lesson learned for Ferguson. By his own admission he made the mistake of not changing his side for the replay. United clearly took more from the first game than Aberdeen did, and they responded by taking an early lead that the Dons never recovered from. It was a bitter loss, 3-0, and one that hit Ferguson hard: 'I remember coming back up the road from Dens Park and feeling worse than I had ever felt. It was a strange feeling. I could not sleep that night because the season promised so much as we handed United a first ever trophy. The great thing though is how to handle adversity and how to recover from such a defeat. I gathered myself the next day and welcomed each player as they arrived at Pittodrie. It was a time to look forward.'

The following Saturday the Dons' lowest crowd of the season turned up in wretched weather for the visit of St Mirren. It proved to be a turning point as John Hewitt made his debut in a 2-0 win, and on 12 January the visit of Rangers would prove to be a pivotal moment in the league campaign. Aberdeen were ten points adrift of leaders Celtic and that gap looked to be heading beyond the Dons as Rangers took a 2-1 lead just after the break. Utility player Derek Hamilton made the difference in the closing minutes, first setting up Steve Archibald to level and then scoring a last-minute winner. Ferguson sensed a change, 'There was now a sense of direction about us, as if we knew we were getting where we wanted to be.'

By March 1980, due to their cup commitments and postponements the Dons found themselves nine points behind Celtic but with five games in hand. Celtic were still clear favourites with points in the bag. The winter conditions continued when Morton came north on 22 March and the Dons' clash was the only top flight game to beat the weather. It was an opportunity to reduce the deficit at the top and Ferguson was desperate to put as much pressure on Celtic as he could, so much so that he and assistant Pat Stanton joined the fleet of pensioners who volunteered their time at the ground to clear the playing surface to get the game playable. Their efforts were rewarded when a solitary Drew Jarvie goal was enough to give Aberdeen both points; they were beginning to gain some momentum.

The first week in April was crucial. Aberdeen were down to play Kilmarnock at Rugby Park on the Tuesday ahead of the first of their double header at Celtic at the weekend. If the Dons were going to be serious about winning the title then they had to win these games. The 4-0 victory over Kilmarnock provided an indication of what was to come. Described as their most complete performance of the season, the Dons' form that evening was outstanding. Ferguson later recalled that several English managers had been at the game and some contacted him afterwards to compliment him on his team, 'They turned up to look at some of our players and were surprised at how good we were. It was good to hear that kind of praise coming from English managers, who often tended to underrate Scottish football.'

The result and performance set Aberdeen up for Parkhead. Aberdeen had a great record at the Glasgow ground and there was no doubt the pressure was all on Celtic. The Glasgow club were also protecting an unbeaten record at home that season; this was the acid test for Aberdeen. On a baking-hot day with a fiery surface, conditions were in stark contrast to the wretched winter just gone. Ferguson brought Drew Jarvie back into the side after resting him at Kilmarnock. His experience in such a game would be vital. One Aberdeen player who thrived in the hostile Parkhead atmosphere was Doug Rougvie. The big defender ignored his manager's pleas to warm up in the shade by instead going right in front of the gathered Celtic support in their well-known 'Jungle' part of the ground. Rougvie would strut along the touchline, almost baiting the home fans. There was no malicious intent, but it did show the Celtic support that this Aberdeen team meant business and would not be intimidated. Ferguson was relieved he had no fresh injury worries ahead of a game he knew his side simply had to win, 'We did some additional work on Thursday in preparation for the game. We know it is a huge challenge for us, but we have belief. Nobody expected we would be in this position a few weeks ago, but here we are, and we will give our all. I think we can do it.' Ferguson had also been in attendance for Celtic's win over Rangers the day after the Dons' win at Rugby Park.

Aberdeen began well and created some good openings in the early stages. Celtic were a confident side and backed by their noisy support they began to put pressure on the Dons, but the visitors opened the scoring in 19 minutes to silence Parkhead. Mark McGhee rounded keeper Peter Latchford to set up Jarvie to score from close range. The Dons were under immediate pressure and the home side levelled four minutes later with a clever back-header from John Doyle. Aberdeen were defending high up the field and that allowed the more creative promptings of Strachan and Scanlon to cause the Celtic defence plenty of problems, and in 56 minutes they again took the lead. Mark McGhee was again involved, and he was on hand to score after Scanlon's shot was blocked. For Celtic, this was not part of the script. They piled on the pressure as they knew a point would be enough to see off the Aberdeen challenge. Keeper Bobby Clark was inspired, and it was his heroics that ensured the title race would continue, although Celtic were awarded a dubious penalty when Clark pushed Frank McGarvey. Ferguson later recalled, 'It is the type of decision that the likes of Celtic and Rangers always seem to get in Glasgow.' It was down to Celtic's Bobby Lennox to take the penalty. Lennox and Clark had plenty of 'previous' dating back to a controversial dive in a 1967 League Cup tie, as well as Lennox's antics in the 1970 Scottish Cup Final when he knocked the ball out of Clark's hands in another act of gamesmanship. On this occasion Clark dived full length to save the spot kick. That spurred the Dons on for the remainder of the game and the 2-1 win was no more than they deserved. The title race was on.

There was no time for Aberdeen to recover as Dundee visited Pittodrie in midweek. A win would put them three points behind Celtic with the same games played. Former Dons striker Ian Fleming had been discarded by Ferguson and he was now leading the line with the Dens Park side. Fleming scored after only three minutes, volleying past Clark. The pressure was again on Aberdeen. In an unchanged starting 11, the Dons laid siege to the Dundee defence but could not find the breakthrough until a brilliant run from McGhee that ended with him being brought down in the box after the hour mark. Gordon Strachan scored from the penalty against his old side. The Dons drew confidence from that and Jarvie scored the vital winner in 74 minutes. It was a real test of character for Aberdeen. Coming so soon after their Parkhead heroics, they showed real resolve to come from behind to put pressure on Celtic, who had now gone eight league games undefeated. Ferguson recalled a sensational save by Clark that proved crucial, 'Bobby made one of his best saves that night when the score was level. I turned to Pat Stanton and told him, "That save will win us the league." Minutes later we went up the park and scored the winner. Things were going our way.'

As Aberdeen were now closing in on Celtic at the summit, they squandered the opportunity to pile the pressure on the Parkhead side by dropping a vital point at home to Hibernian on 16 April. The visitors were already doomed to relegation and were playing out their remaining fixtures looking towards First Division football. Hibernian also paraded George Best, once of Manchester United and regarded as one of the best players in world football. The Irishman, however, was a pale shadow of his former-self and contributed little to the game apart from being booked for talking back to referee Murdoch. There was also rumours ahead of the game that Steve Archibald was on the verge of a move to Tottenham. The distractions did not help Aberdeen, who struggled for long periods. Despite controlling the match, chances were few, and when Gordon Rae put the visitors ahead in 66 minutes the Dons' Premier League chances looked in ruins. Aberdeen came back to level through a rare Andy Watson goal in the closing minutes. This was little consolation for Ferguson, who thought that his team had blown it: 'We were shocking. In fact, it was embarrassing. I remember blowing my top in the dressing room after the game. We had thrown it away.' So, the Aberdeen players experienced the Ferguson 'hairdryer' treatment for the first time. There would be more of that to come.

Three days later came a definitive day in the race for the title. Aberdeen were faced with another long trip to Ayrshire for their second visit to Kilmarnock that month. Celtic made the trip to the east coast to face a Dundee side destined to join Hibernian and being relegated. Kilmarnock had been trounced by the Dons in the earlier meeting but did give them more of a fight on this occasion. Both sides exchanged penalties in the opening 15 minutes before Aberdeen took control. Two goals in two minutes from McGhee and Archibald ended the game as a contest before the break. An injury to Willie Miller was a concern and despite the management team wanting to take him off, the captain refused and played on. Miller typified the spirit and fight that had evolved in the squad.

As Aberdeen held what they had in a relatively subdued second half, the several hundred Dons supporters at Rugby Park were turning their attention to what was happening 70 miles away at Dens Park. As the Aberdeen players emerged for the second half, Chris Anderson told Ferguson that Dundee were leading Celtic 3-1 at the break. This news was relayed to the players. In the days of transistor radios bringing the earliest news of events elsewhere, the scenes of joy among the Aberdeen fans was perhaps not lost on the players as news came through that Celtic were beaten at Dundee. Not just defeated but hammered 5-1. It was a sensational result and most welcome for the Dons. After the disappointment of midweek against Hibernian, the title pendulum was swinging towards Pittodrie and the stage was set for what was rightly billed as a league decider at Parkhead in midweek. The Glasgow press were almost in meltdown as the *Daily Record*, *The Sun* and the *Glasgow Herald* all cast doubts as to the Aberdeen capabilities and opined that it would be impossible for them to win twice at Parkhead in a matter of weeks.

Alex Ferguson wrote in his weekly column in the local *Green Final*, 'If ever there is going to be a test of character, then this is it. Going to Celtic on Wednesday will tell me if Aberdeen can deal with what will be a cauldron. This is the league decider, of that there can be no doubt. And I can give you a million reasons for wanting to win. Winning the championship means everything to any manager. Despite our disappointments this season I am optimistic about Wednesday. A draw would suit Celtic but it's win or bust for us, and that may not be a bad thing. The crowd will be noisy and emotional. Celtic will have a huge support but no matter how big, a support will never beat an Aberdeen team. We will be looking for our own supporters, outnumbered as they will be, we will be playing for them.'

As a postscript to the Dundee result, it was announced that their manager Tommy Gemmell, a former Celtic player, would leave his post as soon as the Dens Park club's relegation was confirmed.

To emphasise the task ahead, the Celtic home record that season was impressive. They had beaten Real Madrid and they had only suffered two home defeats all season; significantly both were against Aberdeen, in the League Cup tie in November and the first league game in April. Manager Billy McNeill was aware of the test his side would face against the Dons, 'The destiny of the title is still within our own hands. It is frustrating that we have let such a lead slip in recent weeks. We are in a position we should never have been in and it is up to ourselves to get out of it. Aberdeen have hit form and they do present us with a big challenge, but I remain confident we can take care of them at home. It is time for everyone at Celtic Park to stand up and be counted.' McNeill was absent from Celtic Park following the Dundee defeat as he was in Ireland taking in the FAI Cup Final in Dublin. In contrast, Aberdeen prepared by travelling south on the Tuesday and staying in a Glasgow hotel. Ferguson took a 16-man squad, adding Ian Scanlon, Alex McLeish, John Hewitt, Doug Bell and Willie Garner to the team that started at Kilmarnock.

Ferguson later recalled his team talk ahead of the game, 'If we were to win the league, we wanted to do it the right way. That was to go to Parkhead and be positive and attack them. Nothing else would be good enough. We so wanted to beat Celtic on their own ground, in front of their own people. It was so important to me and the players because at the end of the day the stature they would gain by winning the way we wanted to at Celtic Park would be immense. If they had done it once, we could do it again.'

The Aberdeen dressing room that balmy evening was relatively quiet before the game; no boom boxes back in those days. The players were ready for anything, including the anticipated delay to the kick-off to let the crowd in. If this was a move to unsettle the Dons, it failed. Experienced full-back Stuart Kennedy had seen it all before and as Celtic chairman Desmond White came into the Dons' dressing room to let them know of the hold-up, Kennedy was stretched out on a bench and not even stripped to play. If Celtic thought they would unnerve this team, it had the opposite effect.

The attendance that night was given as an estimated 48,000. The game was not made all-ticket and it was clear that several thousand fans gained entry by 'other means'. In Scotland it was not uncommon for supporters, usually the younger ones, to be lifted over the turnstiles to gain entry without paying or a click at the gate. Some reports after the match suggested that the actual crowd was nearer 60,000. Nevertheless, it was the biggest crowd Aberdeen had played in front of all season, and the most volatile.

The pressure was all on Celtic and their unforgiving support who had been expecting to pop the champagne corks weeks earlier, such was their lead at the top of the table.

Aberdeen started well and took the game to Celtic, who looked nervous in those early stages. The Dons took a deserved lead after nine minutes when Steve Archibald was left in glorious isolation eight yards out to prod the ball past Latchford. The striker celebrated in front of the Parkhead 'Jungle' in a real statement of intent but the dream start for Aberdeen did not last as Celtic, backed by their crowd, came back into it, albeit through a debatable decision when Alex McLeish was adjudged to have impeded George McCluskey in the penalty area. The Celtic forward took the kick himself to level matters. More anguish followed for the visitors when Gordon Strachan saw Latchford save his penalty. Ferguson recalled, 'Celtic got back into the game with a very doubtful penalty. Over the years Aberdeen have got used to penalties being given against them at Celtic Park.'

Crucially, just before half-time Aberdeen regained the lead. McGhee kept up his scoring streak against Celtic to beat Latchford from close range at the far post from a Kennedy cross. In 65 minutes, Strachan made up for his penalty miss by scoring a third to stun the home support. A quick move on the left involving Scanlon and Archibald let Strachan in to slide the ball into the net. Aberdeen were in complete control and saw the game out after Bobby Clark pulled off a great save from McCluskey.

Ferguson was keen to keep his players grounded despite their fantastic double win over Celtic, their third over the Glasgow club on their own ground that season, telling the *Evening Express*, 'This championship is not over yet. It was a game we had to win, and we did that. Now we must look towards getting both points off St Mirren on Saturday. As far as I am concerned it is the next game that counts. That will stay until the end of the season. I feel we have the right attitude in the side, and I have great faith in the lads. We are in a good position, but so were Celtic a few weeks ago. The St Mirren game is our final home game of the season and we want to hear our great support get behind the team and together we will get the points we need.'

With four games left, the Dons were now looking at securing their first league championship for 25 years. The win saw St Mirren come back into the reckoning. With Aberdeen and Celtic both having to face the Buddies in their closing games, it was all to play for.

Premier League table at 23 April 1980

	P	*W*	*D*	*L*	*F*	*A*	*Pts*
Aberdeen	**32**	**17**	**8**	**7**	**59**	**34**	**42**
Celtic	33	16	10	7	57	37	42
St Mirren	32	14	11	7	51	44	39

Crestfallen Celtic manager Billy McNeill was clearly hurting. 'They [Aberdeen] knew what they had to do; beat us twice at Celtic Park. They came here and got on with the job. Now we are in a position where we are chasing Aberdeen.'

Interest in events at Celtic Park from back in Aberdeen was at fever pitch. As the bars and clubs in the city were listening in on how the Dons were getting on, Grampian Television were also involved as they flashed up progress of the game. Highlights were being shown later that evening and Grampian received 19 calls of complaint from armchair fans who were keen to watch the game without knowing the final score. A Grampian spokesman told the *Evening Express*, 'We recognised this as such a vital match for Aberdeen that it would be a service to viewers to be kept informed of events as they happened. Some people prefer not to know the score, whereas a lot of others do. It is an area where we were never going to please everyone.'

On the back of the win and the performance of Gordon Strachan in particular, the midfielder was set to be announced as the Scottish Football Writers' Association Footballer of the Year. Strachan emerged as the clear favourite and would become the second Aberdeen player to win the award, following on from Martin Buchan in 1971.

With four games still to play the Dons' last home game of the season was against St Mirren on 26 April. With Aberdeen clawing back the Celtic lead to now be in pole position, the visitors were also still not out of the running. With the Paisley club due to face Celtic at home the following week, this clash was vital. The pressure was now all on Aberdeen, but Ferguson was having none of it, 'Our support will play a huge part in helping the players today. They have been magnificent all season and as we look to take the title to Pittodrie we will need one final push. Celtic are still very much in this and if we are to succeed it will take another huge effort from us. I have full faith in the players to see the job through. Some may make us favourites, but it is still very much a race that can go either way.'

On a warm Easter day, the city was immersed in a carnival atmosphere, not just for the events at a packed Pittodrie but also the Aberdeen Students' Charity Parade would take place that evening. The event, which began in 1921, was popular and always well received in the city. The students would dress up in all sorts of clothing and the parade of trucks in the evening as it crept through the city centre was always a highlight in the city calendar. Many of them found their way to Pittodrie as the Dons got down to the more serious business of securing the Premier League title. The ground was full with the capacity cut due to the South Terrace preparatory work beginning before the end of the season. Secretary Ian Taggart declared, 'We decided in January to begin the work early as we did not anticipate that the boys would do so well and go on that unbeaten run. The attendance was limited to 19,000, but such was the interest we could have had double that amount wanting to see the St Mirren game.'

Jim Clunie was manager of St Mirren at the time. The former Aberdeen centre-half was aware of what was at stake, 'Everyone knows that I still have a lot of time for Aberdeen. I spent some great years at Pittodrie as a player and I know what a championship would mean to the club and their support. That is for another day though as we still must believe we can win. If we don't then any hopes we still have of catching the Dons will be gone.'

If there were any nerves in the Aberdeen team then they didn't show it as they pressed St Mirren from the start. Their controlled aggression was exactly what Ferguson was looking for and they took a deserved lead in 25 minutes. Mark McGhee made one of those mazy, unpredictable runs that forced a corner, from which Ian Scanlon was well placed to head Aberdeen in front. Just before the break the Dons struck again. St Mirren keeper Billy Thomson could only parry an Archibald flick and Doug Rougvie scored from close range. St Mirren were simply swept aside and never looked like getting back into the game. The Dons applauded the Pittodrie support at the end of the game as their home campaign came to a close, but there was still work to do. For a side that looked desperately out of form and bereft of any confidence following their League Cup Final replay defeat in December, an unbeaten run had taken Aberdeen to the brink of an unexpected title.

The Dons then played their game in hand at Tannadice, always a tough venue but one that they had traditionally done well at against Dundee United. Their manager Jim McLean was also a close friend of Ferguson but a fierce rival too, as was brutally shown in that League Cup defeat earlier that season. For Aberdeen, anything other than a defeat would keep them on course for the flag. United had little but pride to play for, their season having faded out following their first major cup success. Former Dundee player

Strachan scored the goal of the season after 16 minutes, his 30-yard effort sending the sizeable travelling support into scenes of joy. It was the first goal that United had conceded in the league for 16 hours. The club's match programme notes declared that not many at Tannadice would begrudge Aberdeen taking the title, but nobody told United midfielder John Holt, who levelled after 49 minutes. The 1-1 draw was frustrating for Aberdeen, but the point meant that if they won at Easter Road at the weekend and Celtic failed to do likewise at St Mirren then the Premier League title would be heading north. That was following Celtic's narrow win against Dundee the day after the Dons' clash at Tannadice. Billy McNeill claimed his side were back in control, trying to pile the pressure on Aberdeen: 'The pendulum has swung in our favour again. The Dons have a game in hand, but of more importance we have that point in the bag. The Dons still have to win their game and Saturday will be interesting. It is a case of seeing what develops and if necessary, sit back until Wednesday for their game at Partick.'

All the attention then turned to the trip to Edinburgh and to face Hibernian on 3 May 1980, a definitive day not only in Aberdeen FC history but for Scottish football. No side out of Glasgow had won the title for 15 years. In the modern era that period may not seem as alarming, considering that Aberdeen were the last provincial winners of the title in 1985. Such has been the change in the Scottish game as the financial clout of the two Glasgow clubs has widened the gap between the rest like never before. In 1980, there was a far more level playing field and under Alex Ferguson, Aberdeen took full advantage.

They had an injury scare with Gordon Strachan struggling following the game in Dundee. Strachan was laid low with a stomach bug and following a day of rest the solution was found in the bracing sea air of Stonehaven, the coastal town 15 miles south of Aberdeen. An impromptu game of baseball on the beach was exactly the boost that Strachan and his team-mates needed as they prepared for the crunch game against Hibernian. Ferguson stated, 'The trip to the beach did the lads a lot of good. Gordon has not managed to eat all week and if the run about on the beach does not give him an appetite, nothing will!' Despite McNeill's claims, as far as Aberdeen were concerned nothing had changed. They knew that regardless of what Celtic did, if they won their final two games then they would be champions. There was also an additional factor – the Dons' superior goal difference, which before the Easter Road game stood at four in their favour.

More than 8,000 Aberdeen supporters made their way to Edinburgh. Traditionally Easter Road was a tough venue, but this Hibernian side was in turmoil. From the aborted signature of George Best to an extensive injury list, they were already condemned to relegation. They also handed a debut to rookie keeper Dave Huggins. After 30 minutes all attention turned to events at Paisley as by that time Aberdeen had taken a two-goal lead through Archibald and Andy Watson. Ferguson recalled, 'After 15 or so minutes I just could not see Hibernian scoring. When we went ahead with two goals in as many minutes we were on our way.' Three second-half goals put Aberdeen on the brink. Bobby Clark was a virtual spectator as the Dons played the entire closing period in the Hibernian half. Clark would turn to the Aberdeen support packed in the terrace behind him for updates from Paisley. St Mirren were still holding Celtic at 0-0 as the game went into the final minutes, then came news that they had been awarded a penalty. After 78 minutes St Mirren defender John Young clashed with Tommy Burns amid howls from the 7,000 travelling supporters. The tension among the Dons fans was unbearable. No VAR back then but there was an astute linesman in Paisley who spotted that the infringement was outside of the area. No penalty! Confusion reigned as conflicting news came through. The full-time whistle went at Easter Road as Aberdeen completed their 5-0 rout of Hibernian. Seconds later the game ended in Paisley and St Mirren held Celtic to a 0-0 draw. Aberdeen were champions.

The chaotic scenes at full time were understandable. Ferguson went straight to embrace veteran keeper Bobby Clark as several hundred fans gathered on the pitch among the jubilant players. This was new territory for Aberdeen, their first league title for 25 years. There was no trophy presentation, no helicopter to carry the trophy between Paisley or Edinburgh. Just a jubilant set of players and fans at Easter Road, on this occasion, all as one.

Captain Willie Miller recalled, 'We strolled the game in the second half, but our attentions turned to events in Paisley. After an uncertain interlude as our game finished, our fans erupted in celebration. The Celtic game had finished 0-0, Aberdeen were Scottish Premier League champions, and I felt a wondrous achievement. We celebrated on the pitch, chanting "Here we go, here we go." We enjoyed our moments of glory. The boss was jumping all over the place, hugging anyone who would accept his embrace, but I was shedding tears of joy with most of the senior players and heading back to the dressing room to be interviewed by Arthur Montford of Scottish Television. He was a likeable presenter of the long-running *Scotsport*, and I presented my own views as the champagne flowed. Arthur moved on to Alex McLeish, who claimed he was speechless, but proceeded to talk for about ten minutes about our victory. Our Alex was never a shrinking violet.'

When the dust had settled, it was still mathematically possible for Aberdeen to have been caught, but they would have had to have lost 10-0 in their final game at Partick in midweek. Alastair MacDonald, the meticulous reporter for the *Press & Journal* who had been following Aberdeen fortunes since the war, wrote, 'Forgive me if the foregoing sounds less objective than it should be, but I had a minor role in recording the Dons' last league win in 1955 and a quarter of a century is a long time to wait for the thrill to recur. Aberdeen's league success, however long-overdue, is something which must be welcomed throughout Scotland by anyone unprejudiced enough to recognise that for Celtic and Rangers to have imposed domination on the league title for as long as 15 years is an unhealthy trend. The benefits accruing to Aberdeen in general and the Pittodrie club are considerable. The city always experiences a spin-off from sporting success in various business aspects and in business.'

Aberdeen vice-chairman Chris Anderson pointed towards the future, 'I am sure that breaking the Glasgow stranglehold on the title will encourage other clubs to emulate us. We have shown that it is possible that Celtic and Rangers can be beaten on their own grounds and relegated to lower positions in the league table. If other clubs can follow our example it will be good for Scottish football. We are greatly encouraged by this success and hope it will prove a launching pad in our quest for more honours. We see winning the title as the vindication of our club policies over the past decade. We are proud of this achievement, but realise it is only a step in the right direction. It must be followed by further success.'

The title victory was a timely one for Bobby Clark as he completed his full set of domestic winners' medals; the decisive game at Easter Road came 15 years to the day since he signed for Aberdeen, 'Winning the championship is a tribute to all the hard work put in by everyone at Pittodrie, not least by the manager.'

The Scottish League announced that only 15 medals would be awarded to the club, but they did declare that additional medals for players who made a contribution would be allowed at the club's own expense. The last word on Easter Road; Alex Ferguson was being reported to the SFA following remarks made to referee Brian McGinlay at half-time. Ferguson declared, 'It was just a comment I made in the heat of the moment, possibly an indication of the tension I was under. I should have known better.'

Meanwhile, plans were announced by the club that the players would parade through the city and show off the league trophy at Pittodrie. The procession would take place on Sunday, 11 May, begin at the Bridge of Dee and travel along Holburn Street, Union Street and past the Town House before continuing down King Street to Pittodrie where the trophy presentation would take place.

As Aberdeen were basking in Premier League success, the domestic football season ended in controversial circumstances. The Scottish Cup Final was still the showpiece that it always had been, and Celtic would be battling it out with Rangers in a desperate bid to lift some silverware that season. With Aberdeen and Dundee United already winners in the Premier League and League Cup respectively, there was an air of desperation around Hampden as the Glasgow clubs would meet to save their season.

It was in the full glare of live television, showcased to audiences outside of this country that shame was brought to Scottish football on 10 May. As a cup final it failed to reach any heights. On a dry, fiery surface it was a game of attrition and it took a deflected goal in extra time for Celtic to consign Rangers to another barren campaign.

The SFA in their wisdom allowed the winning side to take their bow in front of their support at full time. While this practice is accepted for any teams outside of Glasgow, for Celtic and Rangers such displays are usually forbidden, such is the toxic hate that surrounds these clubs. The reason the authorities relented for this game was down to the 10ft fences that had been built around the stadium perimeter to prevent any supporter invasions. In the current environment in football, it seems almost barbaric to erect fencing within stadiums. In '80s Britain it was more common. The reason behind this archaic move was mainly down to previous fan incursions from the terraces to the playing field. Rangers were culpable; the mindset being that such invasions would cause so much havoc and lead to games being postponed, often when the Ibrox side were struggling. One such occasion occurred at Pittodrie on Christmas Eve in 1977 as the Dons were cruising to a 4-0 win over the Ibrox side. The police and stewards at Pittodrie were prepared that time and the few supporters that did get on to the field were swiftly removed.

After Celtic were presented with the Scottish Cup they did indeed celebrate in front of their fans, but unfortunately some of them breached the confines of the fencing, which was proving inadequate. As more followed, some went on to the pitch. The Rangers supporters who were still in the ground reacted and that led to pitch scenes that brought shame to Scotland. On-field fighting with bricks and bottles was described by experienced Scottish football commentator Archie MacPherson as being like a scene from *Apocalypse Now*. The police did not escape scrutiny. They took the view that the fencing would ensure crowd 'safety' within the stadium so most of the officers on duty that day were directed to the streets outside of Hampden after the game. The result was carnage on the pitch in full view of the sizeable television audience.

The SFA, who were far from free of responsibility over events at Hampden, fined both clubs £20,000 as more than 200 arrests were made. The subsequent fallout reached the government and a law was passed in Scotland to ban all alcohol sales in all Scottish sports grounds. It was a far-reaching law which remains in place to the present day, although the Scottish Rugby Union were granted a reprieve in 2007. The loss of revenue over more than 40 years is incalculable. At the time the Aberdeen directors were livid at the ruling. There had already been plans to install corporate boxes at Pittodrie, the first club in Scotland to do so. There was also their belief that Aberdeen, along with other clubs, were being penalised for what was essentially a Glasgow problem. Within the Main Stand at Pittodrie had been a sizeable bar which was packed out at every home game. The club, with Chris Anderson at the forefront, were investigating all kinds of different revenue streams. The ban on alcohol was a retrograde step and a move that would have no long-term positive effects on the game.

The team took their bow through the city as Alex Ferguson and his players were presented with the Premier League trophy at a packed Pittodrie. The celebrations were tempered by the confirmation that Steve Archibald had agreed to join Tottenham Hotspur in a £1m deal. The Dons did everything they could to hold on to their striker by offering Archibald a bumper deal to remain. However, Spurs boss Keith Burkinshaw had thrown everything at Archibald to ensure he would switch to London, 'Steve was our first-choice target for many months, and we are delighted he has agreed terms to join us.'

Another departure was Pat Stanton, who played a significant role in the Premier League success. Ferguson was disappointed but understood Stanton's position, 'I am sorry to see Pat move on. He has been great for me and the club since he came here. Pat intimated that he wanted to branch out on his own and I totally understand that. He will be missed.'

Aberdeen also announced that they accepted an invitation to take part in a pre-season tournament in Lyon. The invitation came through a German agency who suggested that they would be ideal participants following their matches against Düsseldorf and Frankfurt in Europe. Aberdeen would then finalise their preparations at Gordonstoun where Ferguson would put his players through it, 'The one thing guaranteed up there is that it brings pain to footballers. There is no easy way out.'

As the squad went their separate ways for a deserved summer break the builders moved into Pittodrie. Plans were approved for the construction of a cantilever roof over the South Terrace. On completion, an ultra-modern Pittodrie would be ready to host European Cup football for the first time.

4

Lessons Learned

AS PREMIER League champions the Dons' elevated status brought new challenges. As the first team to smash the Glasgow monopoly of the Scottish championship since 1965 they were now the team to beat. There was little doubt the club had ruffled Glasgow feathers and noises from Celtic and Rangers were on reflection an endorsement of Aberdeen's success. As the Dons looked ahead to defending their crown and a first European Cup campaign, the latest stage of the Pittodrie development was completed over the summer. The last part of the ground to be covered was the South Terrace, an area that could now seat more than 9,000 spectators with the majority under cover. The £500,000 investment into the facilities was the biggest development at Pittodrie since 1968 when the old enclosure was demolished to make way for new seating and dugouts as the name of the ground changed from Pittodrie Park to Pittodrie Stadium.

Aberdeen began their pre-season training as the draws for European competitions were made in Zürich on 9 July. The Dons were unseeded and accepted that they could face tough opposition in the opening round. As previous European opponents Honvéd came out in the preliminary round, Linfield were drawn against Nantes. Aberdeen were the fifth club drawn out of the hat and they were to face Austrian champions Austria Vienna. With the first leg due at Pittodrie in September, Alex Ferguson was happy enough with the tie: 'It is certainly not an easy one, but it could have been a lot worse. Austria has produced many fine players down the years, so I know they will be strong. The fact that the first game is at Pittodrie is no disadvantage to us. We know what we must do, we must be perfect at home. I think I would have preferred a preliminary round to get the younger players used to the competition, but we must concentrate on this one. It is a great tie.'

Other seeded sides in the European Cup that season included Ajax, Club Brugge, Liverpool, Nottingham Forest, Real Madrid, Bayern Munich, Inter Milan and Nantes. There seemed to be some confusion as to the correct name of the Dons' opponents. Best known as Austria Wien, the Vienna club had been sponsored by cigarette firm Memphis for the past two seasons and were known as Austria Memphis in their homeland. They had won the Austrian championship for the past three seasons and were by far the dominant force in their country.

There was one change in the Pittodrie boardroom as Ian Donald, son of chairman Dick Donald, was appointed as a director following the passing of Charles Forbes in April. Forbes had been a player and director with the club since making his debut in May 1922. He also served as chairman from 1959 to 1970.

One Pittodrie staff member who was busy over the summer was physio Roland Arnott, having swapped footballs for strawberries and cream as he was engaged as one of the physios at Wimbledon for the annual lawn tennis event. Arnott treated eventual winner Björn Borg daily as the superstar Swede overcame a niggling injury to win his fifth Wimbledon men's title.

Aberdeen prepared for the new season in the familiar setting of Gordonstoun. It was a facility that Ferguson enjoyed, although that was not shared by the players. In what were spartan but very adequate surroundings with no external distractions, it was a punishing schedule for the squad as conditioning work was the prime focus. Among the new arrivals to the squad were youngsters Neale Cooper, John Hewitt, Eric Black and Bryan Gunn. Aberdeen opened their season with a rare trip to the Faroes, where they warmed up with a 5-1 win over local side Tórshavn. Ahead of friendlies against Forres and Nairn in the Highland League, the manager had to laugh off rumours that he was about to sign former England keeper Peter Bonetti, 'Really, I think some Sunday papers must get "Oor Wullie" [a fictional character in the *Sunday Post*]. The stories are absolute nonsense. Bobby Clark has three weeks to get fit and we have Jim Leighton already establishing himself as a great young keeper.' After two low-key victories in the Highlands where the Dons rattled in 12 goals, the revamped Drybrough Cup was up for grabs. The sponsored competition had followed in similar fashion to the Watney Cup in England. Aberdeen were first winners in 1971 and Ferguson was keen to get his side off to a winning start, 'The Drybrough Cup gives us the opportunity to lay a marker down for the new season.' Aberdeen opened their campaign at Pittodrie with a visit from Airdrie in the opening round. A 4-1 win on 26 July set the Dons up for a midweek trip to Greenock to face Morton in the semi-final. In between times Alex Ferguson flew to Vienna to see the Dons' European opponents at first hand, in a friendly against Manchester United. Ferguson was surprised to discover that Memphis coach Hermann Stessl had left Vienna on the eve of the season to take over FC Porto in Portugal.

The club had arranged a Pittodrie friendly against Arsenal on Sunday, 3 August as they were also set to unfurl the Premier League flag and parade the title trophy. Ahead of the visit of the Gunners the Dons made time for lifting the first trophy of the season. After a tough semi-final in Greenock in midweek which went to extra time, Aberdeen progressed to meet St Mirren at Hampden the day before the Arsenal visit. The choice of the national stadium for the Drybrough final was far from ideal. The quickfire tournament may have been perfect preparation for the new season but it was never the crowd-puller that the sponsors had hoped for. In what was the last ever Drybrough Cup clash the Dons again prevailed with a 2-1 win over the Paisley side. For Ferguson it was important that his side continued on their winning ways, 'We will be the side they all want to beat this season and we accept that. It is vital for us to keep up our high standards, I will not accept anything else.'

Arsenal were no strangers to Pittodrie having visited Aberdeen in 1908, 1959 and again in 1975 for friendly fixtures. Included in the Gunners' side was new £1.25m signing Clive Allen, a prolific striker who joined Arsenal from Queens Park Rangers. For reasons unknown to Allen he only played in three pre-season matches for Arsenal and after 62 days he was transferred to Crystal Palace. For Aberdeen it was a gala occasion as Ferguson and captain Willie Miller were on hand when the league flag was unfurled in a Main Stand ceremony before kick-off. The flag was later flown from the flagpole at the south corner of the King Street end of the ground and remained there for the duration of the season. The 2-1 win over Arsenal completed an excellent weekend for the Dons. Ferguson was happy with the way the pre-season programme had gone, 'There are bigger targets than the Drybrough Cup, but the competition was part of the programme I had mapped out. Nothing succeeds like success. The look of pride on the faces of the players at Hampden after they had given the opposition a goal start was worth a million. Just 24 hours later we were beating Arsenal, one of the strongest teams in England.'

The club also announced details of the Joe Harper testimonial match. Aberdeen would be playing an International XI made up of some of the best-known players in Scotland and England. It was also announced on 25 August that Archie Knox had agreed to join Aberdeen as assistant manager. Knox would replace Pat Stanton, who left the club in the summer. Knox hardly knew Ferguson before his appointment, their paths barely crossing as both were now in management and coaching. Knox recalled his move to Aberdeen, 'Alex took his young reserve side to Forfar where I was coaching. He asked to speak with me before the game and offered me the opportunity to join him at Pittodrie. I agreed immediately and he asked me when I could start. I told him I could be there the next day. Less than 24 hours later I was at Pittodrie for a friendly against Twente Enschede and agreed terms with Aberdeen chairman Dick Donald.'

Aberdeen had opened their defence of the Premier League with a narrow but deserved win at St Mirren before being held at home to Dundee United. It was a source of frustration at the club that as champions the Dons were not handed a home match to open their season. In the modern era it would be unheard of. The Aberdeen management did not make their feelings known in the media, choosing to raise the matter with the authorities privately.

The unbeaten start continued with a routine two-legged win over Berwick Rangers in the League Cup. The format of the competition once again reverted to a home and away basis in the early rounds which irked Ferguson, 'I don't see any value in these games being played over two legs. Against Berwick we won the first game 8-1 and gained no value from the formality of a second game down there.' The return in Berwick was anything but routine. The 4-0 win was easy enough, but it will be remembered for an astonishing goal from Dons' reserve keeper Marc De Clerck. The Belgian, making his debut, scored against the only English-based team in Scottish football. His hefty, wind-assisted clearance took one bounce and flew over the Berwick keeper and into the net.

In the next round Aberdeen were paired with Rangers and the bitter rivalry between the two clubs continued. During the first leg at Ibrox, Rangers winger Willie Johnson viciously stamped on the neck of John McMaster. The Ibrox player had plenty of previous, having been sent home from the Scotland squad after failing a drugs test in Argentina in 1978 and also receiving various red cards throughout an eventful career. On this occasion Johnston raked his studs down McMaster's neck and chest as he was on the ground injured. The quick thinking of the Dons players and medical staff prevented what could have been a far worse outcome. It was a spiteful act which earned Johnston another red card but no further sanction. McMaster recalled the incident, 'If big Doug Rougvie had got hold of him [Johnston], he would not have seen daylight. I got four stud marks, I didn't need the kiss of life, although that was reported. I was lucky. If he had caught me on the throat it might have been very different. I used to love watching Johnston play, he was brilliant, but he went down in my estimation as a man. There was no apology, nothing. He just walked away and went up the tunnel. I don't know what he was thinking to be honest.'

The incident was another in what was to be a continued feud between the clubs that has endured to the present day. Ferguson at the time refused to speak about it but was more determined than ever to not only overturn the one-goal deficit but to lay down a marker to Rangers that his team were not going to be intimidated or bullied.

Aberdeen faced a crucial spell towards the end of September with a first European Cup tie and domestic clashes against Rangers and Celtic, all at Pittodrie in the space of ten days. The first leg against Austria Vienna was a historic occasion for the club, and for some it came 25 years too late. Back in 1955 when Aberdeen won their first league title the new European Cup came into force the following season. As champions, they expected the call from the SFA to become the first Scottish club to play in Europe. It never came. That first season was by invitation only and the Scottish authorities put forward Hibernian, a team who had been inferior to Aberdeen during that period. The competition was amended the following season as respective league winners were asked to compete. It came too late for the Dons who were treated shabbily by the SFA, which soured relations between the club and the governing body. It can only be imagined how Alex Ferguson would have reacted to such manipulation. The European Cup of course has given way to the current Champions League. One can only wonder what the astute Gabriel Hanot, the French footballer and later journalist who was behind the formation of the European Cup, would have made of what the competition has evolved into with its current form: a monster closed shop and cash cow for the most wealthy clubs in Europe.

Ahead of the tie Ferguson was in Sweden as part of the television media team who were taking in Scotland's opening World Cup qualifier in Stockholm. The manager was delighted to see Gordon Strachan finish off a fine move to score the winning goal and get the Scots' World Cup campaign off to the perfect start. With Alex McLeish and Willie Miller also involved, the Aberdeen presence in the national side was growing.

The tie against the Austrian champions was only the Dons' 29th in Europe, and their fourth in different competitions, following on from the Inter-Cities Fairs Cup, the Cup Winners' Cup and UEFA Cup. Of the 28 games played, 12 had been won with 11 defeats and five draws. Mark McGhee was brought in by Ferguson to realise his huge potential. It was his goal in 31 minutes that gave Aberdeen a vital and welcome one-goal first-leg lead. The Austrians were a proper side, certainly worthy of their European status, and in Walter Schachner they had one of the best forwards in Europe. Despite the threat the Austrians posed, Aberdeen as a team in Europe were not only evolving, but learning. Ferguson declared afterwards that any lead would be a great result to take to Vienna and so it proved as the Dons held Memphis to a 0-0 draw in the second leg in what was arguably their finest defensive display in Europe. The imposing Praterstadion held few fears for Aberdeen and the 500 travelling Red Army. The visitors were dealt a blow ahead of the tie when Alex McLeish failed a late fitness test. Willie Garner deputised and with Willie Miller at the back the Dons not only held their own but created four great opportunities to finish the tie. Miller recalled, 'I had a hunch we could defend well and frustrate them over there. There was about 37,000 of a crowd and they were expecting a home victory, but by the end they were jeering their side. We thoroughly deserved to travel home with a 0-0 draw, and our performance in Austria proved that we could defend well under any circumstances.

It was important to get at least one European Cup win behind us.'

In between times the Dons had unfinished business with Rangers. Pittodrie was at fever pitch for the League Cup second leg following the events at Ibrox. John McMaster exacted immediate revenge for his treatment at Ibrox with a thunderous drive from 25 yards to level the tie after five minutes. The toxic atmosphere piled the pressure on referee Smith, who was willing to let some hefty challenges go as both sides were fully committed. This was tribal. Strachan put Aberdeen ahead before McAdam squared the tie on aggregate early in the second half. As the game entered the closing minutes John Hewitt was taken out by Jackson on the edge of the box. No VAR back then and a brief conversation between the referee and linesman resulted in a penalty to Aberdeen. Strachan did the needful and put his team through to the quarter-final. As victories over the Glasgow clubs go, this one was right up there.

The euphoria following that victory continued until the next round when Aberdeen were shocked by Dundee. After missing numerous chances in both ties, the Dons were hit with a late Dundee goal against the run of play to end their League Cup hopes. Ferguson was disappointed, 'Over the two games it is quite unbelievable that we have not scored. We missed so many chances at Dens and again at Pittodrie. That's football, they took the one chance they had, and we were careless.'

After their European Cup win over Vienna, the Dons were keenly anticipating the draw for the second round. They were unseeded and came out against Liverpool, the plum draw of the round. With the likes of Bayern Munich, Ajax, Inter Milan and Real Madrid in the last 16, it was always going to be a tough task for Aberdeen.

Alex Ferguson was delighted with the draw: 'So now we know, it's Liverpool for Pittodrie in the European Cup. It is a great draw for us. Liverpool is the club that has dominated the English game since the 1960s, and they have won the European Cup on two occasions. Archie Knox and I will be at Anfield next week to watch them, just as we always intend doing, no matter the opposition. It is a formidable task for Aberdeen, but many said that when we went to Vienna.'

Liverpool manager Bob Paisley was unhappy with the draw: 'We would have preferred a continental team. We regard Aberdeen as one of the best teams in the European Cup and it is a real test for us so early in the competition.'

Liverpool captain Phil Neal said after the draw, 'This is what the football fans want. It will set everyone talking on both sides of the border debating who is the best in Britain, and it will be down to us or Aberdeen to prove that point. We will certainly not underestimate the Scottish champions and our management will have them watched before we meet them. Aberdeen are clearly a very good side after their result in the last round.'

SIMPLE SECRET OF A LAUGHING CAVALIER

Interest in what was billed as the 'Battle of Britain' was nationwide. Tickets for the Pittodrie clash were due to go on sale on 13 October, nine days before the game. The *Evening Express* reported, 'Aberdeen and the north-east went football mad yesterday when news of the draw came through from Zürich. Aberdeen secretary Ian Taggart was inundated with interest: "I have never known anything quite like it. The phone was ringing often enough before the draw but when Liverpool came out of the hat things just went wild. Friday is a busy enough day for us, but it was quite unbelievable. Our capacity is 24,000, but we could have sold that amount three times over. We have had interest from Scotland, England and Wales but we will only consider applications from our season ticket holders then a general sale."

Liverpool Football Club

LIVERPOOL

versus

ABERDEEN

(Champions of Scotland)

5th NOVEMBER, 1980

Ticket and Match Information:
051-260 9999 (24 hour service)

KEMLYN ROAD STAND
Block "G"

Row	Seat No.
Nº 4	42

This portion to be retained

'The Pittodrie club contacted Liverpool FC to discuss arrangements for the tie and the allocation of tickets for visiting fans. UEFA rules at the time only stated an "adequate" number should be released to away sides in the European Cup.'

Liverpool were already making their travel plans and had requested that Aberdeen Airport remain open later than normal to allow their fans to return home after the game. The Anfield club were only expecting to take around 600 to Pittodrie. Secretary Peter Robinson explained, 'Liverpool has been hit hard by economic recession and this has influenced the club. Many fans simply cannot afford to go and see their team. Average gates are down from 45,000 to 37,000.'

The economic situation in Aberdeen was in stark contrast to down south as the oil industry was on the verge of a boom time for the area. That was not reflected in some of the city infrastructure. The fact that the airport still closed before 10pm was ridiculed within local business. It was not until 2005 that the airport was changed to a 24-hour operation and latterly became Aberdeen International Airport.

In 1980 Aberdeen only had several hundred season ticket holders. They were all seated in the Main Stand at Pittodrie. Scottish clubs in that era did not prioritise season ticket sales like they do today, as the main source of income was still the 'gate' money, with sponsorship still to make a significant impact. The club had become used to all-ticket games at Pittodrie in the past but the Liverpool tie was something else. The general sale of tickets went ahead on Saturday, 11 October. Many fans had queued outside Pittodrie all night, the first ones setting up camp at 4pm on the Friday. Fans began to converge on the stadium through Friday and into the early hours of the Saturday. At one stage the queue was more than a mile long.

For those who turned up as early as 6am, their wait was futile. The Pittodrie turnstiles began to close less than 45 minutes after the sale commenced, leaving thousands of supporters frustrated. There were chaotic scenes as fan fury threatened to boil over. The club, on reflection, made the error of allowing four tickets per person. This eventually led to a significant number of 'fair-weather' fans obtaining tickets as several thousand Pittodrie regulars missed out. This well known part of the Aberdeen support, those who would pick and choose games throughout the season, were those who privately infuriated Alex Ferguson. In his programme notes for the visit of Kilmarnock later that day he said, 'The sale of the Liverpool tickets should have brought a lot of Aberdeen fans to the ground today and I trust it reflects the crowd that took the opportunity to watch the match against Kilmarnock. I will be really disappointed if we do not get a big gate this afternoon.' A crowd of just over 11,000 turned up to see Aberdeen create a club record of going 23 games unbeaten. Chris Anderson defended the ticket sale, 'The board gave this a lot of consideration and we felt that four tickets per head was a fair allocation. Looking back it could have been one or two each. We had around 60,000 fans wanting after just 20,000 tickets and there was no way we could guarantee our regular supporters a ticket. It was like putting a quart into a pint pot.'

The whole episode reflected badly as Aberdeen were clearly caught out by the level of interest. On reflection, as Scottish champions, such a scenario was always possible. Lessons were learned, however, as later that season the club announced a new system whereby certain games would see vouchers issued to fans who in turn would get priority for all-ticket games in the future. The ticket fiasco aside, the Dons then had to deal with a Liverpool side that was at that time the best in Europe, if not the world. The pre-match rivalry was intense. Notwithstanding the obvious Scotland v England tag, Liverpool boasted the likes of Kenny Dalglish, Graeme Souness and Alan Hansen, all famed Scotland internationals. Former Celtic player Dalglish recalled, 'When the draw was made and it was Aberdeen the whole mood in the dressing room changed. We had to win. Graeme, Alan and I kept telling each other that if we did not get a result we were going to be crucified, completely slaughtered, every time we went back to Scotland. They would rub it in forever.'

Bob Paisley made sure that Aberdeen were watched on each of the four occasions they would play before the first leg. Ferguson and Archie Knox watched the Reds against Middlesbrough on 7 October, where they met Bill Shankly in the Anfield directors' box. The former Liverpool manager was full of praise for what Aberdeen had achieved but remained indignant when it came to his old team, 'You are down to have a look at our great team? They all try that.' Shankly did acknowledge what the Dons had achieved, 'Aberdeen are a credit to the Scottish game. They have been for a number of years. Last season they got the championship they deserved. Now they have shown that they are capable of dealing with the extra demands of European Cup football. Their win over the Austrians was pure European copybook stuff straight from the manual used by Inter Milan in the '60s.'

The atmosphere at Pittodrie reached fever pitch as Liverpool were given the 'treatment' from the massed ranks in the Beach End. Their Anglos got the worst of it. Dalglish recalled that it was 'horrendous, real vitriol from the terraces'. Aberdeen made a dreadful start and were caught out after five minutes when a clever lob from Terry McDermott deceived Jim Leighton. They were up against it, even at that early stage. Liverpool to their credit gave Aberdeen full respect but controlled the tie for long periods. The task was made all the more difficult when influential midfielder John McMaster was on the end of a shocking challenge from Ray Kennedy. Willie Miller recalled, 'That foul was one of the worst challenges I ever witnessed.' The loss of McMaster disrupted the Dons' tactics and approach and although they applied plenty of pressure on the Liverpool defence, they could not find a breakthrough.

The Reds were seasoned European campaigners and familiar with being faced with hostile away crowds. For Aberdeen, it was the first part of a painful European lesson from the side that would go on to win the European Cup later that season.

In the immediate aftermath of that home defeat the Dons recovered well with a 3-1 win over Dundee United at Tannadice and a convincing victory over Airdrie at Pittodrie. Walker McCall had rejoined the Dons in a surprise move from Atlanta Chiefs. McCall grabbed a hat-trick in the Airdrie clash but it was his two goals against Celtic at Parkhead on 8 November between the top two sides in the country that once again was full on controversy. On this occasion it was not so much the Celtic players who couldn't lay a glove on an imperious Gordon Strachan but a home fan who ran on to the field to confront the midfielder. Fortunately for Strachan, other players managed to intervene before the situation got out of hand. Unfortunately for the Celtic fan, Dons defender Doug Rougvie was one of them. The unsavoury incident was just another in a series of nasty moments when Aberdeen were doing the business in Glasgow.

Premier League table at 22 November 1980

	P	*W*	*D*	*L*	*F*	*A*	*Pts*
Aberdeen	**15**	**11**	**4**	**0**	**34**	**10**	**26**
Rangers	15	8	7	0	33	10	23
Celtic	15	9	2	4	31	18	20
Dundee United	15	5	6	4	19	18	16

The return European Cup clash in Liverpool was a watershed moment for Aberdeen and Alex Ferguson. Liverpool were almost unbeatable at Anfield, having only conceded eight goals at home in the league the previous season. They had not lost at home in three years, stretching to an incredible 75 games. The Dons' injuries were also piling up. With McMaster and the experienced Stuart Kennedy missing, the lack of depth in the squad was brutally exposed against Liverpool. The 4-0 defeat was the worst Ferguson endured in his time at Pittodrie. Andy Dornan was making only his second first-team appearance and two substitutes, Neale Cooper and John Hewitt, were still not old enough to vote. Despite the overwhelming odds, Aberdeen did have one great chance to level the tie on aggregate when Mark McGhee robbed Phil Thompson and evaded two challenges before going clean through on goal. England keeper Ray Clemence saved McGhee's effort and there ended any faint hopes of Aberdeen getting back into the tie. After Willie Miller had the misfortune to slice the ball into his own goal, the Dons were looking at limiting a rampant Liverpool. The Anfield defeat was a chastening experience for Ferguson and his players. Their newfound invincibility in Scotland was swept aside by the English champions. It hurt. The Aberdeen support, limited to 2,000, certainly backed their team but it was a night not to forget, instead to learn from.

Ferguson was livid during and after the game but on reflection he realised that however good his side were in Scottish football, in European terms they had some way to go. Captain Willie Miller declared that the Liverpool tie came too early for Aberdeen, 'We had hardly kicked a ball over the two legs. At the time we made all the right noises about being able to bounce back, but it came as a blow to our collective confidence. The boss had influenced us to think we could beat any side on our day, but the truth was Liverpool were streets ahead. They passed the ball better and took their chances when they came. The boss of course took it personally and on the coach on the way home from Merseyside his face was like thunder. I maintain to this day that no side could have lived with that Liverpool team. For context in season 1980/81 we did not lose by more than one goal in all our away games, so Liverpool's achievement in putting four goals past us at Anfield was quite superb.'

There was little doubt the Dons' exit from Europe had an effect on manager and players, although that was not reflected in the league as the team continued to remain unbeaten. That was all to change by the end of the year. Aberdeen were five points clear at the top of the Premier League and well on course to retain their title. On 30 December in the traditional new year clash with Dundee United, Gordon Strachan was injured in a clash with United midfielder Ian Phillip. The injury at the time seemed innocent enough but it was later revealed to be a stomach tear and Strachan would be out for the rest of the season. Ferguson recalled, 'It was a bad blow for us, coming on top of the long-term injuries to Bobby Clark and John McMaster. Our midfield was well and truly scuppered at a vital stage of the season. Gordon more than any other would be missed as a source of inspiration. I believe we would have taken the title that year if we had been able to field a full-strength side and if we hadn't had to play those two games against Liverpool which hurt us physically and psychologically.'

The busy festive period was to prove crucial. Celtic came north on 27 December and were totally outclassed by Aberdeen with Willie Miller and Alex McLeish scoring in a 4-1 win. Three days later the injury to Strachan left a depleted team to face St Mirren in Paisley on 3 January. The Dons were held to a 1-1 draw. There was little doubt that Aberdeen were the team they all wanted to beat; as reigning champions that came with the territory. Scottish football and its tribal nature made any success a grudging one.

With Aberdeen going 31 games without defeat, there was almost a desperation from opponents to see that record come to an end. That fateful day came on 31 January against Rangers at Ibrox. Aberdeen were missing Clark, McMaster, Strachan, Kennedy and Miller, who was suspended. They went down 1-0 to a late Johnstone goal against a Rangers side that were well off the pace at the top of the table. Two weeks later came a crucial Scottish Cup defeat at Greenock of all places. The Morton ground at Cappielow was the one venue that was hated by most visitors and Aberdeen, more than most, traditionally struggled there. It was a sparse, ageing facility that had not seen any improvements since the war. Greenock at that time was a desolate town, economically ruined by the demise of the shipbuilding industry and an uncaring Tory government. Cappielow was no place for the Dons' fluent passing game. Morton played to their strengths and that came in the uncompromising frame of Andy Ritchie, a languid player with uncanny natural ability. Ritchie had the knack of embarrassing opponents. On this occasion Aberdeen defender Doug Considine was turned inside out before Ritchie scored the only goal of the game.

By the end of February the Dons' title hopes were all but gone. A rare home defeat to St Mirren was an eighth game without a win. During that disappointing and unexpected run they also went down to Kilmarnock at Rugby Park. What was ironic was the 2,500 attendance was less than the 3,000 who had turned out at Pittodrie for a reserve game to see Joe Harper return from injury in a 10-2 win over St Johnstone. The decline was halted with a convincing 4-1 win over Hearts at Pittodrie as the Tynecastle side were heading for relegation. Any lingering hopes that Aberdeen could catch Celtic were ended when the sides fought out a 1-1 draw at Parkhead on 28 March.

Premier League table at 28 March 1981

	P	*W*	*D*	*L*	*F*	*A*	*Pts*
Celtic	30	22	3	5	71	31	47
Aberdeen	**29**	**15**	**9**	**5**	**51**	**32**	**39**
Dundee United	30	15	8	7	56	32	38

Aberdeen managed to keep Celtic's champagne on ice until 22 April, when Rangers held the Dons to a goalless draw at Pittodrie. The title gone, and out of the Scottish Cup, the campaign was winding down with the focus certainly on next season.

The club were also making plans for further improvements in the South Stand as new individual seating was to be installed. This would enable them to offer season tickets in that area. The demand for these was never higher, following the poor handling of the sale of the Liverpool tickets in October. There were also plans to introduce a new computer system to handle ticket sales. Aberdeen also announced that they would be hosting their own tournament as a curtain-raiser for the new season. England international Kevin Keegan was invited north to make the draw for the tourney to be held at Pittodrie over the first weekend in August. With £30,000 of prize money up for grabs, Aberdeen were drawn to face West Ham while Southampton would take on Manchester United.

Alex Ferguson remained positive as the season came to a close, 'We want to conclude season 1980/81 with a reminder to all fans what we have endeavoured to achieve over the last nine months. The evolvement of a championship-class side to promote the club and our future ambitions. Although the season has been a disappointment as we failed to become the first team to retain the Premier League, it has in no way shaken the confidence we have for the future. A record of finishing first, and then second, is hardly that of a club who has failed by overall standards. No side outside of Glasgow has ever retained the league since Hibernian in 1952. It is guaranteed that the Aberdeen squad will return full of ambition for 1981/82, ready to compete for all the major trophies.'

Season 1980/81 was statistically one of the Dons' strongest on record but bereft of a major trophy or cup final. There was no doubt the Liverpool tie dominated the Aberdeen season, for all the wrong reasons. Ferguson stated many years later that the Liverpool games effectively ruined the campaign, a major distraction that had a profound and negative effect on the club. The alarming decline at the beginning of 1981 was down to the adverse reaction to Liverpool and the season-ending injuries to John McMaster and Gordon Strachan. In an era of Scottish football when losing three games in succession would usually end any title challenge, the positive form of Aberdeen through to the end of 1980 suggested that further success would follow. Ferguson certainly believed that and in the final analysis he was bitterly disappointed.

The final league game of the season ended with a lacklustre 2-0 defeat at home to a relegated Kilmarnock side. It also brought the curtain down on a Pittodrie legend. Joe Harper had battled back from a long-term knee injury but at 33 years of age, it was time to finish what had been a memorable Pittodrie career. Harper remains the club's record scorer and his two spells at Aberdeen brought him hero status with the support. The 'King', as he was known, never really found favour with Alex Ferguson and his departure from Pittodrie was tinged with sadness and disappointment.

Harper was left in tears as his Pittodrie career came to an abrupt conclusion: 'I had been told at one stage that the knee injury could finish my career, but I was never a quitter and pushed myself harder than ever in an effort to get fit, hoping Fergie would renew my contract, which was due to expire in July 1981. My hopes were raised when I eventually made it back into the first team for the Kilmarnock game in May. I was clinging to the hope that the manager would grant me the opportunity to end my Aberdeen career on a high. My hopes were dashed when Teddy Scott, the club trainer, entered the dressing room and told me the gaffer wished to see me. The instant I entered his office and saw that Archie Knox was also there, I knew that it would not amount to a pleasant conversation. Alex Ferguson avoided eye contact and declared that he was not renewing my contract. He also told me that he never wanted to see me back at Pittodrie again. So ended my career with Aberdeen Football Club. I was shedding tears of bitterness and disappointment as I walked from the stadium for the last time as a Don.'

5

Silver Lining

THERE WAS no disguising the bitter disappointment of going through season 1980/81 without success. The cynics suggested that Aberdeen as reigning champions could not handle the pressure of their lofty status, but Alex Ferguson was having none of it and he put the Dons' demise down to several key players suffering a loss of form, and long-term injuries to John McMaster and Gordon Strachan.

On 7 July, before the Dons returned for pre-season training, the draw for the first round of the UEFA Cup was made in Zürich. With Aberdeen unseeded there was always the possibility of coming up against one of the tournament favourites. Ferguson declared the draw to be an 'exciting prospect' but privately he was hoping for a more favourable outcome. There were some glamorous opponents in the UEFA Cup that season with the likes of Atlético Madrid, Valencia, Feyenoord, Stuttgart, Hamburg, Inter Milan, Napoli, Arsenal and Real Madrid all with hopes of going deep into the competition.

Back at Pittodrie with the League Cup reverting to a group stage format, the Dons' pre-season activity was truncated to a couple of low-key away friendlies and then hosting their own tournament. It was Chris Anderson who was in full support of the new venture; similar tourneys had been seen in Britain and beyond. With Pittodrie now being regarded as one of the most modern grounds in the country the directors were keen to showcase the club and facilities to a wider audience. Aberdeen invited Manchester United, West Ham and Southampton north for the two-day pre-season event.

Alex Ferguson took time to survey his squad over the summer and the club did sanction one major piece of transfer business. Ferguson identified the lack of natural width in his squad. He was well covered on the right with Gordon Strachan fulfilling his potential as one of the best midfielders in the game, but he was never seen as an out-and-out winger. Ian Scanlon had been at Pittodrie since 1978, signed by Billy McNeill from Notts County. Under Ferguson the left-winger failed to secure a regular starting place and it was a position that the boss identified as a weakness. After some tense conversations with the directors, Ferguson was delighted to agree a deal that brought Peter Weir from his old club St Mirren. Weir had been an Aberdeen supporter as a young boy and by the time he was travelling north to sign for the Dons he had become a Scotland international. The transfer broke Scottish records. A fee of £330,000 was paid with Ian Scanlon moving to Paisley as part of the deal. With Scanlon being valued at around £110,000, the deal totalled £440,000 which at the time was a record fee between two Scottish clubs. If ever there was an indication that the game in Scotland was on a more level playing field, it was that transfer with no Celtic or Rangers involvement.

Ferguson was looking forward to the new season, 'We rounded off our pre-season with our own tournament and it was a great success. We beat West Ham in the first game then gave Southampton a real roasting in the final, beating them 5-1 on the Sunday. Peter Weir made a substantial impact and so too did Doug Bell, a player with tremendous skill. He played so well in our tournament. Eric Black was also introduced to the first team in our tournament. Overall, I feel we have real quality in the squad and with the Weir signing, [it] encourages me to look forward to the new season with optimism and ambition. We now have a good, solid base to the club and a good working appetite among the players and the staff. The season can't come quick enough.'

The League Cup campaign was relatively straightforward as Aberdeen qualified from a group that included Hearts, Airdrie and Kilmarnock. With four wins from their first five games, the Dons had already confirmed their place in the latter stages by the time they travelled to Airdrie for their final group game. Watching from the Broomfield stands was Bobby Robson, the Ipswich Town boss; Aberdeen had been drawn to face the UEFA Cup holders in the opening round of the 1981 competition. Robson left at half-time, frustrated as the Dons rested five of their first-team squad for what was a dead rubber.

It was also a time of reflection for captain Willie Miller. After ten years of service the club awarded Miller a testimonial against Tottenham on 16 August. Such games usually signal the end of a long playing career; however, Miller was in his prime and with much more to come, he went on to enjoy a second benefit match in 1990.

The Ipswich tie gave Ferguson and his team the opportunity to exorcise their Liverpool experience. When the draw was made the Dons were immediately written off by the English media. On reflection that was perhaps no real surprise. Aberdeen were unceremoniously swept aside by Liverpool in 1980 and the Ipswich team of 1981 was as good as any down south. Keeper Jim Leighton was not fazed. 'Like most people I felt it was a tough draw when I heard it was Ipswich. Now it has sunk in, I am looking forward to playing them. I don't think they will give us as many problems as some are suggesting. Just look at who is playing in front of me and you will see what I mean. Against England at Wembley, Alex McLeish had Peter Withe in his pocket, and I rate him better than Paul Mariner at Ipswich. Willie Miller can also take care of Alan Brazil. Tony Woodcock and Trevor Francis could not get the better of Willie at Wembley.'

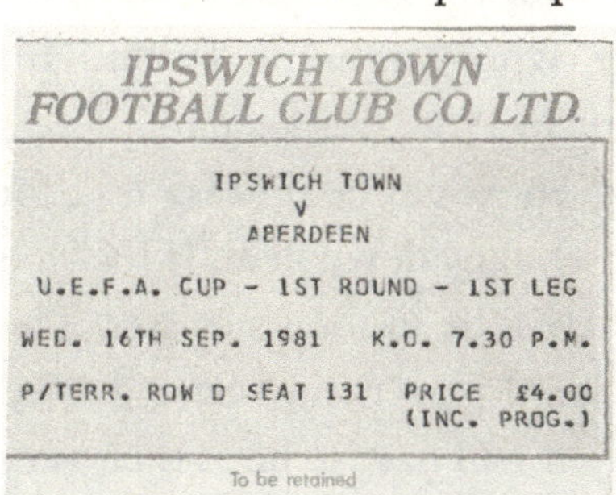
IPSWICH TOWN FOOTBALL CLUB CO. LTD.
IPSWICH TOWN
V
ABERDEEN
U.E.F.A. CUP - 1ST ROUND - 1ST LEG
WED. 16TH SEP. 1981 K.O. 7.30 P.M.
P/TERR. ROW D SEAT 131 PRICE £4.00 (INC. PROG.)
To be retained

Scotland midfielder John Wark was an integral part of the Ipswich midfield and he was keen to face the Dons: 'Let's just say I'm eager to get going against Aberdeen. That is the way I have been feeling since the draw was made. I suppose it goes without saying but we have every intention of holding on to this trophy. I and the other Scots at Ipswich know all about how good Aberdeen are and we have no intention of underestimating them.'

Preparations ahead of the first leg were as meticulous as usual and Alex Ferguson was as ever heavily involved. From choosing the team hotel or base before any tie to deciding whether a chef and bringing their own food was necessary, ahead of European ties, Ferguson had a say in everything. However, on this occasion the choice of team hotel was suggested by Liverpool secretary Peter Robinson, who contacted the Dons after the draw was made suggesting that they use the same base as Liverpool used for their visits to Suffolk.

With the capacity at Portman Road set at 24,000, the Dons were allocated 2,000 tickets for the tie and they were snapped up within an hour. Such was the demand that several hundred Aberdeen supporters obtained tickets for the home areas.

Former Don Steve Archibald, who was with Tottenham Hotspur after his move from Pittodrie in 1980, was keen to impress upon the English media that Aberdeen would be no easy task for Ipswich, 'My former club will surprise many down here. If Ipswich do not show Aberdeen respect, they will be in for a surprise. The Dons have some seasoned international players and have gained valuable experience in Europe. Ipswich will have to be at their very best over both games if they are going to go through. Aberdeen manager Alex Ferguson is a winner and knows the game well.'

Aberdeen began well and their 'early defence' approach stunned the home side. Ipswich had been familiar with visiting teams coming to Portman Road to sit in and defend in numbers. The Dons took a different approach and despite going behind they equalised early in the second half through John Hewitt. It was a game they deserved to win but instead settled for taking the tie back to Pittodrie all square. The proud Ipswich record of never having lost a home tie in Europe was intact, but only just. Never had the Suffolk side been so stretched on home soil.

Bobby Robson did pay tribute to the Dons after the first leg but took comfort that he was convinced his team could improve on their Portman Road showing. Aberdeen certainly surprised Robson and his team by taking the game to the cup holders. Ferguson recalled, 'Our tactics at Ipswich were spot on. We played a 4-4-2 with Strachan and Weir playing deep and wide so they could get to their full-back and tighten our midfield. This meant [Arnold] Mühren and [Frans] Thijssen would have to move infield, where they would be faced with the strength of Simpson and Cooper. The game went well for us. We had plenty of good possession and Strachan and Weir presented them with all sorts of problems. It was a good performance and we deserved to win but to come away with a 1-1 draw was perfectly acceptable.'

Ahead of the second leg at Pittodrie the club's distribution of tickets was welcomed as the new voucher system kicked in following the fierce criticism received after the Liverpool tie.

Ipswich were clearly stunned in the first leg as doubts from the English press piled pressure on the holders. Speaking to the *Derby Daily Telegraph* before the trip north, Ipswich captain Mick Mills was defiant, 'Aberdeen are the most adventurous side we have faced at home in Europe. They really impressed me. But the onus is now on us to score and that is when we are at our most dangerous. We showed last year the sort of damage we can do away from home.' Bobby Robson added, 'Aberdeen played as well as any side we have faced in the last nine years. I don't think they could play any better than they did that night.'

Ipswich warmed up for the return leg with a 2-0 win over Liverpool as they headed towards the top of the English First Division.

A tense opening period in front of what was a hostile atmosphere was exactly what Ferguson had anticipated. He urged the Aberdeen support to be patient and back his team to the hilt.

The first half ended with the tie level on aggregate as both sides exchanged penalties. Aberdeen needed something special, so up stepped record signing Peter Weir whose two second-half goals put his team through in what was an incredible Pittodrie European night. Weir tormented Mills, whose bold pre-match claims made him an easy target for the Pittodrie support. Weir, with socks rolled down, was unplayable in a torrid second half. Aberdeen could also afford to miss a last-minute penalty which was taken twice by Gordon Strachan. It was redemption following that defeat to Liverpool.

Willie Miller was delighted at getting one over the English league leaders, 'The Ipswich players and manager Bobby Robson realised what had hit them at full time. It was a win that I relished deep down, as it showed English football and their media that Aberdeen Football Club deserved respect.'

Doug Rougvie was clearly miffed at further comments from Mills ahead of the Pittodrie clash when the England defender dismissed the Scots entirely as the war of words escalated ahead of a sold-out Pittodrie encounter. Some years later, the *Evening Express* reported, 'Mills had made claims about Aberdeen players fearing his reputation as a tough-tackling defender. However, he was found wanting when coming up against Rougvie, "The ball bounced between us in front of the Main Stand. It was probably more 70-30 in his favour, but I wasn't going to back out after all the things he had been saying. I decided just to get stuck in and charged forward. Mills surprised me as he was backing away. We never had any problems with him after that and we ran out easy winners."' Scotland international Alan Brazil had a different take on Rougvie, 'He kicked everything that moved. Launching himself at people. Fuck me, he was taking you out chest-high! He looked as if he had just escaped from Barlinnie Prison.'

England international defender Terry Butcher was dejected, 'Weir diddled Millsy twice. He just turned on the magic. Bobby Robson wasn't happy that night. I think we stayed at the Thistle Hotel in Dyce after the game and we just got absolutely smashed.'

The Dons' stunning win was also a boost for Scottish football; it was the first Scottish success over English opponents in Europe since Celtic defeated Leeds United in 1969.

The victory was welcome as Aberdeen had made a poor start to their Premier League campaign. After early setbacks against Dundee United and Celtic the Dons recovered by beating Partick at Firhill and then inflicted a first defeat of the season on Hibernian at Pittodrie following their trip to Ipswich in midweek. Aberdeen were looking at a more favourable draw in the UEFA Cup as they looked to get past the second round of any European competition for the first time; news came through from Zürich that they would face Romanian side Argeș Pitești. Regardless of the strength of any opposition, any trip to eastern Europe back then was always difficult. Argeș were an unknown quantity to Ferguson but he was quick to note that they stretched Nottingham Forest in the European Cup in 1979 and they would present Aberdeen with a different problem from the superstars of Ipswich.

One thing was certain – the second leg in Pitești would be played in the afternoon as Romania was in the midst of an energy-saving programme that did not allow the use of any floodlighting at football matches. Alex Ferguson was philosophical about the draw: 'There is no doubt we could face some difficulty in travelling to Romania, but this is the kind of draw that is always likely to happen in European competition. I don't know much about them at this stage and with the first game at Pittodrie we will have to do our business at home.'

One landmark that almost went unnoticed at Pittodrie was the formation of the original Aberdeen Football Club exactly 100 years earlier, on 8 October 1881. That was the first time the 'Association Game' came to Aberdeen after the club was formed; it would play out of the Holburn Cricket Ground. It was the original Aberdeen along with local sides Orion and Victoria United who went on to form the present Aberdeen Football Club on 14 April 1903.

Progress was made in the League Cup as the Dons defeated Berwick Rangers for the second year in succession to reach the semi-final, but the two-legged tie ended in bitter disappointment and defeat against rivals Dundee United. It was all the more painful as the Dons won the first leg 1-0 in Dundee with Peter Weir scoring in a game that they should have won by a wider margin, such was their superiority. However, as was the trend back then in games against the Tannadice team, the away team would often fare better, and the Dons went out after a disastrous second leg at Pittodrie.

What was significant at the time was that Aberdeen and Dundee United were both progressing in Europe, as both the Glasgow clubs were eliminated in the first round. There was no doubt the power was beginning to shift east, much to the dismay of the Glasgow football establishment. For how long that would prevail would be down to Alex Ferguson and his good friend and fierce rival Jim McLean, his counterpart at Dundee United. Progress in Europe was essential as both clubs were not only making their mark in Scotland but were now respected on the continent.

Aberdeen were in the unusual position of being favourites to progress to the third round of the UEFA Cup when Argeș Pitești arrived at Pittodrie on 21 October. Ferguson made it clear that he wanted his team to do the business at home to save any potential problems behind the Iron Curtain. The Romanians were a decent side but did not travel well and Aberdeen brutally exposed them in a torrid first half that brought three goals. The Dons failed to add to that advantage in a stale second half that brought a typically furious reaction from the manager: 'The second half was dreadful. I made the mistake of telling them at half-time they had done well, and we let it slip.' On any other European evening a first-leg 3-0 lead would be welcomed but not for Ferguson; on the back of their win over Ipswich expectations were high. The return leg in north-west Romania was always going to be difficult. Aberdeen had struggled in their European Cup

Winners' Cup tie in Bulgaria in Ferguson's first European tie in charge of the club in 1978.

The Aberdeen charter flight landed in Bucharest on the Monday where the team would be based. Pitești was 72 miles north-west of the Romanian capital and the club could not find any suitable accommodation in the city, a bland and agricultural area that seemed to be stuck in time. The anticipated hostility that usually comes with ties in eastern Europe never really materialised. The game was played in bright sunshine on a pleasant afternoon; the stadium was anything but imposing with shallow terraces and a running track around the pitch. The small covered area was where the 50 or so Aberdeen fans were housed. They were even bolstered by a couple of Ipswich fans who decided to follow Aberdeen after their side were humbled in the first round.

The home support were small in numbers but certainly made plenty of noise and they were rewarded with two sensational first-half goals, the second, a superb free kick from Ilie Bărbulescu, piling pressure on the Dons. By half-time the tie was suddenly in the balance. Captain Willie Miller recalled, 'Through the years I had watched the boss kick a variety of items, such as kit hampers, in frustration when we were failing to produce the goods, and I could never work out why he never did break his toes while venting his wrath. In the dressing room in Romania, a big tea urn was placed on the table. It was a massive item and after he had sent the teacups flying, the manager turned his attention to the urn. He gave it a forearm smash, hoping it would fly off the table, but it didn't move. Not even a centimetre. He grimaced in pain the moment he contacted the tea dispenser. I was sitting among the shattered cups trying to stifle my laughter. You could see his face turning a shade of pale, but he was doing his damnedest not to show he was in pain.'

Young midfielder Neale Cooper had to stop himself from laughing: 'I couldn't believe Fergie did that, it must have been so painful. He was raging at Gordon [Strachan]. My reaction was to piss myself laughing but knowing the boss I had to hold it in. Looking back, it was hilarious.'

For all of Ferguson's pains, it had the desired effect. Despite the home side being buoyed by their first-half showing and a German referee who was clearly favouring the Romanians, the Dons dominated the second half and came back to level, finishing with a 2-2 draw in a game they really should have won. With the match being played in the afternoon, the charter flight was arranged to fly back to Dyce Airport immediately from Bucharest. What was not lost on the flight home was the fact that Aberdeen had qualified past the second round of Europe for the first time. The flight back to Aberdeen was a happy one – even Ferguson and Archie Knox were in fine fettle seated at the rear and enjoying some evening drinks. Unknown to the party was the inclement weather conditions as the captain announced, 'Sorry to inform all but due to strong headwinds we will not be able to reach Aberdeen by the 10pm deadline and will divert to Edinburgh.' Within seconds Ferguson breezed through the aisle and approached the cockpit. Another announcement soon came, 'It's your captain again. I am pleased to announce that we will be landing at Aberdeen Airport and we are due to touch down around 10.20pm.' All's well that ends well. Despite a tetchy reception from some customs officials there was a better welcome from the 100 or so Aberdeen fans waiting to welcome the team home.

The Premier League looked to be heading towards Parkhead after Aberdeen returned from Romania to face Celtic in Glasgow. The game being described as a great advert for Scottish football did not help the Dons much as they went down 2-1 to allow Celtic the opportunity to extend their lead at the top. Aberdeen struggled through November as they looked forward to a third-round clash with SV Hamburg in the UEFA Cup. They were looking to reach the quarter-finals for the first time. Alex Ferguson was confident, 'Hamburg are one of the most experienced sides left in the competition who will certainly present as tough a task as we have faced in Europe. It is going to be a real test of character and ability for the players, a challenge we respect. There will be no hiding place for us against a top European side. Hamburg are considered as tournament favourites, but we will look to approach the game with the dedication and concentration that served us so well against Ipswich.'

The Germans had an array of internationals in their side with Franz Beckenbauer marshalling their defence. With Manfred Kaltz, Horst Hrubesch and Felix Magath in their ranks, the Dons' task was always going to be a tough one. Pittodrie was once again at fever pitch in freezing conditions. Aberdeen adopted an 'early defence' approach, aware that Beckenbauer liked to have time on the ball in his own half. The classic German approach of building up play was something that Aberdeen targeted. In the modern game it is known as the 'press'; in 1981 it was Ferguson's early defence, light years ahead of his time. The home forwards were all over Beckenbauer and his defence as soon as the ball was passed out from keeper Uli Stein. Ferguson recalled, 'Archie [Knox] had been over to see them play and with them using Beckenbauer as a sweeper we felt it was important that we got at them early and didn't allow Beckenbauer arrogance to spur on his team-mates. I made tactical changes. I left out Doug Bell and played Simpson and Watson as my two central midfielders.'

Unfortunately for Aberdeen, in what was one of their finest performances in Europe, two moments of madness cost them dear and the 3-2 first-leg lead was scant reward for effectively playing the Germans off the park. Ferguson was livid, 'A throw-out from Jim Leighton brought confusion between him and Stuart Kennedy and we lost a goal. Then we were down to ten men with Doug Rougvie being carried off. Eight of our players touched the ball during this time and not one had the sense to kick it out of play to allow Cooper to come on as a sub. And of course, Hamburg scored their second goal with three minutes left.' That cost Aberdeen in the second leg in Germany as a depleted side went down 3-1 and their European campaign came to a frustrating end. Ferguson later admitted he got his starting line-up wrong with the out-of-sorts Mark McGhee left on the bench.

The tie in Germany would be the last game the Dons would play until 23 January, some seven weeks later. After a defeat at Greenock they were well off the pace in the Premier League.

Premier League table at 5 December 1981

	P	*W*	*D*	*L*	*F*	*A*	*Pts*
Celtic	15	11	3	1	34	15	25
Dundee United	14	7	4	3	26	12	18
St Mirren	15	7	4	4	23	18	18
Aberdeen	**15**	**7**	**4**	**4**	**21**	**16**	**18**

With their European campaign ending and the Dons playing catch-up in the league, a wretched spell of winter weather hit the country with a succession of pitch inspections and subsequent postponements. Aberdeen did manage three friendlies during their enforced lay-off. A hastily arranged friendly at Pittodrie went ahead against Hearts, who were in the First Division that season, before travelling to Norwich in the new year. The 4-1 win was the perfect preparation for a week-long stay in Benidorm, where the squad enjoyed some training in warm weather and a comfortable win over the local Spanish side.

The draw for the third round of the Scottish Cup was not as favourable for Aberdeen as it could have been. Aberdeen were down to face Motherwell at Fir Park, the Steelmen as they were known. Although they were in the First Division, they were well clear at the top and certain to get back in the Premier League. They were also defending a long unbeaten run and were confident of taking on the Dons on home soil. Their manager Davie Hay, a former Celtic midfielder, signalled his intent ahead of the match, 'Everyone at Motherwell has been looking forward to this tie since the draw was announced. Aberdeen are one of the best football teams in Scotland and will be difficult to beat, but we do not intend to let them have things their own way.'

After several weeks in cold storage the Dons' return to competitive action got off to an incredible start. After 9.6 seconds, John Hewitt swept the ball past Motherwell keeper Hugh Sproat to put the visitors ahead. The goal remains the quickest ever in Scottish Cup history. For Aberdeen it provided the platform to progress to the next round after the 1-0 win. Motherwell's intentions were clear; they adopted a physical approach that bordered on brutal as they tried to stop Aberdeen from playing in their usual fluent style. Several players were booked in what became a bad-tempered game with trouble on the terraces throughout. It was a time when Aberdeen were followed by the Aberdeen Soccer Casuals, who were out in big numbers at Fir Park. Motherwell had their own set of casuals so the likelihood of trouble on terraces was high. Ferguson was happy to get through: 'I thought the referee at Fir Park had a good match having to be on his toes because of the competitive nature of the tie. We earned the win by competing well and facing up to their physicality although Neale Cooper and Gordon Strachan both suffered injuries which will keep them out of action for a while.'

The draw for the fourth round was made after the third-round ties concluded and Aberdeen were given a home tie against Celtic in what was without doubt the match of the round. It was not the draw Ferguson wanted as the Dons' record against Celtic that season had been woeful. Nevertheless, with the tie at Pittodrie they would fancy it against any side. By the time the game came around their fortunes had not improved, and the general belief was the Scottish Cup was the Dons' last hope of silverware that season. For Celtic it was an opportunity to end Aberdeen's season – by February. As far as the Premier League challenge was concerned even Ferguson had given up the chase ahead of the cup tie, 'The return of Celtic in the cup is a real opportunity to show what we are all about. It is our last chance of winning anything this season and there is no reason why we can't show the quality we had earlier in the season.'

Pittodrie was once again full for the tie and Aberdeen reacted in typical fashion to recent criticism by defeating Celtic. It was John Hewitt again, this time in 19 minutes with an acrobatic overhead kick, that was enough to put the Dons through to the quarter-finals. The significance of the cup win cannot be overstated. Not only did it keep the season very much alive, in the wider context of what would follow, it was a definitive day for Aberdeen. With Celtic in what most observers thought was an unassailable lead in the Premier League, they still had to get over the line. For Aberdeen it was the hope over probability. The Scottish Cup was now the prime target, in the knowledge of qualifying for the European Cup Winners' Cup the following season. The detail in which Ferguson went into preparing for such a game included a discussion with captain Willie Miller about which end to play to if he won the toss of the coin before kick-off: 'If Willie had the choice, we were to play to the Beach End from the start. When Willie lost the toss, which meant Celtic had won it on the last three occasions at Pittodrie, I immediately thought, here we go again, it was going to be one of those days.'

The win over Celtic gave Aberdeen the confidence to re-energise their league campaign. With Kilmarnock due at Pittodrie for the Scottish Cup quarter-final, there was no danger of Ferguson allowing his players to show any complacency, 'It is imperative we treat the visit of Kilmarnock as the biggest match of the season. It will be a crime if we are not in the right frame of mind.' The boss still had no thoughts of any Premier League success at that stage, 'We must realise, now, that the cup is really the one ambition left this season.' Perhaps it was some early Fergie mind games, the sort of which he became expert at in his later career. Kilmarnock were in the First Division, a far cry from the side that won the league and reached the latter stages of European competition in the 1960s. A decade of decline had seen the Rugby Park club languish in the lower leagues for several seasons. The Pittodrie tie was a rare opportunity for them to revive their fortunes. They got off to a great start and shocked Aberdeen by taking an early lead. Unfortunately for them the Dons responded well and dominated. Not unlike what Motherwell attempted in the opening round, Kilmarnock turned the tie into a brutal encounter with Gordon Strachan in particular on the end of some rough treatment. That only got the home support right behind the Dons, who cruised to a deserved 4-2 win. Kilmarnock were not the first and certainly not the last side who would try to mix it with Aberdeen. This was something the Dons management recognised and took steps to ensure their team would not be bullied on the park. With the likes of Doug

Rougvie, Alex McLeish, Stuart Kennedy and Willie Miller, and the emergence of the young midfield duo of Neale Cooper and Neil Simpson, there was no prospect of any side imposing their physicality over this team.

With a Scottish Cup semi-final to look forward to against St Mirren, the Dons began to put some results together. By the end of March, a narrow 1-0 win over Celtic had the Glasgow side once again looking over their shoulder. The Dons also defeated Rangers at Ibrox and talk of a repeat of season 1979/80 brought some nervous glances from Parkhead. A run of ten games undefeated had Ferguson in a more positive mood, 'A couple of months ago the outlook, in respect of any material rewards from this season, was about as bleak as the winter we have just had. Our fate by the end of January for all but eternal optimists of any serious Premier League challenge put us nine points behind Celtic. Although we have staged a very impressive recovery, the weeks ahead will be as demanding as ever.'

The priority for Aberdeen though was the Scottish Cup, a trophy they had not won since 1970. With Muirton Park in Perth being suggested as a neutral venue the club were disappointed that the semi-final would take place at Parkhead. In terms of any neutrality it was a farce. Not for the first time Aberdeen were given little consideration when it came to selecting neutral venues. These days, due to the investment the SFA have put into Hampden, the national stadium hosts both semi-finals and the final. For years the Dons had been subjected to several venue choices that were anything but neutral. In the 1972 League Cup semi-final Aberdeen faced Celtic at Hampden. That trend continued in 1976 v Rangers (Hampden), 1978 v Partick (Hampden), 1979 v Hibernian (Hampden), and 1980 v Rangers (Parkhead). The one exception was the 1978 League Cup semi-final against Hibernian that was played at Dens Park in Dundee. The club were never hesitant to voice their concerns when it came to these 'neutral' venues, but on reflection they knew they were wasting their time. The SFA and Scottish League were never known for being flexible in this regard.

The Dons went into the clash with St Mirren on 3 April as favourites to reach the final. But the Parkhead pitch was a real concern. The unusually hot conditions and a fiery bare surface did not help Aberdeen with any fluent football. St Mirren adapted well and relied on long balls to their front players. The breakthrough came in 61 minutes when Frank McDougall escaped at a corner to open the scoring for the Paisley side. The pressure was on Aberdeen but five minutes later they got a break. St Mirren keeper Billy Thomson clashed with Mark McGhee in the six-yard box. To the delight of the Aberdeen support behind the goal, referee Alexander awarded a penalty. It was a dubious decision at best, but one that favoured Aberdeen. Gordon Strachan scored to level the tie. Minutes later the midfielder was hacked down by Billy Abercrombie, who was sent off. With no further scoring, both teams settled for a second game, which took place four days later, and the choice of Dens Park suited the Dons. They were assured of the bigger support and the Dundee ground was a venue they enjoyed playing at.

Conditions were in stark contrast to the first game as heavy rain made the pitch virtually unplayable. Backed by a large support, the Dons came through a sensational tie, progressing 3-2 with Peter Weir scoring the winner in 74 minutes. Conditions were poor and mistakes were made, crucially by Paisley keeper Billy Thomson, who let Weir's winning goal slip through his grasp. It was a welcome victory for Aberdeen and a return to Hampden. Four years on from the day the Dons had disappointed in their last Scottish Cup Final against Rangers, they were now presented with an opportunity to atone. The Ibrox club were coming to the end of an era; their side was an ageing one with several of their stalwarts playing their last games for Rangers. For Aberdeen this was no time for sentiment. Under Alex Ferguson this team was emerging as one of the finest ever seen in Scotland. However, doubts remained so on this occasion the pressure for once was all on Aberdeen. Not since 1959 had Aberdeen gone into a Scottish Cup Final as favourites. On that occasion they again disappointed, going down with a whimper against St Mirren. In the other semi-final Rangers overcame lowly Forfar Athletic, but needed a replay to see off the Angus club.

As Aberdeen looked forward to the final, they still had not given up on what had become the most unlikely of league challenges. Not unlike the closing weeks of 1980, the Dons had gradually closed the gap on Celtic.

Premier League table at 17 April 1982

	P	*W*	*D*	*L*	*F*	*A*	*Pts*
Celtic	30	20	6	4	35	14	46
Aberdeen	**28**	**15**	**7**	**6**	**26**	**13**	**37**
Rangers	30	13	10	7	19	21	36

Aberdeen kept up their unbeaten run by beating Rangers, Airdrie, Dundee, Partick, Dundee United and St Mirren as they approached the final league game of the season. Any slip-ups in those matches would have had Celtic popping the champagne corks. From a position that even had Ferguson accepting the gap was too much for his side, Celtic were nervy and it showed as the Dons incredibly took the destination of the title down to the final day. It was still very much a long shot. Aberdeen would welcome Rangers to Pittodrie, while Celtic were playing St Mirren. The Dons not only had to win but hope St Mirren would do something special and assist with a six-goal swing in favour of Ferguson's men. The manager was still looking at the Scottish Cup as a realistic target, 'Naturally enough Pittodrie is alive, expectant and excited at the prospect of being involved in a truly memorable last page to the season. We have not won anything yet and just getting to the cup final is not good enough. The last half-dozen matches have been a challenge and an opportunity for us to extend our successful run.'

On Saturday, 15 May the Premier League came to a dramatic close. Incredibly, by half-time the impossible was still very much on. Aberdeen set about a fragile Rangers side, backed by a passionate home crowd who relished another opportunity to put one over the Glasgow club. John Hewitt was unplayable, scoring a first-half hat-trick. With Aberdeen-born Rangers pivot Colin Jackson putting through his own goal, the Dons went in at half-time 4-0 ahead. Back then, Ferguson often turned to the supporters in the Main Stand at Pittodrie, your author included, to find out results from elsewhere. As Celtic were being held 0-0 at home to St Mirren, the title was still not done. On learning of the score at Celtic the boss raised his eyebrows and walked quickly towards the home dressing room. The second half failed to bring further misery for Rangers as Celtic hit three goals to finally clinch the Premier League title. For Aberdeen it was all about the Scottish Cup. The Dons had destroyed the Ibrox club, brutally exposing their defensive fragility and ripping through Rangers with pace and power. Aberdeen simply had to turn up at Hampden the following week to lift the Scottish Cup, surely.

The build-up to Hampden was along usual lines for the Dons, taking a relaxed approach as Ferguson always seemed to do before any big final. Staying clear of any distractions and media intrusions was important for the Aberdeen manager. With Aberdeen expected to beat Rangers with ease, Ferguson was guarded, 'We know what we need to do. If this team is to get to where we want to be then we will need to show that on the big stage.' For Ferguson, winning was everything. In his playing career he had learned the hard way; in the 1969 final Rangers were favourites to beat Celtic but were humbled 4-0 and Ferguson was heavily criticised.

The management also had to handle the media in the days before Hampden. There was no doubt that Ferguson was learning how to deal with the Scottish press and media. He was only too aware that just about every national paper reporter had leanings towards either of the Glasgow clubs. It was no surprise to see the media go big by questioning Aberdeen's ability to deal with the big occasion. The *Sunday Mail* declared, 'Aberdeen are the team in form, talented and skilful, they look stronger in every respect, yet do they have the temperament?' One other factor was the expected crowd. For Aberdeen the 140-mile trip to Hampden was always going to be well taken up with around 25,000 following them.

However, with the national stadium on Rangers' doorstep they were taking far more in numbers. With three parts of the stadium still terraced, there was no restriction on allocating tickets. For generations Rangers sides leaned heavily on their big and noisy support. Intimidating as that may have been for some opponents, it was something Ferguson realised and was acutely aware of from his early days at Pittodrie. If Aberdeen were going to realise their ambitions and take the next step, then beating Rangers in the Scottish Cup Final in Glasgow was vital. Anything less than a victory could have set the Dons back years and provided more ammunition for the doubters.

Aberdeen prepared in their traditional stay for big games at the Gleneagles Hotel, while Rangers took their squad away to Troon in Ayrshire. The Aberdeen management team spent several hours talking to the players as to what to expect on the day. Special emphasis was placed on moments of adversity and even going a goal behind and how to react. It was such meticulous preparations that Ferguson became renowned for. The Dons were hit with an injury to Peter Weir which ruled him out.

Rangers manager John Greig looked to the mercurial talents of Davie Cooper, their talented winger with an eye for goal. Cooper, though, was inconsistent and Greig did his utmost to get the best out of his star man. He knew how difficult Aberdeen would be to beat and he had to look to his experienced players and hope the occasion would have an adverse effect on the Dons.

Aberdeen dominated the early stages but just when they were beginning to impose themselves on the game, against the run of play Rangers took the lead after 15 minutes through a John MacDonald header. The Dons hit back in sensational style after 33 minutes.

From a corner Neil Simpson had his shot blocked. The ball broke to the edge of the box and it was Alex McLeish who curled a shot into the top corner of the net. It was not only spectacular but vital for Aberdeen as they regained the initiative. Despite dominating the rest of the final, the Dons could not make the breakthrough, so it went into extra time. Ferguson gathered his players on the Hampden turf and made sure they looked across to the Rangers players, 'Look at them! They are on their knees, finished. Get out there and show everyone what we are all about.'

The extra time period proved to be as significant a spell in Aberdeen FC history as any other. After several big-game disappointments in recent years, this was the opportunity for Ferguson's team to not only lay down a marker, but to crush one of their most bitter rivals. Aberdeen were a fit, vibrant side hungry for success, driven on by a manager who despised losing at anything. Rangers were a side from the past, still embracing memories of previous success. The reality was that they were ageing and Aberdeen were the one team who would brutally expose them. It seemed that the two previous cup final defeats in 1978 and 1979 against the Ibrox club were not forgotten as the Dons hit three goals in extra time to win the Scottish Cup. For Aberdeen it was a sweet moment; for Rangers it was utter humiliation. For once most of the Rangers support stayed to witness their side being torn apart.

After Mark McGhee headed Aberdeen ahead early in extra time it gave the Dons the confidence to go on and finish the job. Just before the first period ended, McGhee totally embarrassed a struggling Alex Miller near the touchline, and he slipped the ball across to Gordon Strachan. The midfielder with his socks rolled down had an open goal and he slotted the ball into the net from all of two yards. Before the humiliation was complete, young Neale Cooper showed more endeavour than his more experienced team-mate when he was presented with an open goal after the ball broke kindly to him when keeper Jim Stewart attempted a clearance. In front of the Rangers support Cooper hammered the ball into the net from a yard out before rejoicing with a forward roll and clenched fists. Cooper was part of the new breed of Aberdeen player, too young to have been involved in previous cup defeats but aware of the rivalry that had developed between Aberdeen and Rangers. Cooper later recalled, 'I just remember the vast number of Rangers fans behind the goal. I was a yard out with the ball at my feet. It was pure instinct, but I just had to smash it. The forward roll I can't remember much about, but it was funny.'

Willie Miller lifted the trophy in his typical one-handed fashion that became synonymous with the Dons' cup success back then. With the Rangers support leaving in their droves to lick their wounds, Hampden that day belonged to Aberdeen. It was a scenario that was to become very familiar for the Dons and the Red Army.

The Dons retired to their base at the Gleneagles Hotel that evening. One surprise guest was a certain Burt Lancaster, the Hollywood legend who was in Scotland for the filming of *Local Hero*. Lancaster was keen to learn of what the team had achieved and mingled with the squad. As was the tradition the following day the players would be welcomed back to the city with an open-topped bus through Union Street, to the Town House and down King Street to Pittodrie. Alex McLeish commented on his incredible goal, 'You might not believe it but that was exactly the kind of goal I scored in a training match at Cruden Bay ahead of the final. When the ball rolled away from the corner, I chased it out and saw John McMaster in a good position and thought about passing to him. The fact that we were a goal down prompted me to have a go.' Mark McGhee, who put Aberdeen ahead in extra time, was delighted to score, 'Gordon's cross was brilliant, and I had plenty of time to pick my spot. I was delighted to repay Gordon by laying on the third goal for him.' Strachan could not miss when he scored, 'I swear the goal started to shrink as soon as that ball came across from Mark. Apart from getting a pass from Mark, my mind was in turmoil as I was unsure whether to stop the ball first or just hit it.'

For midfielder John McMaster it was a sweet success. McMaster had missed most of the previous season after his injury against Liverpool in the European Cup. McMaster recalled the spray painting at Pittodrie in December 1980 after the Dons lost the League Cup Final, 'We went out for training and saw the door painted, "You have let us down again – three in a row". The defeat back then was hard enough to take but we made up for it in style.'

Alex Ferguson reflected on the success and looked forward, 'Winning the title two years ago was a big step forward but failing to build on that last season taught us that we can't take anything for granted. The bonus of winning the Scottish Cup is that it gives the younger players their first taste of success and sharpens their appetite for more. It also makes them realise that Celtic and Rangers are not invincible.' Defeated Ibrox boss John Greig had no complaints, 'Aberdeen played well and at the end of the day, deserved to win the game. They are a good side and worthy winners of the cup.' It was not often any Rangers manager was so magnanimous in defeat. Indeed, previous incumbents were never known for lavishing praise on the likes of Aberdeen. On this occasion, though, it was almost impossible not to. Such was the gulf in class between the teams, the usual inquest at Ibrox would certainly follow. It was something that Rangers were going to get used to.

It did not take long for the Glasgow press to crank up the pressure. After the cup final, reports and summaries had rightly praised Aberdeen for their win, and on the back of that came unfounded speculation. First up was Alex Ferguson as the *Daily Record* speculated that some of the big English clubs would come calling. Attentions then turned to Willie Miller, whose contract was coming to an end in June. The reports were not uncommon and certainly in the main very much fabricated to make a headline and keep their west coast readership interested. Ferguson swept aside such talk, 'I am not speaking about players' contracts at the moment. Willie will be joining the Scotland squad for the World Cup finals in Spain. There will be plenty of time for us to discuss terms when he returns from Spain.'

The last word on the Scottish Cup win comes from chairman Dick Donald as he told the *Press & Journal*, 'It was a great occasion and the team did the club and city proud. The future looks bright for us. I'm delighted.'

1982 Scottish Cup Final statistics

Shots on target: Aberdeen 5; Rangers 1
Headers on target: Aberdeen 2; Rangers 2
Shots off target: Aberdeen 7; Rangers 3
Headers off target: Aberdeen 2; Rangers 6
Free kicks: Aberdeen 21; Rangers 29
Corners: Aberdeen 11; Rangers 6

6

Dining at Europe's Top Table

THE ABERDEEN squad returned for pre-season training in the familiar surroundings of Seaton Park. The leisure park was close to Pittodrie and although open to the public, it was not the busiest of areas. It was far from ideal but with no plans for any long-term training ground, it was down to business for Alex Ferguson. As news came through in the afternoon that Aberdeen would have to face Swiss side Sion in the preliminary round of the European Cup Winners' Cup, there was an immediate fixture concern. Of the 34 clubs who entered the 1982/83 Cup Winners' Cup, four would face a preliminary round. Aberdeen, as an unseeded club, faced that possibility. Vice-chairman Chris Anderson and director Ian Donald were present at the draw and also learned that if Aberdeen were able to get past the Swiss Cup winners, they would face Albanian side Dinamo Tirana in the first round. Sion were not considered as big a threat as the better-known FC Zürich and Grasshopper, but they were an emerging club. Swiss football was also on the up and the national

side had recently defeated England and Portugal and drawn with Brazil.

Ferguson had more pressing matters at home with contract negotiations with captain Willie Miller his priority. The manager was directly involved in such discussions. In the modern game such involvement would be unheard of, but at Pittodrie he remained in control of just about everything that went on at the club. Miller had been at Aberdeen since 1971 and after 11 years and a testimonial, negotiating a new deal was vital to both club and player.

Before negotiations were held, Ferguson travelled to France to see Sion in action against Lyon in an Aloes Cup clash. The Aberdeen squad were on their way for a week-long stay at Gordonstoun School where they would take in some pre-season outings. Meanwhile, speculation over Miller leaving the club again came from the usual sources in Glasgow. As Miller returned to training along with Alex McLeish and Gordon Strachan, who had been given additional time off due to their involvement in the World Cup, claims that Manchester United were looking to sign the skipper were simply fabrication. Miller, now a free agent, did declare that there had been interest from other clubs, but that Manchester United were not one of them. He told the *Press & Journal* ahead of the talks, 'I have put to the club a deal which would tie me to Aberdeen for the remainder of my playing career. So far, they have not agreed to it, but talks will continue.'

It emerged that Miller had rejected an offer to join Rangers. That decision suggested he would remain at Pittodrie. Miller put forward his reasons for turning down the Ibrox club, 'I received a really good offer from them. I rejected it for several reasons. I have never hidden my ambition of helping to break the Glasgow stranglehold in Scottish football, and my decision has gone a long way towards that aim. I also owe my testimonial committee and the Dons fans. Going to a rival club would not have went down well and that also played a part in my decision.'

Following their short stay in the north the Dons opened their Pittodrie season with a testimonial for the long-serving Drew

Jarvie. With Miller still not agreeing terms, Ferguson indicated that the captain would miss the game against Ipswich and that a final decision from Miller had to be made by the following Tuesday. After a final offer was made, Miller was given the weekend to decide his future, and he admitted, 'I intend to think things over in the next couple of days. I have many things to consider, including the fact that I like living in Aberdeen. I thought we were getting close to an agreement, but we are not quite there. I have a difficult decision to make and will let the club know my decision on Monday.'

With Aberdeen being involved in the preliminary round tie against Sion, the Scottish League helped them prepare by bringing forward their opening League Cup tie against Morton at Greenock, three days ahead of the official opening day of the season.

On the eve of the first match, there was great news after Willie Miller agreed to sign the new contract that would tie him to Pittodrie for another four years. In the context of what followed, the decision by the captain was significant. Miller recalled, 'I had asked the club for an additional £20 per week that would have taken me to £220. They said no and came back with £10 per week, and I accepted that, as I think they had sussed out that I would stay, come what may.' In an era when clubs held the power when it came to contracts and transfers, it was a source of frustration for many players. The Bosman ruling was still some years away.

The Dons were given a favourable League Cup draw in Section 2 along with Dundee, Morton and Dumbarton. Progress from that group was expected and achieved as Aberdeen were undefeated in their six outings. They were held by Morton and Dundee but their 3-0 win over the Greenock side on 25 August proved crucial. That was followed by a 5-1 demolition of Dundee at Dens Park. It was a personal triumph for Gordon Strachan, still fresh from his World Cup exploits, returning to his former club and scoring four of the goals, including an outrageous chip from 35 yards. Strachan was fulfilling his undoubted potential just at the right time for Aberdeen.

Ahead of the tie against Sion at Pittodrie, the Swiss club's coach Jean-Claude Donzé watched the Dons in their 3-3 draw against Dundee in the League Cup and was hopeful his team would compete favourably, 'Aberdeen are an impressive side, with many players who are experienced in European football. I would say we are not as strong as Aberdeen but better than Dundee. Strachan, we know about from the World Cup, and I thought McGhee worked very hard up front. I think Eric Black with his three goals was very impressive. It is not possible for us to play a defensive game. We can only play our natural game going forward. If we go into defence it will be because Aberdeen have forced us into that position.'

It soon became clear that Sion were nowhere near the standard of Aberdeen as they were blown away in a 7-0 drubbing in the first leg. Aberdeen signalled their intent when Doug Bell came close to opening the scoring after only 50 seconds with Sion keeper Pierre-Marie Pittier scrambling the ball away. The new 'four-step' rule for keepers was introduced that season and Pittier was at fault when he overstepped the mark, an indirect free kick inside the box leading to Eric Black opening the scoring. Aberdeen totally dominated and the goals continued to come with six different scorers in the rout. The big win delighted Ferguson as he spoke to the *Press & Journal*, 'The second leg will be a bit of a break for us, a trip to enjoy and it gives me the chance to change the side around a bit as we prepare for the Premier League. We must now aim to take a similar advantage when we play Dinamo Tirana in the first round.'

The return leg in Switzerland provided a welcome and unexpected break as the Dons finished the job with a 4-1 win in a stadium that was arguably among the most picturesque and stunning surroundings the club have ever played in. The facilities in Sion matched the beautiful area and provided Ferguson with the chance to get additional preparations completed ahead of the bigger challenges that lay ahead. On reflection it looked as though Sion were a poor side and although they never troubled Aberdeen, they were far better than most Scottish observers believed; they had drawn with Grasshopper days before the Dons tie, against a side that included seven Swiss internationals.

Black reflected on the trip to Switzerland, 'Sion's [Stade de] Tourbillon stadium was stunning. It was like a setting out of a Walt Disney film. The sheer beauty of those massive Alps slipping down to the ground left you breathless.' The 50 or so members of the Red Army who made the trip were treated to a sporting gesture from the home crowd, who stayed behind to applaud the Aberdeen players as they left the field.

Despite the ideal conditions and circumstances that the trip to Switzerland had brought, the Dons began their Premier League campaign with a disappointing defeat against Dundee United at Tannadice. It brought a 17-game unbeaten run to an end. After League Cup rivals Morton were beaten 4-1 at Pittodrie as the Dons got their first league points on the board, attention turned to the visit of Dinamo Tirana in the first round of the European Cup Winners' Cup. For once, Alex Ferguson went into a European tie with little knowledge of his opponents. Not for the lack of trying; ever since the draw was made the Albanians had proved evasive and unhelpful. Albania in the 1980s was a secretive, isolationist country, steeped in communism. With talk of journalists being denied entry to the country for the return leg, it was a step into the unknown, literally. For Ferguson, a good lead in the first leg was vital: 'It has been a difficult game to approach, the unknown is always a problem and it leaves a peculiar feeling that there may be something we do not know about. Despite the intrigue they present, I am confident Aberdeen will adapt to whatever happens during the game.'

The only morsel of information Ferguson discovered was gleaned from the Yugoslav referee from the game in Sion, who had officiated Tirana previously. He told Ferguson that they were a decent side; certainly, better than the Swiss. The unknown factor also spread to the Aberdeen support as the match programme from the night could not even list the Tirana players' names as nothing had been forthcoming. Although Tirana had proved elusive, Aberdeen as a club provided the best of Scottish hospitality, as they always have done for any visiting clubs. The Albanians were put up in a top hotel with the best of food, even steaks for breakfast. In the modern era such secrecy would not be allowed. With current UEFA guidelines and criteria setting a high bar, the Albanians of the '80s would be nowhere near European competition.

Despite John Hewitt scoring early for the Dons, they failed to add to their one goal which meant a precarious lead was taken to Tirana. Aberdeen dominated but came up against a side that stuck gamely to their task. With several missed chances and some dogged defending the visitors held out. If this had been a boxing bout it would have been stopped, but Tirana were to a man delighted to come away from the first leg still very much in the tie. Ferguson was without doubt frustrated, 'We enjoyed all of the possession and on another night, we would have had four or five more goals which would have been a better reward for our efforts.' It left the Dons' European hopes very much in the balance. Although Dinamo were an average side in terms of quality, they still had the distinct advantage that a home game can present in European competition.

Progress in the Premier League was modest, but Aberdeen were still very much in the mix. They did slip up against Rangers at Pittodrie, a 2-1 defeat that was the Ibrox club's first Premier League win in Aberdeen in 14 attempts. The fact that the visiting support stayed behind for more than 30 minutes celebrating a rare victory only confirmed the hold that Aberdeen had over Rangers. Meanwhile, the Dons' reserve side were faring well as they clinched the Reserve League championship after a two-legged play-off against Rangers. The competition was held over from the previous season. Aberdeen won both legs, with a 2-1 success at Ibrox confirming the Young Dons as champions.

Aberdeen travelled to Tirana for the return leg of their Cup Winners' Cup tie with a very much depleted party on their charter flight. The playing squad and backroom team were issued visas with only six journalists accompanying the team. With the visas only arriving from the Albanian Embassy in Paris the day before the party was about to leave, preparations were far from ideal. Alex

Ferguson was for once apprehensive, 'It is going to take a very good performance to get us through. I know from my experience as a player the variety of ways in which these teams can make things difficult for a visiting side, off the field as well as on it.'

One obvious factor was the 2.45pm kick-off time. There was no doubt this was a deliberate ploy by the Albanians. With temperatures expected to peak at around 100°F (38°C), the stifling heat would certainly make it difficult for Aberdeen. It was going to take a disciplined, professional display. Aberdeen had to adapt and abandon their fast, high-paced approach against opponents like Dinamo. The Albanian side were experienced and without doubt the best side in the country for many years. The searing heat made for an uncomfortable 90 minutes but in a game of attrition this Aberdeen team were now well versed in European football and set out to ensure there was no way through for the hosts. Although the conditions favoured the home side, the Dons sucked the life out of Dinamo and sat deep and controlled the game for long periods in their own half. Limited as Dinamo were, they battled on backed by a noisy 20,000 crowd but Aberdeen held out, more comfortably than they had expected, for a 0-0 draw and progress to the last 16.

Willie Miller recalled his experience of Tirana, 'When we arrived at Aberdeen Airport there were press reports of Albania being at the centre of a political coup. We flew into Tirana Airport expecting mayhem, but all was quiet. As we made our way into the city, farmers with bad teeth were waving at us. No tanks, no riots, no dissent. We checked into our hotel and everything was fine. This was the one decent hotel, thank goodness. As visitors we seemed to offer entertainment value, for Albania did not receive many foreign visitors. Shadowy figures in leather coats gazed at us as though we were from another planet. A very strange experience, and the match against Dinamo was as off-putting as the country. It was boiling hot, an uncomfortable heat. This was one of the many football challenges in which the tactical acumen of Alex Ferguson shone through. He decided to play Gordon Strachan and Peter Weir as out-and-out wide men, as the pitch was extensive and in good condition. He told us to keep possession and let Tirana tire themselves out. It proved a masterstroke, and as the game progressed, they became fatigued, and we were in complete control.'

The draw for the second round was made in Zürich the day after the Dons returned from Tirana. Ferguson declared that there would be no easy ties at this stage, but he was keen to avoid the likes of Inter Milan. The Dons were once again drawn to face another trip to eastern Europe against Polish league leaders Lech Poznań, with the first leg at Pittodrie once more. Ferguson was happy enough, 'It is going to be another difficult journey. Poland have produced several top players and they finished third in the World Cup. I would have preferred the first game away from home, but it means we have to get among the goals at Pittodrie.' Other ties in the draw included AZ Alkmaar v Inter Milan, Red Star Belgrade v Barcelona, Galatasaray v Austria Vienna, Real Madrid v Újpesti Dózsa and Tottenham Hotspur v Bayern Munich.

The battle for the Premier League was also taking shape with Aberdeen involved in a three-way scrap with Celtic and Dundee United. On 9 October the Dons inflicted a first defeat of the season on Celtic, 3-1 at Parkhead. Once again, this Aberdeen side had shown their growing resolve when it came to the big matches in Glasgow. When Mark McGhee scored the third goal in the closing minutes, it was too much for Celtic manager Billy McNeill, who came on to the pitch to remonstrate.

For the third round in a row the Dons were at home in the first leg of their European Cup Winners' Cup tie against Lech Poznań. Archie Knox had travelled to Poland to see Poznań in action and although they would present a tough challenge, they were a side that Aberdeen could do very well against. Knox watched them go down 2-1 to Widzew Łódź. Alex Ferguson was again keen to take a lead for the return leg, 'It is important we get a reasonable first-leg lead. I would settle for 2-0, but 3-0 would be perfect. The important thing is we learn from previous mistakes. We missed chances against the Albanians in the last round. My players know exactly what is required now, and we must get it right on the night.' The Poles, meanwhile, were confident they could keep things tight. Manager Wojciech Łazarek declared, 'We are looking for a draw or a single-goal defeat. We would like to score an away goal. Gordon Strachan is a key player for them, and we know about Willie Miller and Alex McLeish.'

Despite dominating from the outset, for long periods the Dons once again were left to rue several missed chances in a first half that saw Eric Black twice hit the woodwork. Two goals in two minutes early in the second half opened the game up and Aberdeen were good value for their first-leg advantage. Mark McGhee scored from the Dons' ninth corner and Peter Weir added a second when he got on the end of good set-up play by Strachan. The last eight of the competition was taking shape as other first-leg results that evening saw Vienna, Waterschei, Real Madrid, Barcelona and Paris Saint-Germain all taking a lead into their second legs. Inter Milan were behind in Belgrade while Tottenham and Bayern Munich were level after a 1-1 draw in London.

Following the difficulties encountered when the Dons travelled to Tirana, there were more concerns for the trip to Poland. The country was effectively in political turmoil. In 1980 in the Lenin Shipyards in Gdansk the first trade union in a Soviet-bloc nation was founded by Lech Wałęsa. The Solidarity movement gave rise to an anti-communist social union that went on to attract more than nine million members. In 1981 the Polish government declared martial law throughout the country in a bid to destroy the union.

Aberdeen arranged another charter flight as once again the visas were late in arriving. Unlike Albania there was no restriction on allowing supporters to attend, but only through the club. Around 30 Dons fans accompanied the team on their flight to Poznań in what was again as brief a stay as was allowed. Poznań was covered in a light blanket of snow as the party touched down. With the country under martial law, the anti-aircraft guns were on show and the Polish army manned the municipal facilities. Situated in the industrial west of Poland, the area was as bleak as the weather. Ahead of the game, Poznań boss Łazarek came out with the now familiar mind games, 'Aberdeen will see a different Lech team tomorrow. We will be backed by a big crowd and the Scottish players will not like that. We rarely fail on our own ground and we expect to unsettle Aberdeen and give them a tough time of it.' Such claims from European opponents were not unexpected. For Alex Ferguson it was nothing new. He honed his legendary pre-match quotes at Pittodrie. European ties apart, Ferguson used the trips to the bigger games in Glasgow to unsettle opponents and the occasional referee, a craft he was to master in time. In Europe, such claims only steeled Ferguson and his players.

The Stadion Miejski had a capacity of around 30,000 for the Dons' visit. The stadium was uncovered and with no floodlights the leg had an afternoon kick-off. Although the local supporters proved hostile, Aberdeen began well and controlled the game for long periods. With Jim Leighton rarely troubled the home crowd grew frustrated as did Poznań as they came up against an Aberdeen defence as solid as the city's granite. When Doug Bell bundled the ball over the line from a Mark McGhee header in 59 minutes, the tie was over. Aberdeen had again shown a maturity and tactical nous that augured well for European football. After 15 years of continental competition, Aberdeen had reached the quarter-finals for the first time.

The team flight home was delayed for several hours after the Polish authorities were reluctant to let the party board their flight due to some players leaving with more money than they came in with. Card schools were just about the only recreation the players were allowed during their brief stay in Poznań. With the local Złoty currency virtually worthless due to spiralling inflation, any UK sterling or US dollars was extremely sought after. For Aberdeen it was job done and they could not get out of Poznań quick enough, despite the warm reception the club received from the Polish people. With a vital Premier League game at the weekend against Dundee United, returning to Aberdeen immediately after the game was important.

For Ferguson, the performance was as good as he had seen, 'It was a proud moment for the team and Scottish football as the partisan crowd applauded us at the end. I look forward to the next stage and hope our progress can be maintained. I believe it was the most impressive performance away from home in Europe that I have seen. We will know our next opponents on 10 December when the draw is made. Will it be Real Madrid, Barcelona, Inter Milan, Juventus? We are now in that company and Aberdeen will not be overawed by such lofty reputations.' One thing for sure was that there would be no Celtic or Rangers interest in the European draws as both were eliminated in their respective European ties. It was left to Aberdeen and Dundee United to carry the flag in Europe for Scotland. The shift of power was moving east.

The visit of Dundee United on 6 November offered Aberdeen the opportunity to avenge their recent exit in the League Cup. Although Ferguson had prioritised the Premier League, Cup Winners' Cup and Scottish Cup as his prime targets, any defeat against United was hard to take for the boss. United arrived at Pittodrie unbeaten that season and had only conceded three goals in nine matches. After a thrilling 90 minutes that record was in tatters as Aberdeen routed the Tangerines 5-1. Gordon Strachan was at his imperious best, scoring in 85 minutes as he calmly slotted the ball past a beleaguered Hamish McAlpine to round off a superb Aberdeen performance. Ferguson was delighted, 'The destruction of Dundee United was a result and victory that has been accepted as everything which we deserved on the day. For me it was a reward and tribute for the team who have stuck to the basic principles I have preached. I thoroughly enjoyed it.'

Premier League table at 6 November 1982

	P	*W*	*D*	*L*	*F*	*A*	*Pts*
Celtic	10	8	1	1	26	12	17
Aberdeen	**10**	**6**	**2**	**2**	**20**	**10**	**14**
Dundee United	10	5	4	1	18	8	14
Rangers	10	4	5	1	21	11	13

The quarter-final draw for the European Cup Winners' Cup was eagerly anticipated as the players gathered for training on Friday, 10 December. Another factor was that the ties were not due to be played until March 1983 so there was plenty of time to look forward to what was always going to be a huge occasion for the club. The draw was held in Zürich and the *Evening Express* exclaimed as a result, 'IT'S BAYERN MUNICH'. Alex Ferguson expected a tough draw and they didn't come much bigger than the German giants, 'A lot will depend on our form at that time. We will really need to be at the top of our game, but the experience many of our players have had against top German opposition in the last few years should help us meet this great challenge.'

This would be no step into the unknown for Aberdeen as Bayern were a world-class side, full of internationals and World Cup winners. Beaten European Cup finalists the previous season, they had never lost to a foreign side on home soil in Europe. For Aberdeen and their supporters, it was a tie to relish. With so much time to prepare, Ferguson would plan thoroughly for what promised to be a magnificent occasion for the club. That school of thought was not shared in Germany as almost immediately the Scots' chances were dismissed. Franz Beckenbauer, who was in the Hamburg side that faced Aberdeen in 1981, declared that Bayern would progress with ease: 'Aberdeen are a good side, more so in Scotland but they will struggle in Munich. The Bayern players will have too much for them and it is a good draw for Bayern.' That view was not shared by Bayern general manager Uli Hoeneß who stated that he would rather his side had drawn Barcelona than Aberdeen: 'Before the draw I believed Inter Milan would be the perfect tie for us. Not Aberdeen. It is entirely different with your Scottish club. For a start, I don't know anything about the Aberdeen players. Inter have their World Cup players and Barcelona have signed Diego Maradona, but I have no fear over Maradona, we know all about him. At Aberdeen there could be better players and I will be coming to Scotland to see them for myself.'

For once Aberdeen were the unknown quantity. That was something that Ferguson picked up on and intended to use to gain any advantage over the Germans. Aberdeen were in uncharted territory, involved at the business end of a European competition and facing world-class opposition with world-class players. It was where Ferguson wanted to be.

The full quarter-final draw was Austria Vienna v Barcelona, Bayern Munich v Aberdeen, Inter Milan v Real Madrid and Paris Saint-Germain v Waterschei of Belgium.

With the glamour tie to look forward to in March, it was back to domestic issues as Aberdeen concentrated on the Premier League and opened their defence of the Scottish Cup through the winter period. On 11 December they went down 2-1 to Celtic at Pittodrie in a game they dominated for long periods but were undone by two deflected goals. Ferguson was seething, 'It ended as a painful exercise and the players and myself all thought we beat ourselves on the day.' The boss also took a swipe at the media, a trend that was to escalate throughout his time at Pittodrie, 'There was certainly a penalty incident that went against us when Gordon Strachan was brought down. For reasons unknown, it was never highlighted on television as one of the main incidents in the game. In terms of previous meetings with Celtic, I remember a penalty claim they had which was re-run several times when we beat them in October. The impression it leaves me with is that the media are no friends of Aberdeen. When we beat either Celtic or

Rangers, we fail to get the credit we deserve. Mind you, the last thing I suppose we should expect during that Celtic match was a penalty. I still remember a glaring example of a spot kick that we didn't get against them when Tom McAdam grabbed the ball with both hands a couple of years ago. The same referee didn't see that one, therefore it was no surprise when he missed the one against Celtic last week.' The official in question was Kenny Hope. Ferguson was certainly no shrinking violet when it came to his relationships with referees. While most observers viewed Hope as one of the more competent referees around, that view was not shared by Ferguson.

Following the defeat to Celtic, Ferguson declared his side were already playing catch-up and that they would need to be near perfect if they were to win the Premier League. Those hopes were boosted with four straight victories over the festive period. Dundee were beaten 2-0 at Dens Park before Christmas in another huge confidence boost. The Dark Blues were aggrieved after the first of Mark McGhee's two goals was contested as both Simpson and Cooper were yards offside. The new year fixture saw the return of Pat Stanton, who had left Pittodrie in 1980, as manager of Hibernian. Aberdeen began 1983 in style as McGhee scored after only 20 seconds, a sign of things to come. Two days later the much-heralded Dundee United defence, swept aside in November, suffered more pain when Aberdeen inflicted another decisive defeat on the Tannadice side. The 3-0 scoreline was United's first defeat at home since May 1982, when Aberdeen were again their conquerors. The Dons had now scored eight times in three matches against the Tangerines, who had only conceded six goals in their other 15 outings. Ferguson was full of praise for the travelling support: 'The side had an invincible feeling about the Tannadice clash, a game that capsulated all the necessary commitment and determination needed to prevail. It was a great day for the club and our wonderful support which was around 8,000 in number.' For Aberdeen it was not uncommon for their support often outnumber home fans on their travels in the '80s. Certainly at both Dundee venues, the Dons would often benefit from having more support when there was a lot at stake. In those days games were rarely all-ticket and segregated areas were usually terracing with ample room to accommodate large travelling supports. Dundee was also the nearest Premier League venue to Aberdeen, a mere 70 miles.

The club took the opportunity to take the squad for a week-long break to the Costa del Sol following their fine form over the festive period. Ferguson was behind the trip, 'We have found in the past that a spell of training in more favourable weather can have a positive effect on the players and if we can reproduce the success which followed our visits to Belenenses and Benidorm, it will have been worthwhile.' Such was the intensity of Alex Ferguson so he could focus fully on the squad and their training and conditioning, he refused to pen his usual programme notes during their break. The first-team squad of only 14 players flew out to Málaga in preparation for the tough schedule ahead. In transfer news the Dons sold Andy Dornan and Andy Harrow in a double deal with both joining Motherwell for a combined fee of around £40,000. Harrow had been brought in as a replacement for Steve Archibald but never really established himself as a regular in the side. Dornan came through the ranks and the young right-back had the tough task of replacing the established Stuart Kennedy in the first team.

Aberdeen returned from Spain to welcome Rangers to Pittodrie and the Dons looked refreshed as they comfortably defeated the Ibrox side 2-0. Mark McGhee marked his 200th appearance for the club by scoring in the win. Doug Rougvie relished games against Rangers and after he opened the scoring, he danced a jig all the way back to the Dons' half to the delight of the capacity crowd. Aberdeen only had two goals to show from a game in which they outclassed Rangers as the gap in class between the clubs was widening with every passing week. At no stage of the season were Rangers challenging for the Premier League title; the consensus was it would be between Aberdeen and Celtic, although Dundee United were still very much in the mix.

The defence of the Scottish Cup began against Hibernian at Easter Road. It was a tough draw for the Dons, coming up against Premier League opposition away from home, and it was without doubt the tie of the round. On reflection it was no surprise that Aberdeen were drawn against the Edinburgh side – they had faced Hibernian on 22 occasions previously in the Scottish Cup, more than any other opponents. Ferguson took the view that irrespective of the opposition they are there to be beaten, at any stage, 'Of course it is a difficult opening to the cup campaign, but we have had hard draws in the past and got through. Even allowing for the unpredictability of Scottish Cup ties, there is no reason why we should have any concerns about going to Easter Road.' Meanwhile, with the German Bundesliga due to resume from its winter break, Ferguson was making plans to watch Cup Winners' Cup opponents Bayern Munich against Karlsruhe in the Olympic Stadium.

Gordon Strachan was missing through a hamstring injury, but Aberdeen proved too strong for Hibernian. Two goals in quick succession in the first half laid the foundation for a comfortable 4-1 win and progress to the fourth round. The Dons were backed by a large travelling support in the 20,000 attendance. The only other tie of note that day was St Mirren knocking Dundee United out in Paisley.

There was some mischievous talk ahead of the Cup Winners' Cup visit to Munich as rumours circulated that Bayern were preparing a £1m bid for Strachan. For once the usual culprits from the Glasgow press were not at fault for this one. It emerged that an unofficial agent acting neither for Strachan nor Bayern was behind it. Uli Hoeneß commented, 'Strachan was one of the players who has been offered to us through an agent. I have since discovered that Strachan is contracted to Aberdeen until June 1984 so we can't have him anyway. That's it then. I will have to look elsewhere to get a replacement for Paul Breitner [who was retiring at the end of the season].'

Aberdeen were now approaching a critical period that would define their season. A week after their Scottish Cup win, they travelled to Parkhead to face Celtic for a match that many believed would go a long way in deciding the destination of the Premier League. The game was important enough to tempt a delegation from Bayern Munich to attend and watch Aberdeen for the first time. Described by many who were there, the Dons' 3-1 win was the complete performance and one that put the team a point ahead at the top of the table. The Parkhead crowd were at their vitriolic worst as they targeted the Aberdeen players before, during and after the game. The Dons were backed by a sizeable away support, scattered throughout the Parkhead terraces and stands.

Eric Black was the Aberdeen player who caught the eye with a hat-trick, his two goals just before half-time putting his team in control. Ferguson was proud of his players, 'All the superlatives in football's dictionary have virtually spilled out in print since Aberdeen proved there may now be only Ben Nevis to conquer this season. It might be an idea of having a crack at that one. Rest assured, the final third of the season will have the team under so much additional pressure to maintain the current momentum. The result at Parkhead was without doubt a high point in our season and to enjoy a fabulous win against a side that has been at the top for the last two years. A good percentage of the 43,000 crowd were patriots from Pittodrie and I was immensely pleased for them and we gave them a day to remember.'

Black became the first Aberdeen player to score a hat-trick against Celtic at Parkhead since Dons legend George Hamilton scored four in a 5-1 win on 2 January 1947. Uli Hoeneß, the Bayern Munich general manager, led the German delegation to Parkhead, and he returned to Munich with a warning for his players: 'Aberdeen were very good. They handled the occasion well and did not look in trouble at any stage of the game. The striker Black was exceptional. Aberdeen were technically better than we expected. They play with Scottish passion and fire; add their tactical awareness they will be a dangerous opponent. Bayern will need to take a lead from the first game.'

Premier League table at 12 February 1983

	P	*W*	*D*	*L*	*F*	*A*	*Pts*
Aberdeen	**24**	**17**	**4**	**3**	**51**	**16**	**38**
Celtic	23	17	3	3	60	27	37
Dundee United	23	14	6	3	53	19	34

Ahead of the trip to West Germany the Dons prepared with a double header against Dundee at Pittodrie in the league and Scottish Cup. They dominated both games to maintain their winning run and progress to the last eight of the cup.

Ticket sales for the return leg against Bayern at Pittodrie were going well. Following the chaos and criticism that came from the Liverpool tie in 1980, the club voucher system was working so that regular supporters would get first option on big match tickets. There were hardly any complaints that the club were charging between £3 and £5 for the Bayern tie.

Ahead of the trip to Munich, Tottenham manager Keith Burkinshaw, who saw his side heavily defeated by Bayern in the previous round, declared, 'It is a big stadium over there and it could be frightening for the younger Aberdeen players, but I am sure they have enough experience to overcome that. Make no mistake about it, Bayern are a very good side and they have skill right through their team. Aberdeen must remain compact as a team and not get dragged about. Aberdeen will go there with a lot of confidence and they have a few young players who will run their socks off and get in about them. Bayern will not like that. [Karl-Heinz] Rummenigge is the best striker in Europe now and he must be stopped. He is strong and quick and very accurate. He would be a threat against any side in the world just now. You have got to congest the area in front of him to stop him and close him down quickly.'

West German Bundesliga table at February 1983

	P	*W*	*D*	*L*	*F*	*A*	*Pts*
SV Hamburg	18	10	8	0	45	17	28
Bayern Munich	18	10	5	3	37	13	25
Stuttgart	18	10	4	4	41	23	24

Hamburg captain Manfred Kaltz, the German international right-back, also voiced his admiration for the Dons, 'Aberdeen were undoubtedly our hardest opponent last year in the UEFA Cup. They could have scored seven goals against us in Scotland.' Paul Breitner was determined to play after picking up a knock. 'Even if I have to play on crutches I will play against Aberdeen,' he said on the eve of the game.

Uli Hoeneß told the *Evening Express*, 'I have spoken to Paul about his decision and he wants to bring more success to the club before he leaves. He has put the Cup Winners' Cup at the top of his list.'

In financial terms this was certainly a mismatch. Bayern Munich were European royalty and they were pulling in the riches to match that. Breitner's intended retirement came after he turned down a two-year contract offer from Bayern worth £250,000 to continue playing. In contrast, Aberdeen captain Willie Miller was on just over £200 per week. The German bonuses were also eye-watering. To beat Aberdeen, they were on £1,300 a man with additional money if the home attendance topped 40,000.

The Dons would be followed by around 2,000 fans in Munich. It was by some way the largest away support to follow the team in Europe. The task for Aberdeen in the imposing Olympiastadion in Munich was daunting; with Bayern unbeaten in Europe against foreign opposition, Ferguson had told the media ahead of the tie that he would settle for a two-goal defeat. Mind games perhaps but Ferguson was expecting a far better outcome. He had identified Karl-Heinz Rummenigge as a real danger. The European Footballer of the Year in 1980 and 1981 was a class act and presented the biggest danger for Aberdeen. Willie Miller was delegated to pick Rummenigge up. Ferguson had told his skipper to stay close and stay on his feet. As for Breitner, young Neale Cooper would look after him when he came forward. Ferguson had faith in his midfield of Cooper, Neil Simpson and Doug Bell. Gordon Strachan was still not fully fit to start so he took a place on the bench. Aberdeen deployed the now accepted tactics away from home in Europe of defending deep and hitting on the break. Ferguson recalled, 'Our whole preparation was based on that this was going to be a real test for us. We had learned from experience in the previous year after throwing the tie away against Hamburg. Much of our tactical talk centred around holding the ball and taking the sting out the game. We played tremendously well, our best away performance in Europe. We dominated the middle of the park and Willie Miller was magnificent. The players took inspiration from their captain.' There was one significant moment that epitomised the Aberdeen performance. Breitner, the majestic Bayern captain, resignedly stepped aside to allow Cooper to dispossess him in a manner that embarrassed the World Cup winner. In that moment, it appeared that Cooper had brought forward Breitner's retirement.

On reflection the 0-0 draw could have been even better for the Dons, who were desperately unlucky not to take a lead back to Pittodrie. The *Press & Journal* declared 'BAYERN MASTERED AT THEIR OWN GAME' in a reference to a superb tactical display that paved the way for an excellent team performance. German fans have always been known for their appreciation of the game and their generous applause at full time towards the Aberdeen players was vindication for the Dons and confirmation that they had 'arrived' in Europe. Even Beckenbauer was impressed, 'I just could not believe that was the same Aberdeen team who played against us in Hamburg. In a tactical sense they have improved so much in a short time.' The German legend was correct, and Ferguson and his players had taken a huge step forward in what was exalted company.

Uli Hoeneß was another who was not that shocked, 'When I went to watch Aberdeen, I did say that they were better than Real Madrid, Inter Milan and Barcelona. I do not think anyone took me seriously, but they will now.' Alex McLeish, along with Miller, was immense and supremely confident, 'It was a good performance from us. I felt we could have played for a fortnight and they would not have scored.'

Austria Vienna against Barcelona was also goalless after the first leg, while Inter Milan and Real Madrid drew 1-1 in Italy, and

Paris Saint-Germain took a 2-0 lead over Waterschei ahead of their visit to Belgium.

Aberdeen prepared for the return leg by progressing to the semi-finals of the Scottish Cup after a bruising narrow win over Partick Thistle in Glasgow. The Firhill club had in their team a young Mo Johnston, who declared ahead of the clash that he was 'going to get in about Aberdeen'. Thistle were intent on making a fight of it, literally. What they, like so many other opponents, discovered about this Aberdeen side was that they could handle themselves. Not many would come up against the likes of Stuart Kennedy, Alex McLeish, Willie Miller and Doug Rougvie and intimidate them. Aberdeen went through after a marvellous free kick from Peter Weir as attention turned to Europe.

Alex Ferguson was acutely aware of the dangers that Bayern would present at Pittodrie. Munich were a world-class side, full of seasoned pros who had seen it all before, and the manager said, 'I think we gave them a real scare over there so I expect them to be hurting a bit as they were criticised by their own media. They may come out snarling at us, but we will be ready.' The club's new ticket voucher system came into use. Main Stand tickets would cost £5 with the South Stand at £4, the Beach End and Merkland Road at £3 each, with child and OAP admission at £1.50. With Munich only taking a minimal allocation of 350 tickets, Pittodrie would be packed with home supporters, confident that it was going to be one of those famed European nights at the stadium. The general belief was that the tie was on a knife-edge, and despite the result in Munich the bookmakers could not separate the sides.

Bayern received a pre-match boost from German national coach Jupp Derwall, 'The Scots will not be able to mark Breitner and Rummenigge so well as they did in Munich. Because they must win, Aberdeen must go forward, and this will certainly give Munich chances to counter.' Uli Hoeneß was counting on his team reaching the semi-finals. The gate money would provide the nucleus of more than £560,000 needed to buy Danish international Søren Lerby from Ajax at the end of the campaign. By contrast Aberdeen were looking at making a modest profit from their European exploits that season. They had incurred significant costs from their earlier trips to Switzerland, Albania and Poland. That all changed with the two games against Bayern that attracted widespread interest across Europe. With television coverage and a guaranteed full house at Pittodrie, Aberdeen were set to cash in. The stage was set for a classic.

The Pittodrie atmosphere matched the occasion. Bayern were a team full of seasoned international players but even they looked unsettled as Aberdeen began well, backed by a passionate crowd, which Ferguson craved. Despite a positive start the Dons went behind in ten minutes. Breitner set Klaus Augenthaler up from a free kick and his shot was too good for Jim Leighton. The away goal hushed Pittodrie and with Aberdeen now needing at least two goals the Germans looked in control, but the Dons came back into the tie and were piling on the pressure. In 22 minutes Black saw his header come back off the bar from a Kennedy cross, and after 38 minutes they were back in it. A McGhee cross was headed back across goal by Black. Augenthaler looked suspect as he tried to clear, only for the incoming Neil Simpson to pounce on the loose ball and slam it into the net from close range.

Bayern were happy to take the sting out of the game and knowing that Aberdeen had to score they were happy to sit in and use Karl Del'Haye on the break. Just on the hour, however, it was disaster for the hosts. Del'Haye crossed into the box and although it was headed clear, Hans Pflügler volleyed past Leighton with a superb shot that went in at the post.

Aberdeen were now staring at defeat, once more looking for two goals. At that stage Ferguson was forced to change things and take a risk, 'I had to do something, I was not going to sit back and accept defeat. We were struggling against their wingers, so I took off Stuart Kennedy and put John McMaster into midfield. Rougvie switched to right-back and Neale Cooper went on the left.' The substitution and positional changes had an effect as Aberdeen regained the initiative, and after 75 minutes they introduced John

Hewitt for Neil Simpson. It was a last throw of the dice, a forward on for a midfielder. A minute later Aberdeen scored. For regular Pittodrie patrons it was not unfamiliar to see Gordon Strachan and John McMaster 'mess up' their free kick routine by both going over the ball, suggesting confusion. As the Bayern defence relaxed, Strachan turned quickly and crossed for Alex McLeish to head past keeper Manfred Müller. The master tacticians of Munich were undone by a classic routine, made in Pittodrie.

The visitors barely had time to argue among themselves when Aberdeen regained possession from the kick-off and took a sensational lead. A deep cross found Black again and his header was only parried by Müller. John Hewitt stooped to slip the ball home to put the Dons in dreamland. If Pittodrie had been quiet for periods when Bayern were strutting their stuff, the crowd rose to the occasion, literally. With 15 minutes left, the supporters, anticipating a Bayern response, created an atmosphere never seen before or since at the old place. This was history in the making. It was back in 1929 that Aberdeen winger Alec Cheyne scored direct from a corner for Scotland to defeat England in the closing minutes and give his side the victory. That day the noise after that goal was so profound that legend has it the 'Hampden Roar' was born. At Pittodrie in 1983 the crescendo of noise helped Aberdeen see the game through to a remarkable conclusion. The Dons finished the tie by retaining possession, much to the frustration of the Germans. When French referee Michel Vautrot blew the final whistle, scenes of joy on and off the field seemed to last an eternity. Bayern were stunned as the Aberdeen players and supporters celebrated a famous victory. The scenes at full time were chaotic with some supporters on the pitch celebrating with the players and staff. Among it all was a stunned Uli Hoeneß, who looked visibly shocked as he made his way down the touchline.

Captain Willie Miller recalled, 'It was a victory to cherish. That night set up the most intense atmosphere that I had ever experienced. I remember the din made by the crowd at the final whistle, and Fergie's little dance on the pitch. I was not present at Pittodrie in the 1950s when 45,000 fans roared approval. In the modern era I had not experienced an atmosphere like that on that magnificent night. We had beaten Bayern Munich, an iconic organisation.'

If the Aberdeen result had sent shockwaves through Europe, then Belgian outsiders Waterschei were doing their bit as they eliminated Paris Saint-Germain, overturning a two-goal deficit to knock the French side out. Although back then PSG were not the force they are these days it was still an incredible result for Waterschei. The other shock came in the Camp Nou as Spanish hopes of a Real Madrid v Barcelona final were extinguished when Austria Vienna held the Catalans to go through on away goals. Real Madrid were now the bookies' favourites after they defeated Inter Milan in the Bernabéu. The results certainly opened up the competition and Aberdeen were now well placed to go further.

Aberdeen were now carrying the flag for British football after Aston Villa, Liverpool and Dundee United were all knocked out of their respective European ties. It was a clear source of pride for Alex Ferguson, 'It was a great night for us on what was a bad evening for British football. We now carry the additional weight of expectation following our win over Bayern, but it is something that we will relish and thrive on. I don't think any side will fancy playing us.'

As so often happens following a European victory, the Dons struggled three days later against a Dundee United side they had defeated with ease in their previous two meetings. The exertions of the European tie clearly had an effect and United were fortunate enough to take advantage. The Premier League was now a three-horse race with Aberdeen, Celtic and Dundee United all looking to be crowned champions. The Tannadice club had been knocked out of the Scottish Cup and failed to progress in the UEFA Cup following drawing a blank against Bohemians of Prague, who went on to be well beaten by Anderlecht in the semi-final. At that stage Dundee United had a clear advantage with only the Premier League to play for. By contrast, Aberdeen were still on target for an incredible treble.

Premier League table at 19 March 1983

	P	*W*	*D*	*L*	*F*	*A*	*Pts*
Aberdeen	**27**	**19**	**4**	**4**	**57**	**20**	**42**
Dundee United	27	17	7	3	65	25	41
Celtic	26	19	3	4	68	29	41

There was no doubt that the prime target for Aberdeen was going all the way in the European Cup Winners' Cup. Their chances were given a boost when they were drawn against Waterschei in the semi-final. With the powerful Austria Vienna and Real Madrid clashing in the other tie, it was clear that the Dons had a great opportunity to reach their first European final. Ferguson wanted the Belgians, and while privately he was delighted, publicly he was praising his opponents, 'We are happy with the draw but at this stage any side making it this far has to be strong. Waterschei had a fantastic result against Paris Saint-Germain in Belgium so we will need to be at our very best to reach the final.'

Four days before the visit of Waterschei, the Dons' title chances were handed a hammer blow when St Mirren escaped Pittodrie with a 1-0 win. Aberdeen dominated the game in dreadful conditions. As the snow fell, Gordon Strachan missed a penalty and from that point on their championship hopes were slim at best. It was hardly the best preparation for their first European semi-final, which now took on huge significance. Archie Knox took the opportunity to look at the Belgians in action, and reported back, 'They are a very experienced side with a good understanding within their team. They like to keep possession as much as possible. It would be a mistake for us to take them lightly, even if they do not have the glamour names of Bayern Munich. I think we will beat them, but we will have to play a bit to get through.' Waterschei prepared for the trip to Scotland with a 2-0 win over Tongeren.

Belgian First Division table at 6 April 1983

	P	*W*	*D*	*L*	*F*	*A*	*Pts*
Anderlecht	26	16	7	3	59	27	39
Antwerp	26	16	5	5	43	24	37
Standard Liege	26	15	6	5	58	29	36
Waterschei	27	13	8	6	41	32	34

Eight months on from their opening tie against Swiss side Sion, Aberdeen now had the chance to head for the final in Gothenburg. Pittodrie was once again full and there was an air of expectancy as the Dons were favourites to progress. Ferguson looked ahead to the tie, 'We all know what is at stake and what is needed if Aberdeen are to continue on a path that affords no respite but is nevertheless creating a situation that is there to be enjoyed as a reward for all of the hard work which everyone within the walls of Pittodrie has produced. The size of the task as we represent Britain as the only surviving club this season will not be underestimated by anyone.'

Within four minutes there was bedlam at Pittodrie. Aberdeen started the first leg with an intensity that matched the fevered atmosphere by taking a two-goal lead that the Belgians never recovered from. Doug Bell weaved his way through the Waterschei defence to set up Eric Black for the opener before a superb run of pace and power had Neil Simpson cutting through the shell-shocked visitors to put Aberdeen on their way. It was a dream start and the Dons continued to build on that. After the break Bell set up Mark McGhee for the third while Peter Weir stooped to head a fourth goal in 69 minutes. Lárus Guðmundsson pulled a goal back before the rout was completed with a bizarre fifth as McGhee, on the ground, took three attempts to get the ball into the net. The 5-1 win was no more than Aberdeen deserved. Although they had to face Waterschei at a difficult venue in the second leg, the Dons were as good as in the final. The result even surprised Ferguson, 'It was a marvellous night for us, and our supporters were behind us all the way. We started so well, and we knew the Belgians were intent on sitting deep. Our two early goals forced them into changing their tactics and we took advantage of that.'

Striker Eddy Voordeckers, who was expected to be a real threat, was clearly shattered, leaving Pittodrie with head bowed and not speaking to the waiting press. However, the Waterschei players had to return to the stadium the next morning for 'penance' training under coach Ernst-August Künnecke. Voordeckers declared, 'We are certainly out of it now for no team can pull back four goals at this stage of European competition. We were almost out of this one before the game started. We were supposed to keep it tight until half-time and then try and grab a goal. But that all changed when we were two down after some of our players were waiting for their first touch of the ball. We then had to scrap our prepared plan, and that was not easy for us. We must now improve and show the Scottish fans in the second game that we are a good team.'

UEFA also announced that the draws for the European competitions for the following season would take place in the Hotel Intercontinental in Geneva on 6 July 1983 and that Aberdeen, by virtue of reaching the Cup Winners' Cup semi-finals, would be a seeded club for the next five years.

Ahead of the trip to Belgium the Dons returned to Scottish Cup action and a semi-final against old rivals Celtic at Hampden. The punishing schedule was beginning to reflect on their Premier League chances, so retaining the Scottish Cup was important to Ferguson. The capacity at the national stadium was restricted to 53,000 due to redevelopment works. Such was the dominance of Aberdeen and Celtic that both Ferguson and Celtic manager Billy McNeill agreed that their clash was the final before the final. Ferguson was looking forward to it: 'Hampden will provide another great platform for my players and they certainly will not need motivation from me. We have an excellent record against them down there. We will be ready for them, all right.' McNeill agreed, 'There is no doubt this semi-final has got everything going for it as it involves the two top teams in Scotland. Aberdeen's season has turned out to be an exciting one and they will be on a high after their great result in Europe.'

Any expectations that the Hampden clash would provide a spectacle showcasing the Scottish game evaporated in the early stages. It was clear from the outset that Celtic were looking to take advantage of the busy Aberdeen schedule by making the tie a physical one. There was no doubt the pressure was on the Dons as they were still going for three trophies. Celtic looked to unsettle them and after some brutal early exchanges the tone was set. Not for the first time the Dons were faced with opponents intent on stopping them at all costs. Chances were few and a game of attrition was settled in 65 minutes when substitute Peter Weir headed a Black cross in at the far post. Aberdeen were left to salute their sizeable support with the Celtic fans long gone as the holders were on course to retain the Scottish Cup for the first time in their history. The Dons were also looking at a roll call over the weekend as the bruising encounter had taken its toll. Ferguson was concerned, 'It was a cup tie and a final in one match because of the pressure on both sides not to lose. After Neale Cooper's hospital trip for a broken nose there was the necessity of a visit for Doug Bell who needed an X-ray to determine the full extent of the damage on his ankle. So, we were looking to the midweek trip to Belgium. There were also injuries to Eric Black and Gordon Strachan. The rich consolation was the fact that Aberdeen won the right for a place in the final.'

It can never be said that a European semi-final would be a formality but with Aberdeen protecting a 5-1 first-leg advantage, they were supremely confident as they travelled to Genk to book their Cup Winners' Cup Final place in Gothenburg. Aberdeen were based in nearby Maastricht in the Netherlands, and were greeted with the familiar sound of the bagpipes from four members of the Gordon Highlanders who made the 150-mile round trip from their Hemer base in West Germany to support the Dons and pipe them on to the field. With four first-team players missing, the Dons looked on course to reach the final without losing any of their matches in the tournament.

Aberdeen controlled the game for long periods and missed several chances before the dangerous Voordeckers scored late on for Waterschei. The injury crisis deepened when Stuart Kennedy caught his studs in the turf. The injury was far worse than first feared and ultimately would end his career. Ever the perfectionist, Ferguson had a few choice words for his players after they suffered their first defeat in Europe that season, and the fact that Aberdeen became the first Scottish club outside of Glasgow to reach a European final was almost lost on the players as they emerged from the dressing room. Willie Miller was annoyed, 'We should have murdered them. We all know it.' The Waterschei pitch was also the worst the Dons had played on all season. Mark McGhee had to change his footwear at half-time as the hard surface made any decent football more difficult. Ferguson reflected on the game, 'The lads wanted to get to the final undefeated and they were pretty sick about going down to the Belgians. The dressing room was certainly a dull place at the end. But I am proud of every one of them for it is a remarkable achievement to get a place in a European final.'

Willie Miller

Waterschei manager Künnecke joined the growing list of coaches who had heaped praise on that Aberdeen side, 'I believe Aberdeen are good enough and strong enough to win this European final, whether it is Madrid or Vienna. They are so organised, probably the best in Europe, they are strong but also very fair. Not many sides could lose four players like they did and still go through. They made several changes from the first game yet were still a formidable team in Belgium. European football is now very interested in Aberdeen and I believe they will take the cup back to Scotland.'

There was little time to dwell on it as the next day Ferguson was on his way to Madrid to watch the conclusion of the other semi-final between Real and Austria Vienna. Ferguson was up early to drive from their base in Maastricht to Brussels and catch a flight to Madrid. With the Dons' tie being played on the Tuesday after Aberdeen agreed to the change requested by Waterschei, it offered Ferguson the ideal opportunity to see Madrid in action. The Spaniards eased past Vienna to book their place in Sweden against Aberdeen. Ferguson didn't see a lot to worry him, 'On my return to my hotel I called Archie Knox to tell him not to say anything but believe me, what a chance we have. I believed that we could beat Real Madrid.'

With the Dons' cup commitments taking priority, something had to give in what was a punishing schedule. The injuries were piling up and the squad had to be utilised to the full. Willie Falconer, the 17-year-old forward, made his debut when he came on against Waterschei, while the likes of Ian Angus, Derek Hamilton, Brian Mitchell, Steve Cowan and Ian Porteous were all called into first-team action in the closing weeks of the season. Ferguson had at one stage given up on the Premier League but a run of victories over Celtic, Motherwell and Dundee kept the Dons in the mix. Crucially in the build-up to Sweden the club had to play two games in three days, so they had a full week to prepare for the final in Gothenburg. On Tuesday, 3 May they failed to open a stubborn Hibernian defence in Edinburgh. Gordon Strachan missed a penalty and the 0-0 draw meant that Aberdeen had almost blown their title hopes. Two days later Kilmarnock were hammered 5-0 at Pittodrie as only six of the team that would start in Sweden took the field against the Rugby Park side. Briefly the Dons were top of the table but in order to stay there, results would have to go their way on the final day of the Premier League season, three days after Gothenburg.

With three games left the Dons were preparing to face Real Madrid in Sweden, their final league game at home to Hibernian and the Scottish Cup Final a week later, fixtures that would define their season.

What is less known was the meticulous planning and preparation that Alex Ferguson and Archie Knox had gone through ahead of the

European Cup Winners' Cup Final. This was of course uncharted waters for Aberdeen and the management. What was significant was that most of the squad had been through so many European ties in recent years, from the hard lessons of Liverpool and Hamburg to the famous wins over Ipswich and Bayern Munich. That experience would be vital. After the Kilmarnock game the players were given two days off. Aberdeen had arranged a reserve match against Hibernian in Edinburgh on the Sunday so that the fitness of Doug Bell and Eric Black could be assessed. Knox took the team south while Ferguson trained the first team. At that stage Ferguson was still undecided as to his starting line-up. That dilemma was eased when Bell was not fit enough to take any part, but Black came through the game and was all set to lead the attack in Sweden. It was heartbreaking for Bell, who had contributed so much in the run to the final. With Kennedy and Bell out, the starting line-up almost picked itself.

Ferguson also brought the players' wives in for a meeting at Pittodrie on the Sunday, 'Despite all the players' mumblings about how the wives would soon tell me a thing or two and what the women would say to me, they were as good as gold about the situation. I asked them to support their husbands as much as possible and not to cause any problems as the players would be nervous and edgy. Above all, understand what was going on, the greatest day in a player's career, playing in a European final against the most famous team in the world. Everything was right. The atmosphere among the players was positive and the build-up was good.'

The city was, not surprisingly, in a frenzy. The excitement ever since Real Madrid confirmed their place in Sweden captured the imagination of the locals, with their team coming up against the winners of the first five European Cups. By contrast, Aberdeen were a provincial Scottish club appearing in their first final. In 28 years of European competition Real had only failed on one occasion to qualify, amassing 173 appearances, including ten finals and six European Cup triumphs. Aberdeen, with 12 European adventures and 48 games, were certainly breaking new ground by reaching the final.

After Aberdeen confirmed their place in the final it was announced by P&O Ferries that the *St Clair* ferry would be used to take 493 Dons fans to the Swedish port for the big game. The *St Clair* was the regular ferry between Aberdeen and Lerwick in Shetland. All berths and cabins were taken up within hours of going on sale. The 4,500-ton ship left Aberdeen Harbour at 1pm on Monday, 9 May for the 27-hour journey to Sweden. Alex Ferguson was on hand to see the ferry off and promised the travellers that he would be back to welcome them home with the cup. Thousands gathered at the quayside as the ferry slipped out of the harbour. Dozens of oil rig supply vessels joined in as they gave the fans aboard a tremendous send-off. P&O manager Eric Turner was delighted, 'It was out of this world, way beyond what we were expecting.' Duty free bar prices made the early part of the journey go very smoothly. Generous nips were going for 40p and it was the same price for the 25,000 cans of beer on board, with more in Sweden if needed for the trip home. The staff would not miss out as the fans among the 67 crew all had tickets for the game. The ferry arrived in Gothenburg in early evening the following day.

Back in Aberdeen more than 20 aircraft, including private charters, left the airport for Sweden on Tuesday, 10 May with the same amount leaving on the morning of the match. Cup fever was hitting Gothenburg as rival fans began to gather in the Swedish port. The Swedes were well prepared and news from the Ullevi stadium was that more than 20,000 tickets had been sold and a crowd of around 40,000 was expected. The main daily paper, *Göteborgs-Posten*, asked if Aberdeen would be strong enough to handle Real Madrid. One local radio commentator predicted a narrow win for Madrid and spoke of his concern for 'English' supporters and their reputation abroad.

The club had engaged with a travel agent since the 1981 UEFA Cup tie against Ipswich and owner Harry Hynds was a busy man, 'We did all the travel for the club, from the supporters to the team and officials. We started taking bookings for Gothenburg as early as September. I wouldn't say it was blind optimism, the team were playing so well, and the manager had a Midas touch.' Hynds was tasked with finding a suitable base for the team ahead of the final, 'The manager and directors left it in my hands, but I knew they were perfectionists and the travel arrangements had to meet their standards. I had seen a few sides to Alex Ferguson, but he was a true master at what he does. When it came to choose a place to stay, I travelled across and found the Hotel Fars Hatt which was about 15 miles outside of Gothenburg. The city was going to be too busy, so the countryside location was ideal. As soon as I visited the hotel, I called Pittodrie and said they had to take it.' The Fars Hatt which translates to 'Fathers Hat' remains open to this day, even for some intrepid Aberdeen supporters for a nostalgic visit. Its name also had a significance in the north-east of Scotland. The name in local dialect equated to 'Where's that?' The hotel dated back as far as 1684 and had evolved into a first-class holiday destination. Ferguson was delighted, 'The base was in the small hamlet of Kungalv and we also had access to a superb training ground at an amateur club there.' By contrast, Real Madrid opted to stay in the city centre at a hotel that had seen better days.

The squad flew out to Sweden on the Monday. Ferguson took up the story, 'We felt that the proper thing to do was go out there on the Monday and get ourselves settled in. The airport was handing out rosettes and the players received a singing telegram from their wives before we set out. It was a carnival of excitement.' The manager was keen to ensure the players were as relaxed as possible and after speaking to Archie Knox, both were keen not to show any nerves. Ferguson was convinced his players could handle the big games and get the better of Real Madrid.

The day before the game the squad went through an extensive training session at the Ullevi with as much variation as possible. The press was out in force as was the Madrid squad who were due to train after Aberdeen. When the Spaniards came out, they used the time to practise penalty kicks before taking turns to speak to the Spanish media at great length. Madrid had been under pressure that season and before the white handkerchiefs would be waved around, they simply had to defeat Aberdeen to save their season. After leading La Liga for many months, they lost out on the title on the final day. Needing a point from their final game, they went down 1-0 to Valencia, which allowed Bilbao's Athletic Club to become champions. It was hardly ideal preparation for the final.

Ferguson also invited Jock Stein to travel with the party. Stein's experience in European football had no equal. He guided Celtic to become the first British club to win the European Cup in 1967 and reach the final three years later. Ferguson had the utmost respect for Stein, who at that time was one of the most revered managers in world football. Stein advised Ferguson to give Alfredo Di Stéfano a bottle of the finest Scottish malt whisky when they met. The thinking behind that was that Ferguson would be seen to be in awe of the Real Madrid legend, who was by now managing the club. Of course, the boss was full of admiration for Di Stéfano, ever since a young and aspiring Ferguson was in the crowd at Hampden to see the iconic forward stamp his class all over the European Cup Final in 1960. Whether the gift had the desired effect or not, Ferguson recalled that Di Stéfano seemed very happy about it.

As the Aberdeen players went through their final training session on the morning of the game at their base, the city was awash with red and white favours. The weather forecast proved accurate as heavy, persistent rain would hit the Gothenburg area throughout the afternoon and into the evening. The general belief was that the conditions would suit Aberdeen, but with the likes of McMaster, Strachan, Black and Weir in the side, the rainfall was of no real advantage.

Alex Ferguson, at his final press briefing before the final, was confident, 'Yes, we have a marvellous chance to do it and I know each player will give his last ounce of energy to win the cup. We intend to play our normal game. That is to attack. It would be foolish if we were to suddenly try a pattern that is foreign to our nature. We are not in Gothenburg to finish as losers.'

How they reached the final

	P	*W*	*D*	*L*	*F*	*A*
Aberdeen	10	7	2	1	23	5
Real Madrid	8	5	3	0	17	8

Aberdeen scorers: McGhee 6; Hewitt 4; Simpson 3; Black 2; Weir 2; Bell 1; Kennedy 1; McLeish 1; Miller 1; Strachan 1; own goal 1

Real Madrid scorers: Santillana 8; Juanito 3; Gallego 1; García Hernández 1; Isidro 1; Metgod 1; Salgureo 1; Isidoro San José 1

PRELIMINARY ROUND
Aberdeen 7 (Black, Strachan, Hewitt, Simpson, McGhee, Kennedy, Ballet OG) Sion 0
Att: 12,000
Sion 1 Aberdeen 4 (Hewitt, Miller, McGhee 2)
Att: 2,400
Aberdeen won 11-1 on aggregate

FIRST ROUND
Aberdeen 1 (Hewitt) Dinamo Tirana 0
Att: 14,600
Dinamo Tirana 0 Aberdeen 0
Att: 18,000
Aberdeen won 1-0 on aggregate

Baia Mare 0 Real Madrid 0
Att: 20,500
Real Madrid 5 (Juanito, Isidro, García Hernández, Santillana, Metgod) Baia Mare 2
Att: 27,500
Real Madrid won 5-2 on aggregate

SECOND ROUND
Aberdeen 2 (McGhee, Weir) Lech Poznań 0
Att: 17,600

Lech Poznań 0 Aberdeen 1 (Bell)
Att: 33,000
Aberdeen won 3-0 on aggregate

Real Madrid 3 (Santillana, San José, Juanito) Újpesti Dózsa 1
Att: 35,000
Újpesti Dózsa 0 Real Madrid 1 (Santillana)
Att: 100,000
Real Madrid won 4-1 on aggregate

QUARTER-FINALS
Bayern Munich 0 Aberdeen 0
Att: 25,000
Aberdeen 3 (Simpson, McLeish, Hewitt) Bayern Munich 2
Att: 24,000
Aberdeen won 3-2 on aggregate

Inter Milan 1 Real Madrid 1 (Gallego)
Att: 75,248
Real Madrid 2 (Salguero, Santillana) Inter Milan 1
Att: 85,000
Real Madrid won 3-2 on aggregate

SEMI-FINALS
Aberdeen 5 (Black, Simpson, McGhee 2, Weir) Waterschei 1
Att: 24,000
Waterschei 1 Aberdeen 0
Att: 13,600
Aberdeen won 5-2 on aggregate

Austria Vienna 2 Real Madrid 2 (Santillana 2)
Att: 60,000
Real Madrid 3 (Santillana 2, Juanito) Austria Vienna 1
Att: 80,000
Real Madrid win 5-3 on aggregate

From the world of entertainment, politics and sport, messages of support and goodwill flooded in for the Dons ahead of the final.

'This must be one of the greatest moments in club history. From all the ex-Dons; good luck lads and have a REAL go!'

Former Don Joe Harper

'My thoughts will be with the Aberdeen lads and I am hoping Gordon Strachan will score a hat-trick. All the best.'

Rod Stewart as he was rehearsing in Los Angeles

'They have brought honour not only to themselves but also to the city of Aberdeen we all love. We as citizens can take great pride in the players and officials of Aberdeen Football Club.'

Alex Collie, the Lord Provost of Aberdeen

'Real Madrid have a lot of things in their favour, but the Aberdeen players are fitter than Real and that could be a deciding factor. Whatever my head may say my heart still says it is Aberdeen for this cup.'

Scotland manager Jock Stein, who was with the official Aberdeen party

'I will be in a television studio in London doing my best to give an impartial commentary on the big game, but it's going to be difficult when I am rooting for my hometown team. In my schooldays in Aberdeen I was no different to any other kid; to play against Real Madrid was one of my ambitions. I finally made it twice, but now I am just as proud that Aberdeen have made it too. Good luck boys and go win it.'

Aberdeen-born Denis Law, the former Manchester United legend

'I hope Aberdeen win it; I really do. I always thought they were capable of going all the way.'

England manager Bobby Robson

'All the best for the final and thanks to everyone in Aberdeen for a fabulous five shows we did there. Rock on Dons.'

Entertainers Tommy Cannon and Bobby Ball

'I wish the Dons every success in the final. I have followed their fortunes ever since I was a loon [local dialect for boy] in Aberdeen and more particularly when I was at Aberdeen University. Get in their lads and win the cup!'

Newsreader Sandy Gall

'I feel sure just as we were on the brink of European success in 1967, the same situation is going to happen for Aberdeen. My best wishes to them and I am confident they will get the result they deserve.'

Celtic manager Billy McNeill

'Good luck from everyone at Old Trafford, even the Sassenachs, although I am not too sure about Laurie Cunningham [who was on loan from Manchester United to Real].'

Manchester United defender Martin Buchan, the former Dons captain

'I wish them all the best. It must be fantastic to be in Aberdeen just now. The atmosphere will be tremendous. I remember what it was like when I was there when we won the league. All the best lads.'

Former Don Steve Archibald, who was with Tottenham Hotspur at the time and joined Barcelona in 1984

'Congratulations to the Dons on reaching the European Cup Winners' Cup Final. You have my admiration for what you already have achieved. I hope you capture the cup.'

Prime minister Margaret Thatcher

Torrential rain continued to fall and at one stage the game was in doubt with pools of water forming on the playing surface. Aberdeen lined up with their special kit and tracksuits for the occasion. With around 15,000 members of the Red Army in the Ullevi they outnumbered the Madrid support which only totalled around 1,300. It is difficult to know the reasons why Real were not backed in big numbers. Certainly, in the '80s they did not command a large travelling support for European ties. Also, Gothenburg was not that accessible from Spain, but the main reason put forward was that Real Madrid that season were staring down the barrel at a succession of failures. Aberdeen were in no mood to change that trend.

The Dons began on the front foot as Ferguson expected that Real would sit deep in the early stages. They signalled their intent after only three minutes when an acrobatic volley from Eric Black came back off the bar. The young striker was not to be denied, however, and he opened the scoring in six minutes from a classic Aberdeen set piece. Alex McLeish would take his time moving forward as Gordon Strachan would look for McLeish coming in late from the edge of the box for a free header. The ball broke to Black, who pounced to slip it past Agustín.

Parity was restored in 14 minutes in what was a personal disaster for McLeish. The conditions played their part as a pass back to Jim Leighton fell short and Santillana went down as he got to the ball first, and Juanito scored from the penalty spot. In the modern era Leighton would have been red-carded for sure, but back in the '80s the penalty award was deemed appropriate. There was not much between the sides in the first half. Ferguson had a few concerns so a tactical switch at the break was to prove crucial, 'I felt that [Uli] Stielike was being given too much space and despite our dismissal of him in our team talk he was turning out to be a real eye-opener. He was the one Madrid player who we could not get the better of, he was the one that kept them going. To combat that we asked our two strikers to work towards the game more quickly to force Stielike forward towards Neale Cooper, who was playing in front of the back four. I also told Peter Weir to play further forward and take their full-back with him.'

The changes worked well for Aberdeen. In the second half they 'battered' Madrid, but some good goalkeeping and bad luck saw the game go into an extra-time period. Ferguson was convinced at that stage that the Spanish side would settle for penalties. Another change had to be made and it was an important one as John Hewitt would come on and score the winning goal in 111 minutes. Peter

Weir began the move on the left and set Mark McGhee away towards the Madrid area. His cross was met by Hewitt, who headed into the net after Agustín failed to get a hand to the delivery.

The closing minutes were tense as Aberdeen were on the verge of club history. Real Madrid had one last opportunity when Willie Miller committed a foul on the edge of the box. The free kick had to be retaken as the Aberdeen defensive wall had been encroaching. José Antonio Salguero fired in a fierce shot that missed the target by inches. Did Jim Leighton have it covered? Many tales since have suggested he did. In the rain-soaked Ullevi that night the collective sighs of relief from the Red Army were palpable. The scenes of unbridled joy when referee Gianfranco Menegali blew the final whistle have remained part of Pittodrie folklore. Ferguson slipped on the trackside as he rushed out of the dugout and the Aberdeen bench joined their rain-soaked team-mates on the pitch.

Captain Miller was calm enough to accept the trophy which was presented on the pitch and his now familiar one-handed grasp of the European Cup Winners' Cup has been immortalised in club history.

Alfredo Di Stéfano seemed to distance himself from the defeat, 'I was looking forward to the game being decided by penalties, but my players wanted to go all out for the victory. I think I was right as Aberdeen finished the stronger team.' The Madrid manager also agreed that the Dons deserved their victory, 'Aberdeen surprised many with their skill and strength. They are now one of Europe's top teams.'

The *Press & Journal* summed up the game, 'Aberdeen produced their own version of scaling Everest last night, setting the seal on a glorious record-setting season by winning the European Cup Winners' Cup in the rain-lashed Ullevi stadium in Gothenburg. This was really the greatest triumph yet for the outstanding teamwork of this Aberdeen side.'

1983 European Cup Winners' Cup Final statistics

Shots on target: Aberdeen 7; Real Madrid 3

Headers on target: Aberdeen 4; Real Madrid 0

Shots off target: Aberdeen 3; Real Madrid 6
Headers off target: Aberdeen 4; Real Madrid 3
Free kicks: Aberdeen 22; Real Madrid 20
Corners: Aberdeen 4; Real Madrid 5

The players took their lap of honour as the supporters celebrated like never before. Eventually in the relative calm of the dressing room the players were singing as the rest of the Aberdeen party were housed in their own room close by. It was only when Alex Ferguson emerged from the dressing room that he realised the enormity of what his side had achieved: 'It was like a whirlwind. Our wives and families were at the reception upstairs, while we waited for Willie Miller and Gordon Strachan to return from the mandatory dope tests. The press was shouting for quotes, the cameras were clicking, and the television lights were flashing, there seemed to be bodies everywhere. The occasion engulfed us.'

Back in Aberdeen the city centre was swamped by joyous fans who gathered in Union Street. Cars blew their horns and the ships in the harbour were also heard. The good-natured atmosphere lasted well into the early hours as the reality of what the team had achieved was beginning to sink in.

Willie Miller recalled the reception the team received on their return to Aberdeen, 'We had been wonderfully supported in Sweden, and we were prepared for a stupendous welcome home, but I just did not expect the massive numbers who spilled on to the streets. The plane touched down just before 3pm, and the minute we emerged we were swamped. Photographers and TV crews met us as soon as we left the plane. The open-top bus snaked its way through the city towards Pittodrie. I had been on the go for 24 hours with little sleep, and by the time we reached the stadium, I was shattered and running on adrenaline. We had put so much effort into beating Real Madrid, had celebrated in the appropriate fashion afterwards, and we were mentally and physically drained.'

As the city celebrations continued the 'Red Armada' that was on the *St Clair* had managed to drink the ferry dry. A helicopter was brought in to replenish supplies and drop off special editions of the *Evening Express* that had covered the team's return. The journey home, however, was tinged with sadness with the death of a young Aberdeen fan, Philip Goodbrand, who tragically collapsed at the game. Five days on from leaving Aberdeen Harbour the *St Clair* arrived back late Friday morning. Alex Ferguson kept his promise by turning up with Mark McGhee and the trophy to welcome the supporters home.

For many fans the season could have finished right there and then. However, the final two games still held huge importance. Pittodrie was once again full as Hibernian were reduced to bit-part players in what was another day of celebration. Winning the Premier League was still possible, but it was a long shot as Aberdeen had to win and hope Dundee United and Celtic both lost. The Dons were applauded on to the pitch by a Hibernian side that had effectively ended their title hopes earlier in the month. Aberdeen turned in a champagne performance in what was a carnival atmosphere and the 5-0 win saw them finish third in the table and set them up for their final game of the season and the Scottish Cup Final against Rangers.

The build-up to the Hampden showpiece was no different by ways of preparation. The last competitive game of an exhausting season was the Dons' 60th. For the likes of Willie Miller, Jim Leighton, Gordon Strachan and Alex McLeish who were all involved in the World Cup in Spain the previous summer, the Scottish Cup Final would provide a welcome conclusion to a remarkable campaign. Aberdeen went into the final as overwhelming favourites to retain the Scottish Cup. Rangers had been blitzed in the 1982 final and had barely improved since. The Dons would also be backed by an estimated 30,000-strong support, at least on a par with what Rangers could muster.

The hot conditions on a hard surface did not help the Dons, who looked weary for long spells in the game. Rangers were desperate to take something from what was another barren season and with Jim Bett in their midfield they posed a real threat. As so often happens when great teams are not 'at it' they find a way to win. Despite Rangers' exuberance, they rarely threatened to win the game and the destination of the Scottish Cup was decided four minutes before the end of extra time. With a replay looking the most likely outcome, Rangers were careless in their own half and gave the ball away to Mark McGhee. His cross spun up in the air after striking a defender and fell perfectly for Eric Black to head home the winner. If there was ever one Aberdeen player who could be relied on when it came to heading, it was Black. The striker had perfected the knack of 'hanging' in the air when it came to heading, and in Scottish football he had no equal when it came to scoring important goals in the big matches.

The scenes of joy among the Aberdeen support were now becoming a familiar sight at the national stadium and beyond. On this occasion it was as much relief as ecstasy. The thought of returning to Hampden four days later was far from appealing so when Black netted it completed a remarkable double for Aberdeen. The Dons had become the first team to retain the Scottish Cup outside of Glasgow, and they also secured two trophies for the first time in the club's history.

There is a general belief that any manager is at his most vulnerable in that 30-minute period after any game. Speaking to the press and media after a cup final was essential. On this occasion Ferguson showed a rare error of judgement by criticising his team for their performance. On live television the boss declared, 'Miller and McLeish won the cup for us.' It was an outburst that not only shocked the watching viewers and gathered journalists, but the Aberdeen players who were then castigated in the dressing room. There was no doubt that Ferguson was seeking perfection. His desire to see his European winners 'show everyone what we are all about' was, on reflection, wishful thinking. The efforts from a gruelling season had taken a toll on a squad that had clearly peaked in Sweden.

The Aberdeen party broke with tradition and stayed at the Old Course Hotel in St Andrews after the game. The hotel staff had bedecked the building in red and white. The door handles had red and white streamers while the staff were also dressed in Aberdeen colours. That could not detract from what proved to be a sombre occasion among the squad, still reeling from their manager's comments. The next morning Ferguson gathered the team at breakfast and apologised for what he had said after the final. On reflection it was a clear error on his part which he recognised belatedly. The west coast press were always a headline away from putting pressure on any successful side outside of Glasgow. The Aberdeen team of that period was as good as any Scottish football has produced and the Dons' superiority had a profound effect on the establishment in Glasgow. Any opportunity to question Ferguson or his team was invariably seized upon. The Sunday papers after the final led with Ferguson's outburst, which was another reminder for the manager that he could not let his guard down and needed to stick with his siege mentality approach.

As the players travelled through the streets of Aberdeen, the citizens turned out in their thousands and Alex Collie, the Lord Provost, was on hand from the balcony of the Town House to welcome the victorious team as the Dons' most successful season came to another triumphant conclusion. The group completed their parade at a packed Pittodrie, taking their bow in front of their support, ten months on from where it all started against Sion in the preliminary round of the European Cup Winners' Cup.

7

Dons Double

THE SUMMER of 1983 may have been a time for basking in success for the Aberdeen support, but for Alex Ferguson his prime focus was on keeping his record-breaking side together. That was going to prove difficult as Gordon Strachan had intimated to his manager that he was looking to move on when his contract was to end in June 1984. That allowed Ferguson to once more go back to St Mirren for a replacement for Strachan; the boss was keen to get the transfer of Billy Stark completed before his month-long holiday in Florida. The Dons had already sold Andy Watson to Leeds United in a £60,000 deal. Stark was keen to come to Aberdeen and a fee of £75,000 was agreed.

With Walker McCall and Derek Hamilton already moved on, the club were still waiting on the fitness of Stuart Kennedy, who underwent a split cartilage operation during the close-season.

Aberdeen had arranged a pre-season tour of West Germany, a busy schedule with eight games in 13 days. Ahead of the team returning for training, Ferguson set out his targets for the new season, 'The Premier League and retaining the European Cup Winners' Cup are our prime targets. League success is important and winning the league would continue our development and stature within the game.' With Aberdeen now seeded in Europe they expected a favourable draw when they opened their defence of the Cup Winners' Cup. Icelandic side ÍA of Akranes were not expected to present any problems for the holders.

On the back of their European success the club's elevated status was reflected in a high-profile pre-season campaign. The trip to Germany was more intensive than anticipated, with some of the lower-league opponents looking at Aberdeen as a real scalp. Some of the squad were given additional time off having been away with the Scotland full and youth groups in Mexico. The training camp conditions were ideal but with Europe in the midst of a heatwave, it made things difficult.

Aberdeen then played three friendlies against top English opponents in the week before the start of the Premier League. Arsenal visited Pittodrie to play in the Boys' Brigade Centenary fixture. One familiar face in the Gunners' line-up was former Celtic star Charlie Nicholas. The Dons then travelled south to complete their preparations by playing in two testimonial matches. The first against Ipswich at Portman Road ended in a disappointing 3-0 defeat to mark George Burley's service to the Suffolk club. Two days later Aberdeen visited Manchester United to pay tribute to one of their own, former captain Martin Buchan. The Scotland international had the distinction of being a winning captain in the Scottish Cup for Aberdeen, in 1970, and then the FA Cup for Manchester United in 1977. The Old Trafford side were also FA Cup winners in 1983 and at half-time Buchan joined Steve Cowan, John Hewitt and Neale Cooper to parade the Cup Winners' Cup, Scottish Cup and FA Cup. Aberdeen fought back from two

Manchester United Football Club
OLD TRAFFORD
MANCHESTER M16 0RA

TICKET AND MATCH INFORMATION
Telephone 061-872 7771
(24 HOUR SERVICE)

MARTIN BUCHAN TESTIMONIAL
V. ABERDEEN F C KICK OFF 7-30
STAIR 10 H MID BLOCK 19
ROW SEAT
8 180 £3.50 170810721

SHARP ELECTRONICS (UK) LTD

goals down to draw 2-2 as Gordon Strachan and Peter Weir were outstanding. Buchan paid tribute to his old club, 'I was delighted Aberdeen came down to play in my testimonial. The club means so much to me and they made it a great night for me. I think the United support also got a look at how good this Aberdeen side is.'

By winning the Cup Winners' Cup, Aberdeen had qualified to play the European Cup winners to contest the European Super Cup. With domestic and international fixtures taking up most available slots, the Dons were in talks with Hamburg and UEFA to agree suitable dates. The format was decided to be over two legs, but Hamburg were keen for a one-off final, in Tokyo. Alex Ferguson could not discount that outcome, 'I can only stress that ideally we would prefer to face Hamburg in front of our own fans. We will exhaust every avenue to resolve this. If not, then we will have to look at Tokyo.' Hamburg were keen to play in Japan as they were already confirmed to face South American champions Grêmio there to contest the World Club Championship.

Aberdeen opened their domestic campaign with an impressive 3-0 win over Dundee at Pittodrie, easing Ferguson's early season worries: 'Some of our pre-season work was a concern. Injuries did not help, and I was worried that we would struggle to get off to a positive start.' Those fears were swept aside as the Dons began in style, following up their opening-day victory by engaging in some shooting practice in the League Cup against Raith Rovers as Eric Black scored four in a 9-0 win. The format of the League Cup had been changed once more, much to the frustration of Ferguson: 'Although it is not a competition I have won yet, the League Cup has suffered through the years with so many changes. Beginning in August with the final not until the following March, supporters seem to switch off. It's unfortunate.'

In their opening five games the Dons scored 24 goals, conceding none before dropping their first point away to Motherwell on 10 September ahead of travelling to Iceland to open their defence of the European Cup Winners' Cup.

Expectations in the European arena were far removed from when Alex Ferguson took charge of the Dons for the first time in Europe in 1978 against Marek Stanke Dimitrov. Five years on and Aberdeen were now seen as one of the top sides in European football. It was a position that a fiercely ambitious Ferguson had craved. Reaching such heights in a relatively short space of time was more than even he had expected. Such notoriety, however, came with new challenges. As holders Aberdeen were coming to terms with being among the favourites. The 1983/84 Cup Winners' Cup was again full of some top European clubs. The Dons were joined by Barcelona, Manchester United, Paris Saint-Germain, Juventus and Cologne as possible winners. No team had ever retained the Cup Winners' Cup, so Aberdeen were looking to not only make club history but to create a first in European competition.

ÍA were part-time but still one of the top sides in Iceland. It is not very often that a club gets criticised after winning away in Europe, but the Dons' 2-1 victory there was anything but comfortable. ÍA took a shock lead through Sigurður Halldórsson to the delight of the home crowd. Although Mark McGhee equalised within a minute and scored the winning goal, the Dons had Jim Leighton to thank for saving a penalty.

The return leg was another reminder to Aberdeen that they would have to at least maintain their high standards if they were going to reach the latter rounds. ÍA scrapped and battled gamely and they earned the respect of the Pittodrie crowd by scoring a last-minute penalty to earn a 1-1 draw. By their own standards the Dons had found it difficult to raise their game as they were protecting a first-leg advantage. It was something Ferguson was acutely aware of, 'All credit to Akranes who put so much into stopping us playing our usual brand of free-flowing football. There are no easy ties in

Europe these days and we need to ensure that we maintain our intensity in situations like that.'

Aberdeen kept up their Premier League title challenge with a convincing 2-0 win at Rangers. In what was another unsavoury, hostile clash, the Ibrox faithful turned on manager John Greig following defeat for their team. They seemed to have difficulty in accepting that in Aberdeen they had come up against a far superior opponent who not only expected to win at Ibrox, but to do so in some style. The toxic atmosphere even spilled into the corporate areas. It emerged that Ferguson prevented captain Willie Miller from accepting his man of the match award from sponsors Tennent Caledonian after the game finished. It followed comments made by the company representative in the directors' box at the game, calling Aberdeen 'hooligans'. The company's later unreserved apology was accepted by Ferguson: 'We have always cooperated with sponsors and will continue to do so. Having taken a stand on this and received their apology the matter is now closed.'

The draw for the next round paired Aberdeen with KSK Beveren. Belgian football was enjoying a fruitful period at club and international level, with four teams progressing in Europe. Beveren, along with Standard Liege, Anderlecht and Antwerp provided the backbone for the national side. The Belgians were due to play Scotland at Hampden in October and Ferguson was keen to see some of the Beveren players in their national side.

On the domestic front progress was made in the elongated League Cup but following a first away defeat to Hibernian on 15 October, Ferguson was left with a lot to ponder, 'I certainly was perturbed by the disappointment at Easter Road and the manner of certain players in the side that afternoon. Aberdeen have been through testing experiences and demanding circumstances to rise above the silly business of throwing away a certain two points which we had on a plate at half-time. What happened after the break was a sore subject of discussion between me and certain players.' Ferguson's reaction after a defeat was not that unusual; however, it was the ferocity of his anger which he described as the 'Hibernian scandal' that really stood out.

While that may have been disrespectful to the Edinburgh side, it was also an indication of Ferguson's thinking. He was so incensed that he was considering breaking up the team, something he had given some thought to since the start of the season. He had looked at clubs like Liverpool, Manchester United and Real Madrid and when they would overhaul their squads. Whether he had made his thoughts known to his players, his outburst had the desired effect as Aberdeen embarked on a period that would define another incredible season.

They travelled to Belgium without Gordon Strachan and Eric Black and there was no doubt Aberdeen were feeling the pressure. Beveren were in good form and were leading the Belgian league, confident they could eliminate the Dons. Belgium international manager Guy Thys warned Aberdeen they would be in for a tough time of it, 'Beveren will be a great danger to Aberdeen in the Cup Winners' Cup. They are a very strong side who play as one unit and are almost impossible to beat at home.' Beveren were also looking at their volatile home support to help them unsettle Aberdeen. Their 21,000-capacity Freetheil stadium, nicknamed 'Little Hell', was compact with the crowd close to the pitch. One local newspaper was confident, 'Aberdeen will receive a hostile reception. Beveren are a better side than Waterschei [who the Dons had beaten in the previous season's Cup Winners' Cup] and are top of the league on merit. Beveren also defeated Inter Milan in their previous European adventure and it took two penalties from Barcelona to eliminate them.' Beveren midfielder Paul Theunis declared, 'Our style is suited to beat Aberdeen. When the draw was made last month, people favoured Aberdeen to go through. But I don't think that is the way it is now. We have gone ten league games without defeat. Our defence is the best in Belgium, and I believe Aberdeen's style is tailor-made for us to beat them.'

Aberdeen were getting used to their favourites tag in the European arena and called on their more experienced players to negotiate the Belgian challenge and hold a lively Beveren side to a 0-0 draw that set up the Dons to finish the tie at Pittodrie. It was the first occasion that season that Beveren failed to score.

Before the return leg the Dons had defeated Celtic and Dundee to regain top spot. Gordon Strachan was back from injury and was outstanding against the Parkhead club. His return was significant in what was a crucial period in the season.

Premier League table at 29 October 1983

	P	*W*	*D*	*L*	*F*	*A*	*Pts*
Aberdeen	**10**	**7**	**1**	**2**	**26**	**7**	**15**
Dundee United	9	7	1	1	22	8	15
Celtic	10	6	2	2	27	13	14
Hearts	10	6	2	2	13	8	14

As Aberdeen regained top spot in the league, all was not well with rivals Rangers: John Greig was sacked after a series of poor results and vitriol from the stands. With the Ibrox club looking for a new manager they were convinced that Alex Ferguson would join them. The usual press reports soon emerged with Ferguson being touted for Ibrox; the west coast tabloids were on a feeding frenzy. Aberdeen chairman Dick Donald understood his manager would be targeted by other clubs. To head off any Rangers interest Aberdeen made Ferguson the highest-paid manager in their history as a new five-year deal was agreed. For Donald, it was a masterstroke. 'Alex Ferguson is very much the Aberdeen manager and will continue to be so. We have agreed a new five-year contract.'

For Rangers it was near humiliation. Their support could not believe one of their former players would turn down the opportunity to manage the club. At Pittodrie the news was kept under wraps and announced on the day of the return leg against Beveren. The atmosphere that evening provided another of those famed European nights in Europe for the Dons. It was all too much for Beveren, top of their league but swept aside as Aberdeen cruised to a 4-1 win. Ferguson was delighted, 'I enjoyed the occasion as much as anyone on what was a night to remember, and personally what had been a very big day for me and my family. Archie Knox and I both agreed that the team was back to their best in what was an important game for us.' The win over Beveren was impressive; the visitors were in the form of their lives, with three full internationals in their side, and heading for the Belgian title. Aberdeen made them look second-rate.

The dates for the European Super Cup against Hamburg were finally agreed with Aberdeen travelling to the Volksparkstadion on 22 November and the return at Pittodrie on 20 December. Meanwhile, Aberdeen were now at the top of the Premier League and faced Rangers and Hearts at Pittodrie before their first Super Cup clash. On 12 November Rangers travelled north looking for revenge and were buoyed by the return of ex-manager Jock Wallace. The former Berwick keeper had been at Ibrox in what was a successful period in the '70s. The supporters had treated him like a returning Messiah but the reality was very different.

The appointment of Wallace had a desperate look to it. He was Rangers' third choice, after Ferguson and then Jim McLean at Dundee United showed no interest in the job. Wallace had a reputation as a tough, uncompromising manager, but the game in Scotland was changing. The new guard of younger, more tactically aware managers and coaches like Ferguson, McLean, Archie Knox and Walter Smith, all coming through the highly respected coaching courses at Inverclyde under Andy Roxburgh, were the future. Wallace was still stuck in the past, hopeful of reviving Rangers' fortunes. The Ibrox club turned up at Pittodrie looking more like a side from the past. Wallace insisted that his team changed their socks back to their traditional black and red colours. Rangers' ticket allocation was sold out and around 500 fans were locked outside, while for Aberdeen it was business as usual.

Within nine minutes the Wallace revival was in tatters as the Dons went two goals up. The atmosphere was beyond hostile as the police made several arrests in the away section. Aberdeen cruised to a 3-0 win and in the second half they treated Rangers with disdain by keeping possession, almost at will. This was Aberdeen at their imperious best; totally dominating Rangers from the outset and humiliating them in the latter stages. A routine 2-0 win over Hearts a week later set Aberdeen up for their trip to face Hamburg, a side they had unfinished business with following their UEFA Cup exit in 1981. There was also the opportunity to become the first Scottish side to win the Super Cup. It was a title that Ferguson craved as Aberdeen's stature in Europe was in the ascendant.

With the draw for the quarter-finals of the European Cup Winners' Cup taking place on 9 December, all attention turned to Hamburg. Ferguson looked ahead to the first leg, 'It is important we treat these games like any other European tie.' The Aberdeen approach was like what had brought them goalless draws at Bayern Munich and Beveren in recent months. Their groundbreaking 'early defence' tactic would need to be deployed well if they were to stop the European Cup winners on their own soil. Any talk of Aberdeen looking at winning in Germany when Ferguson took over in 1978 would have been unheard of, but such was the progress made and the club's reputation that Aberdeen had more than a realistic chance of succeeding. They were challenging the European elite and winning the Super Cup would be another step on their way to more recognition in the continent.

Aberdeen had a late scare with Willie Miller injured in training, but he was in his usual place in the starting line-up.

The Dons began well against the European champions and created the better chances before Hamburg began to put pressure on. The Germans handled the Aberdeen midfield better than Ferguson expected so some tactical changes for the second half should have brought a greater reward than the final 0-0 scoreline. It could have been far better for the Dons had John Hewitt reproduced his Gothenburg heroics by taking his chance in the last minute but Ferguson was happy with the draw, 'We can certainly play better but we are still a young team and it showed tonight. It sets us up for a good game in Aberdeen.'

Stone-faced Hamburg coach Ernst Happel was disappointed with his team's failure to score against the European Cup Winners' Cup holders, 'We hope we will get a better result when we go to Scotland next month. There was a big difference from the Aberdeen side we played two years ago. Most of the names were the same but this was a team with an aggressive approach.'

The attendance in Hamburg was a real disappointment for the home side as their support deserted their team. Indifferent form and the game being televised live in Germany were reasons put forward by Hamburg officials. By contrast the Pittodrie clash before Christmas was a guaranteed sell out with 24,000 tickets being snapped up in hours when they went on sale. The return tie was also televised live in Scotland and it was reported that no fewer than 80 countries worldwide were beaming the game on live television.

The draws for the quarter-finals of the European competitions were made in Zürich on 9 December. Aberdeen were handed a favourable Cup Winners' Cup tie when they were paired with Hungarian side Újpesti Dózsa. Hungarian football had a proud history as their wonderful international side of the '50s was hailed as the one of the best in history. However, the current Hungarian teams were far removed from their golden era. Aberdeen were immediately installed as tournament favourites alongside Italian giants Juventus following the draw. With the quarter-finals not being played until March 1984, there was plenty of time for the management to have Újpesti watched. Archie Knox was happy with the draw, 'I saw a tape of their last round against Cologne which they won 3-1 and they impressed me. They have plenty of pace in attack.'

The other Cup Winners' Cup quarter-finals would see Barcelona taking on Manchester United, Porto up against Shakhtar Donetsk, and Juventus meeting the Finns of Valkeakosken Haka.

As the winter period approached the Dons kept up their unbeaten run, stretching to 16 games before Hamburg travelled to Pittodrie. The German side were still smarting from the news that Aberdeen were voted European Team of the Year ahead of the Bundesliga and European Cup winners. Alex Ferguson, Chris Anderson and director Ian Donald attended the gala night in Paris as Aberdeen were presented with another award to display in what was becoming a highly decorated Pittodrie boardroom. Aberdeen came top in the voting with 21 points, ahead of Hamburg, Anderlecht, Juventus and Real Madrid.

Scotland manager Jock Stein attended many Aberdeen games that season. As the Dons continued to progress on all fronts, there was additional recognition at international level. Scotland were to face Northern Ireland in Belfast and after former Don Steve Archibald withdrew with injury, Stein called up Mark McGhee. With the first-time inclusion of Doug Rougvie, the Aberdeen contingent in the squad was a magnificent seven. McGhee and Rougvie were joined by Jim Leighton, Willie Miller, Alex McLeish, Gordon Strachan and Peter Weir. When McGhee came on for the Scots in the second half, there were six Aberdeen players on the field. Had it not been for a rare injury to Miller there would have been all seven in the national side. For one of the other Aberdeen internationals, though, it was not such good news. Stuart Kennedy's long-term injury was causing concern. Following his knee surgery in the summer there were further complications and after further exploratory work, he was advised to rest for at least two months. That prompted the club to go into the transfer market and they secured Stewart McKimmie from Dundee in an £87,500 deal. The Aberdeen-born right-back had been watched for several weeks and was an ideal long-term replacement for Kennedy.

As McKimmie arrived there was a shock when it was announced that Archie Knox was leaving the club. Don Mackay, the Dundee manager, was sacked after a series of poor results. Ironically his last piece of business was to oversee the transfer of McKimmie to Pittodrie. The Dens Park club offered Knox the manager's position which he accepted.

The Dons were also saddened to learn of the passing of former scout Bobby Calder. Regarded as the finest scout in Scottish football, Calder operated in the west of Scotland and was the man behind taking so many great Aberdeen players to Pittodrie. Calder was the referee in the Dons' first Scottish Cup win in 1947 and after retiring from the game he joined the club in 1949. He had a persuasive nature that was legendary in the game as he became known for taking some of the best young players in Glasgow to Pittodrie. Among the players Calder scouted for Aberdeen were Charlie Cooke, Jimmy Smith, Tommy Craig, Arthur Graham, Jim Leighton, Alex McLeish and Willie Miller.

As Aberdeen prepared for the Super Cup second leg, the Hamburg preparations were not helped when they were beaten by Brazilian side Grêmio in their World Club Championship clash in Tokyo. General manager Günter Netzer was still upset at his side missing out on the European Team of the Year accolade: 'We won the European Cup and the Bundesliga. We deserved to be the best. The game in Scotland will give us the opportunity to prove that.' Alex Ferguson was looking forward to the game, 'It is another proud moment in the club's history to welcome Hamburg to Pittodrie to complete Aberdeen's first involvement in the Super Cup. It is all set to produce another of those terrific occasions when the team don their European cloak in the search for another result that will strengthen Aberdeen's reputation in world soccer.'

The back page of the local *Evening Express* the following day said it all – 'CROWNING GLORY!' – after Aberdeen comfortably defeated Hamburg with two second-half goals. The game was beamed live to more than 80 countries worldwide; Aberdeen's profile had never been so high. After an even first half, the Dons dominated the second period. Goals from Neil Simpson and Mark McGhee secured a famous victory as a second European title in 1983 came to Pittodrie. Ferguson was a proud manager, 'I had told the players before the game that we had the worldwide football stage to ourselves and that was the perfect incentive. Things went well enough in the first half; Hamburg had a lot of the ball but created little. In the second half I wanted the ball played quicker into the last third and get our full-backs to push up.' The *Evening Express* declared, 'Hamburg were pounded into submission and were staggering around Pittodrie punch drunk long before the Austrian referee kindly put them out of their misery with the final whistle.'

As the Aberdeen players took their bow after being presented with what was a plaque to mark the occasion, Pittodrie was in buoyant mood. To round off a fantastic year that had the boardroom enriched with the European Cup Winners' Cup, the Scottish Cup and now the Super Cup, the atmosphere that evening was as much of pride as joy. By contrast Hamburg were crestfallen. Having already been knocked out of the European Cup, they had lost the World Club Championship and now the European Super Cup. As the Aberdeen players and management were happy to speak to the gathered media from across the world, the visitors left without comment. Netzer told the German press their bus was waiting while the Hamburg players departed in silence. It was reported, however, that one of the senior Hamburg players was overheard saying that he wished he could play in an atmosphere like that every week.

The German press were not too kind on Hamburg. The national team had been struggling and with their European Cup winners being outclassed by Aberdeen, there was no shortage of criticism. The general mood of despair following their defeat in Tokyo continued after their defeat in Scotland. Despite being held in Germany, there was a perceived expectation, almost arrogance, in the German media that Hamburg would prevail in Scotland.

Aberdeen came through November and December in sensational form, winning 12 of their 14 games, with the other two drawn, away to Hamburg and Celtic. The Dons completed their most memorable year by defeating Dundee 5-2 on Hogmanay. For Aberdeen these were the best of times. Incredibly the final fixture of 1983 was match number 45 from that season, including friendlies. The exhaustive schedule continued when St Johnstone visited Pittodrie on 3 January 1984. In what was a sign of things to come, the game was abandoned after a blizzard hit the area and knocked out the power. Scottish football never did get around to winter breaks until a few years ago, but back in the '80s any breaks were enforced by the weather. With no competitive action for four weeks, the club went away to the Costa del Sol for a week-long break. On reflection it was an ideal opportunity to enjoy the break and look ahead to what was certainly going to be a defining period in the season.

Aberdeen resumed with a crucial game against Celtic at Pittodrie on 4 February. In his programme notes, Alex Ferguson believed any Aberdeen v Celtic clash had taken over top billing in Scotland, with the traditional Celtic v Rangers meetings falling behind by way of stature and importance. Such claims in the modern era would be unthinkable, such is the ever-widening gap between the two Glasgow clubs and the rest. John Hewitt scored the only goal, a result that stretched the Dons' lead at the top of the Premier League to eight points. Progress was made in the Scottish Cup, but Kilmarnock did shock Aberdeen by holding the Dons to a draw at Pittodrie in the third round. Two days later Aberdeen won 3-1 at Rugby Park in the replay before easing past Clyde in the next round several days later.

With Archie Knox now at Dundee, Alex Ferguson announced that former Don Willie Garner would be his new assistant. Garner had been with the club since 1975 and joined Celtic for a brief spell before he went into management with Alloa Athletic. Ferguson declared he had taken his time with the appointment, 'I had always known I was going back for Willie. What I had to judge was that I was making the right decision, and that was why there was a delay in the announcement. In your career there are players you know would make good managers and Willie comes into that category.'

After 27 games undefeated the Premier League title was Aberdeen's to lose as attention then turned back to Europe and the European Cup Winners' Cup quarter-final with Hungarian side Újpesti Dózsa. At that stage Aberdeen looked unbeatable, going 27 games since the 'Hibernian scandal' and their last defeat. They were still going for a remarkable quadruple with the Super Cup already in the bag, but as so often happens with great teams something had to give. Injuries to key players for once made the team look vulnerable. In the space of three days, a first-leg defeat in Hungary was followed by an exit from the prolonged League Cup, bringing the unbeaten run to a shuddering halt.

Budapest had been a city with unhappy memories for the older generation of Aberdeen supporters. In 1970 the Dons became the first team to be eliminated on penalties in Europe when they went out of the Cup Winners' Cup against Honvéd. Újpesti Dózsa were not seen as a side that would be expected to lay a glove on the holders. They had just emerged from a winter shutdown and coach Miklós Temesvári declared that Aberdeen were the best team that had visited Budapest for many years. Mind games perhaps, but there was no doubt that Aberdeen were strong favourites to reach the last four. However, on a dreadful surface and in front of a hostile home crowd it was a rare night to forget. Several missed chances cost them in a second half that brought two goals for the Hungarians. Ferguson was rightly livid but kept his cool after what was one of the most frustrating of European ties. Mark McGhee came in for criticism as he missed from a yard out, and VAR was not around to aid the striker as one of his efforts was clearly over the line. The only positive was that Aberdeen had the opportunity to atone at Pittodrie.

The new format for the League Cup was never favoured by Ferguson and playing the semi-final over two legs only added to an already congested fixture list. Aberdeen were still licking their wounds after returning from Budapest and went down to a contentious penalty at Celtic after the Pittodrie clash ended goalless. Far from being dejected, Ferguson took a more balanced view, 'I believe despite the defeat we were the better team. We were missing Kennedy, Stark, McMaster, Weir, McGhee and McKimmie. Our younger players did well – 12 of the 13 players on duty came through our ranks.'

He then turned to a call to arms as he demanded his players make up for their dismal showing in Europe, 'As far as Aberdeen are concerned it is a challenge of a lifetime. Újpesti Dózsa are going to have one of their hardest matches in their entire history.' Aberdeen had never managed to claw back a two-goal deficit in European competition before. Újpesti made their intentions clear from the outset by sitting deep and deploying classic European tactics away from home by time-wasting, feigning injury and surrounding the referee at every opportunity. That only managed to noise up the Pittodrie crowd and when Mark McGhee opened the scoring in the first half, the pressure was on the Hungarians. The Dons were again missing chances but with two minutes left it was McGhee again who scored to level the tie on aggregate. He then became the first Don since Frank Munro in 1967 to score a hat-trick in Europe two minutes into extra time. The 3-0 win was a remarkable show of Aberdeen resolve and the Dons were now through to the last four of the Cup Winners' Cup for the second year in a row. McGhee recalled the crucial third goal in extra time, 'Unlike other goals I scored, like in a cup final, it was a feeling of euphoria. There had been a lot said by Alex in the dressing room after the first game; he slaughtered us! When that third goal went in, we knew then that we would go on and win the game.'

The remaining ties saw Barcelona go out 3-2 on aggregate to Manchester United, Porto see off Shakhtar Donetsk 4-3 over their two legs, while Juventus went through 2-0 against Haka.

Following the semi-final draw, Aberdeen were installed as favourites to retain the trophy. They avoided Manchester United as hopes throughout the country for a 'Battle of Britain' final in Basel remained. The Dons were paired with Portuguese side Porto, while Juventus would face the Old Trafford club.

Aberdeen were then back on Scottish Cup duty and faced a difficult replay against Dundee United at Tannadice. Mark McGhee continued his return to form by scoring the winning goal after two minutes as the Dons' unbeaten run in the competition extended to 16 matches. As Aberdeen were preparing for their trip to Porto, they were closing in on the Premier League title. Celtic were still the main challengers as defending champions Dundee United found to their cost, like the Dons did a year earlier, that battling for domestic and European titles was no easy task.

Premier League table at 31 March 1984

	P	*W*	*D*	*L*	*F*	*A*	*Pts*
Aberdeen	**25**	**19**	**3**	**3**	**61**	**13**	**41**
Celtic	27	16	5	6	61	32	37
Dundee United	24	14	6	4	46	22	34

Aberdeen faced a crucial period in the middle of April with the trip to Portugal in midweek followed by their Scottish Cup semi-final against Dundee in Edinburgh three days later. Porto were an emerging force, not mentioned at any stage as likely finalists. That view was not shared by Alex Ferguson as he discussed them with Willie Garner after having them watched. Strong in defence with quick forwards, they would present Aberdeen with a huge challenge. Ferguson declared that his team would need to draw on all of their experience to reach the final, 'Porto are a very accomplished side, probably as tough a task as we could have faced. We will need to prepare well but with so many games in a short period we will need to peak against them over there and at Pittodrie.'

In the first leg the Dons were up against it for long spells and faced a partisan 65,000 crowd in the Estádio das Antas. The last thing that Aberdeen wanted was the loss of an early goal, but disaster struck after 14 minutes when Porto danger man Fernando Gomes headed past Jim Leighton. It was the worst possible start for Aberdeen, who then had to defend in depth against a lively Portuguese side looking to reach their first European final. While Porto dominated the midfield area in the first half, they were restricted to limited opportunities to build on their lead mainly due to stout defending from Miller and McLeish. The renowned Aberdeen defence were given a stern test, but they stood firm and resisted all that the home side could throw at them.

In the second half it was a different story as the Dons began to control the game far better and they in turn created their own chances. Porto keeper Zé Beto was inspired on two occasions to save from Gordon Strachan, then he was once again well placed to turn a ferocious strike from Eric Black away for a corner in 61 minutes as Aberdeen began to look dangerous on the counter. The Dons almost levelled the tie with seven minutes remaining when Strachan's clever lob from 40 yards almost caught out Zé Beto, who did well to recover and make the save.

Despite going behind in the first leg, Ferguson remained confident that the Dons would turn the tie around in the Pittodrie return, 'There was a sense of occasion about our play in the second half last night. We wanted to do something in the game and show our determination. The chance is still there for us to get to the final. If I had been told at the start of the season that we would be coming home with a 1-0 deficit in the semi-final of the European Cup Winners' Cup then I would have gladly taken that. Porto did not bother coming to watch us at Pittodrie; maybe they thought they could have done enough in the first leg. We came through as tough a tie as we have faced away from home for a long time and we still think that Porto will have a hard time of it in Scotland.'

While Aberdeen closed in on a third successive Scottish Cup Final and were well ahead in the Premier League, the return against Porto proved to be one game too far as they failed to ignite their renowned fervour on the night and eventually fell out of the competition with Porto scoring a goal they hardly deserved on the break through Vermelhinho in 75 minutes. It left Aberdeen with the impossible task of scoring three goals and despite dominating possession for long spells and a host of missed chances it was just not their night. There was an eerie atmosphere around Pittodrie as the game was played in a dense spring fog and the capacity all-ticket crowd could not inspire their heroes to scale the European heights once again.

While Aberdeen had due cause to rue some of the decisions by referee Dušan Krchňák it emerged some 20 years later that the Czech official had enjoyed some 'fringe benefits' during his career as a FIFA whistler in that he freely admitted to accepting bribes from certain clubs. While it was never proven that Krchňák had been up to anything sinister in the Dons' matches against Porto, it nevertheless did cast a shadow over the Portuguese club's success.

Eric Black reflected on the disappointing exit, 'It is very hard to look back on the two games and where it went wrong. I was confident we would get the better of them in front of our own fans. It didn't work out that way, and Porto were a better side than most believed. Their control and passing was of a high standard, and we needed to be at our best. Unfortunately, at Pittodrie it was just not our night. We didn't reach the heights we know we can which was disappointing. Overall though it has been a great couple of seasons for the club in Europe. Reaching the final last year and the semi-final this season was some achievement. Now we must target the European Cup.'

After reflecting on their European departure, the club turned to deal with the almost monotonous transfer talk in the press, most of it fabricated, much to the dismay of Ferguson. The boss was as ever involved in all re-signing talks and he was delighted to announce that his defensive trio of Jim Leighton, Alex McLeish and Willie Miller were all on the verge of signing extended deals, 'Willie and Alex have indicated that they want to stay and that is great news for us. Jim Leighton and Peter Weir, who are in their final year, are also keen to sign on again. Overall, I am not that concerned – we could in fact be playing in a European Cup Final next season and the lads who talk about wanting to leave should think about that. Where else could they go to play at that level?' With Gordon Strachan and now Mark McGhee being linked with moves to Europe, the defensive spine of the side being signed up for the long term was welcome news. It was reported that Italian side Verona and the Germans of Cologne were both keen on making bids for Strachan, although Manchester United were interested. Cologne had already tabled a £500,000 offer after vice-president Karl-Heinz Thielen travelled to Scotland to speak with the midfielder.

Following the Porto clash the Dons needed three more wins from their final seven league games to clinch the title. Aberdeen had Dundee at Dens Park at the weekend with St Johnstone and Hearts to face in midweek, so they were looking to wrap up the Premier League to allow plenty of time to prepare for the Scottish Cup Final.

Premier League table at 28 April 1984

	P	*W*	*D*	*L*	*F*	*A*	*Pts*
Aberdeen	**30**	**23**	**4**	**3**	**72**	**16**	**50**
Celtic	34	21	6	7	78	39	48
Dundee United	30	17	7	6	59	32	41

Aberdeen won all three of those matches without conceding a goal, and on 2 May 1984 a 1-0 victory at Tynecastle secured another Premier League title. The Dons were backed by another large travelling support as a rare goal from Stewart McKimmie had them celebrating a championship in Edinburgh for the second time in four years. It was a memorable day for captain Willie Miller. On his 29th birthday, he was earlier named as the Scottish Football Writers' Association Footballer of the Year. Hearts were in no mood to allow Aberdeen to celebrate at their beloved Tynecastle but despite all their efforts, which bordered on the brutal at times, the Dons' class prevailed. McKimmie's goal was the first of his senior career. With four games to spare the championship was secured. Such was the Dons' dominance of the league that season, for some context Aberdeen won 25 of their 36 matches, the same total as Rangers and Hearts combined. They conceded 21 goals with runners-up Celtic 20 worse off. Alex Ferguson took time to praise the Aberdeen fans, 'Our support has been marvellous this season, both here at Pittodrie and on our travels. Take it from me, the players cannot thank our faithful fans enough for the part they have played this season. So, after the title, where do we go from here? We must weld ourselves into an even finer professional unit, strive to get even better and continue to be the best team in Scotland.'

Aberdeen closed their league campaign ahead of the Scottish Cup Final with a surprise 3-2 defeat at St Mirren. The Dons' 'babes' were given a run out as most of the major players were rested. It was the one and only time they conceded three goals in any game that season.

Ferguson's team were now going for their third Scottish Cup in a row in what was the 99th final. They were a side vastly experienced on the big stage, and before the game only Stark and McKimmie were without Scottish Cup winners' medals from the team that faced Celtic at Hampden. In what was another titanic clash between the sides, Aberdeen struck first when Eric Black pounced on a loose ball to beat Pat Bonner from close range in 23 minutes. The dynamic of the game changed just before the break when Roy Aitken was sensationally sent off. Aitken took out McGhee with a dangerously high challenge and referee Bob Valentine flashed the red card; he was the first player to be sent off in a Scottish Cup Final since 1929. Valentine was an experienced referee and was due to take part in the European Championship in France that summer. He was also the first referee to take charge of both domestic finals that season.

Aberdeen looked to take control of the game against ten men, but to Celtic's credit they rallied and made a real battle of it. When Paul McStay took advantage of a mix-up in the Aberdeen box to level with four minutes left, for once the Dons looked vulnerable. Lesser teams may have folded against Celtic's resolve, but this Aberdeen group had seen it all before. A few words from Ferguson at full time set them up for yet another extra-time period. It was McGhee, playing in his final game for the club, who scored the winner in 98 minutes. Aberdeen used the extra man to great effect in that energy-sapping period and the Celtic challenge withered in the Hampden sun.

Aberdeen were worthy winners and for the third year in a row the Scottish Cup was heading north to Pittodrie, the first team outside of Glasgow to achieve that feat.

The Dons' achievements of 1983/84 were quite remarkable following on from the club's first European success in 1983. They won three of the five competitions they entered in a season that ran to 64 matches. Their treble of Super Cup, Premier League and Scottish Cup confirmed Aberdeen's dominance in Scotland. By winning the Super Cup the Dons became the only club in Scotland with two European successes in their honours list.

With Strachan and McGhee leaving, there was still uncertainty around Doug Rougvie, who had not yet agreed terms to remain at

Pittodrie. The not unexpected news also came through that full-back Stuart Kennedy had to quit football at the age of 31. Kennedy was injured in the Cup Winners' Cup semi-final in Waterschei in April 1983 and had not kicked a ball all season following complications to his knee problem. Kennedy said it was not a difficult decision to make: 'It was made for me. If you can't run properly you can't play football. I feel I must get away from football altogether, it's the only way to keep my sanity. Although I was involved in coaching, the injury stopped me giving practical demonstrations. All in all, I decided a complete break was best.'

Stuart Kennedy had been at Pittodrie since 1976 and was a Scotland international with eight caps, described by Alex Ferguson as the 'complete professional'.

8

Champions Again

ALEX FERGUSON was determined to build his side from within. Developing youth players was vitally important and one of his defining principles in management, and during his time at Pittodrie the boss was heavily involved in developing the youth setup. There was little doubt that Ferguson inherited a clutch of the finest youngsters to ever have come through the ranks at Pittodrie. Bryan Gunn, Brian Mitchell, Neale Cooper, Eric Black, John Hewitt and Neil Simpson all went on to play their part at Aberdeen. The close-season of 1984 was a busy period for Ferguson: it was the first occasion that he had to look at rebuilding his team. The departures of Gordon Strachan and Mark McGhee were expected but with Doug Rougvie failing to agree terms, he too was away, to Chelsea. With Stuart Kennedy forced to retire, the squad looked under-strength.

With the players not due back to begin pre-season training until 14 July, the draw for the first round of the European Cup was made in Geneva a week earlier. Aberdeen, as a seeded club, could have expected a favourable draw but being paired with East German champions Dynamo Berlin with the first game at Pittodrie was no easy task. Before the club once again went to West Germany for their pre-season tour, Ferguson and vice-chairman Chris Anderson had the distraction of attending a UEFA commission in Zürich to consider Strachan's move to either Cologne or Manchester United. It took an intervention from the SFA to declare that Strachan was a Manchester United player. UEFA passed the case on to FIFA for a final decision.

With Alex McLeish, Willie Miller, Neale Cooper and John Hewitt all agreeing new contracts the Dons moved into the transfer market and signed Frank McDougall and Tom McQueen. McDougall cost £100,000 from St Mirren, while McQueen was valued at around £50,000 from Clyde, the pair coming in as direct replacements for McGhee and Rougvie. A 16-strong squad departed for West Germany with both new signings included. The Dons were also looking to sign Polish World Cup star Zbigniew Boniek from Juventus. Ferguson was left frustrated as the Italian club were prepared to let him go and Boniek was keen to sign, but Juventus changed their mind before a deal could be completed. The Dons were based in a converted monastery near Koblenz. With five games in as many days the tour was intense, including a friendly against Bayer Leverkusen. Injuries to Peter Weir and Neale Cooper dampened spirits and the news that both would be missing for several weeks made for a disappointing start to preparations. With John McMaster out for months, Ferguson did not have his troubles to seek. The Dons completed their fourth signing of the summer when 20-year-old Brian Grant moved for £50,000 from Stirling Albion.

Aberdeen opened their season at home to Dundee as the Premier League flag was unfurled before the game. Scottish minister for sport Allan Stewart completed the formalities as he congratulated chairman Dick Donald on the Dons' achievement. The SFA also announced that Alex Ferguson would be assisting Scotland manager Jock Stein in the international setup. It was another mark of recognition for Ferguson and Aberdeen.

The League Cup format had changed once more following criticism of the lengthy competition with too many games. That did not have any bearing on Aberdeen, who were sensationally knocked out by Airdrie at their tight Broomfield ground; the hosts were managed by former Dons boss Ally MacLeod. Aberdeen went into the tie with six first-team players out and after missing several chances in the first half they turned in what Ferguson described as the worst performance from his team since he joined the club. By contrast the champions won their opening five Premier League games, leading from the front, including away wins at St Mirren and Dundee United. Before the European Cup tie, Ferguson was away with the Scotland squad as he took his place alongside Jock Stein for the international against Yugoslavia at Hampden on 12 September.

Premier League table at 15 September 1984

	P	*W*	*D*	*L*	*F*	*A*	*Pts*
Aberdeen	**6**	**5**	**1**	**0**	**14**	**3**	**11**
Rangers	6	3	3	0	6	1	9
Celtic	6	2	4	0	8	2	8

Preparations for the visit of Dynamo Berlin were hampered by an injury list that was growing in every passing game. With Weir, Cooper and McMaster all out long term, strikers John Hewitt and Eric Black were the latest casualties. Ferguson looked forward to the European tie, 'Both Willie Garner and I have taken the opportunity to watch Dynamo and their record speaks for itself: six times East German champions in a row, a lot of experience and good individual players. They will be tough opponents for us.' Dynamo were seasoned campaigners in Europe, having been narrowly beaten by Nottingham Forest and Aston Villa in previous European ties. With six of their squad East German internationals, Aberdeen would need to be at their best to progress.

There was one omission from the team – which the club were aware of – and that was Frank McDougall. After being banned for four European ties when he was with St Mirren, McDougall had to bide his time to make his bow in Europe for the Dons. It was down to Eric Black and John Hewitt, the Dons' Gothenburg scorers, to spearhead the attack against the East Germans in what was Aberdeen's 60th game in European competition. Once again Pittodrie was full in anticipation of another great European adventure. All tickets had been sold apart from a section in the Beach End where a cash turnstile would be in operation. The *Press & Journal* declared the tie was a 'Supreme Test for the New Look' Dons, as the report referred to a first European tie without Strachan, McGhee and Rougvie, who had all moved on. For more than 70 minutes it was all going to script. Black once again showed his majestic heading ability by scoring twice, both headers against the giant 6ft 6in keeper Bodo Rudwaleit. The Belgian referee Marcel Van Langenhove did not endear himself to the Pittodrie support as Berlin's robust approach was often overlooked. In an era in European football where away goals were crucial, the Dons paid dearly for a late lapse that allowed Schulz to head past Jim Leighton from a corner in 82 minutes. From a position of relative comfort, the tie was now finely in the balance. Alex Ferguson was in a defiant mood after the game, 'They will have to come out a bit over there and that will suit us. I believe that we will need to score over there. If we do, we will have a great opportunity to go through.'

In the return leg in what was then still eastern Europe, the boss got his wish when Ian Angus scored in 67 minutes, but only after Dynamo had taken the lead early in the second half. Aberdeen were in control and looking to see the game out. Dynamo responded by taking risks to rescue the tie but once again they were helped by Aberdeen gifting them a late goal that took it into extra time. Willie Miller looked to have scored but his effort came back off the bar, so it was down to penalties. With Porteous, McQueen, Hewitt and Stark scoring the first four for Aberdeen, the Dons were on the brink after Bernd Schulz missed Dynamo's third. Captain Miller had the chance to put his team through but his penalty was saved, and after Black missed it was all over. There was time for reflection, difficult as it was, but Aberdeen had blown it. Dynamo were a competent side but over the two legs they were clearly inferior to the Dons, which made the exit more painful. Miller recalled what was a night to forget, 'At Aberdeen, we never did practise penalties, so in seeking volunteers to take the penalties in Berlin, I could not find five men who fancied taking a spot kick. As I could only muster four, I felt it was my duty to give it a go. I was our final penalty taker, and me scoring would see us through to the next round. I committed the cardinal sin by changing my mind in the run-up. I had intended to put the ball to the right but changed my mind and the keeper guessed correctly. It went to sudden death and after Dynamo scored first, Eric Black had to score to keep us in it. Unfortunately, he missed, and we were out.'

Alex Ferguson was disappointed, 'I don't think there was much doubt that over the two games we were the better side and to lose it as we did on penalties was a real sickener. To be honest the tie should never have needed to go to spot kicks. We should have wrapped it up long before it got to that stage.' Ironically for Aberdeen and Ferguson, a month after their exit from the European Cup the boss was in Paris collecting the Adidas Bronze Award for the Dons' overall performances in 1983/84. Aberdeen were just edged out by Liverpool and Juventus for the gold and silver prizes.

With Aberdeen out of the European Cup and League Cup in the first rounds, the pressure was on and they were once again under the scrutiny of the press down south who were questioning how strong they were as their great European side was beginning to break up. Ferguson was defiant, 'We have been through difficult periods in the past, all great teams suffer from that, it's how we respond that is the main thing. Nobody at Pittodrie will be feeling sorry for themselves, that's for sure. It is a challenging time now. We have introduced several new players into the squad this season so it is to be expected that there will be a transitional period.'

The cup exits were hard to take, more so as Aberdeen were eliminated by inferior opposition. That questioned the aura of invincibility that had been around Pittodrie for the previous three years. As the Dons returned from Berlin, they faced Celtic at Parkhead in their next outing and suffered their first league defeat of the season in another bad-tempered clash. Aberdeen had lost two games in succession; a crisis, cried their doubters. It was a mere blip as they confirmed their lead at the top of the Premier League by winning their next eight league games with Frank McDougall scoring nine goals from as many appearances. Included in that run was a 2-1 victory over Rangers at Ibrox. The Glasgow club had certainly improved on recent seasons and they were desperate to land a blow on Aberdeen. Ferguson was happy with the win, 'I thought it was a competitive game as it usually is down there. We found ourselves a goal down, but we got back into it through Billy Stark and we began to impose ourselves on the game. One pleasing aspect about our play is that we always look capable of scoring. With McDougall, Black and Stark in our side we have three natural finishers. My thanks also go to the marvellous support we had down at Ibrox. We had around 4,000 behind us and it was a great boost for the players to see that level of support.'

Premier League table at 8 December 1984

	P	*W*	*D*	*L*	*F*	*A*	*Pts*
Aberdeen	**17**	**15**	**1**	**1**	**42**	**11**	**31**
Celtic	17	11	4	2	43	16	26
Rangers	17	7	8	2	29	9	22

Before the end of the year, long-term injury victims John McMaster and Doug Bell were back in training. With Peter Weir back from several months out the squad looked strong for the second half of the season, and with Ferguson also being involved with the national setup, the Aberdeen representation for Scotland remained strong. A 3-1 win over Spain at Hampden on 14 November put Scotland in a great position to qualify for the World Cup in Mexico in 1986.

Aberdeen began 1985 with a short break in Egypt where they put in some hard work with the sun on their backs and played a friendly against local side Ismaily. Frank McDougall kept up his scoring streak by grabbing both goals in a 2-2 draw. It was the ideal preparation for the visit of a rejuvenated Rangers to Pittodrie on 19 January. McDougall relished the opportunity to take on a Rangers defence that lacked pace and their Pittodrie record in recent years had been lamentable. The former St Mirren striker scored his first hat-trick for Aberdeen, who humiliated Rangers in a 5-1 win. The game boiled over when Stewart McKimmie and Rangers' Ally Dawson were sent off after a clash in the first half. The victory put Aberdeen eight points clear in what was a crucial part of the season.

The Dons began their defence of the Scottish Cup against Alloa Athletic, looking at a record-breaking four Scottish Cup wins in a row in what was the 100th year of the competition. The meticulous planning that the management carried out back then was not just reserved for European opponents. Alloa had been watched on several occasions according to Alex Ferguson. A 5-0 win put Aberdeen through to a tougher assignment, away to Raith Rovers in Kirkcaldy. The Fife side had improved considerably from their previous clash against the Dons, when they were beaten 12-0 over two legs in the League Cup in 1983. On this occasion Raith made Aberdeen work for what was a hard-earned 2-1 victory with McDougall scoring both goals for the holders.

As the final set of league games approached, the Dons were still on course for a league and cup double, matching their achievement from the previous season. The month of March was going to be decisive; the Dons were again drawn away from home in the Scottish Cup with a trip to Tynecastle to face Hearts. Aberdeen prepared for the quarter-final in Edinburgh with a 3-0 win over St Mirren at Pittodrie. Ferguson said, 'We were in control throughout the game and that was pleasing. St Mirren never make things easy, but we never really let them get into the game. I was pleased Ian Porteous put in such a good shift and he took his opportunity to show what he is all about. Given our horrendous injuries this season, our younger players have had to step up and they have not let us down.'

Aberdeen travelled to face Hearts on 9 March in the Scottish Cup backed by another large away support. It had been more than four years since they had lost a Scottish Cup tie. Another bruising encounter saw the holders fall behind to a Sandy Clark goal in 51 minutes. As Hearts sensed an upset it was Eric Black who rose to head a late equaliser to take the tie back to Pittodrie four days later, where it was redemption in the replay as Ferguson was disappointed following the game in Edinburgh, 'We never really got going and what made it disappointing was the fact that we were followed in big numbers again and we let them down. However, we are presented with a chance to make up for Saturday and secure our place in the last four. Overall, the game was a good one, played in a fair spirit. Hopefully we will be able to put our game together in the replay. The players know what is at stake. We have a proud record in the Scottish Cup over the last few seasons and we will not let our hold on the trophy go without a fight.' As it turned out it was Hearts centre-half Roddy MacDonald who carried the fight as he was sent off in 15 minutes after leaving his elbow in Black's face. Billy Stark then scored what proved to be the winning goal in a game in which Aberdeen were rarely troubled against the ten men of Hearts.

Stark was proving to be a great signing, filling the role left by the departure of Gordon Strachan; his winner against Hearts was his 15th goal of the season and he was the Dons' top scorer in the cup. He was delighted to win over some of the doubters in the Aberdeen support, 'I would be a liar if the criticism didn't get to me, but I am a bit older and more experienced to handle these situations. I am just happy to continue to contribute. I made my first appearance in the Scottish Cup for Aberdeen when I came on in extra time in the final against Celtic for my first winners' medal.'

As Alex Ferguson looked towards the closing games of the season, he told his players to relax, 'That's my advice to my squad as we enter the most crucial stage of the season. I know there are only seven league games and we are in the Scottish Cup semi-final against Dundee United. Our priority is to win the Premier League, then the cup. After losing a few influential players, many had written us off before a ball was kicked this season. Despite the early cup exits, the team has done better than I expected. Some individual performances have been exceptional and certainly a bonus to me. Tom McQueen has come on so well in his first season as a full-time player and Stewart McKimmie is developing into one of our most important players. Frank McDougall came here and proved he can score goals. Then Neil Simpson is having a magnificent season. He has matured this term and there have been times he has carried our midfield. Eric Black was expected to be our main threat up front and he has been outstanding. Eric has been a full-time professional for over five years now and all he needs now is to add experience to his ability. Over the last few years, we have grown used to experiencing an exciting and demanding run-in to the season. It is almost second nature to our more experienced players. The younger lads know all about life with Aberdeen and exactly what is required from an Aberdeen player.'

Aberdeen moved a step closer to the Premier League title on 16 March following a 4-0 win against Dundee at Dens Park. The game had been in doubt with heavy snow falling in the Tayside area, but the pitch was cleared in time for the players to turn on the style and two goals in a minute just before half-time made it a comfortable afternoon. As news came through that Celtic had lost at home to Hibernian, the Premier League was the Dons' to lose as they went six points clear of the Glasgow club, who had a game in hand.

A week later Hibernian welcomed Aberdeen to Easter Road looking to build on their Parkhead success and steer themselves away from a relegation battle. The visitors left Hibernian in no doubt who were the champions-elect with a majestic display in a 5-0 win. Ferguson was doing the maths, 'I reckon we need to take at least seven points from our remaining six matches to have the title in the bag, no matter what Celtic achieve from their final fixtures. That should not be that difficult a task, particularly when we show the kind of commitment we displayed against Hibernian. We went into the game with the right approach and I was delighted with the way we took our chances.'

In an era when crowd trouble was the scourge of British football, after Aberdeen's third goal some of the home support spilled over and threw objects at Jim Leighton and Alex McLeish. Leighton was struck with a bolt while bottles narrowly missed McLeish. Hibernian were well known for having a sizeable 'casual' element, intent on causing trouble. The Dons were also followed by the Aberdeen Soccer Casuals who had gained notoriety across the country after forming the first 'firm' in Scotland. Most of the violence was carried out away from stadiums, at motorway cafes and train stations.

Aberdeen returned to Pittodrie at the end of March looking to defeat Dundee United, the only side to beat them at Pittodrie that season. Two points would edge them closer to the title and lay down a marker for the forthcoming Scottish Cup semi-final in Edinburgh. John Hewitt had returned from injury and his two first-half goals set up a 4-2 win, a result that was kind on the visitors. The Dons dominated the Tangerines and with 16 goals in four matches, Aberdeen were now racing towards the title. Celtic were relying on United doing them a favour but even the Tannadice support didn't share those hopes with only a few hundred in attendance at Pittodrie. With only five points needed from their final five league outings, it was now a matter of when Aberdeen would retain the Premier League for the first time.

The Dons then travelled to Ibrox ahead of their semi-final against Dundee United. Rangers were well off the pace in what had been a battle between Aberdeen and Celtic for several months. The Dons had found Ibrox a happy hunting ground in recent years. Ever since Alex Ferguson berated his first Aberdeen side in 1978 for being happy with a late equaliser at the Glasgow ground it was a priority for the boss to address that. The toxic atmosphere at Ibrox always threatened to boil over as the Rangers supporters were never a group to accept defeat with any grace. Aberdeen were going for their eighth win from their last 13 league games at Ibrox.

When Eric Black scored their second goal just before half-time it was enough for many of the 23,437 crowd as the Ibrox stands began to empty. Black's goal was also the Dons' 79th in the league that season, a new Premier League record which beat the one set by Aberdeen a year earlier. With relegated Dumbarton due at Pittodrie in their next league game, it looked likely that the final home match of the season against Celtic would prove decisive.

The recent defeat of Dundee United at Pittodrie suggested that Aberdeen were slight favourites to continue their incredible four-year undefeated run in the Scottish Cup. The selection of Tynecastle in Edinburgh as a neutral venue seemed an odd choice, 130 miles from Aberdeen but half of that from Dundee. Dens Park in Dundee could still have the capacity to accommodate both sides although had it been played there it certainly would have been an all-ticket sell-out. As it turned out over 18,000 were at Tynecastle to see another stalemate. Not unlike the 1979 League Cup Final, the Dons were the better side, taking the game to United and passing up the more presentable chances to score. The best of them came when John Hewitt missed from close range and Billy Stark was unlucky to see his header come back off a post. It was a frustrating game for Aberdeen, who were now looking at a midweek replay at the same venue. The SFA came in for criticism for not taking the replay away from Tynecastle. The pitch was bare and rock hard in places. Despite calls to move the replay to Dundee, the authorities seemed oblivious to what appeared to be an obvious choice. That was confirmed when the teams met again on 17 April with less than 11,000 returning for the tie, and it was a fateful night for Aberdeen as their long unbeaten run came to an end in controversial circumstances. The Dons were again the better side but fell behind to an early United break. The game erupted on the hour mark as Neale Cooper was sent off for a lunge at Ralph Milne before Stuart Beedie scored a decisive second for the Tangerines. Aberdeen never gave up and both sides were down to ten men when Davie Dodds was expelled for a dreadful challenge on Willie Miller. Ian Angus pulled a goal back for the Dons before a late rally ended with United defender Maurice Malpas clearly handling in the box. It seemed a certain penalty, but referee Hugh Alexander didn't agree. On reflection it was a shocking decision and one that compounded Aberdeen's frustration. Alexander had not been a referee who had done many favours for the Dons in the past, and he had plenty of 'previous' when it came to controversial decisions. Ironically the last time Aberdeen lost a Scottish Cup tie before the United defeat was at Cappielow in 1981, when Alexander was again in charge.

The Scottish Cup exit completed a season of disappointment in the three cup competitions; Aberdeen had high hopes of going all the way in them all. What was even more frustrating was the general belief inside Pittodrie that Aberdeen went out to inferior opposition in each one. Certainly, Airdrie of the First Division came into that category in the League Cup, as did Dynamo Berlin in Europe. Dundee United may claim some sort of parity with Aberdeen, but the honours won suggested otherwise.

There was no time for licking wounds as Ferguson's top priority that season was still to be won, and Dumbarton offered little resistance as they were swept aside 4-0 at Pittodrie. That gave Aberdeen the opportunity for another first, the chance to secure the championship in front of their own fans. Alex McLeish looked forward to the visit of Celtic, 'Although we still have two matches after today, the Celtic game will be decisive. We are all determined to go out and secure the title in front of our own support. We have clinched titles before away from home in recent seasons so it would be tremendous to win the Premier League at Pittodrie. We were disappointed going out in the European Cup so early and getting back into Europe as champions again would be an obvious target.'

Celtic arrived at Pittodrie determined to keep the Dons' champagne on ice. They had managed to see off Motherwell in a replay to reach the Scottish Cup Final but held few hopes of catching Aberdeen. Manager Davie Hay was aware of the task in hand, 'We know we have got to go to Pittodrie and win to make things go as long as they can. We still cannot give up hope, and we will battle away until it is impossible for us. A big factor in Aberdeen this season has been the sheer professionalism of Willie Miller and Alex McLeish. They have been together a long time and that is important for Aberdeen. We have changed a few things around this season while Aberdeen have been far more settled.'

With away games against Hearts and Morton to follow it was only a matter of time before Aberdeen wrapped up the title, but Alex Ferguson was keen to do it in front of a capacity home crowd. Celtic were in no mood to allow the party to begin at their expense so they came at Aberdeen in the early stages and as the tackles flew in Neil Simpson was booked for a late challenge on Murdo MacLeod. It was frantic stuff and the game exploded minutes before the break when Celtic were awarded a penalty that bordered on the ridiculous. Frank McGarvey for once evaded his shadow in Willie Miller and his cross to the back post looked innocent enough. Mo Johnston and Billy Stark challenged for the ball and Stark got there first to head it out for a corner. Amazingly referee George Smith, no stranger to dubious decisions in Aberdeen matches, pointed to the spot. Not even the Celtic players could believe their luck but amid chaotic scenes at the King Street end Roy Aitken hammered the ball high past Jim Leighton. The Celtic captain celebrated behind the goal in front of the Aberdeen support, which led to police intervention.

Aberdeen began the second half in a more positive frame of mind and began to pile on the pressure. Ferguson sensed this was no game for the faint-hearted so he withdrew Doug Bell on the hour and sent on Neale Cooper. That change paid an immediate dividend as Cooper played his part in the equaliser. Cooper dispossessed Peter Grant in midfield and sent Stewart McKimmie away on the right. The full-back was chopped down by MacLeod as Celtic were now desperate to stop Aberdeen at any cost. Ian Porteous floated in the free kick and Willie Miller stooped to head wide of Pat Bonner as the ball went in off the far post. Miller then embarked on a celebratory run down beside the South Terrace as the Aberdeen crowd rejoiced. It was a display of passion from the skipper that remains a special moment in Pittodrie folklore. Once Miller's team-mates caught up with him, he was unceremoniously

Pittodrie

hauled to the ground as the celebrations continued. Miller recalled his historic goal, 'On the hour mark I went up for a free kick from Ian Porteous, launching myself at the ball and beating Roy Aitken in the air, which was no easy task. The ball went in off the post to the delight of the Aberdeen support as I was swamped by my team-mates.'

Aberdeen could have had a deserved victory had John Hewitt scored from a great chance in the final minute, but the 1-1 draw was enough for the players to take their bow in front of their own fans at full time; they were now six points clear at the top with two games left to play. The first of those was a quick return to Tynecastle to face Hearts. Aberdeen had clinched the league title there in April 1984, and this time they were in Edinburgh to turn on the style in what was almost exhibition football of the highest quality. It was a personal triumph for Frank McDougall, returning from injury to bag all three goals in the 3-0 win. His third, a volley from just inside the box, rounded off a classic move in what should have been the goal of the season. Even the Hearts faithful were in awe, and their manager Alex MacDonald agreed, 'That game just illustrated how short we were in comparison to Aberdeen. Look at the players

Aberdeen had missing, yet they were still far superior.' McDougall scored his three goals in a blistering 13-minute period in the first half as the Dons visibly eased up in the second half, passing the ball around with ease.

Aberdeen completed their season by coming from behind to defeat Morton 2-1 at Cappielow and reached the 59-point mark, a new Premier League record. The Greenock ground was never a favourite venue for Aberdeen. Cappielow was, and still is, one of the most antiquated grounds in Scotland. It was a vivid reminder that on the same day in Bradford, tragedy struck with 56 fatalities as fire broke out in the grandstand at their Valley Parade ground.

The presentation of the Premier League trophy was arranged to take place at Pittodrie as the Aberdeen youth side were to face Celtic in the BP Scottish Youth Cup Final. They had beaten Dundee, St Johnstone and Ayr United to reach the final of the competition, which was now in its second year. With the entire first team in attendance it was a marvellous club occasion; the family traditions that were so important to chairman Dick Donald and Chris Anderson were shining as bright as the Northern Lights that evening. For the youngsters it was an incredible game. On the hour mark Celtic went 3-0 ahead and looked well in control. However, the young Aberdeen players drew inspiration from the seniors as they battled back and three goals in 20 minutes took the final into extra time. There was nothing going to stop those young lads as Aberdeen ran out 5-3 winners by scoring two more goals in that additional period. The crowd of around 6,000 gave the young players a standing ovation as they were presented with the trophy.

Alex Ferguson recalled the occasion, 'I was more excited by the prospect of the match than by the presentation. It was a time for examination of our youngsters, a time to judge progress, assess character and temperament. It was the best youth game I had ever seen, played with all the enthusiasm and innocence that only young players can exhibit. As both sets of players abandoned their inhibitions the game reached a frightening standard. Celtic were ahead at half-time and I decided I wanted to know what these lads were really made of and I let them know Aberdeen FC expected far more. If they froze on the big occasion as youth team players, then what chance had they as first-team players playing in front of a 60,000 crowd in a cup final? After we scored the boys' confidence soared and we went on to win convincingly. As the young ones had done their lap of honour they were met at the dressing room by every player, ground staff and office workers. Willie Miller went around every player congratulating them as did others. The sight of that unity moved me. It made me realise that my seven years with the Dons was not the completion of an achievement but only the start.'

As most of the Aberdeen players took a well-earned rest for the summer break, there was still some international business for Ferguson and the defensive trio of Jim Leighton, Alex McLeish and Willie Miller. All three were in the side that defeated England at Hampden to lift the new Rous Cup before the Scots travelled to Reykjavík and a vital World Cup qualifier against Iceland. Scotland midfielder Jim Bett was familiar with the Reykjavík surroundings having played there previously. Bett had been a target for Aberdeen for several months and transfer speculation intensified after he scored the winning goal from the penalty spot to keep Scotland on course for the World Cup.

9

Silver Darlings

'I WANT to assure our support that while on one hand we are proud to have won the Premier Division, there is no way we were satisfied to have won just one major trophy,' said Alex Ferguson as he looked ahead to the new 1985/86 season. It was a clear measure of the progress that had been made and standards reached. It was perhaps normal for either of the two Glasgow clubs to make such bold claims to appease their entitled support, but the pendulum of power had shifted north. It hurt Celtic and Rangers, and Ferguson was revelling in their demise.

Aberdeen added two new players to their squad in the summer. Jim Bett arrived at Pittodrie from Belgian side Lokeren in a £285,000 deal; he had been a long-time target for Ferguson and the former Rangers midfielder was a regular in the Scotland national side. Brian Irvine also joined Aberdeen from Falkirk. The young centre-half turned down the opportunity to go to England to join the Scottish champions. It was another indication of just how powerful Aberdeen had become when it emerged that Rangers tried to tempt Bett back to Ibrox with a last-ditch bid to thwart Aberdeen. Rangers manager Jock Wallace declared the Ibrox club had submitted a substantial offer to Lokeren for Bett. The transfer fee was never an issue for Aberdeen as they were prepared to match anything that Rangers could offer. Ferguson was unconcerned, 'We are in touch with the situation. What Rangers do does not concern me.'

Ferguson was keen to keep his squad together and avoid a repeat of the previous summer when Gordon Strachan, Mark McGhee and Doug Rougvie left the club. For the new season the manager was happy with his squad, 'The fact is we have a nucleus of players who have been bred to win. This means we have the ammunition to do the job, but we will not win anything unless we prepare properly. Our pre-season tour of Switzerland was a worthwhile exercise though only as a means of achieving fitness, not as a guide to form in the competitions that lie ahead.' Aberdeen went into the new season with 38 registered players.

The signing of Bett was another indication of Aberdeen's ambition. Bett was also being targeted by Southampton, but he declared after signing for the Dons, 'I would not have returned to Scotland to play for any other team but Aberdeen or any other manager than Alex Ferguson. This club has set such high standards and they have a great squad of players and it is natural to want to be a part of that. In the last few seasons, they have got used to the idea of success and they want more of it. There are so many challenges ahead, especially the European Cup, that is an exciting prospect. You only have to look at the teams involved to see the quality and we look forward to doing well.'

The European Cup, along with the European Cup Winners' Cup and UEFA Cups would have no English representation. Following the tragic events in the Heysel Stadium in Brussels at the European Cup Final between Liverpool and Juventus, English clubs had been banned from competing indefinitely. They were later allowed back in 1990, with Liverpool's exile continuing for a further year. Aberdeen had been proud of the behaviour of their travelling support to European ties but still issued a statement on the back of the English ban, 'The supporters of Aberdeen FC have earned an excellent reputation for good behaviour at home and in Europe. The success of the club in recent years has been enhanced by the good humour and behaviour of our supporters and we want this to continue. In the aftermath of the Heysel Stadium tragedy, crowd behaviour in European matches will be under scrutiny. Your loyal support and good behaviour are essential for the success of Aberdeen FC.'

Aberdeen left for a ten-day tour of Switzerland on 20 July, taking in five matches. Peter Weir, who had been sorely missed through injury for almost the entire previous season, was back in action, which was a welcome boost. The Dons finished off their tour with a 6-2 win over Lausanne in which debutant Brian Irvine scored his first senior goal. They completed their preparations with friendlies at Meadowbank and Inverness Caley over the first weekend in August.

Pittodrie had undergone more stadium improvements over the summer with a new roof being constructed over the King Street end of the ground. Traditionally the home of the Dons' 'songsters' for many years, it was first covered in 1934. It was also the first part of the ground outside of the Main Stand to have bench-style seating fitted, that work having been done in 1973. The latest project also included new kiosks, stairwells and lighting. For the opening games of the season that area was still under construction with completion due in October.

Aberdeen opened the defence of their Premier League crown at home to Hibernian on 10 August. Ahead of their visit, Steve Cowan was sold to the Edinburgh club in a £45,000 deal. Aberdeen were content to allow the transfer to be completed so that Cowan could face them three days after his switch to Hibernian. Pittodrie was near capacity due to the King Street end works and Scottish League secretary Jim Farry was on hand to present the club with the 1984/85 Premier League flag as it was unfurled in the Main Stand. The Dons began their league campaign with a convincing 3-0 win that was pleasing for Ferguson in itself, but it was the performance that had him delighted: 'It wasn't the fact that we won so well, although that was welcome, the thing that pleased me was that it was a smashing game in which both sides played good football.' Jim Bett announced his arrival with a superb opening goal in the second half.

One long-term issue for Ferguson was the one domestic trophy that had eluded him in his seven years at Pittodrie, the League

Cup. It had frustrated Ferguson and at no stage was winning the League Cup a prime target, but that changed in 1985: 'I hardly need to remind our supporters the League Cup is the one domestic trophy that we have not been able to win since I came here. We will regard it this season as important a feat as the other competitions. Maybe the fact that we haven't won it in seven years will inspire us to put that right this season.' Aberdeen eased past Ayr United and St Johnstone in the opening rounds to reach the last eight without conceding a goal.

One unexpected departure in August was Gothenburg hero Doug Bell. The midfielder, who had been signed twice by Ferguson for St Mirren and then Aberdeen, did not get much sympathy from his mentor when he indicated he was now unhappy at the club. Ferguson, throughout his managerial career at Pittodrie and Manchester United, was never one for holding on to players who were unhappy: 'We would all like to wish Doug Bell all the best in his move to Glasgow Rangers. As I have said I would have been happy to keep him but he was not content so there was little point in standing in his way when the opportunity came to release him with a large fee [£125,000] involved. Unhappy players in the club can spread discontent in the dressing room so it is always my policy to capitalise where possible.'

For Bell it was a decision he later regretted, although the circumstances around his move could be traced back to a serious rib injury sustained in 1984. Bell was convinced that Ferguson, although very helpful through his recovery, had become too protective of his injury. With Bett arriving and Neale Cooper and Neil Simpson regulars in midfield, Bell decided to leave and join Rangers and years later he declared, 'To leave Aberdeen was without doubt the biggest mistake of my life. I had never considered it and I fully expected to see out my career at Pittodrie.' Despite all of Bell's insecurities, Ferguson wanted him to remain at Aberdeen. Bell recalled that his manager was disappointed, 'He asked me sarcastically if I was fed up winning trophies. I believed him when he said that he wanted me to stay. I am certain he would have looked after me, repaying my loyalty with his own loyalty. Nothing I did subsequently in football could compare to my time at Pittodrie.'

While Bell was on his way, fellow Gothenburg hero John McMaster was enjoying his testimonial year. The club announced that McMaster's testimonial match would be played on 16 December. Former Dons manager Billy McNeill agreed to manage a side made up from Manchester United and Manchester City players to face Aberdeen.

Alex Ferguson identified September as a crucial month for the club. With seven games to play in three different competitions, the Dons were due to face Hearts twice in the space of four days, a European Cup trip to Iceland, away matches at Celtic and Rangers as well as Alex Ferguson and international players being involved in the crucial World Cup clash in Wales. They began well with a double success over Hearts at Pittodrie. In the League Cup quarter-final an Eric Black goal was enough to send them through to the last four. Days later Hearts were beaten again, on this occasion more convincingly, a 3-0 win that frustrated Ferguson: 'Although the result was a positive one, it was an uneasy afternoon for us as we were put under pressure for long spells. We didn't play well but at least we scored the three goals.' Ever the perfectionist, Ferguson's remarks still seemed harsh on an Aberdeen side that was once again heavily involved in four competitions. Following their League Cup tie the Dons were paired with old rivals Dundee United in what was now a two-legged clash at the semi-final stage.

On the international front, Scotland faced a vital World Cup qualifier against Wales in Cardiff. They were looking to reach the finals for a fourth time in a row, and a draw would be enough to go through to a play-off against the Oceania group winners. Four Aberdeen players were in the side that earned the 1-1 result, which was enough. However the game will always be remembered for the tragic passing of Jock Stein. The Scotland manager had been seen to be struggling during the match which was noted by Alex Ferguson and team doctor Stuart Hillis, who were both keen to keep an eye on things. After Davie Cooper scored a late penalty the pressure was intensified, and Stein collapsed at the end of the game. Stein was carried into the dressing room and Ferguson told his players to remain on the pitch. After the tragic news that Stein had not survived it was down to Ferguson to inform the players: 'I managed to keep my feelings in check. I didn't shed a tear until we had flown from Cardiff to Glasgow the following day and set out on the drive up to Aberdeen. On the way up I pulled into a layby and I just broke down. At Ninian Park I had absorbed what Jock said about maintaining dignity and I was making sure the players were all right.' Ferguson was asked by the SFA to take over as Scotland manager in an emergency capacity for the two play-off games against Australia.

Aberdeen opened their European Cup campaign on familiar ground with a return to Reykjavík to face ÍA of Akranes, the Icelandic champions. The Dons had clashed with ÍA in the 1983/84 European Cup Winners' Cup campaign. As the team boarded their charter flight to Reykjavík, Ferguson was cautious: 'We can't afford to underestimate Akranes. There's no way we can look on this as our easy passage to the next round.' Ferguson was perhaps thinking back to the Dons' exit in 1984 when they went out of the European Cup in Berlin. With Jim Bett in their ranks, who was very familiar with Icelandic football having played there previously, the Dons were well prepared to get their European Cup campaign off to a winning start. ÍA coach Hörður Helgason was taking inspiration from local rivals Valur, who had beaten French side Nantes 2-1 in the first leg of their UEFA Cup tie, 'Valur have shown what can be done against a top European side. Now it is up to us to do the same. I believe we were unlucky to go out to Aberdeen the last time.'

Aberdeen had no such difficulties in avoiding a potential shock with a 3-1 win that got their campaign off to a great start. ÍA were confident of an upset and they took the lead in 36 minutes after a ridiculous penalty award from the Norwegian referee Thorbjørn Aas. Aberdeen responded with three second-half goals and it could have been more as they hit the woodwork on three occasions.

Before the return leg, Aberdeen went to Tannadice and came back with a one-goal lead in the first leg of their League Cup semi-final. They also clashed with a rejuvenated Rangers for the first time that season at Ibrox. Doug Bell was in the Rangers side who were desperate to land a blow on Aberdeen. For the first time in several years Rangers were considered as serious challengers for the title and after six games they were at the top ahead of Aberdeen and Celtic. The Ibrox side, under Jock Wallace, had improved but they still had to prove themselves against Aberdeen. Their chance came on 28 September in front of one of their biggest home attendances of the season. Rangers sensed their opportunity and Wallace, known for his robust approach, had his players keen to at last get one over the Dons. It is not often a manager after his side won 3-0 away from home would declare that all he wanted for his team was to get away up the road unscathed. However, Alex Ferguson just wanted this most unsavoury of matches to end, 'Looking back on our 3-0 win over Rangers, I can only say in all honesty I have never been so pleased in my career to see a match end and get on the way home. The reaction was nothing to do with the scoreline. The fact was I had a genuine fear for people's safety and as problems developed it was a relief to get it all behind us. I have no intention of responding to comments made by Jock Wallace after the game.'

Those comments from Wallace were perhaps typical of a well-beaten Ibrox manager after watching his side lose their discipline and their heads. The Dons' victory was never in doubt after Rangers had two players sent off in what was a brutal clash. The game was also held up for several minutes at the start of the second half as some Rangers fans invaded the pitch. This was nothing new from the Ibrox faithful. Wallace made his outburst immediately after the game, calling some Aberdeen players 'cheats' and accusing some of feigning injury. It was a bitter tirade from Wallace that Ferguson and Aberdeen ignored. The busiest Aberdeen staff member was physio David Wylie as Stewart McKimmie, John Hewitt, Neale Cooper and Billy Stark were all on the end of Rangers' brutality. With Jim Bett and Peter Weir already missing, the Dons came through the crucial period with a near perfect report card, but a growing injury list. Billy Stark recalled Ferguson's words at half-time, 'Make sure the game gets finished. Don't be scoring six or seven goals, make sure we stay in control of the game and get up the road.' Following the volatile clash Aberdeen were incensed that the SFA fined them £1,000 for their 'part' in the match. Rangers were fined £2,000. Ferguson was livid, 'We went out to win a game and within 20 minutes three players were booked, all of them Rangers players. What they are saying, in effect, is don't beat Rangers at Ibrox because you might cause trouble. This decision sets a terrible precedent.' The most favoured opinion on the Wallace comments was that he was trying to deflect the pressure away from himself, mindful of the fractured relations between the club and their supporters.

Premier League table at 28 September 1985

	P	*W*	*D*	*L*	*F*	*A*	*Pts*
Celtic	7	5	2	0	15	4	12
Aberdeen	**8**	**4**	**3**	**1**	**16**	**6**	**11**
Rangers	8	5	1	2	12	7	11

Aberdeen progressed in the European Cup with a 4-1 second-leg defeat of ÍA, the highlight being three second-half goals in four minutes. After a favourable draw in the opening round Aberdeen were paired with Swiss champions Servette in the second round with the first leg in Geneva. One boost was that top scorer Frank McDougall would at last be available after serving his four-game European ban.

The League Cup return against Dundee United at Pittodrie presented Aberdeen with an opportunity to reach another major final against their Tayside rivals. Despite carrying a slender lead from the first meeting in Dundee, it was a tie that had Ferguson on his guard, 'We know all too well from past cup ties with them that we can never take anything for granted. If I say that I believe that this time is to be our turn in the League Cup after seven years, it won't happen unless we make it happen.' Frank McDougall had proved to be an inspired signing and ready-made replacement for Mark McGhee. The former St Mirren striker had a different style from McGhee, where he was quick and more direct and keener to take his chances 'early'. It was something that Ferguson liked and encouraged Eric Black to do likewise: when a chance came, take it as soon as you can, often catching opponents by surprise.

The atmosphere was enhanced by the near-capacity crowd and that the new Merkland Stand was now open again following extensive works over the summer. McDougall scored the only goal of the game in 68 minutes as both teams missed several chances, and Aberdeen were now into their first League Cup Final since 1979. They had reached Hampden after five ties and had yet to concede a goal. It was exactly what Ferguson wanted as he continued to push his players on to success, 'We kept playing our football and sticking to our principles. This has given a good deal of confidence at the right time. We kept our patience against Dundee United and made sure we did not slip up like we have in the past.' Aberdeen would face Hibernian, who reached the final by beating both Celtic and Rangers in previous rounds.

The fixture schedule in October was another hectic spell; the Dons also had to face Servette in Switzerland four days before the League Cup Final. It was hardly ideal preparation for a major final, and it was thought that more care should have been given to the scheduling. Servette were not seen as one of the better sides in the European Cup but they were experienced with several Swiss internationals in their line-up. Aberdeen were now a very experienced team in European football and after their disappointing experience in Berlin in 1984, they were keen to keep Servette at bay in the first leg, looking to then finish the tie at Pittodrie. The

Dons, with their Gothenburg backbone of Leighton, McLeish, Miller, Simpson and Cooper, held the Swiss in a 0-0 draw. They defended for long periods and could have grabbed an away goal as a McLeish header came back off the bar. The Swiss crowd were unimpressed, but Ferguson was in no mood to entertain them: 'We came here to make sure we did not concede. Servette are a very good side with some terrific players so we could not allow them space to get in behind us. On another night we could have come away with a victory, but we are happy to take them back to Pittodrie.'

Attention now turned to Hampden and the first silverware of the season. John Hewitt had been outstanding in recent weeks, even prompting Ferguson to say that a Scotland call-up was possible; the Dons boss was of course now in temporary charge of the international side for the games against East Germany and the vital World Cup clashes with Australia. Hewitt was preferred over Peter Weir to start the final against a confident Hibernian side who had held Ferguson's men in a Premier League fixtures earlier in the month. That confidence was shattered after only 12 minutes, by which time Hewitt had two assists with Eric Black and Billy Stark scoring to put Aberdeen in early control. Experience was the key for the Dons, who went on to score a third in the second half in a game they controlled throughout. As cup finals go it was a masterclass from Aberdeen and they went through the whole competition without conceding a goal. For Hibernian it was a sobering experience. At no stage did they ever give up the battle, but they were outclassed against a side that was very streetwise in the big matches. After the final, Ferguson was delighted and even took a veiled swipe at the absence of either Glasgow side, 'The game was a great occasion. A great crowd, a superb match. This made it a great event for the supporters and a family, and for any neutrals who went along to see a great football match.' The manager's comments clearly touched on the family atmosphere that was clearly apparent when clubs outside of Glasgow competed in a national final. Aberdeen were presented with two trophies on the day. Along with the League Cup, the tournament sponsors

Skol also had a trophy struck which was awarded to the winners. Willie Miller had to amend his traditional one-handed trophy lift. The *Press & Journal* headline leaned towards the sponsors – 'ABERDEEN SKOLARS ARE TOP OF CLASS'.

Man of the match John Hewitt was in the form of his career, 'It's probably the best thing that's happened since Gothenburg, and it is a great feeling. The manager has kept faith in me and that has helped. I should have scored, Frank McDougall set me up beautifully, but I maybe hit the ball too well and Alan Rough made the save.' Eric Black revealed he was struggling all week to make the game, 'Towards the weekend I got better, and I am indebted to the manager for giving me the chance. Nothing can compare with Gothenburg, but I really enjoyed scoring against Hibernian.'

Hibernian manager John Blackley claimed, 'We will be back here. You can't afford to give a side like Aberdeen two goals of a start and expect to come back. We were left with a mountain to climb. It was a great occasion and we were delighted to be involved.' The *Burton Daily Mail* reflected on the Dons' 'Gothenburg Double Act', reporting, 'Eric Black and John Hewitt revived memories of Gothenburg 1983, when they combined to turn Hibernian's Skol Cup dream into a grim nightmare. Aberdeen's resident double act played the roles of goal-maker and goal-taker as their side lifted the trophy with a 3-0 triumph over the Edinburgh team. Black and Hewitt again proved that they have the appetite for the big occasion.'

1986 Scottish League Cup Final statistics
Shots on target: Aberdeen 5; Hibernian 4
Headers on target: Aberdeen 3; Hibernian 1
Shots off target: Aberdeen 6; Hibernian 8
Headers off target: Aberdeen 2; Hibernian 0
Free kicks: Aberdeen 13; Hibernian 19
Corners: Aberdeen 5; Hibernian 5

With a domestic treble an obvious target, the Dons were still looking at the European Cup but as so often happens after a team has won a cup, they slipped up three days later in a narrow defeat at Hearts. Despite dominating they could not force an equaliser. Aberdeen had to get their league campaign back on track and the visit of Celtic on 2 November proved crucial. The Glasgow club had been struggling for form and they came up against Frank McDougall who went on a goal rampage against their fragile defence. McDougall, became the first Aberdeen player to score four goals against Celtic since George Hamilton hit four of the five at Parkhead in January 1947. Ferguson was impressed, 'Those who witnessed Frank McDougall's brand of finishing against Celtic were fortunate, because you have to go a long way back to find anything to match it. His four goals added up to a superb performance and confirmed he is the most lethal finisher in Scotland.' While McDougall's tally was a joy for the Aberdeen support, his efforts were not seen by a wider audience. The game was never televised due to an ongoing dispute between eight Premier League clubs and the Scottish League. The Scottish League were out in the cold as cameras were not being allowed in the grounds of the dissenting clubs. It was all about the rebel clubs being against the proposed live coverage of league games in Scotland.

McDougall kept his goal glut going by scoring the winner against a Servette side who earned many plaudits for their second-half performance at Pittodrie. McDougall scored with a typical header in 23 minutes to put Aberdeen ahead, but the Swiss knew that one goal would be enough to take them through on away goals. In the end Aberdeen, for once, were lucky. Ferguson described the Servette performance in the second half as the best he had seen from any side in Europe at Pittodrie. High praise indeed, but it was Aberdeen who progressed to the last eight of the European Cup.

Scotland were on the cusp of qualifying for the World Cup in Mexico but were faced with a final qualifier against Australia. Just why FIFA decided that the Oceania group winners would face Scotland, runners-up in a European group, was questioned. With the first game at Hampden, Ferguson was looking for a two-goal lead to take to Melbourne. A crowd of 61,920 filled the national stadium for what was a physical encounter, which was expected by the Scotland manager. Two second-half goals earned the lead the boss was looking for. After the game Ferguson had mixed feelings: 'I don't know whether to be happy we got the result we wanted or disappointed we didn't score more goals. I think that the relief of scoring the goals contributed to a drop in our play towards the end. We have an outstanding chance of getting to Mexico now. The Australians must change their tactics for the second leg. I feel it was important we did not concede – that threat will now hang over the Australians.' Frank Arok, the Australian side's coach, paid tribute to Scotland, 'I admire Alex Ferguson's vision and courage he showed in leaving out established players. The Scottish team are extremely talented, but when they are in a strange environment, anything can happen.'

That change of scenery was the Olympic Park in Melbourne, a vast arena but one that rarely housed first-class football. Along with Leighton, McLeish and Miller, the Aberdeen contingent was strengthened as Stewart McKimmie and Neale Cooper were included in the travelling party. Jim Bett was not there after being injured at Hampden. Scotland were going to be boosted by the support of around 20,000 which delighted Ferguson, 'No other team could travel 12,000 miles and find more than 20,000 Scottish fans waiting to support them.' That backing was vital as Australia launched all they had at the Scottish defence, but their robust, physical approach did not faze McLeish and Miller, who had seen it all before. Scotland remained calm in the hostile atmosphere and held on with relative comfort in a 0-0 draw. Ferguson's visit to Australia was in stark contrast to his previous trip as part of a Scottish League squad that toured in 1967. Scotland played nine matches against Israel, New Zealand and Australia and at the same Melbourne Olympic Park venue, he scored both goals in a 2-0 win over Australia on 3 June 1967.

With Aberdeen safely through to the last eight of the European Cup and ties not due to be played until March 1986, the winter period allowed some respite. On 16 December the Dons paid tribute to the long-serving John McMaster with his testimonial game. Ferguson had been critical in the past when Drew Jarvie's big day was poorly attended in 1982. Billy McNeill, who oversaw the select side to face Aberdeen, paid tribute to McMaster: 'When I went to Aberdeen in 1977, he was one of the first people I met when I arrived. Even in the close-season he was in training in the morning and helping the ground staff in the afternoon. Despite a series of bad injuries, I was delighted to see John playing for Aberdeen in the club's most memorable day against Real Madrid in Gothenburg.' As a crowd close to 17,000 turned out to pay tribute to McMaster, the draw for the World Cup was made. Scotland were in the proverbial 'Group of Death' along with West Germany, Uruguay and Denmark.

As Alex Ferguson looked back on the year it was a time for reflection: 'It has been a satisfactory one in terms of winning two major trophies. Also of course we were proud to win the Youth Cup and Reserve League Cup, ensuring our future is in good hands. Looking ahead we see a most exciting period coming for the club and a momentous year for Scottish football. The fact that representatives from Pittodrie will play a huge part in the World Cup in Mexico gives an added dimension for our supporters and the club's stature. We must defend our Premier League title, correct last season's lapse when we missed out on the Scottish Cup and make new ground in the European Cup.'

The new year also brought with it new league leaders. Surprise package Hearts had embarked on an unbeaten run as others slipped. The Dons' away form was a concern to Ferguson and ultimately it was points dropped on the road that proved crucial. Losing to lowly Clydebank and Dundee United over the festive period was a hammer blow for the Dons' chances of retaining the league title, while they had also been drawn to face IFK Gothenburg in the quarter-final of the European Cup. The return leg in Sweden would be a poignant return to the Ullevi stadium, scene of their finest hour in 1983.

Ferguson announced that Teddy Scott, the Aberdeen kit man, would be part of his backroom team for Scotland in Mexico. It was a great gesture by the manager, whose respect for Scott was enduring. Teddy recalled, 'I have been in football for more than 30 years and this is the first time I have received any international recognition.' Ferguson completed his team by appointing Archie Knox and Clyde manager Craig Brown as his assistants.

Hearts' revival from being a promoted side in 1983 to league challengers continued after a narrow win at Pittodrie. It was a defeat that annoyed Ferguson, 'We had them watched several times and our feelings were that provided we played well we would beat them. They have been fortunate to avoid injury and despite their good run they are not a side that we should be losing to. As it turned out a few of our players were not at their best and we suffered because of that.' The league form at the turn of the year was a concern as Aberdeen had slipped to fourth place, six points off the top but with two games in hand. There was some respite when the Scottish Cup campaign opened with Montrose visiting Pittodrie. On the face of things it was a great tie for the Angus club, who were expecting to take around 2,000 fans north. As it turned out the game was postponed and played days later in a blizzard which kept the crowd down and perhaps the Dons' goal count too in a comfortable 4-1 win and a safe passage to the next round. Angus neighbours Arbroath were next, and this time Aberdeen had to travel down the A92 to Gayfield. Having drawn both near neighbours from lower divisions was favourable although Aberdeen did get through with young Joe Miller scoring the only goal in a tie that was played in arctic conditions.

The away form that had irked Ferguson continued to see the Dons fall further behind in the league race. They did defeat Hibernian at Easter Road on 22 February, incredibly their first away win in the Premier League since September. Too many points dropped ultimately cost Aberdeen the title, not that Ferguson was giving anything up, but with the chances of retaining their title slipping away, attention again turned to Europe and the Scottish Cup. IFK Gothenburg presented a huge hurdle for Aberdeen if they were going to reach the last four of the European Cup for the first time. The Swedes had a pedigree in Europe that was certainly on a par with Aberdeen. Coming from one of the less popular leagues in Europe, Gothenburg were UEFA Cup winners in 1982 and regular Swedish champions. They were also emerging from their winter break and they prepared for Aberdeen by playing Wimbledon and West Ham United in friendlies.

Ahead of kick-off there was a minute's silence for Swedish prime minister Olof Palme who had been assassinated earlier that day, then Willie Miller opened the scoring with a spectacular effort in 16 minutes in his 50th European tie for Aberdeen. Gothenburg showed they were a quality side and levelled just before the break. John Hewitt seemed to have given the Dons a vital lead to take to Sweden, but a last-minute error allowed Johnny Ekström to equalise. Ferguson was angered at the late lapse, 'I can't pretend the European result was the one we wanted and for that we can blame that moment of madness in the last minute. Conceding that late goal when we were looking at an advantage has put us under tremendous pressure. Having said that I am convinced we can still get through. Despite the result, they will still have to come out and win it in front of their own fans.'

On this occasion Ferguson was wrong. In the return leg at the Ullevi the Swedes adopted a safety-first approach and defended in depth on their own patch. The frustration for Aberdeen was apparent as they came up against a side that limited them to few opportunities. As a spectacle it was painful viewing. The home crowd, in excess of 44,000, were almost relieved as anything at full time. A game of attrition and petty stoppages made for a night to forget for the couple of thousand Aberdeen supporters who made the trip. For Gothenburg, it was job done after a goalless draw; for Aberdeen it was another tale of woe having lost another late goal in the first leg. Going out on away goals compounded Aberdeen misery.

With Hearts leading the Premier League, Aberdeen were still very much in the mix. In the Scottish Cup for the third time in succession the Dons were drawn to meet east coast opposition, Dundee at Dens Park in the quarter-final. The Dark Blues had improved under Archie Knox and were proving to be a real handful. The cup tie stretched the Dons to the limit in a pulsating game, with John Hewitt again on the mark in a 2-2 draw. The replay proved as tough and it took extra time for Aberdeen to finally see off the Dundee challenge. Peter Weir excelled and it was his clever lob that finally put them through. The last four presented a refreshing change with all four semi-finalists from the east; Aberdeen were joined by Hibernian, Hearts and Dundee United. Although both Edinburgh clubs had suffered relegations in recent years, all four competitors were accepted as the main challengers to the two Glasgow clubs. The prospect of an all-Edinburgh final was what many observers in the game were hopeful of and following the draw that was still on as Aberdeen would face Hibernian at Tynecastle and Hearts would face Dundee United at Hampden. In an era when both games were played on a Saturday at the same time, it was a special day in the Scottish football calendar.

Hibernian had the advantage of playing in their home city and they were keen to avenge their League Cup Final defeat to the Dons earlier in the season. What was significant, though, was that this was Aberdeen's seventh Scottish Cup semi-final in eight seasons under Alex Ferguson. The big-game experience they had gathered in recent years made them a formidable force in the games that mattered. Hibernian surprised the Dons by forcing the pace early on, probably mindful of their humbling Hampden experience in October. However, after that early pressure it was Groundhog Day for the Easter Road side as they were hit by a Dons double. Two headed goals by Billy Stark and Eric Black replicated the torment Aberdeen hit Hibernian with in the League Cup Final. From that stage Aberdeen's big-game management experience kicked in and Joe Miller added a third in 81 minutes to set them up for the final with Hearts, who had beaten Dundee United by a solitary goal in a dull game at Hampden. Ferguson was happy that his two-trophy target was very much on, 'Once Billy Stark and Eric Black put us ahead there was no doubt we would win. It was an excellent game and we improved as the game went on. The third goal by Joe Miller came from a fine footballing move involving six of our players. We deserved the win.'

Premier League table at 5 April 1986

	P	*W*	*D*	*L*	*F*	*A*	*Pts*
Hearts	32	18	9	5	54	30	45
Dundee United	30	15	10	5	49	27	40
Celtic	31	15	10	6	55	38	40
Aberdeen	**30**	**14**	**10**	**6**	**51**	**25**	**38**

The Premier League title was now very much unlikely to come north as an ever-growing injury list and hectic fixture schedule once again proved decisive. It was on 12 April that the top four clubs were in action against their rivals. Aberdeen faced Celtic at Pittodrie while Dundee United welcomed Hearts. For Aberdeen a victory was essential to keep their hopes alive. Hearts hammered United 3-0 while the Dons lost out to a Mo Johnston goal in a 1-0 defeat.

The focus was now on the Scottish Cup. It was a competition that Aberdeen under Ferguson had excelled in. Semi-finalists in his first two seasons, the only real failure was defeat at Cappielow in 1981, a venue that just about every Aberdeen player disliked. The last-four defeat in 1985 to Dundee United that brought an end to 23 unbeaten Scottish Cup ties and three successive trophy wins hurt Ferguson. In 1986 the Dons were going for a first domestic cup double, ensuring that the manager's demand of picking up at least two trophies a season was met. Cup final opponents Hearts were closing in on the Premier League title after an incredible seven-month unbeaten run had taken them to the summit.

On 20 April the sides would clash at Tynecastle in a rehearsal for the final. The game was played on the Sunday and was the first Scottish league fixture to be televised live. Had Aberdeen not lost out to Celtic earlier in the month, the Tynecastle clash could have been a league decider. As it turned out the Dons made a few changes with the final in mind. Hearts were lucky to keep their unbeaten run intact with an equaliser in the final minute after Aberdeen had dominated. If this was a marker for the cup final, then Aberdeen looked supremely confident. It perhaps confirmed Ferguson's opinion that Hearts had been very fortunate to go so long without defeat. Hearts manager Alex MacDonald admitted his side were outplayed, 'Someone up there must like us. We came back from the dead. I thought we had lost it.'

That good fortune ran out on what was a dramatic final day on 3 May 1986. For Aberdeen it was a routine win at bottom side Clydebank before a low crowd of just over 2,000. The Bankies were given a stay of execution along with Motherwell as league reconstruction meant that relegation for that season was suspended. Not surprisingly, it was very much an experimental Aberdeen side with their big players all rested. If cup final squad places were up for grabs, then the players who turned out at Kilbowie did themselves no harm as they strolled to a 6-0 win. While the atmosphere at Clydebank was quite sedate, it was very different at Paisley and in Dundee where the destination of the Premier League was decided. For leaders Hearts, a point against Dundee at Dens Park would give them the title. Celtic had to win handsomely against St Mirren in Paisley and hope for a miracle elsewhere. Celtic went on to win 5-0, but even their support was not optimistic. That was until two Dundee goals in the final seven minutes handed them a league title that seemed unlikely for several months. The scenes in Dundee were quite incredible. The expected Hearts party had turned into a nightmare as their sizeable travelling support were crestfallen; they had lost the title on goal difference. Ironically it was Hearts who had also choked on the final day in 1965 as visitors Kilmarnock won 2-0 to take the championship on goal average. The rules were changed after that from goal average to goal difference and the Tynecastle club lost out on both occasions. Hearts were left to pick up the pieces as a week later they would have to face Aberdeen at Hampden. Ahead of the cup final, the Young Dons retained the BP Scottish Youth Cup with a 2-0 win over Queen of the South in Dumfries.

The general opinion within the game was that Aberdeen would have far too much experience for a Hearts side that were in relatively uncharted territory, the club having not won a major trophy for 24 years. Five out of six Premier League managers thought that Aberdeen would win when asked by the *Press & Journal*. Archie Knox, the Dundee manager, said, 'I just can't see past Aberdeen. When you think of them in four finals in the last five years and they have won three on the trot, everything points to an Aberdeen win.' Hearts manager Alex MacDonald was defiant, 'I know the players will be haunted by us losing the title and it will prey on their minds for a long time. But when we gather as a team the spirit and confidence come through and I have seldom seen a group so determined before any game.'

Aberdeen captain Willie Miller was now 31 years old and regarded as 'Old Man River' at Pittodrie. Miller had made more than 750 first-team appearances for the Dons, 12 of them in major finals in a ten-year period. He looked ahead to the clash with Hearts, 'We certainly played well in the last meeting with them and should have won. But there is no question we can play a lot better than that. That must be worrying for Hearts.' Alex McLeish was confident, 'However Hearts will play I think Aberdeen will be good enough. I remember the days when it was said Aberdeen could not handle the big occasion. That has all changed now. Without being too cocky, we have what it takes to win major trophies. Hearts can't say that. They will be nervous running out at Hampden.' Jim Leighton recalled, 'As soon as we heard Hearts had lost at Dundee we were saying, "We're a shoo-in for the cup final." We had nine international players. We had players who'd played in Scotland–England games, World Cups, cup finals. Hearts didn't have any of that. They were a one-season wonder.'

Throughout his career as a manager, Alex Ferguson took some tough decisions over personnel. The 'no player is bigger than the club' line was one that he showed over the years. Players with big reputations crossed Ferguson to their cost in most cases. In 1986, two weeks before the Scottish Cup Final, striker Eric Black had informed the boss that he had accepted an offer from Metz in France, and he would be moving on. It was a decision that disappointed Ferguson. Black had been with the club as a teenager and had been nurtured and coached into a first-class forward, on the verge of the Scotland international squad. Ferguson was particularly annoyed that Black did not speak with him before agreeing his move, and was convinced that he could have done far better than join a mid-table side in France. Black was told by Ferguson that he would not be considered for the cup final and had played his final game for Aberdeen.

A crowd in excess of 62,000 filled Hampden for the occasion. Hearts had sold 34,000 tickets, such was their enthusiasm to see their team in a final, the Tynecastle faithful turning up still confident they would end their long trophy drought. As Hibernian had discovered to their cost in the League Cup Final, the early stages were crucial and against Aberdeen teams would have to get a foothold in the game. The Dons, with their vast experience of the major occasions, knew that their opponents would be nervous, almost fragile. John Hewitt, in the Dons' first meaningful attack, worked his way through the middle and before any Hearts defenders engaged him, he rifled a low shot past Henry Smith to open the scoring in five minutes. It was a hammer blow for Hearts as their fragility was laid bare in the Hampden sun. They created a couple of chances but Aberdeen dominated, and their game management was a masterclass. When Hewitt finished off a slick move at the beginning of the second half the final was finished as a contest; Billy Stark completed the scoring in 75 minutes.

Aberdeen finished the game keeping possession and far from humiliating their opponents it was down to Hearts captain Walter Kidd to compound Tynecastle misery. It was all too much for

Hewitt scores in the 1986 cup final

Kidd, who had already been booked for a hack at Hewitt when he lost his head midway through the second half. While play had stopped, Kidd hit Neale Cooper on the head with the ball, caught the rebound and threw it into Frank McDougall's face, yards from referee Hugh Alexander. Kidd was sent off, becoming the first captain to be sent packing in a Scottish Cup Final and the third in history after Roy Aitken in 1984 and Rangers' Jock Buchanan in 1929. With several Hearts players booked the Tynecastle club forfeited half of the prize money from the sponsors.

Alex Ferguson was delighted but reflected on missing a domestic clean sweep, 'As far as I am concerned, we should have had the treble. We just lost too many players through injury for too long in the league campaign. It is a pity, but I suppose two cups in the season is a good return.'

The victorious Aberdeen party stayed over in Anstruther that evening before making the now-familiar open-top bus parade through the city the following day.

1986 Scottish Cup Final statistics

Shots on target: Aberdeen 6; Hearts 4
Headers on target: Aberdeen 3; Hearts 0
Shots off target: Aberdeen 3; Hearts 7

Headers off target: Aberdeen 3; Hearts 2
Free kicks: Aberdeen 23; Hearts 13
Corners: Aberdeen 4; Hearts 9

Days after the domestic season had concluded, Ferguson along with his backroom team and international players were heading for the USA to prepare for the World Cup finals in Mexico. Scotland went on to lose narrowly to Denmark and West Germany before being held by Uruguay in a game they had to win to go through from their group.

Although Aberdeen missed out on winning the Premier League title for a third season in a row, Pittodrie attendances were on the increase. The 54 competitive matches the club played produced an aggregate attendance of 860,000 with an average of 15,925, marginally up from 1984/85's figure of 15,455. There was, however, a fall in league attendances at home with an average of 14,326, compared to 15,877 from the previous season. Billy Stark's goal in the Scottish Cup Final was the Dons' 100th of the season.

Aberdeen's results over the previous two seasons:

	P	*W*	*D*	*L*	*F*	*A*
1984/85	45	31	7	7	107	42
1985/86	54	30	16	8	100	39

The Aberdeen family lost one of their own on 27 May when vice-chairman Chris Anderson OBE passed away. Anderson had been diagnosed with motor neurone disease in 1985. After serving the club as a player he was widely regarded as one of the best administrators in the game, joining the board in 1967 and becoming vice-chairman three years later. He was the driving force behind the continued ground improvements at Pittodrie and was the prime mover in the creation of the new Premier League in Scotland in 1975. After taking early retirement from his position at Robert Gordon University in 1984, his focus turned to running Aberdeen Football Club. His passing was a huge loss to the club and the city.

Alex Ferguson pointing the way at Pittodrie in 1985

Alex Ferguson in his office at Pittodrie in 1985

Mark McGhee in action against Ipswich at Portman Road in the Dons' 1981 UEFA Cup first leg clash

Doug Rougvie with the Scottish Cup at Hampden in 1982 after Aberdeen beat Rangers 4-1

Peter Weir and Mark McGhee celebrate in Gothenburg after Aberdeen had defeated Real Madrid in the European Cup Winners' Cup Final

Alex Ferguson shakes hands with Ernst Happel before the 1983 Super Cup Final at Pittodrie

Willie Miller celebrates scoring the goal against Celtic that clinched the Premier League at Pittodrie in 1985

9 May 1983 – Aberdeen supporters get ready to board the St Clair ferry for Gothenburg

Ullevi scoreboard in Gothenburg on 11 May 1983 Aberdeen v Real Madrid

Premier League flag unfurled at Pittodrie in 1980 before match against Arsenal

Maradona famously took on the Belgian defence – Aberdeen's Gordon Strachan did similar against Vienna in 1980

Aberdeen chairman Dick Donald inspects the South Terrace's new seating in 1981

Alex Ferguson meets the players for his first training session at Seaton Park in July 1978

Alex Ferguson at Pittodrie in 1981

Stuart Kennedy with Burt Lancaster at the Gleneagles Hotel in May 1982. Aberdeen were celebrating their Scottish Cup win, while Lancaster was in Scotland filming Local Hero

Willie Miller and Phil Thompson in 1980 before the Aberdeen v Liverpool European Cup tie at Pittodrie

Pittodrie Stadium 1978, the first major all-seated stadium in Britain

Alex Ferguson in November 1985 with the Premier League and League Cup trophies

Aberdeen FC 1978

Donald, chairman of Aberdeen from 1970 until his death in 1993

Tensions are high on the Aberdeen bench in Gothenburg

Aberdeen FC 1979

Aberdeen FC 1980 Premier League champions

Aberdeen players after learning the Dons had been drawn against Bayern Munich in the ECWC

The Aberdeen squad leave Dyce Airport for Tirana in September 1982

Aberdeen v Hamburg 1981 at Pittodrie in the UEFA Cup third round clash

10

The Farewell

THERE SEEMED little indication when the club travelled to Sweden for their pre-season tour in July 1986 that all was not well at Pittodrie. The World Cup in Mexico ended with disappointment and Alex Ferguson's stint as national team manager came to an end after Scotland's elimination. He had indicated when he was appointed that he would take on the role on a permanent basis but only if he had full control on all team matters from all age groups. That was something the SFA could not accept so they turned to staff coach Andy Roxburgh to replace him.

Ferguson had indicated to chairman Dick Donald before the end of the 1985/86 season that he was looking to move on. One of the main reasons was that he believed he had taken Aberdeen as far as he could, and on reflection it is hard to disagree with that view. The Dons had reached the top in Scotland and Europe, and they had the silverware to prove it.

The close-season also brought the return of Archie Knox as co-manager to Pittodrie. Willie Garner had been in that role for two seasons, but Ferguson was not entirely happy. He felt that Garner was too young and too close to some of the senior players who he had played with during his career. He thought that it was too difficult for him to assert his authority. Garner was asked by Ferguson to meet him at Pittodrie along with his plans for the pre-season. Within minutes Ferguson had told him that Archie Knox was coming back and that there was no longer a role for him at the club. It was a hammer blow for Garner, who looked back on his two years with pride, a period that brought the club more success.

As Knox returned, Neale Cooper was another of the Gothenburg side to move on, declining a new deal and joining Aston Villa. It was another blow for Aberdeen, but like many who have left before and since, moves away from Pittodrie do not always work out. The clubs could not agree a fee and when a tribunal was set to decide the compensation, a figure of £350,000 for Cooper was announced. As news came through that Aberdeen had been paired with Swiss club Sion in the European Cup Winners' Cup, John Hewitt signed a new deal as the club left for their tour of Sweden. Sion were still coached by Jean-Claude Donzé, who did not need reminding of his last clash with the Dons. He told the media, however, that Sion had learned a lot from their Aberdeen experience and were a far better side. With several internationals now in their team, they beat Servette to win the Swiss Cup, opposition Aberdeen had struggled to get the better of in the European Cup.

With around £1m in the bank from the various transfer deals, Ferguson was keen to add to his squad. The Premier League had also changed with 12 teams now in the top tier. With the season now extending to 44 games it was highlighted that the likes of Jim Leighton, Alex McLeish and Willie Miller could play 40 competitive fixtures before the end of the year. Ferguson had capped Dundee midfielder Robert Connor the previous season and after negotiations were completed, Connor joined Aberdeen in a £350,000 deal that included Ian Angus going to Dundee in part-exchange.

Dick Donald had been acutely aware for some months that his manager was considering moving on. Donald also knew that only one or two clubs would be able to tempt Ferguson away from Pittodrie, so he was keen to ensure that he would find it difficult to leave. That was made more complicated when Ferguson was made a director of the club, joining Donald and his son Ian. The three-man board, with all having been players in their day, continued with the Ferguson appointment. Ferguson was delighted, 'The Dons are my life now and I welcome the opportunity to assist in any way I can. My appointment maintains the tradition of all of the board having a football background.'

In the League Cup, the Dons were eliminated before they kicked a ball in anger in Europe. After comfortable home wins over Alloa and Clyde, they went out against Celtic in the quarter-final, on penalties after a 1-1 draw. There were more penalty woes for captain Willie Miller, who missed, along with John Hewitt. To compound this defeat the injuries were mounting up. Frank McDougall and Neil Simpson had been out for weeks and they were joined by Alex McLeish, Peter Weir, Jim Bett and Stewart McKimmie on the treatment table. It was hardly the ideal preparation for the visit of Sion in the Cup Winners' Cup. The amount of games being played was contributing to the growing injury list. By the end of September, eight weeks into the season, the Dons had played 14 times.

As predicted, Sion presented a far tougher task than their team of 1982, who were humbled 7-0 at Pittodrie. They arrived well clear at the top of their league and also had five Swiss internationals in their squad along with Moroccan World Cup star Aziz Bouderbala. Aberdeen had to battle back from going behind to turn things around with two late goals from Hewitt and young striker Paul Wright giving a narrow lead to take to Switzerland. With Frank McDougall looking to be out for a prolonged period, the Dons signed former Dundee United forward Davie Dodds. It was not a transfer that caught the supporters' imagination. Dodds had been an adversary for several seasons, was not regarded as a prolific scorer and was very different in style from McDougall. A fee of £215,000 was agreed with Swiss side Neuchâtel Xamax to take Dodds to Pittodrie.

The return in Sion was a night to forget. After losing an early goal, the Dons squandered several chances and eventually went down 3-0 to exit Europe at the first-round stage. Jim Bett was also sent off in a game that was in stark contrast to the Dons' last visit in 1982. Sion had attracted new finance and had evolved into a very useful outfit. Painful as it was for Aberdeen, they were not as strong as the side that conquered Europe in 1983, and their Swiss experience was a reality check for Ferguson: 'We missed chances that should have been put away. We had about half a dozen opportunities when we could have scored but failed. You can't afford that in European competition.'

With Aberdeen out of Europe and the League Cup, they had also slipped from grace in the Premier League. The signing of Dodds looked desperate, although Robert Connor was settling into the midfield and looked impressive. Bryan Gunn completed his delayed transfer to Norwich City in a £100,000 deal. The Gothenburg side was gradually breaking up and the task of rebuilding a second great Aberdeen team was proving to be a formidable, if impossible, task.

Premier League table at 6 November 1986

	P	*W*	*D*	*L*	*F*	*A*	*Pts*
Celtic	15	11	3	1	36	8	25
Dundee United	16	10	5	1	30	11	25
Rangers	15	9	3	3	26	10	21
Hearts	16	7	6	3	19	12	20
Aberdeen	**15**	**7**	**5**	**3**	**25**	**14**	**19**

Perhaps the most telling indicator of the impact made when Alex Ferguson left Pittodrie on 6 November 1986 was the frenzied reaction from opposition supporters and media. The Scottish tabloids, almost triumphantly, were not slow to suggest that Aberdeen would never be as strong again.

In Aberdeen there was an understanding that sooner or later Ferguson would move on. What most fans held on to was the fact that Ferguson had turned down plenty of opportunities to leave the Dons before he joined Manchester United. His boyhood club Rangers tried on two occasions to prise him away from Pittodrie. The Ibrox club had plenty of previous when it came to weakening opponents by buying their best players and managers. When it came to Ferguson they failed. Twice. They were savaged by their own support over their handling of their bids. For Rangers it was uncharted territory to be rebuked by 'one of their own' in such a dismissive manner. Although there were other reasons why Fergie turned down his old club, everyone at Aberdeen was delighted that he committed himself to the Dons for so long, particularly with him becoming a director.

A direct comparison was his predecessor Billy McNeill, who answered the call from his old club Celtic to leave the Dons after only one season in charge. Although Ferguson had not enjoyed such a productive spell at Rangers as McNeill had at Celtic, it was still a coup for Aberdeen that they held on to their manager to see the job through. However, there were compelling reasons why Ferguson shunned the Ibrox club. His period at Rangers was littered with controversy and personal circumstances that should be nowhere near any football club. The Rangers 'tradition' of being a staunch Protestant club had a profound effect on Ferguson, whose wife Cathy was Catholic. Even on the day he signed for Rangers as a player he had doubts after being quizzed on where he got married. His response when he declared his vows were taken in a registry office seemed to appease the Ibrox club but in hindsight it set off alarm bells in his own mind. The doubts and innuendo over his personal life were something that Ferguson despised, and it was never forgotten when Rangers came in for him for the second time in 1984. As Aberdeen were enjoying a hugely successful period, at Ibrox it was very different. Ferguson sought out advice from Scott Symon, an ex-Rangers manager who had the utmost respect from the Aberdeen boss. There was also the issue of Cathy's religion and that was enough for Ferguson to flatly turn down any approach.

Daily Record
SPORTSFRONT
Dramatic swoop on Dons pair
UNITED GRAB FERGIE
ARCHIE KNOX
MANCHESTER UNITED sensationally swooped last night on Aberdeen's winning team of Alex Ferguson and Archie Knox.
By ALEX CAMERON
CHOP YOUR BILLS DOWN TO SIZE
Loans from £1000 to £50000
A MAN BORN TO WIN
10-1 Garry double
Champion Finance
EDITED, PRINTED AND PUBLISHED IN SCOTLAND

Ferguson also turned down offers from Arsenal, Tottenham Hotspur and Wolverhampton Wanderers during his Pittodrie tenure. Ferguson always indicated that there were only three clubs in football that would tempt him away from Pittodrie. Unfortunately for the Dons, one of them, Manchester United, were struggling and sitting second from bottom in the old English First Division.

United had of course proud traditions that has made them one of the most formidable and greatest clubs in world football. Their back story from the solemn days of the Munich air disaster in 1958 to becoming the first English side to win the European Cup in 1968 remains a legacy. Six years after being crowned European champions, however, they were relegated. In the penultimate game of the 1973/74 season an audacious back-heel from Aberdeen-born Denis Law, then of Manchester City, condemned United to a first relegation since 1938, albeit followed by an immediate promotion. The Old Trafford club had regressed and by 1986 under Ron Atkinson there were genuine fears of another relegation battle. On reflection, Ferguson was the ideal manager for the Red Devils. Under the right leadership United's potential was unlimited. They were the perfect fit for Ferguson at the right stage of his managerial career.

Dick Donald, who had become like a father figure to Ferguson at Pittodrie, always told his manager that he would not stand in his way if a new challenge came up. Donald had been a player with the club in the 1920s and went on to become a successful businessman in Aberdeen before becoming a director in 1949. His relationship with Ferguson was a crucial factor in the Aberdeen success story.

In retrospect, Ferguson moving to Old Trafford was a huge compliment to Aberdeen. With other clubs having more stature and resources, the fact that Aberdeen and Ferguson resisted those overtures was a great credit. However, Ferguson did later reflect on his desire to take on a new challenge after being frustrated at some of the support his team was getting. He was disappointed that the 1986 European Cup quarter-final against IFK Gothenburg did not sell out. He suspected that his side had become so successful that apathy had crept into the support. As a relatively young manager with a burning desire to succeed he was always looking to progress. Had he taken Aberdeen as far as he could? There certainly were some rumblings from within, well before Ferguson did agree to join Manchester United. He had taken enormous pride in making Pittodrie a place to fear. He was never against stretching the rules to gain any slight advantage. He craved a partisan support. His ill-fated 'sweetie paper' reference, made after a subdued Pittodrie crowd was not as vociferous as he had hoped, was manipulated by those who opposed him and the club. The inference was that on occasion you hear fans unwrapping their sweets, it was so quiet. For some of the more observant, the counter-argument to that was the claim that Aberdeen fans were among the most knowledgeable in football. There was certainly some merit in that. For many years it had been widely accepted that Dons supporters knew the game inside out and on rare occasions were quietly appreciative of good football from opponents.

The feelings towards Aberdeen at that time from opponents and media alike can never be underestimated. The Scottish media has for generations shown a heavy Glasgow bias. Ferguson was acutely aware of this and would use that favouritism to his advantage. The 'siege mentality' that he had instilled in his players and staff was legendary. Ferguson had no equal when it came to upsetting those who opposed him. Pittodrie, for him, was a vital part of his armoury. He wanted opponents to be fearful when they would travel to Aberdeen. For context, the late former Rangers defender Sandy Jardine told the author of this book some years ago, 'We hated going to Aberdeen as we always knew we were up against it. We tried everything. Sometimes we would travel up the day before and stay in a hotel outside of the city. On other occasions we would be on the coach on the day of the game. I recall one occasion we stopped off at Aberdeen beach and went for a brisk walk. It was not uncommon for some of our players to vomit before these games. Pittodrie back then was the toughest venue we could go to, without question.'

The problem Ferguson had was not so much the games against the Glasgow clubs and near rivals Dundee United. They did not need any motivation for the fans. Any clash with Celtic or Rangers was always keenly anticipated, even long before the Dons' success of the '80s. The animosity between Aberdeen and the Glasgow clubs was nothing new. On the back of Aberdeen's success and dominance over that period, the relations between the clubs and supporters just reached new heights of hatred, almost tribal.

Even the rivalry that exists today between Aberdeen, Hearts and Hibernian was not apparent in the '80s. With both Edinburgh clubs struggling to challenge at any stage and suffering frequent relegations, they were never seen as credible challengers to Aberdeen during that period. Hearts under their chairman Wallace Mercer often made outrageous claims of grandeur, despite suffering demotions in 1979 and 1981. For a club with a rich history they had not won a major trophy since 1962 and that woeful record continued through the '80s. Such delusions angered their core support while opponents would derive pleasure from their plight.

Perhaps it is the perceived underdog tag and provincial status that has been part of the club for generations. Any opportunity to get one over the Glasgow clubs was relished. Ferguson was fully appreciative of how the club and fans approached these games. It was perhaps against lesser opposition that he wanted more from the support. That became more difficult after several years of unprecedented success. There was an almost apathetic approach on occasion and that clearly riled Ferguson. The supporters had been spoiled and that was something he had a real issue with.

Back in October 1980 when Aberdeen were on top of the league, on the back of a 23-game unbeaten run and about to face Liverpool in the European Cup, Ferguson was disappointed at the lack of support, 'As it continues to happen all around us, and Aberdeen command a prominent involvement in all three senior competitions, I just wonder how much more the club must achieve to win the confidence of more supporters. The true Aberdeen supporters have been with us all season and they are a credit to the club. Yet there are far more who follow the team but only voice their opinions on what they hear or see on TV. Right now, Aberdeen is the first name in Scottish football. I say that as the proud manager of the Premier League title holders, and no team can do better. No side has had a more demanding couple of months and no side has matched what we have achieved at Aberdeen. Yet, apart from the games against Celtic and Rangers, our attendances have been disappointing. I believe that the efforts of this club deserve to be better rewarded through the turnstiles.'

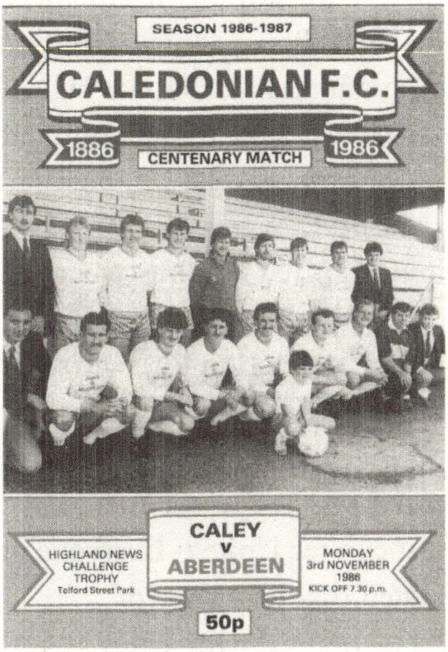

On reflection, it was always likely that Ferguson would move on, even after such a successful period. Aberdeen were a great fit for him and the club at that stage of his career was ideal for a manager keen to establish himself in the game.

The rumours of Ferguson being targeted by clubs in England began in earnest in March 1986 when Arsenal dismissed Don Howe and spoke with him about taking over at Highbury. Those informal talks didn't go that well as Ferguson left the meeting confused as the Arsenal delegation believed he was set on joining Manchester United, which was news to him. With Ferguson manager of Aberdeen and the Scotland national side at the 1986 World Cup, his stock had never been higher so it was inevitable he would attract English attention, but interest was not only coming from down south. When the Scotland team was in Australia for a World Cup qualifying tie, he was approached by an agent representing Inter Milan. In 1985 Terry Venables was the manager of Barcelona at that time and indicated he was stepping down so advised the Catalan club that Alex Ferguson would be the ideal replacement. Talks were held in London with Ferguson, Barcelona president Josep Lluís Núñez and three directors as well as England manager Bobby Robson. Talks were harmonious but the Spanish club never made an offer.

It was at nearby Seaton Park that Ferguson held his final session with Aberdeen on 5 November 1986. Brian Irvine, at the time a young centre-half, recalled that fateful day: 'We were training in the afternoon. I was with the younger players and reserves; Archie Knox was there as well. Secretary Ian Taggart appeared and took the manager away in the back of his car back to Pittodrie. That was it. He was gone. That was the last we saw of Sir Alex in a working capacity with the club. The news then quickly broke that he was going to Manchester United, and it was a shock. He signed me, he was the man I looked up to, so it was a big disappointment for me. I was a young boy and in awe of him.' Ferguson took a call from Manchester United chairman Martin Edwards that afternoon before arranging to meet in Hamilton later that evening, where an agreement was made.

Willie Miller declared, 'The first reaction of course is disappointment that we are losing Alex Ferguson but looking at it from the manager's point of view, it is a step forward for him. It was probably a challenge he could not turn down. It was not unexpected that he would be approached by Manchester United. Everyone at Pittodrie, however, will be disappointed that he accepted.'

Ferguson would be joined by his assistant Archie Knox at Old Trafford after Knox turned down a lucrative offer to take over at Pittodrie. The double departure was described by Dick Donald as a 'shattering blow': 'We have tried everything in our power to keep Mr Ferguson at Pittodrie but the lure of Old Trafford and the chance to manage the biggest club in England has proved too great. Manchester United have agreed to compensate us for the unfulfilled portion of Mr Ferguson's contract, but how can you evaluate the loss of his services?' Aberdeen were to be compensated £60,000 for losing their manager.

Confirming that he had agreed to accept the role at Old Trafford, Ferguson declared, 'Manchester United is the only club in the world I would have left Aberdeen for. After eight years working with Dick Donald and everyone else at Pittodrie, I cannot begin to express the sadness I feel at having to end what for me has been an unforgettable experience. The Old Trafford job, however, was something I could not turn down.' Ferguson's departure was immediate, so much so that no financial package had been agreed, 'I can't see there being any problems as money has not been spoken about yet. It was simply that United were the only club capable of drawing me away from Pittodrie.'

If ever there was any doubt as to why Ferguson opted to join Manchester United it was not for financial gain. Hard to believe as it was, his offer from United was less than what he made at Pittodrie in salary and bonuses in 1986.

Ferguson would travel to Manchester that day and be in the dugout for the Red Devils' game at Oxford United, before returning to Aberdeen to clear up his affairs. On what was a dramatic day in Aberdeen and Manchester, it all began when United announced that manager Ron Atkinson had been sacked, then chairman Martin Edwards and director Maurice Wilkins were on a flight to Aberdeen to meet with the Dons' directors.

Ferguson saw his new side being humbled 2-0 at Oxford before returning to Aberdeen on the Monday to say his final farewell to the players, staff and supporters, and he spoke to the *Press & Journal*: 'I would like to express my deepest gratitude to all the fans for all they have done for the club and myself during my time as manager and would urge them to support my successor. Aberdeen have made Alex Ferguson and the Dons supporters have contributed so much to that platform for any success we have enjoyed. It is never easy to leave a club, particularly one to which you have become deeply attached.'

As Ferguson watched his new side go down, the Dons struggled to a goalless draw with St Mirren at Pittodrie. Emotions were understandably raw, and the club were disappointed that Archie Knox received a poor welcome as he took temporary charge of the Dons before his move to Manchester. Ferguson was disappointed but understood, 'I would have hoped the supporters, although they were hurting, would have understood Archie's position. Archie has worked as hard as anyone for the good of the club in his two spells at Pittodrie, but like me he has his own ambitions. From my point of view, it is natural that I should want someone I trust and can work with me at Old Trafford.'

Knox had no issues about the pre-match reception, 'While it was not something that I enjoyed, I understand and accept the supporters venting their frustration. It was a very tough decision for me to make, whether to stay at Pittodrie or move to Old Trafford.'

When things calmed down it was a time for reflection. The argument that Ferguson had taken Aberdeen as far as he could was a valid one. The game in Scotland was changing with more emphasis being placed on financial clout. While Aberdeen could compete favourably in terms of attendances and transfer fees with the bigger Glasgow clubs, by the mid-'80s that was changing as Rangers, hurting after years of mediocrity, embarked on a spending frenzy that was to change the Scottish game. Could Aberdeen still compete?

On attracting more support, that was always a non-starter. Despite the club looking at increasing the capacity of Pittodrie to 30,000, there was no real prospect that an Aberdeen side, however successful, would attract such large crowds on a regular basis. With television money back then virtually non-existent, the only other revenue stream was sponsorship. With the Aberdeen area enjoying the riches of North Sea oil, those resources never did stretch to the football club. Back then Shell and BP were the big oil companies based in the city. Neither sponsored the club in any substantial way although the Dons certainly knocked on their doors several times. Aberdeen did not agree a shirt sponsor until JVC became the first company to take that position in 1988.

It soon became clear that Celtic and Rangers were now investing heavily in stadia and playing squads, and attracting huge sponsorship. With Rangers spending big on attracting England internationals to Ibrox, Aberdeen simply could not compete on that scale. Gradually, on the back of improving television and sponsorship money, the major clubs across the top European leagues would prosper. With freedom of contract also coming into force, for clubs like Aberdeen it was a perfect storm.

In terms of a replacement for Alex Ferguson the club eventually appointed Ian Porterfield, a Scottish-born manager who was best known for his winning goal for Sunderland in the 1973 FA Cup Final. Porterfield did not know the Scottish game and his personality was in stark contrast to Ferguson; after 18 months he left for personal reasons. Following Ferguson was an impossible task. Even Manchester United have struggled to come to terms following Ferguson's retirement in 2013.

By the time Aberdeen celebrated their centenary in 2003, 20 years on from being the number one-ranked team in Europe, their stock had fallen to a lowly 156 with Real Madrid, Barcelona and, ironically, Manchester United occupying the top three places.

11

Pittodrie People 1978–1986

Aberdeen FC directors:

Dick Donald

Best known for his period as chairman, Richard 'Dick' Donald also played for Aberdeen. Signed as a professional in 1928, he had two spells at Pittodrie, interrupted by a season with Dunfermline in 1933. His playing career ended with the outbreak of hostilities in Europe in 1939. Donald made 16 appearances for the Dons.

In 1949 Donald was appointed as a director, serving the club until his death in 1993. After becoming vice-chairman in 1960 he became chairman in 1970. In August 1993 the completion of the new stand at the Beach End of Pittodrie was opened and named after him. The Richard Donald Stand was officially opened by Princess Anne in a private ceremony. Donald was also among the original inductees to the club's Hall of Fame in 2003. During his 23 years as chairman, the Dons won 14 major trophies. Alex Ferguson looked upon Donald as one of the best, 'As a chairman, he was a colossus, and nobody had to tell me that I had little chance of ever working for his like again.'

Chris Anderson

Another former Aberdeen player who went on to serve the club with distinction on the board. Anderson joined Aberdeen in 1943 after playing for Scotland Schoolboys and had attracted attention from Rangers. Anderson chose his local team. After the war it was not until 1948 that Anderson made his debut. The highlight of his career came in a Scottish Cup win over Celtic at Parkhead in 1950. Aberdeen won 1-0, their first Scottish Cup win at Parkhead, and Anderson scored the winning goal. Injury curtailed his senior career and he ended his playing days with Arbroath, where he went on to coach after giving up playing in 1956.

Chris was appointed a director in 1967 and was made vice-chairman three years later. His period at Aberdeen was hugely successful with Anderson behind the improvements to Pittodrie Stadium and he was also an advocate of the creation of the Premier League in 1975.

His tragic passing in May 1986 was a huge blow to the club and the Dons family. The stadium at Linksfield was later developed and named the Chris Anderson Stadium, just a few hundred yards from Pittodrie.

Charles Forbes

Just weeks before the club posted their record 13-0 victory over Peterhead in the Scottish Cup, Charles Forbes signed for Aberdeen and made his first appearance in a District League game at Buckie. Forbes went on to win a Highland League medal with Aberdeen 'A' in 1924 and made six appearances for the first team in his four years at Pittodrie. After his career finished, he went into teaching in the city. In 1936 Forbes returned to the club as a director and served until his death in April 1980. Forbes was chairman from 1958 until June 1970.

Ian Donald

Son of Richard Donald, Ian began his career by signing for Manchester United as a 16-year-old in 1968. After making his debut in October 1970, it was another two years before he played again. After Frank O'Farrell was dismissed, Tommy Docherty took over and Donald was out of favour. He joined Partick Thistle in January 1973.

In 1980 Donald was appointed as a director at Pittodrie. Six years later he was vice-chairman after the passing of Chris Anderson. Donald took over as chairman in early 1994. After a difficult spell with Aberdeen falling from grace, he remained on the board until 2004 and was then appointed as the Dons' honorary president.

The background team:

Pat Stanton

Alex Ferguson's first assistant manager at Pittodrie. Stanton enjoyed a playing career with Hibernian and Celtic, his only two senior clubs, who played in his testimonial in April 1978. After his playing career finished his first coaching role was at Pittodrie under Ferguson. Stanton was with the Dons when Aberdeen clinched the Premier League title in 1980, at Easter Road where he had enjoyed his best days as a player. After short spells with Cowdenbeath and Dunfermline, Stanton returned to Hibernian in 1982 as manager.

Archie Knox

The most trusted and longest-serving assistant manager under Alex Ferguson during his spell at Pittodrie. Knox had been with Forfar Athletic when Ferguson appointed him in 1980. It was Knox who was entrusted on many occasions to look at the Dons' European opponents. He proved to be a perfect foil for Ferguson and as a duo they were respected and feared, certainly by some of the younger players. After a spell as manager of Dundee, Knox returned to Pittodrie as co-manager in 1986. Knox has the rare distinction of being appointed as Aberdeen assistant manager on three occasions, as he returned in December 2010 with new manager Craig Brown following their move from Motherwell. Knox was inducted into the Aberdeen FC Hall of Fame in 2017.

Willie Garner

Joined Aberdeen in 1975 and was in the side that won the League Cup in 1976. Garner eventually lost his place with the emergence of Alex McLeish. In 1981 he joined Celtic in a £35,000 deal but his career at Parkhead was a short one with only one appearance. In 1982 Garner joined Alloa Athletic as player-manager, where he cut his teeth in coaching. After Archie Knox left Pittodrie at the end of 1983, Garner was appointed as assistant manager to Alex Ferguson in February 1984. His two years brought five major honours but he was let go by Ferguson when Knox intimated that he was keen to return. After retiring in 1992 Garner was involved in coaching in Scottish Junior football. He is currently back at Pittodrie as a non-executive director.

Teddy Scott

'Mr Aberdeen', as he was fondly known by many. Teddy Scott was in the Aberdeen Junior side Sunnybank that won the Scottish

Junior Cup in 1954, the first city club to win it. He was signed by Aberdeen that year but never managed to oust the established Alec Young at centre-half.

It was during the latter part of season 1956/57 that Teddy was loaned to Brechin City and following a free transfer from the club he moved to Elgin City in the Highland League. After one season at

Borough Briggs, Teddy returned to Pittodrie to take up a training role under manager Dave Shaw. That situation altered somewhat when Tommy Pearson took over as manager and Shaw reverted to his previous position as trainer. That left Scott in sole charge of the reserve team and there began an incredible association with the club. In his time Teddy had various titles: trainer, kit man, reserve team coach and physio. For many years Teddy coached and nurtured the young Dons players, always keen to offer a word in their ear. The testimonies that came flooding in after he announced his retirement in 2003 gave some indication of just how much value they had placed on his contribution.

Alex Ferguson remained one of his close friends and could not have paid a higher tribute by taking his full Manchester United side up to play Aberdeen in Teddy's testimonial in January 1999.

David Wylie

After Aberdeen had won the European Cup Winners' Cup in Gothenburg, physio Roland Arnott left in the summer. Aberdeen appointed David Wylie, who had been physio with Motherwell for four years, beginning an association with Aberdeen that lasted for more than 30 years. Wylie may have missed Gothenburg but was around to look after the players who won the European Super Cup and several domestic accolades. Wylie joined Aberdeen when Alex Ferguson, Archie Knox and Teddy Scott made up the entire backroom staff. By the time he retired the game had changed beyond recognition with several physios, sport scientists and video analysts all involved with the players.

Brian Scott

The physio joined Aberdeen in a full-time position after leaving his part-time role at Falkirk in 1977. He enjoyed a full season with the Dons under Billy McNeill before the manager left to return to former club Celtic. Scott served under Alex Ferguson in his first year at Pittodrie. McNeill persuaded Scott to join him at Parkhead in the summer of 1979, where he remained in various roles for 24 years.

Len Taylor

Local schoolteacher Len Taylor had been a scout and coach for Aberdeen for several years, helping to bring through the younger players at Pittodrie. He was highly respected by Alex Ferguson with his attention to detail and his handling of young players. Taylor helped develop the youth system along with Ferguson that brought so many players through the ranks. After leaving to concentrate on teaching, Taylor returned to Pittodrie in 2006, where he remained in a coaching capacity until retiring in 2011.

Roland Arnott

Arnott took over as Aberdeen physio in 1979 after Brian Scott moved to Celtic. Arnott was a surprise applicant for the position, and he had the distinction of looking after the players through their glory period up to and including the European Cup Winners' Cup win in Sweden. Arnott, like the others, leapt from the bench at full time to join in the celebrations. During his four-year spell at Pittodrie, Arnott was vital when it came to tend to the players' wellbeing in the closing weeks of the 1982/83 season when the fixtures were piling up. In the summer of 1983 he left to take up a similar role looking after some of the best tennis players at Wimbledon.

12
Transfers

Players in:

Alex Ferguson only signed 16 players during his eight and a half seasons at Pittodrie. Two of them, Doug Bell and Steve Cowan, were free transfers from his previous club St Mirren. The transfer of Peter Weir in 1981 was at the time a record between two Scottish clubs. During those eight seasons, Aberdeen paid an estimated £1.5m in transfer fees for 13 players. Four of them – Jim Bett, Bobby Connor, Davie Dodds and Peter Weir – were already Scotland internationals, while three went on to play for Scotland when they were at Pittodrie – Brian Irvine, Mark McGhee and Stewart McKimmie.

Bett (Lokeren), Dodds (Neuchâtel Xamax) and Marc De Clerck (Go Ahead Eagles) were transferred in from European clubs; Mark McGhee (Newcastle United) and Andy Harrow (Luton Town) signed from English clubs; Walker McCall (Atlanta Chiefs) was the only player to join from outside Europe.

Doug Bell (St Mirren), Bobby Connor (Dundee), Steve Cowan (St Mirren), Brian Grant (Stirling Albion), Brian Irvine (Falkirk), Frank McDougall (Clydebank), Stewart McKimmie (Dundee), Tom McQueen (Clyde), Billy Stark (St Mirren) and Peter Weir (St Mirren) were the players to join from Scottish clubs. Bell and Cowan were free transfers.

Arriving after 1978 and then departing before 1986 were Bell, De Clerck, Cowan, Harrow, McCall, McGhee and McQueen.

Doug Bell

Arguably the best piece of business Alex Ferguson completed during his Pittodrie tenure, Bell was released by St Mirren on a free transfer

in 1979. He joined Aberdeen just at the right time as he went on to play his part in the success story. It was in European ties that the midfielder excelled, his close control and natural ability to unlock the tightest of defences often being used to great effect by Ferguson. After coming on as a substitute in the 1982 Scottish Cup Final as Aberdeen were demolishing Rangers, Bell was injured against Celtic in the semi-final in 1983. His ankle problem meant he would miss out on the European Cup Winners' Cup Final in Gothenburg and the Scottish Cup Final win over Rangers ten days later. However, Bell was inspired later that year as he played against Hamburg when Aberdeen won the Super Cup.

Jim Bett

Airdrie-born Bett had been in the Rangers side that lost to Aberdeen in the 1983 Scottish Cup Final before he moved to Lokeren after being a standout in what was an average Ibrox team. Ferguson was keen to bring the international midfielder back to Scotland after an impressive spell in Belgium. Aberdeen paid Lokeren £300,000 for his services on 26 June 1985. Guy Thys, the Belgian international manager at the time, declared that had Bett been Belgium-born he would have been a certainty for his World Cup squad. Bett went on to gain 26 caps for Scotland; he was disappointed to be in the 1986 World Cup squad under Ferguson and not have any game time, the only player not to get on the pitch. Bett, however, was an integral part of the Aberdeen side that won Scottish Cup and League Cup doubles in 1985/86 and 1989/90. He left Aberdeen in 1994 and returned to Iceland, where he had previously enjoyed a short spell with Valur before joining Lokeren for his first spell there in 1978. His two sons, Baldaur and Calum, were both professional players. His one goal for Scotland was a vital winning penalty against Iceland in Reykjavík in 1985.

Bobby Connor

One of Alex Ferguson's last signings before he left Pittodrie, Connor began with Ayr United in 1977 before signing for Dundee in a £50,000 deal in 1984. His move to Dens Park brought him full international recognition, capped by Ferguson when he oversaw the national team. His move to Aberdeen came at a time of change at Pittodrie. Within three months Ferguson had departed and the Dons were under new management with Ian Porterfield. Connor went on to establish a great partnership with Jim Bett in the midfield that won a domestic cup double in 1989/90. Further international recognition and several appearances in Europe followed and after eight years at Aberdeen, he was released after recovering from a long-term Achilles injury. Connor went on to join Kilmarnock in 1994 and finished his playing career with Partick and Queen of the South.

Marc De Clerck

With experienced keeper Bobby Clark still a long-term injury concern, Belgian De Clerck was brought in as cover for Jim Leighton in 1980 after signing from Go Ahead Eagles. His transfer was never going to be for the long term and during his brief spell at Pittodrie he made an impact by scoring direct from a clearance in a League Cup tie against Berwick.

Steve Cowan

Joined Aberdeen from St Mirren on a free transfer on 28 December 1979. One of the most versatile players in the squad, Cowan played in several positions, even filling in as the goalkeeper in a reserve match. Had the distinction of scoring a spectacular winning goal for Aberdeen in the 1980 Drybrough Cup Final against his old club. Cowan was never a regular in what was a strong front line, but he made enough appearances to gain a Premier League medal in season 1984/85.

Davie Dodds

An adversary of the Dons with his time at Dundee United, Davie Dodds enjoyed his best days at Tannadice before a surprise move to Switzerland. Dodds was Alex Ferguson's last major signing in September 1986 when he joined from Neuchâtel Xamax. Aberdeen had to fend off interest from Rangers to secure his signature. Dodds only played seven games under Ferguson and his spell at Pittodrie was underwhelming although he became a regular in the side under Ian Porterfield. Dodds eventually joined Rangers in 1989 and missed out on Aberdeen winning a domestic cup double.

Brian Grant

Alex Ferguson had learned to build for the future by totally revamping the scouting network at Pittodrie. Recognising the best young players in Scotland was crucial. Brian Grant was one of the most sought-after youngsters with several clubs looking to sign him, including Manchester City, Arsenal and Celtic. It was Aberdeen who secured his signature in a £50,000 transfer in 1984. His first-team debut was one to forget, a surprise defeat at Airdrie in the League Cup. Signed as one for the future, Grant went on to establish himself in the Aberdeen side long after Ferguson had departed. He was part of the double cup-winning side of 1989/90 and in 1996 he was awarded a testimonial by the club when Everton visited Pittodrie before the start of the season. Grant later joined Hibernian in a £75,000 deal and ended his career with Dundee and Stirling Albion.

Andy Harrow

By his own admission, Alex Ferguson's efforts to replace Steve Archibald were in vain. Andy Harrow had been a prolific, emerging forward with Raith Rovers which brought a move to Luton Town.

Harrow joined Aberdeen in a £65,000 transfer in 1981 after only making four appearances for the English side. His debut came at Cappielow in a 1-0 Scottish Cup defeat against Morton. With Mark McGhee established in the side and the emergence of Eric Black, Harrow's first-team appearances were rare.

Brian Irvine

Joined his boyhood team Aberdeen from Falkirk in 1985 in a £50,000 deal. Another young defender who had to bide his time before making an impact in the first team, Irvine was content as a young, up-and-coming centre-half to learn his trade under Alex Ferguson and the two best central defenders in the country in Alex McLeish and Willie Miller. His first-team debut came against Clydebank in May 1986, a week before the Scottish Cup Final. Four years later, after Irvine had been in the side after a long-term injury to Willie Miller, his most famous moment in the red of Aberdeen came in the 1990 Scottish Cup Final. A 0-0 draw saw the Dons go into a first Scottish Cup Final penalty shoot-out and Irvine scored the decisive kick to take the cup north. Irvine went on to earn nine Scotland caps and was awarded a testimonial by the club in 1997 before he signed for Dundee.

Walker McCall

With Andy Harrow struggling to find his scoring touch in 1980 the Dons were looking to strengthen their attacking options. Walker McCall had been with the club previously, scouted by Bobby Calder in 1970 and signed from Hurlford United. It was in 1980 after a spell in the USA that McCall was looking to keep fit and asked to train with the players.

Ferguson offered McCall a short-term deal that lasted for three years as he became a part of the first-team squad.

Frank McDougall

The transfer of Mark McGhee to old European rivals Hamburg after the 1984 Scottish Cup Final paved the way for Aberdeen to once again plunder St Mirren and sign striker Frank McDougall. The £100,000 deal proved to be a bargain as McDougall ended his first season as top scorer in the Premier League with 22 goals and the Dons won the title. During his spell at Pittodrie, McDougall gained hero status after his scoring exploits that included a hat-trick against Rangers and a record-breaking four-goal haul against Celtic. In his two full seasons at Pittodrie he ended as the club's top scorer and completed a clean sweep of domestic winners' medals. A persistent back injury effectively ended his career at the age of 28.

Mark McGhee

The former Morton forward was Alex Ferguson's first major signing when Aberdeen paid Newcastle United £70,000 for him in April 1979. After taking several months to settle, McGhee began to show his value in the side that won the Premier League in 1980. His unorthodox style made him a formidable striker, often excelling in the European games. His hat-trick against Újpesti Dózsa in 1984 took Aberdeen into the semi-finals of the European Cup Winners' Cup. McGhee scored many vital goals, including putting the Dons ahead in the 1982 Scottish Cup Final against Rangers and the winner against Celtic in 1984, his last act for the club.

Stewart McKimmie

Aberdeen-born defender McKimmie was signed in December 1983 and was the natural replacement for Stuart Kennedy. Aberdeen paid £90,000 to Dundee and McKimmie made his debut against Hibernian at Pittodrie on 17 December 1983. Three days later he was in the team that won the European Super Cup against Hamburg. It began the highly successful post-Gothenburg period as McKimmie added to his medal collection with Aberdeen dominating Scottish football. It was not until 1989 that he earned the first of 40 Scotland caps. He also had the distinction of scoring the winning goal against World Cup holders Argentina at Hampden. In 1995, after Aberdeen had struggled in the Premier League, McKimmie captained the team to the League Cup against his former club Dundee in the Hampden final. In 1994 McKimmie was awarded a testimonial by the club as Blackburn Rovers visited Pittodrie to honour the Dons' most-capped full-back.

Tom McQueen

With Doug Rougvie failing to agree terms after his contract ended in the summer of 1984, the Dons signed McQueen from Clyde as a direct replacement, to the disappointment of Hibernian, who had agreed a fee with Clyde for the 21-year-old left-back. McQueen became a regular in the side that strolled to the Premier League title in 1985. He was also a Scottish Cup winner the following season. McQueen took over from Gordon Strachan as the preferred penalty taker. In the early part of the 1986/87 season McQueen was facing competition for a starting place with Brian Mitchell. McQueen then suffered a leg break that kept him out of action for three months. By the time he returned it was all changed with Alex Ferguson gone and his own place being taken by David Robertson. In March 1987 he was sold to West Ham United in a £125,000 deal.

Billy Stark

After Gordon Strachan had informed Alex Ferguson that he would be leaving Pittodrie when his contract expired in 1984, the Dons moved quickly by signing Billy Stark from St Mirren in a £100,000 deal in the summer of 1983. Midfielder Stark proved to be an inspired signing, on occasion never fully appreciated by sections of the Aberdeen support. One of the strange anomalies of the time was that Stark was never recognised at international level. Having been overlooked for the under-21 side, following his form with Aberdeen and a succession of winners' medals, it was a surprise to many that he was never capped for his country. After scoring in both domestic cup finals in 1985/86, Stark left Aberdeen to join rivals Celtic in a £75,000 deal in 1987.

Jim Bett and Peter Weir

Peter Weir

At the time the transfer of Weir from St Mirren to Aberdeen was a record deal between two Scottish clubs. Aberdeen paid £330,000 with Ian Scanlon going the other way in part exchange. Alex Ferguson described the signing of Weir as 'the final piece in the Aberdeen jigsaw'. Weir grew up in the west of Scotland as an Aberdeen supporter following the stunning Scottish Cup win in 1970. Described by many as the best two-footed player in the country, the Scotland international was a vital part of the team that was so successful in the '80s. Weir's finest hour was his display against Ipswich in the 1981 UEFA Cup tie. His two second-half goals and his tormenting of England captain Mick Mills remains one of the iconic moments in Aberdeen's history. Weir was also at the start of the move that ended with John Hewitt scoring the winner against Real Madrid in the 1983 European Cup Winners' Cup Final.

Players out (34):

Ian Angus

One of the Aberdeen substitutes in Gothenburg, Angus never managed to cement a regular place in the first team. His most productive season was in 1984/85 when he made 21 starts in the Dons' successful defence of their Premier League crown. Angus went on to make 105 appearances for the first team after making his debut against Morton in 1980. It can be argued that had he played for the club in any other era he would have been a mainstay in most Aberdeen teams through the years. He scored 12 goals, one of which came in the ill-fated European Cup tie against Dynamo Berlin in 1984. The Glaswegian was also involved in one of the last deals that Alex Ferguson completed for Aberdeen; in 1986 he moved to Dundee as Bobby Connor joined Aberdeen as part of the transfer. In 1990, after Dundee were relegated, Angus joined Motherwell in a £40,000 deal. A year later he scored for the Steelmen in their sensational 4-3 win over Dundee United in the Scottish Cup Final. He later played for Clyde and Albion Rovers.

Steve Archibald

Losing Archibald to Tottenham after the Premier League win in 1980 was on reflection a hammer blow for Ferguson and Aberdeen. Ferguson declared that he never successfully replaced the former Clyde forward until the emergence of Eric Black. Archibald was signed by Billy McNeill in a £20,000 transfer in January 1978. He was an immediate success at Tottenham, finishing as top scorer in his first season and winning the FA Cup on two occasions. The Scotland international later went on to sign for Barcelona in 1984 and helped the Catalan side win their first La Liga title in 11 years. His time in Spain came to an end with the restriction of foreign players as Barcelona signed Gary Lineker and Mark Hughes.

Doug Bell

It was after Aberdeen signed Jim Bett in 1985 that Bell was unsure of his future at the club. He later described leaving as the worst decision of his career. He signed for Rangers before joining Hibernian in 1986. In his career, Bell played for 12 clubs: St Mirren, Aberdeen, Rangers, Hibernian, Shrewsbury, Hull, Birmingham, Partick, Portadown, Clyde, Elgin, Alloa and Albion Rovers. In 2008, Bell was in temporary charge of Clyde for two matches and was sent from the dugout in both games. He later received a ten-game touchline ban.

Eric Black

One transfer that clearly disappointed Alex Ferguson. Black had emerged as a striker of great promise in 1981 and scored the opening goal in the 1983 Cup Winners' Cup Final followed by the winner against Rangers in the Scottish Cup Final. Black was highly thought of by Ferguson and he firmly believed that the forward could have opted for a better option than to agree to join French club Metz in 1986. Black informed Ferguson that he was moving at the end of his contract and was promptly left out of the squad for the 1986 Scottish Cup Final against Hearts.

Bobby Clark

When Aberdeen clinched the Premier League title in 1980, Alex Ferguson ran on to the Easter Road pitch to embrace Bobby Clark, the veteran keeper. Clark had been a record holder in terms of club appearances and Scotland caps for several years before being overtaken by Willie Miller. He had been signed by Eddie Turnbull in 1965 from Queen's Park and earned his first Scotland cap in 1967. Clark was in the Aberdeen side that won the Scottish Cup in 1970 and the League Cup six years later.

Marc De Clerck

The Belgian keeper left Aberdeen after a brief spell in season 1980/81. In only his second appearance against Kilmarnock an injury kept him out of contention, and he was released at the end of the campaign. De Clerck joined SC Heracles and later played for De Graafschap.

Doug Considine

Signed from Huntly in 1978, left-back Considine was never a regular under Alex Ferguson. In his three seasons at Pittodrie he played enough games in 1979/80 to earn a winners' medal and he was also in the side that won the last Drybrough Cup in 1980. After making only 32 appearances he joined Dunfermline in 1981 in the search for first-team football in a £35,000 deal. After two seasons at East End Park, Considine retired from the game at the age of 26. His son Andy went on to become an Aberdeen player and made more than 400 appearances for the club.

Neale Cooper

Once described as a 'young Franz Beckenbauer', Neale Cooper was brought through the ranks at Pittodrie and made his mark in the midfield that went on to succeed in Scotland and Europe, making his debut in October 1980 at the age of 17. In 1982 he gained hero status after scoring the Dons' fourth goal in the 1982 Scottish Cup Final against Rangers. Cooper took advantage of a kind break of the ball and he slammed it into the net from all of two yards before celebrating with a forward roll in front of the Rangers support. His last appearance for Aberdeen was in the 1986 Scottish Cup Final win over Hearts. Cooper joined Aston Villa and later played for Rangers and Dunfermline. On 28 May 2018 Neale Cooper tragically died after being found in a critical condition in a stairwell in flats in Aberdeen. Hartlepool United were one of the sides he managed during his career and they named a stand at their ground in honour of him. In November 2017 Cooper was inducted into the Aberdeen FC Hall of Fame.

Neil Cooper

Local player Cooper was one of the most sought-after teenagers in Scotland when he was still at school in Aberdeen. Aston Villa and Sunderland wanted him to join them, but he opted to learn his trade with Aberdeen. He had been a forward in school football, but he developed at Pittodrie as a central defender. Making his debut in 1975 he never managed to break into the first team as the Alex McLeish–Willie Miller partnership was established. In 1980 he joined Barnsley then later played for St Mirren and won a Scottish Cup winners' medal in 1987. Cooper later returned to Pittodrie, coaching the Aberdeen youngsters.

Steve Cowan

In any other era, Steve Cowan would have certainly gone on to establish himself in the first team. With Cowan up against the likes of Eric Black, Mark McGhee and latterly Frank McDougall, the young forward only made 55 appearances in his six seasons at Pittodrie. Despite his few appearances, Cowan still won a Premier League winners' medal in 1985 as well as the Drybrough Cup when he scored a stunning winning goal against St Mirren at Hampden.

Cowan was sold to Hibernian in August 1985 and to underline his potential he was the top scorer in Scottish football in season 1985/86 with 28 goals, making his transfer fee of £45,000 great value for the Easter Road side. He never managed to get anywhere near that prolific form again and joined Motherwell in 1987, where he made 51 appearances in three seasons at Fir Park. In 1990 he moved to Northern Ireland and enjoyed a successful period with Portadown, where he scored an impressive 66 league goals from only 87 appearances. He also picked up Irish League winners' medals in 1990 and 1991 as well as the Irish Cup in 1991. These days Cowan works in financial services and as a football pundit on radio.

Duncan Davidson

Elgin-born Davidson joined Aberdeen in 1972, his first professional club. Davidson had been with Junior club Lewis United and was spotted by the Dons' Davie Robb, who had been coaching them. Bobby Clark was also his PE teacher so it was almost inevitable that Davidson would sign for Aberdeen. After learning his trade with the successful reserve team under Teddy Scott, Davidson made his first-team debut in 1974. One of his highlights was scoring the winning goal in a Scottish Cup replay at Ibrox in 1975. Davidson also scored the Dons' goal in the 1979 League Cup Final. After failing to secure a regular place in the side, Davidson left in 1981, joining Tulsa Roughnecks in a £30,000 deal. After returning from the USA, Davidson joined his old manager Billy McNeill at Manchester City, playing ten games before a long-term injury forced him to retire at the age of 30.

Andy Dornan

Signed by Billy McNeill in February 1978 after being noticed playing for the Scotland Schoolboys against England at Wembley, Aberdeen-born Dornan never managed to make the breakthrough into the first team. His three appearances all came at the beginning of November 1980, which included coming on as a substitute in the European Cup tie against Liverpool at Anfield. Dornan left the Dons in 1982 along with Andy Harrow with both joining Motherwell in a deal worth around £40,000. Dornan later played for Walsall and had a brief spell as manager at Montrose in 1995.

Ian Fleming

Ally MacLeod's first signing for Aberdeen when Fleming joined from Kilmarnock for a modest £15,000 fee. His five years with the Ayrshire club were followed by three seasons at Pittodrie. Fleming proved to be a tough competitor, often falling foul of officials with his robust approach. Not unlike Alex Ferguson as a player, Fleming was never a favourite with the manager and in February 1979 he was sold to Sheffield Wednesday in a £45,000 deal. After only one season in England, Fleming returned to Scotland and signed for Dundee. He later managed Brechin City, a move that shocked Ferguson who once said he thought Fleming would never be suited to management. Fleming led Brechin to the Second Division title and at the time was the youngest manager in Scottish football at 29 years of age.

John Gardiner

With the injury to regular keeper Bobby Clark in Ferguson's first season, his replacement was a straight choice between Gardiner and Jim Leighton. With Gardiner being overlooked and Clark still to return from injury, there was no long-term future at Pittodrie for the young keeper. Gardiner joined the Dons from Campsie Black Watch and was also selected for the Scotland under-21 side in 1979. He joined Dundee United in 1980 for £25,000 after failing to command a place in the Aberdeen side. After a spell with Motherwell, Gardiner enjoyed success in the Highland League with Huntly.

Willie Garner

The emergence of Alex McLeish in 1979 saw him replace Willie Garner as the regular centre-half. Garner had been in the team that won the League Cup in 1976 after joining Aberdeen in 1975 from Campsie Black Watch. With first-team appearances limited after the Miller–McLeish partnership developed, Garner was a surprise signing for Celtic in 1981 in a £46,000 deal. After a disaster of a debut when he scored two own goals, Garner struggled to make an impact at Parkhead. In 1982 he joined Alloa as player-manager, then in February 1984 he returned to Pittodrie as assistant manager to Alex Ferguson.

Ian Gibson

Signed from Nairn County of the Highland League in 1975, Gibson spent three seasons at Pittodrie. His most productive spell came under Billy McNeill at the end of 1977 when he was given a rare starting place. After making 12 appearances, scoring four goals, Gibson was not included in the Dons' first-team squad under Alex Ferguson and was sold in a £15,000 deal to Kilmarnock in 1978. Gibson later emigrated to Australia, where he turned to teaching.

Bryan Gunn

One of several young players who Alex Ferguson inherited at Pittodrie, Gunn proved to be the ideal deputy for Jim Leighton.

Ferguson claimed that he had the best two keepers in Scotland as Gunn, when called upon, suggested he would eventually move on to get first-team football. Gunn was an unused substitute in Gothenburg and after missing out on the 1986 Scottish Cup with Leighton returning from injury, he went on to join Norwich City in a £100,000 transfer. Gunn spent the rest of his career in Norfolk attaining legendary status at Carrow Road. Gunn was also a Scotland international, and his son Angus is, at the time of writing, Scotland's regular number one.

Derek Hamilton

Another squad player who could not force his way into the first team on a regular basis, most likely undone by his versatility. Hamilton was signed in 1978 as a defender but will be best known at Pittodrie for his occasional appearances in a forward position. In his seven seasons he made 46 appearances, scoring four goals, three of which came in the successful 1979/80 season, including a late winner against Rangers at Pittodrie in January. Hamilton later joined Hamilton Accies in 1983.

Joe Harper

The relationship between Harper and Alex Ferguson was fragile at best. Harper was the Dons' record signing in October 1969 in a £40,000 deal from Morton, and he went on to become the club's record scorer after two spells that ended in 1981 after a knee injury kept him out of action for more than a year. Along with Bobby Clark he was the only Aberdeen player to gain a full set of domestic winners' medals by 1980. However, the manner of his departure from Pittodrie soured relations further between Harper and Ferguson, a rift that has never been healed.

Andy Harrow

In early 1983 after failing to secure a regular place in the side, an unsettled Harrow and Andy Dornan were signed for Motherwell in a dual transfer. It was a deal that Ferguson was reluctant to allow as he was convinced there was better to come from Harrow. He was a regular at Fir Park for four years and later went on to manage Cowdenbeath.

Drew Jarvie

A club record signing in 1971 when he joined Aberdeen from Airdrie in a £72,000 deal, Jarvie played a vital role in the closing weeks of the 1979/80 season as Aberdeen closed in on the Premier League title. After 11 years at Pittodrie, Jarvie was awarded a testimonial against Ipswich in August 1982.

Stuart Kennedy

Signed by Ally MacLeod in 1976 from Falkirk in a £25,000 deal, Kennedy went on to a popular amd respected player at Pittodrie. Described by Alex Ferguson as the 'ultimate professional', the Scotland international was injured in the semi-final of the 1983 Cup Winners' Cup in Belgium and was unable to be considered for the final in Sweden. Ferguson held Kennedy in such high esteem that he included him as a substitute in Gothenburg but he was never fit enough to take part.

Walker McCall

McCall left Aberdeen on a free transfer on 14 March 1983 just before the Cup Winners' Cup tie against Bayern Munich to join Hong Kong club South China AA. After a brief spell in the Far East, McCall ended his playing career at Dens Park with Dundee. When McCall left Aberdeen for the second time – he made appearances between 1973 and 1978 after first signing as a youngster – he was persuaded to head east by Alex Miller, who had just been appointed as head coach for South China. McCall enjoyed his swansong at Dens Park, where he would travel from Aberdeen daily along with a young Stewart McKimmie.

Mark McGhee

It was McGhee's performances in European football that attracted the interest of West German clubs wishing to take him to the

Bundesliga in 1984. His final act for Aberdeen was scoring the winning goal against Celtic in the 1984 Scottish Cup Final. A week later he scored for Scotland in the 1-1 draw against England at Hampden, by which time he had agreed to join SV Hamburg. His time in Germany was plagued by injury and in 1985 he returned to Scotland and signed for Celtic. A Scotland international with four caps, McGhee finished his playing career with Newcastle. In 2009 he returned to Pittodrie as manager, taking over from Jimmy Calderwood.

Tommy McIntyre

After making his debut in the immediate aftermath of Gothenburg, full-back McIntyre struggled to command a starting place in an Aberdeen side that dominated the game in Scotland. After four years at Pittodrie, McIntyre joined Hibernian, making over 100 appearances in seven seasons at Easter Road. He also won a League Cup winners' medal in 1991, scoring for Hibernian in the win over Dunfermline. McIntyre ended his playing career with Airdrie in 1997 and later joined the SFA as head of youth development.

Chic McLelland

Recognised by Ferguson as an honest, professional and reliable defender, McLelland was never going to be in Ferguson's long-term plans. He joined Aberdeen in 1972 and made his debut a year later, one of more than 200 appearances, and was in the side that won the League Cup in 1976. After gaining two Scotland under-23 caps, McLelland joined Motherwell in 1979 for a £10,000 fee. He later returned to Pittodrie to head up the club's youth development.

Steve Morrison

After joining Aberdeen in 1978, midfielder Morrison never managed to play a competitive first-team game for the Dons. Alex Ferguson released him in 1981 and the St Andrews-born player joined Dunfermline. After making over 200 appearances for the

Fife outfit, Morrison played for several clubs including Hamilton, Dumbarton, Clyde, Alloa and Larne in Ireland. Morrison also managed Clydebank and East Stirling.

Doug Rougvie

It was a surprise to Alex Ferguson and the Aberdeen support that Doug Rougvie announced he was leaving to join Chelsea in the summer of 1984. With Rougvie and the club failing to agree terms, the defender moved on after turning down the Dons' final offer. Rougvie had been at Pittodrie since 1972 and was unlucky to miss out on a testimonial match. He made over 300 appearances for the club before his £225,000 transfer. Rougvie won one cap for Scotland, against Northern Ireland in December 1983.

Steve Ritchie

Will forever be known for his freak goal at the end of the 1978 Scottish Cup Final defeat. His mishit shot went high into the air and incredibly dropped under the bar with Rangers keeper Peter McCloy hanging on to the crossbar thinking the ball had gone wide. Ritchie was signed by Billy McNeill in March 1978 from Hereford in a modest £8,000 deal. A left-back who was never a regular in the side, Ritchie was released by Alex Ferguson in 1979 after making only one appearance that season. Ritchie went on to join Torquay United.

Ian Scanlon

Scanlon was a player who frustrated Alex Ferguson. One of the most natural left-footed players in the country, there was always a doubt over his approach and attitude. Signed by Billy McNeill in 1978, Scanlon had been with Notts County after starting out with East Stirling. It was during his spell with County that he considered retiring from playing after making false claims over an inheritance. Ferguson identified Peter Weir as the 'final piece' in his jigsaw and that was the end of Scanlon's time at Pittodrie. Scanlon was transferred as part of the deal that took Weir north, and he finished his playing career with St Mirren in 1986.

Joe Smith

Younger brother of Jimmy 'Jinky' Smith, the midfielder was a vital part of the side that won the League Cup in 1976 and highly rated by manager Ally MacLeod. When MacLeod became Scotland coach, he called Smith up for the Home Internationals and trip to South America in 1977, although he never did better than a seat on the bench. That lofty status did not extend to Ferguson. Smith made his debut in 1972 and made more than 140 appearances for the Dons. When Ferguson arrived in 1978, Smith was not in his plans and after a short loan spell with Arbroath, he signed for Motherwell in a £40,000 transfer. He finished his playing career with Dunfermline in 1984.

Gordon Strachan

Another Billy McNeill signing, Strachan went on to become one of the greatest midfielders to ever play for Aberdeen. His early days were anything but harmonious and there was talk of moving him on, but Alex Ferguson was at pains to find a role for Strachan. It was in the 1979/80 season that the 'wee man' came into his own, playing a vital part in the side that won the Premier League. Strachan was rewarded by being named as the Scottish Football Writers' Association Footballer of the Year in 1980. Thereafter he became a vital part of the Aberdeen and Scotland international teams. It was in 1983 that Strachan informed Ferguson that he intended moving on when his contract was to expire at the end of the 1983/84 season. His transfer when it eventually came was a controversial one. It seemed that an agreement had been reached between Strachan and Cologne in Germany, but when Manchester United became interested in taking Strachan to Old Trafford it took an intervention from FIFA to make a ruling on the transfer. Strachan joined Manchester United in August 1984 in a £500,000 deal. United had to pay £75,000 to Cologne in compensation. Strachan went on to enjoy a lengthy playing career in England with Manchester United, Leeds United and Coventry City before retiring in 1997.

Dom Sullivan
Ally MacLeod signed Sullivan from Clyde for £25,000 in 1976. A Scotland under-23 international, he was in the Aberdeen side that won the League Cup that year. Under MacLeod and then Billy McNeill, the midfielder was a regular in the team that went close to winning the Premier League in 1978. Alex Ferguson was not so keen on Sullivan and he questioned his attitude and work ethic. Any disruptive player would never find favour with Ferguson and Sullivan left in 1980 to join Celtic in a £92,000 move.

Andy Watson
Aberdeen-born Watson played a significant if unassuming part in the Dons' Premier League success in 1980. His 20 appearances and five goals were vital in the closing weeks of the campaign. In his eight seasons at Pittodrie he made 135 appearances, scoring 17 goals. One of the unused substitutes in the 1983 European Cup Winners' Cup Final, Watson was never a regular in the midfield under Alex Ferguson.

FRANKFURT
Eintracht
Die Sportzeitung von Eintracht Frankfurt e.V. Nr.10a/3.Oktober 1979

Welcome Aberdeen

Die Rangers geschlagen

Ribbeck testete gut

Die Bayern kommen

Mercedes-Benz
Ihr Partner in Frankfurt

Bobby Clark, Drew Jarvie and Stuart Kennedy all retired from playing when they left the club during that period, although Clark remarkably played one final game for Clyde before embarking on a coaching career. Clark and Jarvie were both rewarded with testimonial matches after giving more than ten years' service to the club.

13

Records and Statistics

Complete Aberdeen FC honours won, 1978–1986

European Cup Winners' Cup: 1983
European Super Cup: 1983
Scottish Premier League: 1980, 1984, 1985
Scottish Cup: 1982, 1983, 1984, 1986
Scottish League Cup: 1985
Drybrough Cup: 1980
Aberdeenshire Cup: 1980/81, 1981/82, 1982/83
Premier Reserve League: 1981/82
Reserve League Cup: 1978/79, 1979/80, 1984/85
Scottish 2nd XI Cup: 1981/82
Reserve League East: 1983/84

ABERDEEN FC PLAYING STAFF 1978–1986

Name	*Signed from*	*Year*	*App*	*Gls*
Angus, Ian	Eastercraigs	1979	120	12
Archibald, Steve	Clyde	1977	100	42
Black, Eric	Alness Academy	1979	180	70
Bell, Doug	St Mirren	1979	184	14
Bett, Jim	Lokeren	1985	52	6
De Clerck, Marc	FC Twente	1980	2	1
Clark, Bobby	Queen's Park	1965	83	0
Connor, Bobby	Dundee	1986	14	3

Considine, Doug	Huntly	1978	48	0
Cooper, Neale	Hazlehead Academy	1979	220	10
Cooper, Neil	Hilton Academy	1975	10	1
Cowan, Steve	St Mirren	1979	55	11
Davidson, Duncan	Lewis United	1971	32	6
Dodds, Davie	Xamax	1986	7	2
Dornan, Andy	King Street 'A'	1977	3	0
Falconer, Willie	Lewis United	1981	52	7
Fleming, Ian	Kilmarnock	1976	19	2
Gardiner, John	Campsie Black Watch	1976	5	0
Garner, Willie	Campsie Black Watch	1975	53	2
Grant, Brian	Stirling Albion	1984	1	0
Gray, Steve	Irvine	1983	31	3
Gunn, Bryan	Nairn County	1980	18	0
Hamilton, Derek	Beith	1978	46	5
Harper, Joe	Hibernian	1976	65	39
Harrow, Andy	Luton Town	1980	22	4
Hewitt, John	Hilton Academy	1979	250	74
Irvine, Brian	Falkirk	1985	13	0
Jarvie, Drew	Airdrie	1972	131	33
Kennedy, Stuart	Falkirk	1976	240	8
Leighton, Jim	Dalry Thistle	1977	347	0
McCall, Walker	Atlanta Chiefs	1980	37	15
McDougall, Frank	St Mirren	1984	69	44
McGhee, Mark	Newcastle United	1979	250	99
McLeish, Alex	Glasgow United	1976	398	24
McLelland, Chic	Eastercraigs	1969	41	2
McMaster, John	Port Glasgow	1972	237	21
McIntyre, Tom	Fir Park BC	1981	21	0
McKimmie, Stewart	Dundee	1983	140	7
McQueen, Tom	Clyde	1984	66	5
Miller, Joe	St Mungo's Academy	1983	35	10
Miller, Willie	Eastercraigs	1971	429	19
Mitchell, Brian	King Street Belmont	1980	85	1
Morrison, Steve	St Mirren BC	1978	1	0

Porteous, Ian	Eastercraigs	1980	52	8
Ritchie, Steve	Hereford United	1978	1	0
Robertson, David	Deeside BC	1985	13	0
Robertson, Ian	Inverness	1983	6	0
Rougvie, Doug	Dunfermline United	1972	264	20
Scanlon, Ian	Notts County	1978	131	19
Simpson, Neil	Middlefield Wasps	1978	239	30
Smith, Joe	St Gregory's BC	1969	2	0
Stark, Billy	St Mirren	1983	127	54
Strachan, Gordon	Dundee	1977	276	88
Sullivan, Dom	Clyde	1976	52	8
Weir, Peter	St Mirren	1981	206	37
Watson, Andy	Sunnyside	1976	135	17
Wright, Paul	St Andrews	1983	27	3
Own goals				14
TOTALS			5,743	900

WHERE AND WHEN

All the different venues Aberdeen played at between 1978 and 1986

Date	*Opponents*	*Venue*	*Competition*
31/7/78	Elgin City	Borough Briggs, Elgin	Friendly
2/8/78	Buckie Thistle	Victoria Park, Buckie	Friendly
7/8/78	Middlesbrough	Pittodrie Stadium, Aberdeen	Friendly
12/8/78	Hearts	Tynecastle Park, Aberdeen	Premier League
26/8/78	Dundee United	Tannadice, Dundee	Premier League
30/8/78	Meadowbank Thistle	Meadowbank Stadium, Edinburgh	League Cup
13/9/78	Marek Dimitrov	Bonchuk Stadium, Dupnitsa, Bulgaria	ECWC
16/9/78	Rangers	Ibrox Stadium, Glasgow	Premier League
23/9/78	Hibernian	Easter Road, Edinburgh	Premier League
4/10/78	Hamilton Accies	Douglas Park, Hamilton	League Cup
14/10/78	St Mirren	Love Street, Paisley	Premier League
18/10/78	Fortuna Düsseldorf	Rheinstadion, Düsseldorf, Germany	ECWC
23/10/78	Arbroath	Gayfield Park, Arbroath	Testimonial
28/10/78	Morton	Cappielow, Greenock	Premier League

8/11/78	Ayr United	Somerset Park, Ayr	League Cup
11/11/78	Motherwell	Fir Park, Motherwell	Premier League
9/12/78	Celtic	Celtic Park, Glasgow	Premier League
16/1/79	Belenenses	Estádio do Restelo, Lisbon, Portugal	Friendly
14/4/79	Partick Thistle	Firhill, Glasgow	Premier League
14/5/79	Ross County/Brora	Victoria Park, Dingwall	Testimonial
17/7/79	Kolding IF	Kolding Stadion, Denmark	Friendly
19/7/79	Randers	Cepheus Park, Randers, Denmark	Friendly
21/7/79	Skovbakken	Vejby Stadion, Aarhus, Denmark	Friendly
28/7/79	Kilmarnock	Rugby Park, Kilmarnock	Drybrough Cup
29/7/79	Fraserburgh	Bellslea Park, Fraserburgh	Testimonial
4/8/79	Cowdenbeath	Central Park, Cowdenbeath	Friendly
9/8/79	Nairn County	Station Park, Nairn	Friendly
29/9/79	Dundee	Dens Park, Dundee	Premier League
3/10/79	Eintracht Frankfurt	Waldstadion, Frankfurt, Germany	UEFA Cup
24/2/80	Rothes	Mackessack Park, Rothes	Testimonial
19/7/80	Tórshavn	Gundadalur, Tórshavn, Faroe Islands	Friendly
22/7/80	Forres Mechanics	Mosset Park, Forres	Friendly
23/8/80	Airdrie	Broomfield Park, Airdrie	Premier League
30/8/80	Berwick Rangers	Shielfield Park, Berwick	League Cup
1/10/80	Austria Vienna	Praterstadion, Vienna, Austria	European Cup
5/11/80	Liverpool	Anfield, Liverpool, England	European Cup
24/1/81	Raith Rovers	Starks Park, Kirkcaldy	Scottish Cup
25/1/81	Aberdeen University	Kings College Grounds, Aberdeen	Aberdeenshire Cup
25/7/81	Dunfermline Athletic	East End Park, Dunfermline	Friendly
4/8/81	Brechin City	Glebe Park, Brechin	Friendly
16/9/81	Ipswich Town	Portman Road, Ipswich, England	UEFA Cup
4/11/81	Argeş Piteşti	Stadion 1st May, Piteşti, Romania	UEFA Cup
9/12/81	SV Hamburg	Volksparkstadion, Hamburg, Germany	UEFA Cup
6/1/82	Norwich City	Carrow Road, Norwich, England	Friendly
12/1/82	Benidorm	Municipal de Foietes, Benidorm, Spain	Friendly
3/8/82	Inverness Thistle	Kingsmills Park, Inverness	Testimonial
9/8/82	Stirling Albion	Annfield Stadium, Stirling	Friendly
1/9/82	FC Sion	Stade de Tourbillon, Sion, Switzerland	ECWC
8/9/82	Dumbarton	Boghead, Dumbarton	League Cup
29/9/82	Dinamo Tirana	Dinamo Stadium, Tirana, Albania	ECWC
3/11/82	Lech Poznań	Stadion Miejski, Poznań, Poland	ECWC
2/3/83	Bayern Munich	Olympiastadion, Munich, Germany	ECWC
19/4/83	Waterschei	André Dumontstadion, Genk, Belgium	ECWC

11/5/83	Real Madrid	Ullevi, Gothenburg, Sweden	ECWC Final
24/7/83	Salmrohr	Salmtalstadion, Salmrohr, Germany	Friendly
26/7/83	Schwetzingen	Stadion an der Ketscher Landstraße, Germany	Friendly
27/7/83	Luttringhausen	Rontgen Stadion, Germany	Friendly
29/7/83	Offenbach Kickers	Bieber Berg Stadium, Offenbach, Germany	Friendly
30/7/83	Hassia Bizen	Sportzentrum, Bingen, Germany	Kirn Tournament
3/8/83	Eisbachtal	Eisbachtalstadion, Nentershausen, Germany	Friendly
6/8/83	Nuremberg	Frankenstadion, Nuremberg, Germany	Friendly
10/8/83	Forfar Athletic	Station Park, Forfar	Testimonial
17/8/83	Manchester United	Old Trafford, Manchester, England	Testimonial
7/9/83	St Johnstone	Muirton Park, Perth	League Cup
14/9/83	ÍA	Laugardalsvöllur, Reykjavík, Iceland	ECWC
19/10/83	Beveren	Freethiel Stadion, Beveren, Belgium	ECWC
28/1/84	Aldershot	Recreation Ground, Aldershot, England	Friendly
18/2/84	Clyde	Shawfield Stadium, Glasgow	Scottish Cup
7/3/84	Újpesti Dózsa	Megyeri úti Stadium, Budapest, Hungary	ECWC
11/4/84	Porto	Estádio das Antas, Porto, Portugal	ECWC
1/8/84	Viktoria Gogh	Lichterfelde Stadium, Berlin, Germany	Friendly
2/8/84	Bayer Leverkusen	BayArena, Leverkusen, Germany	Friendly
3/8/84	Blau-Weiß 1890 Berlin	Platz an der Rathausstraße, Berlin, Germany	Friendly
4/8/84	Stuttgart Kickers	Gazi-Stadion auf der Waldau, Germany	Friendly
5/8/84	VFL Frohnlach	Willi-Schillig-Stadion, Bavaria, Germany	Friendly
13/8/84	Leicester City	Filbert Street, Leicester, England	Centenary Match
3/10/84	Dynamo Berlin	Friedrich-Ludwig-Jahn-Sportpark, Berlin, E Ger	European Cup
14/1/85	Ismaily	Ismailia Stadium, Ismailia, Egypt	Friendly
21/7/85	Solothurn	Solothurn Stadion, Switzerland	Friendly
24/7/85	Neuchâtel Xamax	Stade De La Maladière, Neuchâtel, Switzerland	Friendly
28/7/85	Schaffhausen	Stadion Breite, Schaffhausen, Switzerland	Friendly
30/7/85	Lausanne	Stade Olympique de la Pontaise, Lausanne, Switzerland	Friendly
4/8/85	Inverness Caledonian	Telford Street Park, Inverness	Testimonial
23/10/85	Servette	Stade des Charmilles, Geneva, Switzerland	European Cup
1/12/85	Deveronvale	Princess Royal Park, Banff	Friendly
10/12/85	Clydebank	Kilbowie Park, Clydebank	Premier League
22/7/86	Gunnilse	Hjällbovallen, Angered, Gothenburg, Sweden	Friendly
24/7/86	Groheds IF	Rimnersvallen, Uddevella, Sweden	Friendly

27/7/86	Vara SK	Sparbankshallen, Vara, Sweden	Friendly
29/7/86	IFK Trollhattan	Edsborgs, Trollhattan, Sweden	Slusscupen
8/10/86	Falkirk	Brockville Park, Falkirk	Premier League

These matches were played at 91 different venues across 19 different countries: Albania, Austria, Belgium, Bulgaria, Denmark, East Germany, Egypt, England, Faroe Islands, Hungary, Iceland, Poland, Portugal, Romania, Scotland, Spain, Sweden, Switzerland and West Germany.

TESTIMONIAL MATCHES

Aberdeen played 16 testimonial matches during Alex Ferguson's period at Pittodrie.

3/9/78	Bobby Clark	Aberdeen v Former Dons Select	Pittodrie, Aberdeen
23/10/78	G. Marshall/C. Murray	Arbroath Select v Aberdeen	Gayfield, Arbroath
14/5/79	Ian Hunter	Ross County/Brora v Aberdeen	Victoria Park, Dingwall
29/7/79	Bertie Bowie	Fraserburgh v Aberdeen	Bellslea Park, Fraserburgh
24/2/80	Gavin Gray	Rothes v Aberdeen	Mackessack Park, Rothes
16/3/80	Tom Cargill	Arbroath v Aberdeen	Gayfield, Arbroath
31/8/80	Joe Harper	Aberdeen v Joe Harper Select	Pittodrie, Aberdeen
3/5/81	Jocky Scott	Dundee v Aberdeen	Dens Park, Dundee
16/8/81	Willie Miller	Aberdeen v Tottenham	Pittodrie, Aberdeen
3/8/82	Ian Cumming	Inverness Thistle v Aberdeen	Kingsmills, Inverness
7/8/82	Drew Jarvie	Aberdeen v Ipswich Town	Pittodrie, Aberdeen
10/8/83	R. Farningham/Ian McPhee	Forfar Athletic v Aberdeen	Station Park, Forfar
15/8/83	George Burley	Ipswich Town v Aberdeen	Portman Road, Ipswich
17/8/83	Martin Buchan	Manchester United v Aberdeen	Old Trafford, Manchester
4/8/85	Billy MacDonald	Inverness Caley v Aberdeen	Telford Street, Inverness
16/12/85	John McMaster	Aberdeen v Billy McNeill XI	Pittodrie, Aberdeen

Alex Ferguson's record as Scotland coach, October 1985–June 1986

	P	*W*	*D*	*L*	*F*	*A*
Home	3	2	1	0	5	0
Away	4	1	2	1	2	2
Neutral	3	0	1	2	1	3
Total	10	3	4	3	8	5

RESULTS

<table>
<tr><td>16/10/85</td><td>East Germany</td><td>0-0</td><td>Hampden Park, Glasgow</td><td>Friendly</td><td>41,114</td></tr>
<tr><td colspan="6">Leighton, Gough, Albiston, Miller, McLeish, Nicol, Souness, Aitken, Cooper, Dalglish, Johnston
Subs: Goram, Speedie, McStay</td></tr>
<tr><td>20/11/85</td><td>Australia</td><td>2-0</td><td>Hampden Park, Glasgow</td><td>World Cup play-off first leg</td><td>61,920</td></tr>
<tr><td colspan="6">Leighton, Nicol, Malpas, Miller, McLeish, Strachan, Souness, Aitken, Cooper, Dalglish, McAvennie
Subs: Sharp, Bett</td></tr>
<tr><td>4/12/85</td><td>Australia</td><td>0-0</td><td>Olympic Park, Melbourne</td><td>World Cup play-off second leg</td><td>32,000</td></tr>
<tr><td colspan="6">Leighton, Gough, Malpas, Miller, McLeish, Aitken, Souness, McStay, Cooper, Speedie, McAvennie
Sub: Sharp</td></tr>
<tr><td>28/1/86</td><td>Israel</td><td>1-0</td><td>Ramat Gan, Tel Aviv</td><td>Friendly</td><td>7,000</td></tr>
<tr><td colspan="6">Leighton, Gough, Malpas, Narey, Miller, Aitken, Bett, McStay, Bannon, Sharp, Nicholas
Sub: Sturrock</td></tr>
<tr><td>26/3/85</td><td>Romania</td><td>3-0</td><td>Hampden Park, Glasgow</td><td>Friendly</td><td>53,589</td></tr>
<tr><td colspan="6">Goram, Gough, Malpas, Narey, Miller, Strachan, Aitken, Souness, Bannon, Dalglish, Sharp
Subs: Nicholas, Hansen, Nevin</td></tr>
<tr><td>23/4/86</td><td>England</td><td>1-2</td><td>Wembley Stadium, London</td><td>Rous Cup</td><td>68,357</td></tr>
<tr><td colspan="6">Rough, Gough, Malpas, Miller, McLeish, Nicol, Aitken, Souness, Bannon, Speedie, Nicholas
Sub: Nevin</td></tr>
<tr><td>29/4/86</td><td>Holland</td><td>0-0</td><td>Philips Stadium, Eindhoven</td><td>Friendly</td><td>14,500</td></tr>
<tr><td colspan="6">Goram, Malpas, Albiston, Narey, McLeish, Miller, Bett, Connor, Cooper, McCoist, Sturrock</td></tr>
<tr><td>4/6/86</td><td>Denmark</td><td>0-1</td><td>Estadio Neza, Mexico</td><td>World Cup (Mexico)</td><td>18,000</td></tr>
<tr><td colspan="6">Leighton, Gough, Malpas, Miller, McLeish, Strachan, Aitken, Souness, Nicol, Sturrock, Nicholas
Subs: McAvennie, Bannon</td></tr>
<tr><td>8/6/86</td><td>West Germany</td><td>1-2</td><td>Corregidora, Querétaro, Mexico</td><td>World Cup (Mexico)</td><td>25,000</td></tr>
<tr><td colspan="6">Leighton, Gough, Malpas, Narey, Miller, Strachan, Aitken, Souness, Nicol, Bannon, Archibald
Subs: McAvennie, Cooper</td></tr>
<tr><td>13/6/86</td><td>Uruguay</td><td>0-0</td><td>Estadio Neza, Mexico</td><td>World Cup (Mexico)</td><td>20,000</td></tr>
<tr><td colspan="6">Leighton, Gough, Albiston, Narey, Miller, Strachan, Aitken, McStay, Nicol, Sturrock, Sharp
Subs: Cooper, Nicholas</td></tr>
</table>

14

The Ferguson Legacy

THERE HAS been an age-old debate among a generation of Aberdeen supporters and observers as to the legacy that was left by Sir Alex Ferguson and his incredible period at Pittodrie. For some it has been argued that such success set the bar so high that those heady days will never be repeated. For others it must be an inspiration and something to aspire to. What is not in doubt is that the game in Scotland since the '80s has changed beyond recognition.

During that period, it was very much a more level playing field. There is plenty of evidence to support that view. In 1981, Ferguson brokered the deal that took St Mirren winger Peter Weir to Pittodrie. The £440,000 transfer, which included Ian Scanlon joining the Buddies, was at that time a record between two Scottish clubs. For some context in season 1978/79, the first under Ferguson, even then the difference between Aberdeen, Celtic and Rangers was not the chasm it is today. Over that season Rangers' aggregate home crowds totalled just over 550,000, with Celtic just behind. Pittodrie attendances that season were in excess of 325,000 and by 1982 that gap was closed significantly. In 1979 Rangers' turnover was £1.132m, with Celtic well behind on £682,000 and Aberdeen generating £520,000.

The amount of players on the payroll was similar, Aberdeen leading the way with 34, ahead of Celtic (32) and Rangers (31).

The financial accounts provided in April 1984 showed that Aberdeen had pushed their operating income towards the £2m mark after breaking through the £1m barrier for the first time in 1982/83. The turnover in 1984 showed an increase of £631,328 over the previous year, which together with an increase in rental value produced a total income of £1,905,859, compared with £1,186,731 from 1983. Despite an increase in operating costs of £488,000, the profit had more than doubled to £459,646. The club also had spent over £250,000 on improving the facilities at Pittodrie that year. Those figures were more remarkable when the sales of Gordon Strachan, Mark McGhee and Doug Rougvie were not included. With more than £1m taken in from those sales, only £200,000 was paid out for signings Frank McDougall, Tom McQueen and Brian Grant.

Staff costs for 1983/84 had risen to £914,453 with six Pittodrie employees now earning in excess of £30,000 per year, compared to two in 1982/83. By contrast Rangers' balance sheet in 1984 revealed a deficit of £932,588 after they had signed several players including Ally McCoist.

By 1986 the turnover at Aberdeen from football activities had increased to £1.6m, with costs rising to above the £2m mark. The average attendance at Pittodrie was just below 13,000 while Rangers' crowds were on the increase above 40,000 after the arrival of Graeme Souness and a host of big-money international players.

When Alex Ferguson left in 1986 the club's accounts for the following April revealed the dependency Aberdeen had on the transfer market. A profit of £577,510 was announced compared to a £118,320 loss in 1986, the difference being almost entirely down to transfer revenue. The departures of Eric Black, Neale Cooper, Bryan Gunn, Brian Mitchell, Tommy McIntyre and Tom McQueen brought in more than £1m in transfer fees.

There is no doubt that Ferguson left Aberdeen in a far better position than when he took over in 1978. Although Billy McNeill had been bold enough in his one season at Pittodrie, he never managed to land silverware. His predecessor Ally MacLeod did guide Aberdeen to a League Cup victory in 1976. We will never know whether MacLeod or McNeill would have brought success to

Pittodrie had they stayed for any length of time. It is almost certain that they would not have come anywhere near what Ferguson achieved. The more cynical observers would claim that Ferguson left at the right time. However, nothing that he said then and since would support that school of thought.

Ferguson thrived on new challenges and pushing the boundaries. That new challenge was coming from Ibrox. Rangers had found themselves to be also-rans in Scottish football since 1979. Ferguson

seized on their plight, exploiting their weakness and instilling an air of supremacy that flowed out of Pittodrie. The infighting and apathy at Ibrox offered Ferguson the chance to not only make a name for himself but put Aberdeen right up there as a force in Scotland that was respected and feared. The tales of Rangers players travelling to Pittodrie in the '80s have become legendary. The Ibrox club tried everything: travelling the day before and staying overnight, travelling by coach on the morning of a game, even a bracing walk along the Aberdeen beachfront. It was also well known that some Rangers players were physically sick ahead of a visit to 'Fortress Pittodrie' as it had become known.

Celtic fared better but were still well behind Aberdeen. Charlie Nicholas, the Celtic striker, who at that time was the new superstar to emerge from Scotland, later declared, 'In the year before my move to Arsenal the team I had begun to dislike was Aberdeen. There was an arrogance about them. Also, at Celtic we found it hard to beat them. That wasn't easy to accept, and our resentment boiled up into a real dislike and brought grudge games between us. There were other reasons. Particularly the tactics used to stop me. That's why I hated Alex Ferguson.

'There were one or two bad incidents involving Aberdeen and myself and I blamed Fergie for them. Neale Cooper flattened me with a crunching tackle before I was out of the centre circle. I was convinced Fergie had sent the big fellow out to hammer me. The jealousy all of us at Celtic felt for Aberdeen, we were going into games knowing that we might be beaten, it would be more honest to say that we were expecting to be beaten often. They seemed to have the Indian sign over us and we didn't take too kindly to that. Tactically they were ahead of us, they were better organised and more patient. Aberdeen were deadly. They were successful. They were arrogant. We couldn't accept that. It was only after I left Celtic that I realised how short-sighted that outlook was.'

Nicholas changed his opinion after being involved with Scotland when Ferguson was manager, 'He was knowledgeable, approachable and friendly. I thought he was sensational. I felt blessed.'

'A very impressive club setup, a super stadium and a club with great potential,' said Ian Porterfield after accepting the offer to take over as Aberdeen manager in 1986. The former Sunderland player continued, 'It must be one of the best clubs in the country and I was very impressed with everything I saw. I remember playing for Sunderland here in a friendly, but the ground has been transformed since then.'

If alarm bells were not ringing after Porterfield's initial comments, they should have been. Before Alex Ferguson departed, he recommended Hearts' Sandy Jardine as his successor. The Tynecastle club headed that off by handing Jardine a lucrative new deal. The Aberdeen board turned to Porterfield, a Scot who had been managing Rotherham United and Sheffield United with moderate success. The Fife-born manager had little or no knowledge of football in Scotland. Having not been to Pittodrie for more than 13 years, it was thought that Porterfield would appoint an assistant with an inside knowledge of the Scottish game. The smart money was on such a move, and even the *Press & Journal* suggested, 'After sizing up the situation at Pittodrie, Mr Porterfield may well decide it would be advantageous to have as his assistant someone with a familiarity of the game in Scotland.' Those observations were not taken on board by Porterfield who turned to Jimmy Mullen, who had been with Cardiff City and was player-manager with Newport County. Mullen, like Porterfield, was not familiar with Scottish football.

To be fair to Ian Porterfield, following Alex Ferguson was always going to be a huge, if impossible task. Just ask David Moyes. However, it was clear, even from his initial comments, that Porterfield did not fully grasp the magnitude of the task. Suggesting that Aberdeen 'had great potential' was an odd assessment. The

Dons, over the past seven years, had not only realised their potential but had reached heights way beyond all expectations. The 'super stadium' had already evolved into one of the best in Britain at that time. The club finances were in a very healthy position. The squad was still one of the strongest in Scotland with eight full Scotland internationals and another four who would go on to win caps in the future. Porterfield lasted until the final game of the 1987/88 season, when he resigned. A succession of signings failed to inspire. A style of football that was far removed from what the Pittodrie faithful had been used to and some difficult personal circumstances led to his departure.

The Aberdeen side that evolved under Alex Ferguson also spawned many who went on to management. Having learned from the master, Steve Archibald, Doug Bell, Eric Black, Bobby Clark, Neale Cooper, Neil Cooper, Steve Cowan, Andy Dornan, Ian Fleming, John Gardiner, Willie Garner, Bryan Gunn, Joe Harper, Andy Harrow, John Hewitt, Brian Irvine, Drew Jarvie, Mark McGhee, Chic McLelland, Alex McLeish, Willie Miller, Joe Miller, David Robertson, Doug Rougvie, Billy Stark, Gordon Strachan, Dom Sullivan and Paul Wright all went on to various coaching and management roles. Three of them – Jarvie, McGhee and Miller – went on to manage the Dons at some point.

Every Aberdeen manager who has followed Ferguson has had to deal with the weight of expectancy. Through the ageing corridors at Pittodrie Stadium there are plenty of reminders of the glory days. It is something that has endured and formed such a memorable period in club history. Aberdeen Football Club has been defined by its achievements in the '80s. It is something that has been celebrated down the years and will remain part of Pittodrie folklore. Since Alex Ferguson left in 1986 there have been 17 permanent managers. During the Ferguson years the club won ten major titles, including the European Cup Winners' Cup and European Super Cup, all condensed in a seven-year period. Since then Aberdeen have claimed four successes on the national stage: one Scottish Cup in 1990, and three League Cups in 1989, 1995 and 2014, in 38 years.

15

Brian Mitchell Remembers

BRIAN MITCHELL came through the youth ranks to establish himself in the first team in 1985. Born in Stonehaven, Mitchell signed for Aberdeen in 1981 from King Street Belmont. Brian made his first-team debut against Hibernian at Easter Road on 10 April 1982. After being part of the Aberdeen side that won the Premier League title in 1985, Mitchell replaced Tom McQueen the following season and was in the team that won the League Cup in October 1985.

After 87 appearances for the Dons, Mitchell joined Bradford City in 1986, making 178 appearances for the Bantams in his six seasons in Yorkshire. Brian recalled his Pittodrie career:

'I joined Aberdeen as a professional when I was 17 and actually played for the Aberdeen reserves while I was still at school. Having supported the Dons as a youngster, I guess it was every boy's dream to sign for their local side.

'It all started when I was part of the development squad under Bobby Clark and Lenny Taylor when I was around 15. In football terms I guess I was a "late developer" as most of the other lads at the time had already been signed up with various teams.

'We used to train a couple of times a week and Bobby and Lenny brought in junior teams for games on the blaes car park outside Pittodrie. That was a tough introduction coming up against older players but helped the development of the boys at the time.

Brian Mitchell

'One evening Sir Alex came along as I think Bobby and Lenny wanted him to look at me so after the game I was delighted and excited to hear he wanted me to sign schoolboy forms. He came along to my house to meet my parents as he does with all the young boys. He was always meticulous when taking on new players at any age. He would visit just to see what kind of family and surroundings we had as that helped him gauge several things about our background.

'After learning my trade in the reserves, I progressed through the years to make my debut in the first team in an away game against Hibernian. It was such a great feeling playing and winning 3-0 and that was the start of a memorable career with the Dons.

'Sir Alex was never scared of having young boys in the team and I was lucky enough to come through a generation that included Neale Cooper, Eric Black, John Hewitt, Neil Simpson, Andy Dornan and Willie Falconer, so it was great he had belief in us to allow us to get the confidence and believe we were good enough to be in the team.

'Fergie and Archie Knox worked us hard with afternoon sessions for the young boys but also with a strong disciplined culture within the club and more so on our social life away from the club. Whenever we went out Fergie used to know exactly where we were at the weekend. It was not unusual for the younger players to be pulled up on Monday to explain what we had been up to. It was all to make sure we adopted good habits and developed a work ethic that would stay with us throughout our careers.

'Fergie wouldn't let any of the boys get their own place until they knew every single ingredient of scotch broth and the recipe always caught you out as he would add in an ingredient no one knew about!

'In training it was always intense, you had to be on your toes all the time. It had to be total commitment as you knew the manager would demand the highest of standards that continued from training into the games. There was pressure every day and more so ahead of matches. It was an exciting pressure knowing you were part of a squad of players who were the best in the country and went on to be the best in Europe.

'The training sessions were as varied and high quality as later in my career when I went on to work in football development with the SFA. A lot of the routines and practices in these courses had a lot of what Alex and Archie had in our training sessions. That was testament to what they had been doing at Aberdeen, with many of the drills and methods being used on the national stage.

'For sure, Alex ruled by fear and there were many examples of that I can remember, especially being one of the younger members of the squad.

'There was one time I got picked to referee a game of what was called "Tips" [a game in the gym where you had one touch of the ball and tried to score in the opposition goals]. Archie and Sir Alex were hard at it and arguing like hell at every decision until I gave a decision against Fergie and he went ballistic! He promptly sent me out of the door and told me to get running around the track until he told me to stop! I trooped out and started running and did a few laps until Teddy Scott came out and asked me what I was doing. After he heard he said "just come in" as he needed some strips taken up to the dry cleaners and he said he would deal with Fergie!

'So off I went and I heard later that Fergie and Archie had played a couple of hours and when he was in the changing room he said to Teddy, "Oh my god, I've had Brian out running round the track so he'd better be called in." Little did he know Teddy pulled me in after five minutes so I didn't do the laps he thought I did! When he was up at the unveiling of his statue, he pulled all the players and me in and told them that story. I was standing there but I was still scared to tell him I only did a couple of laps!

'There were of course many outstanding memories of my time playing for Alex Ferguson and it's only when you look back at your career that you realise how special they were. From the weekly league games leading to league titles to the cup finals, European games and to the countless training sessions that developed you and all the players. The staff and personalities I worked with and all the stories that could be recollected, it really was special moments. Although I was not a regular all the time, I was lucky to be part of the team on many occasions and more so part of the squad that lived those experiences and all the players will look back at those moments knowing those formative years of our careers created a bond for life.

'You don't realise how special Sir Alex was until you encounter other managers as I did throughout my career with Bradford City, Bristol City and Hull City. His attention to detail was amazing. He would brief you on who you were up against and highlight his weaknesses (very rarely his strengths) as he wanted you to feel your superiority over your opponent.

'His team talks were emotive and detailed and at times you felt you were going to war and winning was all that mattered. Once the game was over there was little time to reflect as it was on to the next one and the preparation that went with it. The team was like a juggernaut blowing away opponents and getting better and better and winning more and more but that was just the way with Alex Ferguson, it was a culture that just consumed everyone at Pittodrie.

'Of course, the end was sad when Sir Alex left to join Manchester United. I remember Archie calling us in one by one to the office to talk to us after it had been announced. Alex had left and he gave us encouraging words from Fergie, but the place was never the same again.

'Ian Porterfield came in and I didn't really get on with him so when the chance came along to move to England, I jumped at it. To be honest it was the best thing that happened to me as I had a great time down there playing at many iconic grounds and enjoying success.

'After 15 years in England, I moved back to the Aberdeen area and also carry out media work at the Aberdeen home games. I take my son Matthew along so it does give me moments to reflect back on the Fergie era when I cast my thoughts over the pitch and remember the many fantastic games I was involved in and the glory years I was so lucky to be part of!'

Brian Mitchell
June 2024

16

Robert Connor Remembers

ROBERT CONNOR was one of Alex Ferguson's last major signings for Aberdeen in 1986. With Ian Angus moving to Dundee in part-exchange, Connor went on to become an integral part of the midfield for eight years before leaving in 1994.

How did your transfer to Aberdeen come about?
'When Archie Knox was manager of Dundee, he signed me from Ayr United before the start of the 1984 season. I played for two very enjoyable seasons under Archie at Dens, but he returned to Pittodrie to be Fergie's assistant again in 1986 – the reason being touted at the time was that he felt he'd taken Dundee as far as he could under the financial restraints. The Dundee board would not give him the financial backing for his vision for the club.

'When Archie returned to Aberdeen, his assistant at Dundee, Jocky Scott, took over at Dens. It was only a few weeks into the 1986/87 season that Jocky told me I might see in the newspaper that Aberdeen were interested in signing me, but that would never happen if my team-mate John Brown was transferred to Hearts where, unknown to anyone, he was having a medical that day. As it turned out, John failed his medical at Tynecastle due to his dodgy knees, and the next day after training Jocky called me into his office and told me Alex Ferguson and Archie were on their way from Aberdeen to speak to me. I was totally overawed when speaking with Alex and Archie and agreed to sign a four-year deal for the money they offered. I was very excited at the prospect of playing for Aberdeen, with the players there, the stadium, and the prospects of winning top-level trophies seemed surreal. I was really enjoying playing for Dundee but there was no way I could turn down an opportunity like this. Fortunately, things also turned out to John Brown's advantage too as he signed for Rangers shortly afterwards and went on to have a fantastic career at Ibrox.'

First impressions of Alex Ferguson, the staff and Pittodrie?

'The first day I arrived at Pittodrie, I was immediately taken to see the chairman Dick Donald who welcomed me and, in his own measured way, told me all about the club and how everyone working at Pittodrie played a big part in the success on the pitch. He came across as extremely genuine and generous; it was easy to see why he was held in such high esteem. In the dressing room it was brilliant to see the formidable defensive trio of Leighton, Miller and McLeish and thinking that they would be on my side now! But I'm sure most players would agree that a football dressing room is the same no matter what league or level you are playing at. There are all types of characters that you quickly get to know and learn to live with as you are sharing the ups and downs of football during your time with them. But I did notice one difference in the Aberdeen dressing room, which was a real belief and desire to win every game no matter the opponent. Willie Miller and Alex McLeish embodied this in their leadership and will to win. I saw this in Archie Knox during my time at Dundee where he would regularly turn into a crazed maniac if things weren't going our way in a game, so it did shock me to hear the Aberdeen players say that Archie was a really good guy, but Fergie was a bit of a madman!'

Thoughts when Alex Ferguson left?

'It was a real blow to everyone at the club when Fergie left for Manchester United. Personally, I had been looking forward to playing and learning under him, but the players who'd been at the club for a while did say they'd seen a change in him during the months leading up to his departure in that he was more mellow and calm, as if he knew what was coming. It was a blow to see Archie leaving too as it signalled the end of the way the club had been run under the two of them, and an incredibly hard act to follow.'

Playing for Scotland?

'Playing for Scotland was like something I'd never experienced before. I had played in the international youth setup and a few games for the Scotland under-21s, so I thought it would be like that. But in my Scotland debut, a friendly against Holland in Eindhoven, I experienced something for the first time – shaky legs! For some reason, my legs felt like jelly when the game started but fortunately it only lasted a minute or so and I really enjoyed the game. It was the last friendly before the 1986 World Cup in Mexico and Alex Ferguson told me straight that I would not be going to Mexico as the squad was already picked but that it would be good experience for me going forward. I had no expectations of even playing in the game and was surprised when Alex named me in the team, but I played well in an entertaining 0-0 draw where Ally McCoist also made his Scotland debut. In the first half, I played Ally through on the goalie but, unlike him, he missed the chance to put us in front. I've joked with him on a couple of occasions since that if he'd scored, we'd both have been on the flight to Mexico!'

Players you liked playing with at Aberdeen?

'Even after Alex Ferguson had left, the standard of player at Aberdeen remained very high with established internationals like Jim Bett, Alex McLeish and Stewart McKimmie. The Gothenburg greats had been broken up with only a few remaining, and although the players brought in could never compete with their incredible achievements, the level of player at Pittodrie remained very high. Ian Porterfield pulled off a remarkable signing in Charlie Nicholas, who was sensational and brought a lot of attention to the club. Jim Leighton had moved on with Fergie to Manchester United and, after Ian Porterfield's short time at the helm, Theo Snelders was brought in by new manager Alex Smith. Theo was arguably on a par with Jim, or even better, though I wouldn't like to hold the deciding vote on that, especially if both were standing beside me.

'Alex Smith and Jocky Scott also recruited very well from Holland, among them Hans Gillhaus, one of Pittodrie's finest ever strikers who formed a terrifically entertaining partnership with Charlie and assisted in the development of youngsters Eoin Jess and Scott Booth. This is borne out by the fact that in my eight years at Pittodrie we finished runners-up in the league five times to Graeme Souness and Walter Smith's Rangers, who had been taken by David Murray to a completely different level financially to every other Scottish club. My biggest disappointment in football was losing in the title decider at Ibrox in 1991 after we had a great run up to that game. We missed a couple of good chances in the first half but ultimately fell short on the day. I think if we'd won the league that day, it would have been an unbelievable achievement given the huge financial gulf between the two clubs, but unfortunately it wasn't to be.'

Most difficult opponent?

'The best domestic player I faced was undoubtedly Paul McStay. He was a fantastic midfielder who, for much of his time at Parkhead, carried an indifferent Celtic side. He wasn't only an outstanding player; he was a great sportsman and person too. Internationally, I was lucky enough to see first-hand the difference between a very good international player and a truly world-class player, in Gheorghe Hagi, when I played against Romania at Hampden in a Euro qualifier in 1990. I played directly against Hagi who was one of the top three best players in the world at the time and it was a real eye opener. I couldn't get near him, and although we won 2-1 my memory of the game how brilliant he was.'

Any funny tales from your time at Pittodrie?

'In the days when the players had five or six weeks off at the end of the season, we reported back for the first day of pre-season training and there was a bit of a commotion in the away dressing room where the younger lads changed. Paul Wright ("Bunion"), who had a bit of trouble controlling his weight, had put on a couple of stones during the lay-off and had just taken his shirt off to reveal his new physique and duly received dog's abuse from the rest of the young lads. He only lasted a few minutes in the warm-up run around Seaton Park before he collapsed in a heap lying face down under a tree. Unfortunately for him, a local reporter was there and the photo of him lying prostrate was on the front page of the evening newspaper that night with the headline 'Dons back in training'. From that day Jim Bett christened him "the Chancellor", after the rotund chancellor of the exchequer at the time, Nigel Lawson, which Bunion hated. If you wanted to upset him after that you only had to call him Nigel and he went off his head.'

Thoughts on when you left Aberdeen?

'I suffered from three Achilles tendon injuries which required surgery over a two-year period in the early '90s, and with Willie Miller trying to build a new team after being appointed manager, I understood when he said he would not be offering me a new contract for the new season in 1994. Alex McLeish and Jim Bett would also leave at that time and while my wife and I were sad to leave Aberdeen where we had made many friends and where our two daughters were born, the blow was softened by the fact that I would sign for my hometown team Kilmarnock. I appreciated the fact that I had been part of a real community club at Pittodrie and my family had benefited from living in Aberdeen which was a very family oriented city.'

17

They Said It

Quotes about Aberdeen's golden era:

'It was an opportunity to earn 25 quid a week more and I couldn't miss it.'

Gordon Strachan recalling his transfer to Aberdeen

'We were 1-0 up and they were struggling. They pushed big Derek [Johnstone] up front. The ball was played out to the left and I was standing around the halfway line and he backed into me and just fell. Ian Foote the referee came up and showed me the red card. It didn't surprise me at all. I just wondered if they were in the same [masonic] lodge.'

Doug Rougvie recalling his dismissal in the 1979 League Cup Final

'It was strange being in the away dressing room. I would have loved to have been celebrating in the home dressing room, but it just wasn't to be for me and Hibernian. I didn't chase Alex on to the park; that was his moment. But I was delighted for the players who had worked so hard for success.'

Aberdeen assistant manager Pat Stanton after the Dons had won the Premier League at Stanton's old stomping ground, Easter Road, in May 1980

'I slid in for a challenge on the halfway line and Johnston jumped up and he stood on my chest. There was a lot of damage to my chest, I had all the stud marks. The press asked to speak to me afterwards and I said that it had been a disgraceful challenge, that there was no need for it. They made an issue out of it.'

John McMaster recalling the horrendous challenge from Willie Johnston of Rangers in a 1980 League Cup tie that made for bad press and a deterioration in relations between the clubs

'Come on lads, three quick goals and we are right back in it.'

Drew Jarvie declared at half-time in the dressing room at Anfield in 1980 with Aberdeen already two goals down; Liverpool had only conceded eight goals at home in the entire previous season

'I wouldn't bet a stale haggis on Ipswich's chances in the return leg.'

Daily Star *report following the Dons' 1-1 draw at Portman Road in the 1981 UEFA Cup tie*

'He may be 36, but he is pencil slim and has the looks and fitness of a 19-year-old. Every time he got on the ball there was an air of expectancy in the stadium. He is a player that lived up to his reputation and he was everything I thought he would be.'

Former Aberdeen player Dom Sullivan warning about the dangers of Franz Beckenbauer ahead of the 1981 UEFA Cup tie against Hamburg; Sullivan had been in the Celtic side beaten by Hamburg in a pre-season friendly

'Aberdeen are the best side we have ever seen on this ground. Their football was like from another planet. I fully expect them to go on and win the European Cup Winners' Cup.'

FC Sion general manager Léon Walker after his team were beaten 11-1 on aggregate in the Cup Winners' Cup preliminary round in Switzerland in September 1982

'Neil Simpson is tighter than a dead heat, he loves his money, and he came in with a handful of local currency, boasting about the exchange rate. When it was pointed out to him there was nothing he could buy and he wouldn't be allowed to take that money out of the country, he was absolutely gutted.'

Neale Cooper looking back at the trip to Tirana in 1982

'Are you happy with this? Are you in a comfort zone? Do you want to be watching *Coronation Street* on a Wednesday night instead of playing European football?'

Alex Ferguson challenging his players in 1982

'My memory of that game is that despite scoring three goals, I got bollocked by Fergie in the dressing room afterwards. I can't remember why, I got shouted at most games, and it didn't bother me. That day was very special.'

Eric Black after scoring a hat-trick against Celtic at Parkhead in 1983 in a 3-1 win, as Alex Ferguson was seeking perfection

'Aberdeen are technically inferior to the Bielefeld side who lost 5-0 to Bayern at the weekend. Bayern must outplay them and that is what I think they will do in Munich.'

Franz Beckenbauer dismissed the Dons' chances against Bayern ahead of the 1983 Cup Winners' Cup quarter-final in Germany

'No one before has ever trained here on the morning of a major European tie.'

Bayern manager Uli Hoeneß in 1983 as he watched the Dons go through their paces in the Munich snow

'Maybe that is why no one has won here in the past 55 games in Europe.'

Alex Ferguson responding to Hoeneß

'Aberdeen must be one of the best sides in all European competitions. I had heard they were good, but I hadn't realised they were that good. Bayern are the finest technical team in Germany, but Aberdeen matched them in every way. No Scottish side has played so well in Germany like they did.'

West German national team manager Jupp Derwall after watching the first leg in Munich

'There are no reasons at all why Aberdeen should not go all the way now. They have proved they can beat the best in Europe.'

Scotland manager Jock Stein after watching the win over Bayern Munich

'When Bayern went 2-1 ahead, I didn't think there was a team in the world capable of beating them. The determination we showed last night could be decisive in this tournament.'

Alex Ferguson doing some crystal ball gazing after the Dons had defeated Bayern

'If you think Strachan and McMaster were in any kind of confusion, you're wrong, they were doing this quite deliberately … it was a carefully rehearsed piece of tomfoolery.'

TV commentator Jock Brown back-pedalling on his view of the free-kick routine that outwitted the Bayern Munich defence and led to Alex McLeish scoring at Pittodrie

'Rummenigge was in bad form but Aberdeen deserved to win. They were wonderful, great fighters. They were down but they hit back hard. The biggest asset was their fans, the best I have seen in my life. Those Aberdeen supporters won half the match.'

Bayern supporter Wolfgang Spalleck, shaking his head in disbelief as his side had been beaten at Pittodrie

'What a night! When the first goal went in, Archie Knox turned to me and said, "Book the tickets," when the second goal went in, he says, "Get the plane booked." After the third it's, "Book the hotel."'

John McMaster, an unused substitute in the 5-1 win over Waterschei in the Cup Winners' Cup semi-final at Pittodrie in April 1983

'Aberdeen are a strong side and have surprised many this season. We lost our chance of winning the Spanish title so beating Aberdeen has now become our priority.'

Alfredo Di Stéfano, the legendary Real Madrid coach ahead of the Cup Winners' Cup Final in Gothenburg

'I didn't win any medals as a player and I don't worry about getting medals as a manager. The memories will do fine.'

Alex Ferguson after the Dons won the European Super Cup in December 1983. The club rectified that 40 years on after UEFA agreed on awarding Ferguson a winners' medal from the Cup Winners' Cup Final

'There is no doubt in my mind that man for man, Real Madrid have the edge, but we are going to have to work hard to take the steam out of this Aberdeen team. If we don't then the Scots are going to wear us down. I have been working extra hard to get fit to play in this final. Aberdeen will have our respect, as we all know what they have already done to my fellow countrymen, Bayern Munich.'

Uli Stielike, the Real Madrid midfielder, ahead of the final in Gothenburg

'I told Alex Ferguson after they had knocked us out of the UEFA Cup that they were capable of winning it. But it looks like they have kept their European final up their sleeves until this year. I hope Aberdeen do it, I really do.'

England manager Bobby Robson ahead of the Cup Winners' Cup Final

'I am so proud of him. I was confident that they would do it, but they left it late. Alex deserved the success. He has worked long and hard to achieve success, but it is no surprise to me. He always had the determination to be a winner.'

Elizabeth Ferguson, mother of Alex, after the victory in Sweden

'I believe the experience the Aberdeen players have gained through international matches and in their games away from home in Europe will help them immensely. If Madrid do not respect Aberdeen they will be in for a shock.'

Celtic manager Billy McNeill ahead of the Cup Winners' Cup Final

'I know the support Aberdeen will take with them will be very helpful in Sweden. Aberdeen must be careful though and not get carried away. No kamikaze stuff, and they will win.'

Rangers boss John Greig in full support of the Dons ahead of the Cup Winners' Cup Final

'We had good players at the club and an exceptional manager, [and] an exceptional coach in Archie Knox. It was just a good group of people with an insatiable desire to succeed. I had nothing to compare it with obviously, I just thought that was how it was; you turned up, played a game, got shouted at and won a trophy every year!'

Eric Black looking back on his Pittodrie career

'Aberdeen are one of the best sides in Britain. They have nothing to fear against Madrid, whose reputation could work to Aberdeen's advantage. Real have just blown their league chances and they will be determined to make up for that. Spanish fans tend to turn on their own team when things are going against them.'

Northern Ireland striker Gerry Armstrong, who built a lucrative career as a pundit on Spanish football after scoring against them in the 1982 World Cup, speaking ahead of the Cup Winners' Cup Final

'No matter what happens tomorrow night I am very proud of my players for reaching the final. I am sure they will not let down our tremendous support who are here in numbers and the millions watching on television. We aim to do Britain and those fans proud.'

Alex Ferguson on the eve of the final

'This is the culmination of years of work on behalf of this club and I'm so happy for the manager and players. One thing that really pleases me is that UEFA have told me that Aberdeen Football Club have been a credit to this competition and that above all makes me a very happy man.'

Aberdeen chairman Dick Donald after the Cup Winners' Cup Final

'If you play for a club like Madrid the only thing that counts is winning. To say that people were disappointed in 1983 was an understatement. It was pissing down. Strachan did me a couple of times. He went past me as if I wasn't on the pitch.'

Real Madrid midfielder Johnny Metgod remembering the Cup Winners' Cup Final

'This was Aberdeen's big night and they won it well in the end. They had a tough spell in the first half but once they sorted that out, they never let go of their hold on the game.'

Scotland manager Jock Stein after the final

'I had a feeling I would get the goal and I told that to a few of the lads before the game. I really fancied my chances of scoring when I came on as a substitute. I predicted before the match that Eric Black and I would score against them. It was agony sitting on the bench, particularly when we weren't putting the chances away.'

Aberdeen hero John Hewitt after he scored the winner in Gothenburg

'We have shown that we have learned our lessons from Liverpool and Hamburg and now we must maintain our standards and stay at the top. I sat down in the dressing room after the game and when I looked around there are guys with European winners' medals and they are only 18, 19 and 20 years old.'

John McMaster after the final

'The chemistry was right, and Aberdeen were full of confidence. I thought beforehand that they would win. I am delighted for Aberdeen and the rest of Scottish football.'

Rangers manager John Greig paid tribute to Aberdeen after the final

'When the resources of Aberdeen are compared to Real Madrid it is a tremendous tribute to the board and manager to not only compete but to beat them. Aberdeen have a team made up of Scottish players, without the costly imports of the Spanish.'

St Mirren manager Ricky McFarland paid his after-match tribute

'I was up off my seat when they scored that winning goal.'

Kilmarnock manager and former Don Jim Clunie after the final

'Great, just great, we gave them a right doing.'

Doug Rougvie recalling the Cup Winners' Cup Final win over Real Madrid in his own inimitable style

'Aberdeen are a side feared by everyone on the continent. We all know Aberdeen are a major force in Europe now. I have played against Celtic and Rangers recently and Scottish football has a style of its own. However, I think the greatest respect has been gained by Aberdeen who have become tactically aware and still have that commitment.'

The legendary Johan Cruyff speaking after a friendly against Rangers in January 1984

'I like preaching loyalty to my players, now I have to set an example myself.'

After three approaches from Tottenham to take over as manager in 1984, Alex Ferguson declared that he was going nowhere

'In my book Aberdeen are the best British team I have seen in the last five years, with only Liverpool matching them.'

Ex-Newcastle and England striker Malcolm Macdonald after watching Aberdeen beat Rangers at Ibrox in 1984

'It was a tremendous experience being in the position I was beside Alex McLeish and Willie Miller. It's been a long time since I played at the back in that position and if I did anything silly, Willie and Alex were there.'

Neale Cooper after playing in a back three in the 1985 League Cup win over Hibernian

'Aberdeen was the big game. It was the whole hostility of Aberdeen against Rangers. You thought to yourself, "What the hell have I walked into here? Jesus Christ." There was a nastiness about the Aberdeen fixture, from history, and it seemed to get nastier. When we played Aberdeen it was a war, a bloody war.'

Terry Butcher, the England international, after joining Rangers in 1986

'As a chairman, he was a colossus, and nobody had to tell me that I had little chance of ever working for his like again.'

Alex Ferguson paying tribute to Dick Donald in 1986

'It was Real Madrid, for goodness sake, you can't take that away from us. We beat Real Madrid; we beat Bayern Munich and then we beat Hamburg over two legs. I think we were the best team in Europe at that time, we proved it.'

Gordon Strachan recalling the Aberdeen team of 1983

'Manchester United is the only club in the world I would have left Aberdeen for. After eight years at Pittodrie, I cannot begin to express the sadness I feel for having to end what has been an unforgettable experience.'

Alex Ferguson speaking immediately after he accepted the manager's role at Old Trafford in November 1986

'Fergie's philosophy was simple, Simmy [Neil Simpson] and I were there to protect Weir and Strachan. We were told to win the ball and give it to them. Job done. I was in my element, I just loved it.'

Neale Cooper recalling the wise, and blunt, words from Ferguson in 1984

'Those European games, I felt 20 per cent better a player than I did on the Saturday. There was something extra special when we went to play in those ties, for some reason it charged us up. On those European nights it felt different. We just loved it, and we loved the duty free!'

Mark McGhee reflecting on his European career with Aberdeen, with added perks

'There is no doubt that Aberdeen made me as a manager. I keep a very special place in my heart for Pittodrie. I have to say that the chemistry which brought together that particular talent and character might turn out to be a once-in-a-lifetime happening.'

Sir Alex Ferguson speaking at the club's centenary event in 2003

'That team could play any game, anytime, anywhere. They were like a four-wheel-drive Range Rover. They could handle anything.'

Sir Alex Ferguson speaking about his 1983 Aberdeen team in 2013

Gordon Strachan scores against Rangers in the 1982 Scottish Cup Final

Aberdeen and Liverpool take to the field in their 1980 European Cup tie at Pittodrie

Aberdeen defeated Sion 7-0 in the preliminary round of the ECWC in August 1982

Aberdeen players celebrate at Easter Road in May 1980 after clinching the Premier League

Alex Ferguson statue outside Pittodrie, 2022

Chris Anderson the Aberdeen vice-chairman at the time of Ferguson's appointment

Charles Forbes, Alex Ferguson, Dick Donald and Chris Anderson at Pittodrie in June 1978

Pittodrie Stadium 1983

Aberdeen FC 1983 ECWC and Scottish Cup winners, the third trophy is the Aberdeenshire Cup, the oldest in the north east

16 THE PRESS AND JOURNAL THURSDAY MAY 12 1983

ABERDEEN .... 2 Journal Sport REAL MADRID 1

Extra time goal takes Cup-Winners' Cup to Aberdeen

SUPER–SUB HEWITT SINKS SPANISH ARMADA

ALASTAIR MACDONALD'S GOTHENBURG REPORT

ABERDEEN produced their own version of the scaling of Everest last night, setting the seal on a glorious, record-setting season by winning the European Cup-Winners' Cup in the rain-lashed Ullevi Stadium in Gothenburg.

Substitute John Hewitt, who headed home a Peter Weir cross for a magnificent winning goal in the second half of extra time, was the toast of his native city and the 15,000 Dons fans who flocked to Sweden.

But really this was the greatest triumph yet for the outstanding team-work of the Aberdeen side. The depth of character in the current squad was demonstrated by their never-say-die recovery from the sickening loss of a penalty-kick equaliser after Eric Black had rocked Real Madrid with a sixth minute goal.

Although it took 120 minutes to separate the teams, it was a thoroughly merited victory for Aberdeen against the legendary Madrid club.

Skipper Willie Miller was again a positive inspiration to his side and other outstanding contributions to the greatest night in Aberdeen Football Club's 80-year history came from John McMaster, Neil Simpson and Peter Weir.

For 20-year-old Hewitt it was an action replay of his substitute appearance against Bayern Munich for he grabbed the goal that beat the Germans.

It was John's ninth counter in European competition to make him the most prolific European scorer of the current Pittodrie side.

Aberdeen made a dream start with Eric Black putting them ahead little more than six minutes after the kick-off.

But the Dons suffered a cruel blow eight minutes later when an Alex McLeish pass back, hampered by surface water, left goalkeeper Jim Leighton to take on Real striker Carlos Santillana in a race for the ball.

When the Spanish skipper went flying under Leighton's challenge the referee indicated a penalty, and Juanito levelled the scoring from the spot.

The remainder of the first half developed into a wall of attrition, with neither side gaining control but from the outset of the second half the Dons established a grip on the play and came close to settling the issue on several occasions.

A harassed Real defence, however, held out until the 90 minutes were signalled by which time Hewitt had replaced Black injured in an earlier raid.

Aberdeen maintained their superiority into extra time and eventually their greater fitness contributed to Hewitt's winning goal, which came after a move between Peter Weir and Mark McGhee on the left.

A disappointing attendance of 17,804 had to brave deplorable weather conditions which threatened to ruin the final utterly as a spectacle.

Aberdeen supporters who formed the bulk of the meagre attendance however felt that the misery they endured in torrential rain was all worth while when that decisive extra time goal gave Aberdeen a triumph which only a few seasons ago would have been regarded as being in the realms of fantasy.

The Italian referee, Gianfranco Menegali, a martinet by reputation, obviously made allowance for the underfoot conditions in his control of the game, but he nevertheless seemed to take an over-lenient view of some of the Spanish tackling .

On at least two occasions the Dons might have been awarded a penalty but Senor Menegali just was not interested.

Real's most effective players were in defence, with Johnny Metgod in outstanding form, ably supported by Francisco Bonet.

The Real attack, however, made little impression on the Pittodrie rearguard, with skipper Santillana in particular having a lean time.

The heroes of a wet evening, however, were the entire Aberdeen team, who proved once again that they have the makings of greatness, with a bright future.

Black's early goal

ABERDEEN were first to look dangerous when Strachan made a good interception and, although half checked by a Camacho challenge, he got the ball away to Black who transferred it to McGhee on the right. The latter's cross was

attacking efforts. McMaster sent Strachan away on the left in 21 minutes, but his fast cross sped out of the reach of any of his attacking team mates.

As the game entered the second half of the first 45

Weir broke on the left as the Dons piled on the pressure.

In 59 minutes Augustin had to dive full length to hold a 30-yard drive from Cooper.

Three minutes later a brilliant run by Weir on the

REAL started the first period of extra time with San Jose replacing Camacho and it was the Aberdeen goal which first came under threat. Isidro, however, sent a try wide of the target two minutes after

they sent their supporters into ecstacies of delight when substitute HEWITT gave them the lead in 111 minutes.

Weir started the move with a break on the left before passing to McGhee,

Aberdeen Press & Journal *back page, 12 May 1983*

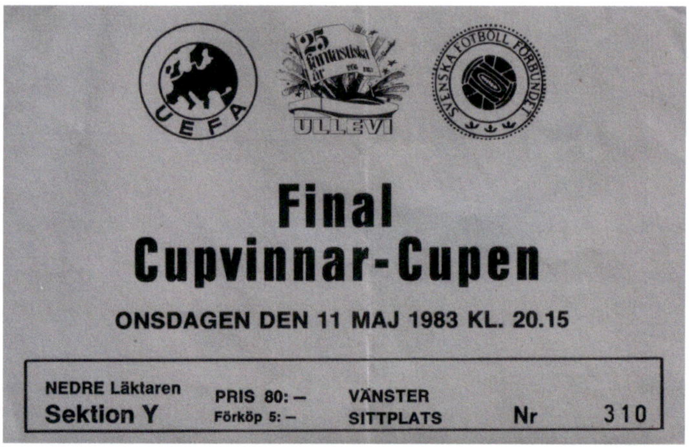

1983 ECWC Final Aberdeen v Real Madrid match ticket

0:0 FC Bayern droht Europacup-Aus!

Dynamo Kiew – Hamburg 0:3

Kaiserslautern – Craiova 3:2

Handball-Team gegen Schweiz 16:16/S. 28-31

Bild *newspaper headline after Aberdeen drew with Bayern Munich in 1983, European Cup Winners' Cup*

KOLEJOWY KLUB SPORTOWY
„LECH - POZNAŃ"
ZAPRASZA
NA MECZ RUNDY PZP W PIŁCE NOŻNEJ
Aberdeen F.C. Szkocja : „KKS LECH" Poznań
KTÓRY ODBĘDZIE SIĘ 3.11. 19.82 R.
O GODZ. 14.00 NA STADIONIE KKS „LECH"
LOŻA HONOROWA - RZĄD –

Lech Poznan v Aberdeen 1982 ECWC match ticket

Bobby Clark warming up ahead of the Dons' crucial clash against Celtic at Parkhead in April 1980

Gordon Strachan in action against Brechin in August 1981

The late Neale Cooper celebrates after scoring against Rangers in the 1982 Scottish Cup Final. His goal remains one of the most iconic moments in club history

Aberdeen line up at Hampden before the 1983 Scottish Cup Final, ten days after winning the European Cup Winners' Cup in Sweden

Mark McGhee in action against Camacho of Real Madrid in the 1983 ECWC Final

The legendary Alfredo Di Stefano leading his Madrid players through their final training session before facing Aberdeen in the European Cup Winners' Cup Final

Gordon Strachan was a marked man in the 1984 Scottish Cup Final against Celtic

John Hewitt celebrates scoring against Hearts in the 1986 Scottish Cup Final rout

Aberdeen fans on board the St Clair ferry on their way to Gothenburg, 9 May 1983

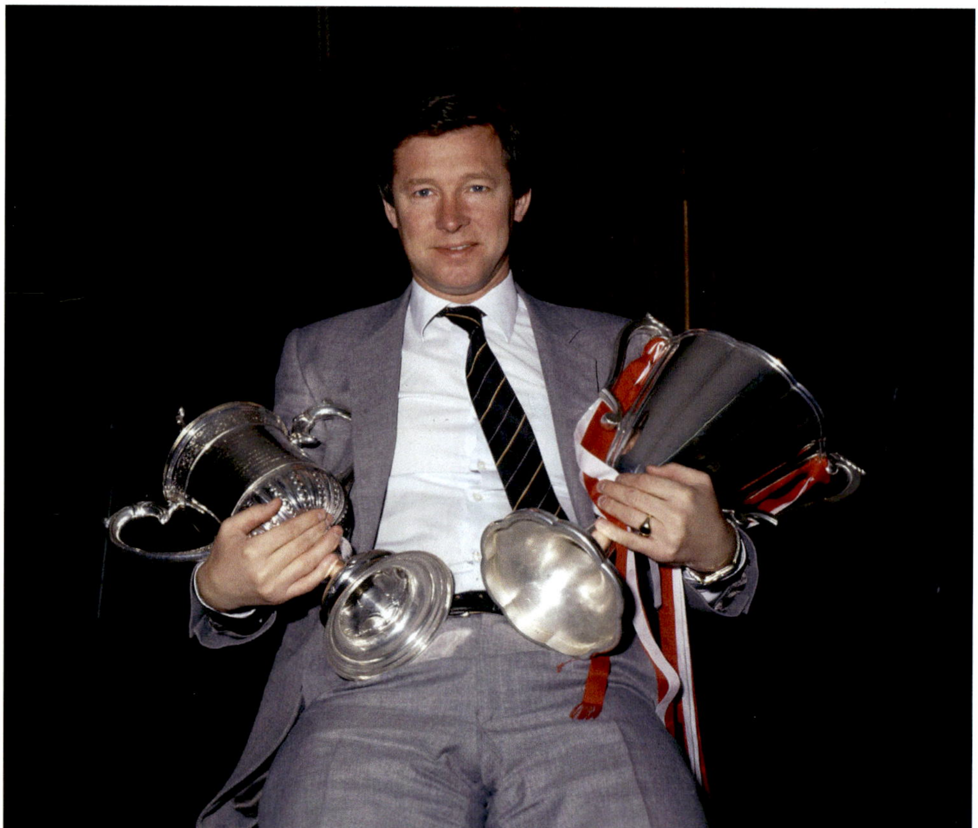

Alex Ferguson with the European Cup Winners' Cup and Scottish Cup in 1983

18

Did You Know?

The new television gantry, built in the summer of 1980 within the new South Terrace, was used for the first time against Morton on 6 September 1980. The cameras were on hand to catch a perfect view of all the Aberdeen goals in their 6-0 win.

After winning the Premier League in 1980 the club discovered the flagpole at the King Street end was not fit for purpose and a new one was fitted to accommodate the championship flag which would be in place all season with the exception of European matches.

Winger Peter Weir had been a lifelong Dons supporter long before he joined the club in 1981. Weir had been brought up in Johnstone but got hooked on Aberdeen after going to the 1970 Scottish Cup semi-final win over Kilmarnock in Perth and then the final victory over Celtic at Hampden. Weir stopped playing football when he was 14 to go and follow the Dons all over Scotland.

When Dinamo Tirana arrived at Pittodrie for a European Cup Winners' Cup tie in 1982, so little was known about the Albanians that the Aberdeen match programme could not include their line-up as no information on their squad had been provided. The only info was that the Tirana team would be announced over the public address system.

When Aberdeen touched down in Tirana for their second leg in 1982 they were unaware of an ill-fated coup to oust the ruling communist government. King Leka I, the exiled ruler of Albania, was behind the Liberation Army that planned to land on the Albanian coast in a bid to overthrow the ruling party. Leka, who was exiled in Johannesburg, advised his commander to cease their plans as it seemed suicidal from the outset. Leka made the claims during a visit to Paris, where it was reported that he had gathered groups of fighting commando units as he was determined to overthrow the communist government in Tirana. Aberdeen were oblivious to all the political instability and went about keeping the precious clean sheet against Dinamo in the searing heat of the capital to progress to the second round of the Cup Winners' Cup.

Aberdeen had to change their shirts at half-time during their Cup Winners' Cup second leg against Dinamo in 1982. With the heat peaking at nearly 100°F the only change kit was an adidas prototype that was never adopted by the club but only ever worn in the second half in Tirana.

Jim Leighton was the recipient of a superb trophy and £500 for his chosen charity when he picked up the *Daily Star* Clean Sheet Award in 1982. He had the most shut-outs in British football to prove he was the hardest keeper in the country to beat.

In September 1982 the Dons boasted of having nine players selected for Scotland duty. Jim Leighton, Alex McLeish, Willie Miller and Gordon Strachan were selected for the full squad while Bryan Gunn, Eric Black, Neale Cooper, John Hewitt and Neil Simpson were in the under-21 squad. Young Willie Falconer was also in the Scotland Youth side for a tournament in Monaco.

Gordon Strachan picked up another sports award in December 1982 when he was named Sports Personality of the Year by the Scottish Professional Sports Photographers' Association. Strachan was at the gala awards ceremony to accept the trophy where several sports celebrities were in attendance. Previous winners included Jim Watt, Sandy Lyle, Allan Wells and Andy Irvine.

When Aberdeen were in Munich for their European Cup Winners' Cup tie, they weren't the only personalities staying at their hotel. The popular women dancers Legs & Co of *Top of the Pops* fame were going through their paces in rehearsals for a show in Munich.

Sir Hugh Fraser, the well-known wealthy Scottish businessman and entrepreneur, was a guest of former Don Jimmy Wilson for the game against Bayern Munich. A charity event in Wilson's pub raised money which was doubled by Fraser, who was delighted to see Aberdeen win, 'This is only the third football game I have been to in my life. You can count on me as a Dons supporter from now on. That last 20 minutes was something I will never forget.'

The personalities were out in force for the Cup Winners' Cup clash with Bayern Munich on 16 March 1983. Among the managers in attendance were Jock Stein, Jock Wallace, John Greig, Jim Clunie and John Clark. TV commentator Ian St John came in for a lot of attention, while several former Aberdeen players were there including George Hamilton, Joe Harper, Tom McMillan, Andy Harrow and Andy Dornan. Tommy Younger and Jock McDonald represented the SFA.

When Bayern Munich visited Pittodrie there was a record 50-strong press contingent. There were also four live radio broadcasts: BBC Scotland, BBC2, Northsound and on German radio.

Aberdeen were fined £880 by UEFA following their win over Bayern Munich at Pittodrie. During the game an umbrella shaft landed on the pitch. It emerged that the offending object belonged to sales manager Dick King, who had been shaking his umbrella when the shaft broke and ended up on the pitch. Mr King was led away by police but was allowed to return minutes later after his explanation of the accident was accepted.

Stuart Kennedy, the Dons' international full-back, actually started his sporting days as a rugby player. Kennedy was outstanding in the Grangemouth High rugby team during his time at the rugby-only school. Kennedy later moved to Murray Secondary, where he was able to play football. It was later revealed that he kicked all the rugby conversions and was never on the losing side.

When Scotland drew 2-2 with Switzerland at Hampden on 30 March 1983, after Alex McLeish came on at half-time for an out-of-sorts Alan Hansen, the Aberdeen contingent was five. Described in the *Evening Express* as the Dons' 'Famous Five', it was the first time the club had five players in the same Scotland side. McLeish joined Jim Leighton, Willie Miller, Gordon Strachan and Peter Weir in the European Championship qualifier.

In March 1983 no fewer than 14 Aberdeen players were called up for Scotland duty. Jim Leighton, Alex McLeish, Willie Miller, Gordon Strachan and Peter Weir were all called up for the senior side. Bryan Gunn, Neale Cooper, Neil Simpson, Eric Black and John Hewitt would represent the under-21s, while Willie Falconer and Ian Porteous were in the under-18s. Steve Smith and Joe Miller were selected for the Scottish Schoolboys' clash with West Germany.

On the eve of the Cup Winners' Cup semi-final against Waterschei, the club announced a new sponsorship deal with local firm Hydrasun. The £20,000 agreement was to supply tracksuit advertising and promotional facilities, for the remainder of 1982/83 and through the following season. In hindsight for Hydrasun the timing could not have been better with the club's profile and standing throughout Britain and Europe at an all-time high.

When Aberdeen travelled to Genk for the second leg of the semi-final, chairman Dick Donald was presented with a batch of strawberries before kick-off. Apparently, they were the first lot of fresh strawberries from the Genk area that year. The Aberdeen substitutes had trouble accessing the away dugout getting past boxes of strawberries.

Alex Ferguson's first game in Europe as a player took place in Gothenburg, ironically the same city as the 1983 Cup Winners' Cup Final. Ferguson was in the Dunfermline side that played Swedish outfit Örgryte IS in the Inter-Cities Fairs Cup.

Following Aberdeen eliminating Bayern Munich, they were then Britain's sole survivors from all three European competitions. Liverpool and Aston Villa had been knocked out of the European Cup while Dundee United exited the UEFA Cup.

The Ullevi stadium in Gothenburg was built for the 1958 World Cup finals and as part of its 25-year anniversary it was chosen to host the 1983 Cup Winners' Cup Final.

Thames TV revealed that the final in Gothenburg was the biggest event it had covered since the wedding of Prince Charles and Diana Spencer. It was reported that 150 million viewers throughout the world were expected to tune in to watch the game.

Real Madrid players were on big money to beat Aberdeen. Having reached the final, they had already been rewarded with a £10,000 bonus per man. If they defeated the Dons a further £5,000 would be forthcoming. Manager Alfredo Di Stéfano's bonus was double that of his players. The Aberdeen players were on a bonus of £2,000 each to win the Cup Winners' Cup.

There was plenty of activity in Gothenburg for the Red Army in 1983 as the city boasted of having one of the biggest carnival fairs in the world. On the Tuesday evening before the final, David Bowie was performing as part of his European tour.

Aberdeen Airport reported that 4,650 supporters were on the 40 flights to Gothenburg over the three days before the game. The duty free areas also enjoyed brisk business. More than 4,500 bottles of whisky and 1,500 bottles of white spirits, mainly vodka, were sold.

Before the final in the Ullevi stadium the largest taxi firm in Gothenburg reported that their booking system had fallen apart. Such was the demand from Aberdeen supporters that it was later revealed that the company's switchboard had blown a fuse after being so overloaded with enquiries.

Supporter banners, or *tifos* as they are known these days, are nothing new. For the final there was a range of banners on show from the Red Army. 'Peter Weir lays on more balls than Emmanuelle' was a reference to an adult film series of the time. 'Doug Rougvie never lets a dago by' was a slightly controversial slant on the Spanish which would not be tolerated these days. 'Gordon Strachan gives out more majestic passes than Dick Donald' referenced the chairman owning the Majestic Cinema in Aberdeen at that time.

The opening goal in the Cup Winners' Cup Final was timed at six minutes and 34 seconds as Eric Black struck following a set piece from a Gordon Strachan corner.

The Dons gained a further accolade in the aftermath of the final as the Red Army were declared the best travelling fans in Europe by the Gothenburg police. The local force reported that the Aberdeen support were 'very nice people' and were no trouble at all. A spokesman said, 'I hope they enjoyed visiting Gothenburg as much as we enjoyed having them and their visit was not spoiled too much by the rain.' The local police also laid on several beds for some fans who could not find their way back to their hotels.

It was announced by the Grampian Region Educational Department that all schools in the area would remain open despite the Aberdeen team being welcomed back on an open-topped bus parade on the Thursday afternoon after the final. Aberdeen Grammar School put forward a petition that attracted more than 100 pupils and teachers to grant a half day to allow everyone to see the parade. It later emerged that hundreds of children reported being sick that afternoon.

The victorious party would parade through the city on their return from Gothenburg on Thursday, 12 May 1983. From the airport, the bus would take the following route: Dyce Drive, Inverurie Road, Auchmill Road, Great Northern Road, Queens Road, Albyn Place, Alford Place, Union Street, King Street and on to Pittodrie.

John Hewitt is not the only Aberdonian to score a winning goal in the Cup Winners' Cup Final. While Hewitt etched his name into Pittodrie folklore in 1983, back in 1966 it was a very different experience for Aberdeen-born Ron Yeats. The Liverpool defender put through his own goal as Borussia Dortmund won 2-1 in the Hampden final.

Aberdeen first installed executive boxes in the summer of 1983. Situated along the rear of the Main Stand, 20 boxes were fitted with heating, armchairs and catering facilities. They were available for £13,500 for a three-year lease, and within four weeks they had all been sold.

Ahead of the European Super Cup meetings with Hamburg in 1983, Alex Ferguson was again meticulous in his preparations. He interrupted his family's summer holiday in Florida to jet off to New York to see Hamburg in pre-season action against New York Cosmos.

The accolade of European Team of the Year was one that Aberdeen accepted in 1983. The much respected *France Football* magazine bestowed that title on the Dons following their stunning Cup Winners' Cup success. SV Hamburg, the European Cup winners, were runners-up. The Germans were disappointed that Aberdeen had edged them out, and all this was before the two sides clashed in the European Super Cup Final.

Aberdeen just missed out on another Team of the Year prize when they were edged out in the annual BBC Sports Review of the Year 1983 awards. That title went to ice skaters Jayne Torvill and Christopher Dean, with athlete Steve Cram picking up the Sports Personality of the Year honour.

Gordon Strachan received a surprise in 1983 when he was invited to Edinburgh as a guest of Her Majesty the Queen. Along with his top hat and tails, Strachan attended the Royal Garden Party at Holyrood Palace.

Willie Miller was named as captain of Scotland against Canada when the Scots toured in the summer of 1983. Miller also led his nation against Belgium at Hampden in October 1983. The Dons' skipper had previously captained the Scottish under-23 side.

Alex Ferguson was named as the first Scottish Sports Personality of the Year by the Variety Club of Great Britain in December 1983. Ferguson saw off some fierce competition, not only from the football world but from all sports in the UK. Lord Provost Alex Collie and the Aberdeen directors were on hand to see the Dons' manager collect the award at a gala dinner in Glasgow.

When Mark McGhee scored against Újpesti Dózsa in the Cup Winners' Cup quarter-final second leg in 37 minutes, it was a landmark in the club's European history. The first of McGhee's three goals that evening was the Dons' 100th in European competition.

Mark McGhee joined Hamburg in 1984 and was sent off in his first friendly outing for the Germans. The former Don faced a potential eight-week suspension.

The Main Stand at Pittodrie saw the removal of the wooden seats in the summer of 1984 as they were replaced with new plastic seating to match the rest of the stadium. The seating had been in place since the stand had been extended in 1934.

When Eric Black scored his third goal against Morton at Cappielow on 8 September 1984, it was the Dons' 600th goal in the Premier League, which was in its eighth season following reconstruction of the Scottish leagues.

A young Aberdeen side travelled to Wembley on 21 November 1984 to take part in a national five-a-side tournament. The Dons' stay was brief as they went down 3-0 to Watford in the opening round. The English club went on to win the tournament.

On 31 December 1984 Alex Ferguson was awarded an OBE in the New Year Honours List. It was a double celebration for Ferguson as the news came on his birthday.

Aberdeen defeated Hearts in a Scottish Cup quarter-final replay at Pittodrie on 13 March 1985, exactly 31 years to the day since they had played the Edinburgh club at the same stage in 1954. On that earlier occasion Pittodrie was packed with a club record attendance of 45,061 as Aberdeen won 3-0 and went on to reach the final.

Assistant manager Willie Garner turned the clock back by playing for Aberdeen 'A' as the young Dons defeated Dundee United to win the Reserve League Cup on 14 March 1985. Aberdeen won 2-0 at Pittodrie after losing the first leg 1-0 in Dundee. Willie, along with John McMaster, Doug Bell and Steve Cowan who all played after coming back from injuries, handed their winners' medals to the younger players who played in the earlier rounds.

Willie Miller made his 50th Scottish Cup appearance for Aberdeen in the semi-final replay against Dundee United in April 1985, overtaking Bobby Clark as making the most appearances in the competition for the club.

Frank McDougall was still serving a European ban in September 1985 but was on hand ahead of the tie against ÍA to receive the adidas Golden Shoe award for finishing as the top scorer in Scotland in his first season, 1984/85.

The new Merkland Stand was opened at Pittodrie in October 1985. The King Street end had undergone many changes through the years, with works including a new roof along with new kiosks, stairways and disabled access. The 'Paddock' as it had been known also had new turnstiles installed for ease of access. The cost was around £1m and the club received part of the funding from the Football Grounds Improvement Trust.

When Aberdeen defeated Hearts in the 1986 Scottish Cup Final, it was their fourth success in the competition in five seasons. The supporters had been used to winning at the national stadium; since losing the 1979 League Cup Final, the Dons never lost another Hampden final under Alex Ferguson. For Hearts it was more anguish as they had thrown away the chance to win the league the week before. Following the Dons' 3-0 win it was all too much for some of the Tynecastle support as the police made 72 arrests on the day.

Acknowledgements

FOLLOWING THAT incredible night in Gothenburg in 1983, it was always my intention to recall not only that evening but the whole seven seasons as the Dons ruled the roost. There have been plenty of references to what Aberdeen achieved in the '80s over the years. For my part I have provided a comprehensive statistical account of the period along with some fascinating quotes, facts and memories.

The resources that I have used to complete this book include:

Ferguson, Alex, *A Light in the North* (Mainstream Publishing, 1985)
Stirling, Kevin, *Aberdeen: A Centenary History 1903-2003* (Desert Island Books, 2002)
Miller, Willie, *The Don* (Birlinn, 2007)
Crick, Michael, *The Boss* (Simon & Schuster, 2002)
Bell, Dougie, *Signed Twice by Fergie* (Archie McLeod, 2020)
Irvine, Brian, *What a Difference a Day Makes* (Mainstream Publishing, 1996)
Grant, Michael, *Fergie Rises* (Aurum Press, 2014)

Other resources that formed a lot of my research included the British Newspaper Archive, and my own personal archive from that period. Several books listed above provided a wealth of information, no more so than Michael Grant's first-class *Fergie Rises*.

Special thanks to Kirsty Smith and David Powell from Aberdeen Journals from sourcing and allowing use of the superb archive at DC Thomson.

My personal thanks to Andrew Morrison, whose statistical knowledge of Aberdeen is second to none. Andrew took the time to go through the statistics with forensic detail. Also, to Malcolm Panton at Aberdeen FC. Former Dons Brian Mitchell, Robert Connor and Willie Garner were a great help, Brian and Robert sharing some of their experiences at Pittodrie and Willie for providing me with an excellent foreword.

Thanks to all at Pitch Publishing for being so helpful, and once again to my son Kevin, whose support for Aberdeen and his old man is quite remarkable. To my wife Bernadette and daughter Joanne for their continued support, my thanks.

Finally, to Aberdeen FC supporters everywhere, I hope you enjoy reading through a period that remains the greatest ever from an era that will never be forgotten. Keep the faith.

Appendix: Records and Statistics

SEASON 1978/79

Date		*Premier League*		*Att*	*Scorers*
12 Aug	A	Hearts	W 4-1	11,500	Archibald 2, Harper, Davidson
19 Aug	H	MORTON	W 3-1	14,500	Harper 3
26 Aug	A	Dundee Utd	D 1-1	10,000	Harper
09 Sep	H	MOTHERWELL	W 4-0	12,200	Archibald 2, Harper 2
16 Sep	A	Rangers	D 1-1	27,000	Sullivan
23 Sep	A	Hibernian	L 1-2	12,086	Jarvie
30 Sep	H	PARTICK TH	D 1-1	11,100	Archibald
07 Oct	H	CELTIC	W 4-1	24,000	Archibald 2, Harper, Davidson
14 Oct	A	St Mirren	L 1-2	10,973	Harper
21 Oct	H	HEARTS	L 1-2	12,750	Harper
29 Oct	A	Morton	L 1-2	6,500	Jarvie
04 Nov	H	DUNDEE UTD	W 1-0	13,850	Harper
11 Nov	A	Motherwell	D 1-1	5,448	Scanlon
18 Nov	H	RANGERS	D 0-0	24,000	
25 Nov	H	HIBERNIAN	W 4-1	13,250	Harper 2, Fleming, Sullivan
09 Dec	A	Celtic	D 0-0	24,000	
16 Dec	H	ST MIRREN	D 1-1	11,700	McMaster
23 Dec	A	Hearts	D 0-0	9,500	
30 Dec	H	MORTON	L 1-2	8,700	Harper
20 Jan	A	Hibernian	D 1-1	4,100	Harper
24 Feb	A	St Mirren	D 2-2	11,500	Archibald, Strachan
28 Feb	H	PARTICK TH	W 2-1	11,500	McMaster, Archibald
03 Mar	A	Celtic	L 0-1	26,000	
17 Mar	H	DUNDEE UTD	L 0-2	10,200	
26 Mar	H	MOTHERWELL	W 8-0	6,300	McMaster, Archibald 2, Harper 3, Davidson, Strachan
01 Apr	A	Morton	W 1-0	6,500	Cooper
07 Apr	H	HIBERNIAN	D 0-0	10,000	
14 Apr	A	Partick Th	W 1-0	6,000	McGhee
18 Apr	A	Motherwell	D 1-1	2,672	McLeish
21 Apr	H	CELTIC	D 1-1	18,400	Strachan
25 Apr	H	RANGERS	W 2-1	19,000	McGhee, Archibald
28 Apr	H	ST MIRREN	L 1-2	10,400	Archibald
02 May	H	HEARTS	W 5-0	6,000	Strachan, Sullivan, McGhee 2, Scanlon
05 May	A	Dundee Utd	D 2-2	7,822	Strachan, Jarvie
07 May	A	Rangers	L 0-2	30,000	
11 May	A	Partick Th	W 2-1	4,000	Sullivan, Harper
League Cup					
30 Aug	A	Meadowbank	W 5-0	1,600	Kennedy, Archibald, Jarvie, Scanlon, Fleming

02 Sep	H	MEADOWBANK	W 4-0	6,850	Harper 2, Archibald, Scanlon
04 Oct	A	Hamilton	W 1-0	5,000	Scanlon
11 Oct	H	HAMILTON	W 7-1	10,000	Harper 4, Kennedy, Rougvie, Sullivan
08 Nov	A	Ayr Utd	D 3-3	6,300	Harper 2, Sullivan
15 Nov	H	AYR UTD	W 3-1	13,000	Archibald, Harper, McLelland
13 Dec	N	Hibernian (aet)	W 1-0	21,048	Kennedy
31 Mar	N	Rangers	L 1-2	54,000	Davidson

Scottish Cup

27 Jan	A	Hamilton	W 2-0	9,400	Miller Harper
21 Feb	A	Ayr Utd	W 6-2	11,500	McMaster, Archibald 2, Scanlon 2, Harper
10 Mar	H	CELTIC	D 1-1	23,000	Harper
14 Mar	A	Celtic	W 2-1	36,000	Archibald, Davidson
11 Apr	N	Hibernian	L 1-2	9,837	Archibald

ECWC

13 Sep	A	Marek Dimitrov	L 2-3	20,000	Harper, Jarvie
27 Sep	H	MAREK DIMITROV	W 3-0	21,100	Harper, Jarvie, Scanlon
18 Oct	A	Fortuna Dusseldorf	L 0-3	10,000	
01 Nov	H	FORTUNA DUSSELDORF	W 2-0	16,800	McLelland, Jarvie

Friendlies

31 Jul	A	Elgin City	W 5-0	1,500	Sullvan, Harper, Jarvie, Davidson, Cooper
02 Aug	A	Buckie Thistle	W 2-0	800	Sullivan, Cooper
05 Aug	H	TOTTENHAM HOTSPUR	W 3-1	18,000	Archibald, Harper, jarvie
07 Aug	H	MIDDLESBROUGH	W 3-2*	10,545	Harper, Davidson
03 Sep	H	FORMER DONS SELECT	L 0-1	21,000	
23 Oct	A	Arbroath Select	D 2-2*	1,200	Smith
22 Nov	H	MOSCOW DYNAMO	W 1-0	11,878	Davidson
16 Jan	A	Belenenses	W 5-0	900	Jarvie 2, Davidson 3
24 Jan	A	Buckie Thistle	W 3-0	750	Simpson, Watson, Hamilton
14 May	A	Ross County/Brora	W 2-0	2,000	Rougvie, McGhee

			Home					*Away*						*TOTALS*					
		P	*W*	*D*	*L*	*F*	*A*	*W*	*D*	*L*	*F*	*A*	*Pts*	*W*	*D*	*L*	*F*	*A*	*Pts*
1	Celtic	36	13	3	2	32	12	8	3	7	29	25	48	21	6	9	61	37	48
2	Rangers	36	12	5	1	32	10	6	4	8	20	25	45	18	9	9	52	35	45
3	Dundee Utd	36	12	4	2	33	16	6	4	8	23	21	44	18	8	10	56	37	44
4	ABERDEEN	36	9	5	4	39	16	4	9	5	20	20	40	13	14	9	59	36	40
5	Hibernian	36	7	9	2	23	16	5	4	9	21	32	37	12	13	11	44	48	37
6	St Mirren	36	8	3	7	23	20	7	3	8	22	21	36	15	6	15	45	41	36
7	Morton	36	9	4	5	34	23	3	8	7	18	30	36	12	12	12	52	53	36
8	Partick Th	36	10	2	6	31	21	3	6	9	11	18	34	13	8	15	42	39	34
9	Hearts	36	5	5	8	19	25	3	2	13	20	46	23	8	7	21	39	71	23
10	Motherwell	36	2	5	11	20	38	3	2	13	13	48	17	5	7	24	33	86	17

Attendance Records 1978/79

Highest Home Attendance	24,000	v Celtic 7 Oct 1978 and v Rangers 18 Nov 1978
Highest Away Attendance	36,000	v Celtic 14 Mar 1979
Highest Overall Attendance	54,000	v Rangers 31 Mar 1979
Lowest Home Attendance	6,000	v Hearts 2 May 1979
Lowest Away Attendance	1,600	v Meadowbank 30 Aug 1978
Average Home Attendance	13,528	All Competitive Matches
Average Away Attendance	12,156	All Competitive Matches
Average Neutral Attendance	28,295	All Competitive Matches
Overall Average Attendance	13,717	All Competitive Matches

Debuts

Leighton, Jim	v Hearts 12 Aug 1978
Gardiner, John	v Meadowbank Thistle 30 Aug 1978
Simpson, Neil	v Hamilton Accies 11 Oct 1978
Considine, Doug	v Motherwell 11 Nov 1978
McGhee, Mark	v Morton 4 Apr 1979
Hamilton, Derek	v Morton 4 Apr 1979

Final Appearances

Ritchie, Steve	v Morton 28 Oct 1978
Smith, Joe	v Dundee United 4 Nov 1978
Fleming, Ian	v Morton 30 Dec 1978
Gardiner, John	v Hibernian 11 Apr 1979
McLelland, Chic	v Rangers 25 Apr 1979

STATS OF THE SEASON

The 8-0 win v Motherwell was the biggest win in the Premier League at that time.
Drew Jarvie scored the Dons' 50th goal in European competition when he netted against Dusseldorf on 1 November

INTERNATIONAL NOTES

Stuart Kennedy capped for Scotland v Austria 20 Sep 1978, v Portugal 29 Nov 1978

Alex McLeish capped for Scotland U-21 v USA 17 Sep 1978

SEASON 1979/80

Date		*Premier League*		*Att*	
11 Aug	A	Partick Thistle	L 0-1	7,500	
18 Aug	H	HIBERNIAN	W 3-0	10,300	McMaster 2, Archibald
25 Aug	A	Dundee Utd	W 3-1	10,982	McGhee, Archibald, Harper
08 Sep	A	Morton	L 2-3	5,540	Archibald, McMaster
15 Sep	H	RANGERS	W 3-1	23,000	Strachan, McMaster, Rougvie
22 Sep	H	CELTIC	L 1-2	23,000	Strachan
29 Sep	A	Dundee	W 4-0	11,817	Jarvie 2, Archibald, Harper
06 Oct	A	St Mirren	D 2-2	9,163	Archibald, Harper
13 Oct	H	KILMARNOCK	W 3-1	12,000	Strachan, Scanlon, Jarvie
20 Oct	H	PARTICK THISTLE	D 1-1	12,000	Davidson
27 Oct	A	Hibernian	D 1-1	7,000	Watson
03 Nov	H	DUNDEE UTD	L 0-3	12,500	
10 Nov	H	MORTON	L 1-2	10,400	McLeish
17 Nov	A	Rangers	W 1-0	18,500	Archibald
15 Dec	H	ST MIRREN	W 2-0	5,000	McLeish, Hamilton
05 Jan	A	Morton	L 0-1	6,000	
12 Jan	H	RANGERS	W 3-2	18,600	Strachan, Archibald, Hamilton
19 Jan	H	CELTIC	D 0-0	24,000	
02 Feb	A	Dundee	W 3-1	7,661	Jarvie 2, Hamilton
09 Feb	A	St Mirren	D 1-1	7,900	Strachan
23 Feb	H	KILMARNOCK	L 1-2	9,600	Archibald
01 Mar	H	PARTICK THISTLE	D 1-1	9,000	Jarvie
15 Mar	H	DUNDEE UTD	W 2-1	10,000	Watson, Jarvie
19 Mar	H	DUNDEE	W 3-0	7,000	Watson, Miller, Jarvie
22 Mar	H	MORTON	W 1-0	7,250	Jarvie
29 Mar	A	Rangers	D 2-2	20,000	Archibald, Jarvie
01 Apr	A	Kilmarnock	W 4-0*	5,000	Kennedy, Strachan, McGhee
05 Apr	A	Celtic	W 2-1	40,000	McGhee, Jarvie
07 Apr	H	DUNDEE	W 2-1	11,600	Strachan, Jarvie
16 Apr	H	HIBERNIAN	D 1-1	15,000	Watson

19 Apr	A	Kilmarnock	W 3-1	3,000	Strachan, Archibald, McGhee
23 Apr	A	Celtic	W 3-1	48,000	Strachan, Archibald, McGhee
26 Apr	H	ST MIRREN	W 2-0	19,000	Rougvie, Scanlon
29 Apr	A	Dundee Utd	D 1-1	12,954	Strachan
03 May	A	Hibernian	W 5-0	12,921	Scanlon 2, Watson, Archibald, McGhee
07 May	A	Partick Thistle	D 1-1*	7,000	

League Cup

15 Aug	H	ARBROATH	W 4-0	6,700	McGhee, McMaster, Davidson, Jarvie
22 Aug	A	Arbroath	L 1-2	2,174	Harper
29 Aug	A	Meadowbank	W 5-0	1,200	McMaster 2, Garner, McGhee, Strachan
01 Sep	H	MEADOWBANK	D 2-2	6,000	McMaster, Strachan
26 Sep	H	RANGERS	W 3-1	18,000	McLeish, Garner, Harper
10 Oct	A	Rangers	W 2-0	28,000	Strachan, Harper
31 Oct	H	CELTIC	W 3-2	24,000	Archibald 3
24 Nov	A	Celtic	W 1-0	39,000	McGhee
01 Dec	N	Morton	W 2-1	11,896	Strachan, McGhee
08 Dec	N	Dundee Utd (aet)	D 0-0	27,173	
12 Dec	N	Dundee Utd	L 0-3	28,933	

Scottish Cup

26 Jan	A	Arbroath	D 1-1	5,764	Archibald
30 Jan	H	ARBROATH	W 5-0	9,127	Scanlon 3, Archibald, Hamilton
16 Feb	H	AIRDRIE	W 8-0	10,410	Archibald 4, McMaster, Miller, Strachan, Scanlon
08 Mar	A	Partick Th	W 2-1	8,584	Archibald, Jarvie
12 Apr	N	Rangers	L 0-1	44,000	

UEFA Cup

19 Sep	H	EINTRACHT FRANKFURT	D 1-1	20,000	Harper
03 Oct	A	Eintracht Frankfurt	L 0-1	20,000	

Drybrough Cup

28 Jul	A	Kilmarnock	L 0-1	2,500	

Friendlies

17 Jul	A	Kolding IF	W 2-1		Archibald, Harper	
19 Jul	A	Randers	W 1-0		Jarvie	
21 Jul	A	Skovbakken	W 7-0		McGhee 2, Archibald 2, Cooper, Garner Jarvie	
29 Jul	A	Fraserburgh	W 3-2	600	McMaster 2, McLeish	
30 Jul	A	Buckie Thistle	W 1-0	650	Watson	
02 Aug	H	COVENTRY CITY	W 4-1*	9,343	Miller, McGhee, Strachan	04
Aug	A	Cowdenbeath	W 3-2		Rougvie, McGhee, Jarvie	
08 Aug	H	TOTTENHAM HOTSPUR	W 2-0	11,500	McGhee, Archibald	
09 Aug	A	Nairn County	W 5-1	250	Jarvie 2, Scanlon, Harper, Cowan	05
Sep	H	LEICESTER CITY	D 1-1	8,123	Watson	
24 Feb	A	Rothes	W 4-1	400	Davidson 2, Scanlon, Hamilton	19
Mar	A	Arbroath Select	L 2-3	750	McGhee, Jarvie	

* denotes own goal

			Home						Away					TOTALS					
		P	W	D	L	F	A	W	D	L	F	A	Pts	W	D	L	F	A	Pts
1	ABERDEEN	36	10	4	4	30	18	9	6	3	38	18	48	19	10	7	68	36	48
2	Celtic	36	13	3	2	44	17	5	8	5	17	21	47	18	11	7	61	38	47
3	St Mirren	36	11	5	2	37	23	4	7	7	19	26	42	15	12	9	56	49	42
4	Dundee Utd	36	9	7	2	23	6	3	6	9	20	24	37	12	13	11	43	30	37
5	Rangers	36	11	5	2	29	16	4	2	12	21	30	37	15	7	14	50	46	37
6	Morton	36	9	4	5	24	16	5	4	9	27	30	36	14	8	14	51	46	36
7	Partick Th	36	6	8	4	24	22	5	6	7	19	25	36	11	14	11	43	47	36
8	Kilmarnock	36	7	6	5	19	19	4	5	9	17	33	33	11	11	14	36	52	33
9	Dundee	36	9	3	6	33	30	1	3	14	14	43	26	10	6	20	47	73	26
10	Hibernian	36	6	4	8	23	31	0	2	16	6	36	18	6	6	24	29	67	18

Attendance Records 1979/80

Highest Home Attendance	24,000	v Celtic 31 October 1979 (LC) and 19 January 1980
Highest Away Attendance	48,000	v Celtic 23 April 1980
Lowest Home Attendance	5,000	v St Mirren 15 December 1979
Lowest Away Attendance	1,202	v Meadowbank 29 August 1979 (LC)
Average Home Attendance	13,339	All Competitive Matches
Average Away Attendance	14,138	All Competitive Matches
Average Neutral Attendance	28,001	All Competitive Matches
Overall Average Attendance	14,795	All Competitive Matches

Debuts

Doug Bell	v Partick Thistle 11 Aug 1979
John Hewitt	v St Mirren 15 Dec 1979

Final Appearances

Neil Cooper	v Partick Thistle 11 Aug 1979
Dom Sullivan	v Kilmarnock 13 October 1979
Steve Archibald	v Partick Thistle 7 May 1980
Bobby Clark	v Partick Thistle 7 May 1980

After 585 appearances (a club record at the time) Bobby finally hangs up his gloves having won all three domestic honours.

STATS OF THE SEASON

15 games unbeaten in the Premier League between March and May 1980

INTERNATIONAL NOTES

Willie Miller capped for Scotland v Belgium 21 Nov 1979, v Wales 21 May 1980, v England 24 May 1980, v Hungary 31 May 1980.

Alex McLeish capped for Scotland v Portugal 26 Mar 1980, v Northern Ireland 16 May 1980, v Wales 21 May 1980, v England 24 May 1980, v Poland 28 May 1980, v Hungary 31 May 1980.

Steve Archibald capped for Scotland v Portugal 26 Mar 1980. (Further caps v N Ireland, Poland and Hungary after transfer to Tottenham)

Gordon Strachan capped for Scotland v Northern Ireland 16 May 1980, v Wales 21 May 1980, v England 24 May 1980, v Poland 28 May 1980, v Hungary 31 May 1980

Gordon Strachan capped for Scotland U-21 v Belgium 20 Nov 1979

Alex McLeish capped for Scotland U-21 v Belgium 18 Dec 1979, v England 12 Feb 1980, 4 Mar 1980

Steve Archibald capped for Scotland U-21 v Belgium 18 Dec 1979, v England 12 Feb 1980, 4 Mar 1980, v West Germany 26 Feb 1980

SEASON 1980/81

Date		Premier League	F-A	Att	
09 Aug	A	St Mirren	W 1-0	7,067	Jarvie
16 Aug	H	DUNDEE UTD	D 1-1	13,729	Strachan
23 Aug	A	Airdrie	W 4-0	5,000	Cowan, McGhee, Jarvie, Scanlon
06 Sep	H	MORTON	W 6-0*	9,485	Miller, Strachan, McMaster, Scanlon, Hewitt
13 Sep	A	Rangers	D 1-1	30,000	Strachan
20 Sep	A	Partick Thistle	W 1-0	6,000	McGhee
27 Sep	H	CELTIC	D 2-2*	23,000	McGhee
04 Oct	A	Hearts	W 1-0	10,873	Rougvie
11 Oct	H	KILMARNOCK	W 2-0	11,164	Jarvie, Scanlon
18 Oct	H	ST MIRREN	W 3-2	11,000	McGhee 2, McMaster
25 Oct	A	Dundee Utd	W 3-1	10,043	Strachan, McGhee, Hewitt
01 Nov	H	AIRDRIE	W 4-1	9,000	McCall 3, McGhee
08 Nov	A	Celtic	W 2-0	29,000	McCall 2
15 Nov	H	PARTICK TH	W 2-1	12,000	Strachan, Bell
22 Nov	A	Kilmarnock	D 1-1	3,200	McLeish
06 Dec	A	Morton	L 0-1	5,000	
13 Dec	H	RANGERS	W 2-0*	22,500	McGhee
20 Dec	A	Partick Thistle	D 1-1	4,000	McCall
27 Dec	H	CELTIC	W 4-1	24,000	McLeish, Miller, Strachan, McCall
30 Dec	H	DUNDEE UTD	D 1-1	23,000	Scanlon
03 Jan	A	St Mirren	D 1-1	11,100	Scanlon
10 Jan	A	Hearts	W 2-0	7,999	McCall, McGhee
31 Jan	A	Rangers	L 0-1	32,500	
07 Feb	H	MORTON	L 0-1	11,000	
21 Feb	A	Airdrie	D 0-0	2,600	
28 Feb	H	ST MIRREN	L 1-2	9,500	Jarvie
07 Mar	H	HEARTS	W 4-1	9,500	Hamilton, Angus, McCall, Jarvie
14 Mar	A	Kilmarnock	L 0-1	2,400	
28 Mar	A	Celtic	D 1-1	35,200	Harrow
01 Apr	H	PARTICK THISTLE	W 3-1	8,000	McLeish, Simpson, McGhee
04 Apr	A	Morton	W 3-1	4,500	Rougvie, Simpson, McGhee
11 Apr	H	HEARTS	W 1-0	5,600	Rougvie
18 Apr	H	AIRDRIE	W 3-0	7,000	McGhee 2, McCall
22 Apr	H	RANGERS	D 0-0	15,000	
25 Apr	A	Dundee Utd	D 0-0	6,369	
02 May	H	KILMARNOCK	L 0-2	6,300	

League Cup

27 Aug	H	BERWICK RANGERS	W 8-1	7,570	McGhee 3, Jarvie 2, Watson 2, Bell
30 Aug	A	Berwick Rangers	W 4-0	1,188	De Clerk, Kennedy, Strachan, Hewitt
03 Sep	A	Rangers	L 0-1	30,000	
24 Sep	H	RANGERS	W 3-1	23,926	Strachan 2, McMaster
08 Oct	A	Dundee	D 0-0	10,500	
29 Oct	H	DUNDEE	L 0-1	14,060	

Scottish Cup

24 Jan	A	Raith Rovers	W 2-1	10,000	Jarvie 2
14 Feb	A	Morton	L 0-1	8,350	

European Cup

17 Sep	H	AUSTRIA MEMPHIS	W 1-0	18,633	McGhee
01 Oct	A	Austria Memphis	D 0-0	37,000	
22 Oct	H	LIVERPOOL	L 0-1	23,926	
05 Nov	A	Liverpool	L 0-4	36,182	

Drybrough Cup

26 Jul	H	AIRDRIE	W 4-1	8,650	Scanlon 3, Watson
30 Jul	A	Morton	W 4-2	4,000	Scanlon 2, McGhee, Strachan
02 Aug	N	St Mirren	W 2-1	7,000	Jarvie, Cowan

Aberdeenshire Cup

25 Jan	A	Aberdeen University	W 7-1	450	Davidson 2, Cowan 2, Angus, Scanlon, Burke
09 Mar	A	Keith	W 4-1	250	Rougvie, Cowan, Angus, Hewitt
19 Apr	H	BUCKIE THISTLE	W 5-1	3,000	McGhee 2, Scanlon, Harrow, Watson

Friendlies

19 Jul	A	Torshavn	W 5-1	200	Scanlon 2, McMaster, Watson,Jarvie
22 Jul	A	Forres Mechanics	W 7-1		Jarvie 3, McMaster 2, Cowan, Scanlon
23 Jul	A	Nairn County	W 5-0	450	Scanlon 3, Strachan, Jarvie
03 Aug	H	ARSENAL	W 2-1	13,698	Watson, Miller
12 Aug	H	TWENTE ENSCHEDE	L 1-2	8,621	McLeish
31 Aug	H	JOE HARPER SELECT	W 8-6	16,000	Cowan 2, Strachan, Perovic, Jarvie, Davidson, Dornan, Leighton
03 May	A	Dundee	W 3-0	3,000	Rougvie, Harrow, Davidson

* denotes own goal

			Home					*Away*						*TOTALS*				
		P	W	D	L	F	A	W	D	L	F	A	Pts	W	D	L	F	A	Pts
1	Celtic	36	12	3	3	47	18	14	1	3	37	19	56	26	4	6	84	37	56
2	ABERDEEN	36	11	4	3	39	16	8	7	3	22	10	49	19	11	6	61	26	49
3	Rangers	36	12	3	3	33	10	4	9	5	27	22	44	16	12	8	60	32	44
4	St Mirren	36	9	6	3	28	20	9	2	7	28	27	44	18	8	10	56	47	44
5	Dundee Utd	36	8	5	5	34	24	9	4	5	32	18	43	17	9	10	66	42	43
6	Partick Th	36	6	6	6	17	17	4	4	10	15	31	30	10	10	16	32	48	30
7	Airdrie	36	6	5	7	19	25	4	4	10	17	30	29	10	9	17	36	55	29
8	Morton	36	7	2	9	24	28	3	6	9	12	30	28	10	8	18	36	58	28
9	Kilmarnock	36	3	5	10	14	31	2	4	12	9	34	19	5	9	22	23	65	19
10	Hearts	36	3	4	11	10	27	3	2	13	17	44	18	6	6	24	27	71	18

Attendance Records 1980/81

Highest Home Attendance	24,000	v Celtic 24 December 1980
Highest Away Attendance	37,000	v Austria Memphis 1 October 1980 (EC)
Lowest Home Attendance	5,600	v Hearts 11 April 1981
Lowest Away Attendance	1,188	v Berwick Rangers 30 August 1980 (LC)
Average Home Attendance	13,920	All Competitve Matches
Average Away Attendance	13,868	All Competitve Matches
Overall average Attendance	13,893	All Competitve Matches
Overall Attendance	666,871	All Competitve Matches

SEASON SUMMARY

	P	W	D	L	F	A
Premier League	36	19	11	6	61	26
Scottish Cup	2	1	0	1	2	2
League Cup	6	3	1	2	15	4
European Cup	4	1	1	2	1	5
Drybrough Cup	3	3	0	0	10	4
Aberdeenshire Cup	3	3	0	0	16	3
Friendlies	7	6	0	1	31	11
TOTAL	61	36	13	12	136	55

Home Wins	14	All Competitive Matches
Away Wins	10	All Competitive Matches
Most wins in a row	4	1 Apr-18 Apr 1981
Unbeaten games in a row	11	6 Sep-18 Oct 1980
Most losses in a row	3	31 Jan-14 Feb 1981
Clean Sheets	18	All Competitive Matches

RECORD

Premier League	Runners-up
Scottish Cup	Fourth Round
League Cup	Quarter-Final
European Cup	Second Round
Other	Aberdeen win the last ever Drybrough Cup

Debuts

Steve Cowan	v St Mirren 9 August 1980
Marc De Clerck	v Berwick Rangers 30 August 1980
Neale Cooper	v Kilmarnock 11 October 1980
Andy Dornan	v Airdrie 1 November 1980
Ian Angus	v Morton 6 December 1980
Andy Harrow	v Rangers 31 January 1981

Final Appearances

Marc De Clerk	v Kilmarnock 11 Oct 1980
Andy Dornan	v Celtic 8 Nov 1980
Willie Garner	v Partick Thistle 20 Dec 1980
Doug Considine	v Airdrie 21 Feb 1981
Duncan Davidson	v Morton 4 Apr 1981
Ian Scanlon	v Dundee Utd 25 Apr 1981
Joe Harper	v Kilmarnock 2 May 1981 Ending his two spells at the club as all-time top goalscorer with 199 competitive goals

The One and Only

Steve Morrison v Berwick Rangers 30 Aug 1980 made his one and only appearance for the club.

STATS OF THE SEASON

Belgian keeper Marc De Clerck scored on his debut from a wind-assisted clearance against Berwick, a League Cup tie played in England

Aberdeen went nine months without suffering a defeat in the Premier League between March and November 1980

INTERNATIONAL NOTES

Willie Miller capped for Scotland v Sweden 10 Sept 1980, v Portugal 15 Oct 1980, v Israel 25 Feb 1981, v Northern Ireland 25 Mar 1981, and 19 May 1981, v Wales 16 May 1981, v England 23 May 1981

Alex McLeish capped for Scotland v Sweden 10 Sep 1980, v Israel 25 Feb 1981 and 28 April 1981, v Northern Ireland 25 Mar 1981 and 19 May 1981, v England 23 May 1981

Gordon Strachan capped for Scotland v Sweden 10 Sep 1980, v Portugal 15 Oct 1980

Strachan scored the winning goal in Scotland's opening World Cup qualifier in Sweden 10 Sep 1980

Andy Watson capped for Scotland U-21 v Sweden 9 Sep 1980, v Denmark 18 Nov 1980

Mark McGhee capped for Scotland U-21 v Denmark 18 Nov 1980

Doug Bell capped for Scotland U-21 v Denmark 18 Nov 1980

Pittodrie hosted the Scotland v Denmark U-21 European Championship match on 18 Nov 1980

SEASON 1981/82

Date		Premier League	F-A	Att	
29 Aug	A	Dundee Utd	L 1-4	10,598	McLeish
05 Sep	H	CELTIC	L 1-3	18,825	Strachan
12 Sep	A	Partick Th	W 2-0	3,606	McCall, Cowan
19 Sep	H	HIBERNIAN	W 1-0	10,852	Simpson
26 Sep	A	Airdrie	W 4-0	3,000	Weir 2, McLeish, Hewitt
03 Oct	H	MORTON	W 2-0	11,007	Rougvie, Watson
10 Oct	A	Rangers	D 0-0	28,000	
17 Oct	A	St Mirren	W 2-1	6,870	Watson 2
24 Oct	H	DUNDEE	W 2-1	11,506	Rougvie, McCall
31 Oct	H	DUNDEE UTD	D 1-1	11,035	Black
07 Nov	A	Celtic	L 1-2	29,326	Strachan
14 Nov	H	PARTICK TH	W 2-1	11,193	Harrow, Watson
21 Nov	A	Hibernian	D 1-1	7,600	Simpson
28 Nov	H	AIRDRIE	D 0-0	8,030	
05 Dec	A	Morton	L 1-2	3,102	Hewitt
30 Jan	H	CELTIC	L 1-3	20,000	McMaster
03 Feb	A	Partick Th	D 0-0	2,317	
06 Feb	H	MORTON	D 0-0	7,217	
20 Aug	A	Airdrie	W 3-0	3,500	McGhee 2, Hewitt
27 Feb	H	DUNDEE	D 0-0	8,961	
10 Mar	H	HIBERNIAN	W 3-1	8,691	Strachan, Cooper, Jarvie
13 Mar	A	Rangers	W 3-1	20,000	Cooper, Cowan, Watson
17 Mar	A	Dundee	W 3-0	6,126	Simpson, Hewitt, Cowan
20 Mar	H	DUNDEE UTD	W 2-1	12,056	McLeish, Hewitt
27 Mar	A	Celtic	W 1-0	30,000	Kennedy
10 Apr	A	Hibernian	W 3-0	8,000	Strachan, McGhee, Jarvie
14 Apr	H	ST MIRREN	W 4-1	12,119	Rougvie 2, Strachan, Simpson
17 Apr	A	Morton	L 1-2	3,000	McGhee
21 Apr	H	RANGERS	W 3-1	15,700	Rougvie, Black, McGhee
24 Apr	H	AIRDRIE	W 2-0	8,000	Black, McGhee
01 May	A	Dundee	W 5-0*	6,415	McLeish, Harrow, Bell, McCall
03 May	H	PARTICK TH	W 3-1	6,000	Watson, McCall, Hewitt
05 May	A	Dundee Utd	W 2-1	6,587	Hewitt 2
08 May	H	ST MIRREN	W 5-1	9,000	Strachan 2, McGhee 2, Cooper
12 May	A	St Mirren	W 2-0	3,942	Rougvie, McLeish
15 May	H	RANGERS	W 4-0*	18,000	Hewitt 3

League Cup					
08 Aug	H	KILMARNOCK	W 3-0	9,000	McGhee 2, Kennedy
12 Aug	A	Hearts	L 0-1	10,500	
15 Aug	H	AIRDRIE	W 3-0	7,000	Strachan, Hewitt, Weir
19 Aug	H	HEARTS	W 3-0	8,600	Strachan, Bell, Hewitt
22 Aug	A	Kilmarnock	W 3-0	3,100	Strachan 2, McGhee
26 Aug	A	Airdrie	D 0-0	3,000	
02 Sep	H	BERWICK R	W 5-0	6,500	Strachan 2, Cooper, Bell, McCall
23 Sep	A	Berwick R	W 3-0	1,200	McGhee, McMaster, Harrow
07 Oct	A	Dundee Utd	W 1-0	15,000	Weir
28 Oct	H	DUNDEE UTD	L 0-3	21,000	

Scottish Cup					
23 Jan	A	Motherwell	W 1-0	12,679	Hewitt
13 Feb	H	CELTIC	W 1-0	24,000	Hewitt
06 Mar	H	KILMARNOCK	W 4-2	12,000	Strachan 2, McGhee, Simpson
03 Apr	N	St Mirren	D 1-1	16,782	Strachan
07 Apr	N	St Mirren	W 3-2	15,663	Simpson, McGhee, Weir
22 May	N	Rangers (aet)	W 4-1	53,788	McLeish, Strachan, McGhee, Cooper

UEFA Cup

16 Sep	A	Ipswich Town	D 1-1	18,535	Hewitt
30 Sep	H	IPSWICH TOWN	W 3-1	24,000	Weir 2, Strachan
21 Oct	H	ARGES PITESTI	W 3-0	22,000	Strachan, Hewitt, Weir
04 Nov	A	Arges Pitesti	D 2-2	8,760	Strachan, Hewitt
25 Nov	H	SV HAMBURG	W 3-2	24,000	Watson, Black, Hewitt
09 Dec	A	SV Hamburg	L 1-3	45,000	McGhee

Aberdeen FC Tournament

01 Aug	H	WEST HAM UNITED	W 3-0	12,500	Weir, Bell, McGhee
02 Aug	H	SOUTHAMPTON	W 5-1	11,000	McMaster, Cooper, Strachan, McGhee, Cowan

Friendlies

25 Jul	A	Dunfermline	D 1-1	1,985	Jarvie
04 Aug	A	Brechin City	D 0-0	850	
16 Aug	H	TOTTENHAM HOTSPUR	L 0-1	11,000	
30 Dec	H	HEARTS	W 2-1	3,000	Hewitt 2
06 Jan	A	Norwich City	W 4-1*	4,000	McLeish, Strachan, Bell
12 Jan	A	Benidorm	W 3-1	200	Hewitt 2, Bell

			Home					*Away*						*TOTALS*				
		P	W	D	L	F	A	W	D	L	F	A	Pts	W	D	L	F	A
1	Celtic	36	12	5	1	41	16	12	2	4	38	17	55	24	7	5	79	33
2	ABERDEEN	36	12	4	2	36	15	11	3	4	35	14	53	23	7	6	71	29
3	Rangers	36	10	5	3	34	16	6	6	6	23	29	43	16	11	9	57	45
4	Dundee Utd	36	10	4	4	40	14	5	6	7	21	24	40	15	10	11	61	38
5	St Mirren	36	8	4	6	30	23	6	5	7	19	29	37	14	9	13	49	52
6	Hibernian	36	8	7	3	23	14	3	7	8	15	26	36	11	14	11	38	40
7	Morton	36	9	6	3	20	12	0	6	12	11	42	30	9	12	15	31	54
8	Dundee	36	7	2	9	28	34	4	2	12	18	38	26	11	4	21	46	72
9	Partick Th	36	4	5	9	19	23	2	5	11	16	36	22	6	10	20	35	59
10	Airdrie	36	5	4	9	24	36	0	4	14	7	40	18	5	8	23	31	76

Attendance Records 1981/82

Highest Home Attendance	24,000	v Ipswich Town UEFA 30 Sep 1981, v Hamburg 25 Nov 1981, v Celtic SC 13 Feb 1982
Highest Away Attendance	45,000	v Hamburg UEFA 9 Dec 1981
Highest Neutral Attendance	53,788	v Rangers SC 22 May 1982
Lowest Home Attendance	6,000	v Partick 3 May 1982
Lowest Away Attendance	1,200	v Berwick Rangers LC 23 Sep 1981
Average Home Attendance	13,082	All Competitive Matches
Average Away Attendance	11,373	All Competitive Matches
Overall Average Attendance	13,097	All Competitve Matches
Overall Attendance	759,608	All Competitve Matches

SEASON SUMMARY

	P	W	D	L	F	A
Premier League	36	23	7	6	71	29
Scottish Cup	6	5	1	0	14	6
League Cup	10	7	1	2	21	4
UEFA Cup	6	3	2	1	13	9
Aberdeen FC Tourney	2	2	0	0	8	1
Friendlies	6	3	2	1	10	5
TOTAL	66	43	13	10	137	54

Home Wins	21	All Competitive Matches
Away Wins	15	All Competitive Matches
Most Wins in a row	9	
Unbeaten games in a row	15	
Most Losses in a row	2	
Clean Sheets	28	All Competitive Matches

RECORD

Premier League	Runners-Up
Scottish Cup	Winners
League Cup	Semi-Final
UEFA Cup	Third Round

Debuts

Eric Black	v Dundee Utd 31 Oct 1981(A scoring debut)
Brian Mitchell	v Hibernian 10 Apr 1982
Peter Weir	v Kilmarnock 8 Aug 1981

Final Appearances

Drew Jarvie	v Airdrie 24 Apr 1982
Andy Harrow	v Dundee 1 May 1982 (A scoring finale)

STATS OF THE SEASON

John Hewitt scored the quickest goal in Scottish Cup history when he netted against Motherwell in 9.6 seconds on 23 Jan 1982

Willie Miller became the most capped Dons player when he played against Brazil in the World Cup. His 18 appearances overtook Bobby Clark's long-standing record of 17.

INTERNATIONAL NOTES

Alex McLeish capped for Scotland v Sweden 9 Sep 1981, v Spain 24 Feb 1982, v Northern Ireland 28 Apr 1982, v Brazil 18 Jun 1982

Willie Miller capped for Scotland v Northern Ireland 14 Oct 1981, v Portugal 18 Nov 1981, v Netherlands 23 Mar 1982, v Brazil 18 Jun 1982, v USSR 22 Jun 1982

Gordon Strachan capped for Scotland v Northern Ireland 14 Oct 1981, v Portugal 18 Nov 1981, v Spain 24 Feb 1982, v Netherlands 23 Mar 1982, v New Zealand 15 Jun 1982, v Brazil 18 Jun 1982, v USSR 22 Jun 1982

Stuart Kennedy capped for Scotland v Portugal 18 Nov 1981

Neale Cooper capped for Scotland U-21 v Denmark 13 Oct 1981, v England 19 Apr 1982, v England 28 Apr 1982

Andy Watson capped for Scotland U-21 v Denmark 13 Oct 1981, v Italy 24 Mar 1982

Jim Leighton capped for Scotland U-21 v Italy 23 Feb 1982, v Italy 24 Mar 1982

Neil Simpson capped for Scotland U-21 v Italy 23 Feb 1982, v Italy 24 Mar 1982, England 28 Apr 1982

SEASON 1982/83

Date		Premier League	F-A	Att	
04 Sep	A	Dundee Utd	L 0-2	11,683	
11 Sep	H	MORTON	W 4-1	7,500	Strachan, Black, Simpson, Hewitt
18 Sep	A	St Mirren	D 1-1	4,800	McGhee
25 Sep	H	RANGERS	L 1-2	20,300	Strachan
02 Oct	H	MOTHERWELL	W 2-1	9,000	Miller, Cowan
09 Oct	A	Celtic	W 3-1	29,733	Strachan, Simpson, McGhee
16 Oct	H	DUNDEE	W 1-0	10,800	Weir
23 Oct	A	Kilmarnock	W 2-0	3,400	Black, Hewitt
30 Oct	A	Hibernian	D 1-1	6,400	Weir
06 Nov	H	DUNDEE UTD	W 5-1	14,000	Rougvie 2, Cooper, Strachan, Black
13 Nov	A	Morton	D 1-1	2,500	Simpson
20 Nov	H	ST MIRREN	W 4-0	10,300	Strachan, McGhee, Hewitt, Black
27 Nov	A	Rangers	W 1-0	23,000	Black
04 Dec	A	Motherwell	W 2-0	4,929	Strachan, Weir
11 Dec	H	CELTIC	L 1-2	24,000	McGhee
18 Dec	A	Dundee	W 2-0	6,528	McGhee 2
27 Dec	H	KILMARNOCK	W 2-0	14,500	Miller, Weir
01 Jan	H	HIBERNIAN	W 2-0	14,000	McGhee 2
03 Jan	A	Dundee Utd	W 3-0	17,851	Weir, Simpson, McGhee
08 Jan	H	MORTON	W 2-0	12,600	Simpson, McGhee
15 Jan	A	St Mirren	D 1-1	4,530	Black
22 Jan	H	RANGERS	W 2-0	21,600	Rougvie, McGhee
08 Feb	H	MOTHERWELL	W 5-1	13,300	McMaster, McLeish, Black, McGhee, Cooper
12 Feb	A	Celtic	W 3-1	42,831	Black 3
26 Feb	H	DUNDEE	W 3-1	11,500	Black, Bell, Weir
05 Mar	A	Kilmarnock	W 2-1	2,400	McGhee, Watson
19 Mar	H	DUNDEE UTD	L 1-2	22,800	Strachan
26 Mar	A	Morton	W 2-1	2,800	Black, Watson
02 Apr	H	ST MIRREN	L 0-1	16,400	
09 Apr	A	Rangers	L 1-2	19,800	McLeish
23 Apr	H	CELTIC	W 1-0	24,000	McGhee
27 Apr	A	Motherwell	W 3-0	6,715	Strachan, McGhee, Hewitt
30 Apr	A	Dundee	W 2-0	10,076	Strachan, Hewitt
03 May	A	Hibernian	D 0-0	8,000	
05 May	H	KILMARNOCK	W 5-0	12,000	Strachan 2, Angus 2, McMaster
14 May	H	HIBERNIAN	W 5-0*	24,000	Strachan, McGhee, Angus, Cowan

League Cup

Date		Opponent	F-A	Att	
11 Aug	A	Morton	D 2-2	3,500	Strachan, McGhee
14 Aug	H	DUNDEE	D 3-3	9,000	Black 3
21 Aug	H	DUMBARTON	W 3-0	6,500	Strachan 2, McGhee
25 Aug	H	MORTON	W 3-0	11,000	Bell 2, Rougvie
28 Aug	A	Dundee	W 5-1	7,000	Strachan 4, McGhee
08 Sep	A	Dumbarton	W 2-1	750	Hewitt, Bell
22 Sep	A	Dundee Utd	L 1-3	14,000	McGhee
06 Oct	H	DUNDEE UTD	L 0-1	11,700	

Scottish Cup

Date		Opponent	F-A	Att	
29 Jan	A	Hibernian	W 4-1	14,289	Simpson, McGhee, Weir, Watson
19 Feb	H	DUNDEE	W 1-0	19,000	Simpson
12 Mar	A	Partick Th	W 2-1	12,092	Cooper, Weir
16 Apr	N	Celtic	W 1-0	51,152	Weir
21 May	N	Rangers (aet)	W 1-0	62,979	Black

ECWC

18 Aug	H	SION	W 7-0*	13,000	Kennedy, McMaster, Simpson, Strachan, Black, Hewitt
01 Sep	A	Sion	W 4-1	2,400	McGhee 2, Miller, Hewitt
15 Sep	H	DINAMO TIRANA	W 1-0	15,000	Hewitt
29 Sep	A	Dinamo Tirana	D 0-0	20,000	
20 Oct	H	LECH POZNAN	W 2-0	17,600	McGhee, Weir
03 Nov	A	Lech Poznan	W 1-0	30,000	Bell
02 Mar	A	Bayern Munich	D 0-0	35,000	
16 Mar	H	BAYERN MUNICH	W 3-2	24,000	Simpson, McLeish, Hewitt
06 Apr	H	WATERSCHEI	W 5-1	24,000	McGhee 2, Simpson, Weir, Black
19 Apr	A	Waterschei	L 0-1	15,000	
11 May	N	Real Madrid (aet)	W 2-1	17,800	Black, Hewitt

Aberdeenshire Cup

20 Feb	A	Buckie Thistle	W 4-0	600	McIntyre, Lyons, Porteous, Falconer
19 Mar	A	Aberdeen University	W 2-0	350	Lyons, McGachie
25 Apr	H	FRASERBURGH	W 1-0	1,100	Porteous

Friendlies

31 Jul	A	Ross County	W 5-0	700	Black 2, Harrow 2, McMaster
02 Aug	A	Nairn County	W 5-0	1,006	Harrow 2, McGhee, McCall, McLeish
03 Aug	A	Inverness Thistle	W 4-0	2,534	Strachan 3, Black
07 Aug	H	IPSWICH TOWN	L 0-1	8,210	
09 Aug	A	Stirling Albion	W 3-0	802	McGhee, Lyons, Hewitt

			Home					*Away*						*TOTALS*				
		P	W	D	L	F	A	W	D	L	F	A	Pts	W	D	L	F	A
1	Dundee Utd	36	13	4	1	57	18	11	4	3	33	17	56	24	8	4	90	35
2	Celtic	36	12	3	3	44	18	13	2	3	46	18	55	25	5	6	90	36
3	ABERDEEN	36	14	0	4	46	12	11	5	2	30	12	55	25	5	6	76	24
4	Rangers	36	9	6	3	32	16	4	6	8	20	25	38	13	12	11	52	41
5	St Mirren	36	8	5	5	30	18	3	7	8	17	33	34	11	12	13	47	51
6	Dundee	36	8	3	7	29	28	1	8	9	13	25	29	9	11	16	42	53
7	Hibernian	36	3	11	4	21	17	4	4	10	14	34	29	7	15	14	35	51
8	Motherwell	36	9	3	6	28	27	2	2	14	11	46	27	11	5	20	39	73
9	Morton	36	4	4	10	14	26	2	4	12	16	48	20	6	8	22	30	74
10	Kilmarnock	36	3	7	8	17	31	0	4	14	11	60	17	3	11	22	28	91

Attendance Records 1982/83

Highest Home Attendance	24,000	v Celtic 11 Dec 1982, v Celtic 23 Apr 1983, v Hibernian 14 May 1983, v Bayern Munich 16 Mar 1983, v Waterschei 6 Apr 1983
Highest Away Attendance	42,831	v Celtic 12 Feb 1983
Highest Neutral Attendance	62,979	v Rangers 21 May 1983
Lowest Home Attendance	6,500	v Dumbarton 21 Aug 1982
Lowest Away Attendance	750	v Dumbarton 8 Sep 1982
Average Home Attendance	15,561	All Competitive Matches
Average Away Attendance	12,059	All Competitive Matches
Average Neutral Attendance	43,977	All Competitive Matches
Overall Average Attendance	15,289	All Competitve Matches
Overall Attendance	917,338	All Competitive Matches

SEASON SUMMARY

	P	W	D	L	F	A
Premier League	36	25	5	6	76	24
Scottish Cup	5	5	0	0	9	2
League Cup	8	4	2	2	19	11
ECWC	11	8	2	1	25	6
Aberdeenshire Cup	3	3	0	0	7	0
Friendlies	5	4	0	1	17	1
TOTAL	68	49	9	10	153	44

Home Wins	22	All Competitive Matches
Away Wins	17	All Competitive Matches
Most Wins in a row	6	
Unbeaten games in a row	16	
Most Losses in a row	2	
Clean Sheets	28	All Competitive Matches

RECORD

Premier League	Third
Scottish Cup	Winners
League Cup	Quarter-Final
ECWC	Winners

Debuts

Willie Falconer	v Waterschei 19 Apr 1983
Ian Porteous	v Kilmarnock 5 May 1983
Bryan Gunn	v Hibernian 30 Oct 1982

Final Appearances

Walker McCall	v Hibernian 1 Jan 1983
Stuart Kennedy	v Waterschei 19 Apr 1983
Derek Hamilton	v Hibernian 14 May 1983
Andy Watson	v Rangers 21 May 1983

STATS OF THE SEASON

Aberdeen win their first European trophy by defeating Real Madrid 2-1 in the final of the ECWC in Gothenburg on 11 May 1983

Aberdeen retain the Scottish Cup, for the first time in club history after a 1-0 win over Rangers in the final on 21 May 1983

INTERNATIONAL NOTES

Jim Leighton capped for Scotland v East Germany 13 Oct 1982, v Switzerland 17 Nov 1982, v Belgium 15 Dec 1982, v Switzerland 30 Mar 1983, v Wales 28 May 1983, v England 1 Jun 1983, v Canada 16 Jun 1983, v Canada 19 Jun 1983

Willie Miller capped for Scotland v East Germany 13 Oct 1982, v Switzerland 17 Nov 1982, v Switzerland 30 Mar 1983, v Wales 28 May 1983, v England 1 Jun 1983, v Canada 12 Jun 1983, v Canada 16 Jun 1983, v Canada 19 Jun 1983

Gordon Strachan capped for Scotland v East Germany 13 Oct 1982, v Switzerland 17 Nov 1982, v Belgium 15 Dec 1982, v Switzerland 30 Mar 1983, v N Ireland 24 May 1983, v Wales 28 May 1983, v England 1 Jun 1983, v Canada 12 Jun 1983, v Canada 16 Jun 1983, v Canada 19 Jun 1983

Alex McLeish capped for Scotland v Belgium 15 Dec 1982, v Switzerland 30 Mar 1983, v Wales 28 May 1983, v England 1 Jun 1983, v Canada 12 Jun 1983, v Canada 16 Jun 1983, v Canada 19 Jun 1983

Peter Weir capped for Scotland v Switzerland 30 Mar 1983

Neil Simpson capped for Scotland v N Ireland 24 May 1983

Mark McGhee capped for Scotland v Canada 12 Jun 1983, v Canada 16 Jun 1983

Neil Simpson capped for Scotland U-21 v East Germany 12 Oct 1982, v Switzerland 16 Nov 1982, v Belgium 14 Dec 1982, v Switzerland 29 Mar 1983

Neale Cooper capped for Scotland U-21 v East Germany 12 Oct 1982, v Switzerland 16 Nov 1982, Belgium 14 Dec 1982, v Switzerland 29 Mar 1983

Eric Black capped for Scotland U-21 v East Germany 12 Oct 1982, v Switzerland 16 Nov 1982, v Belgium 14 Dec 1982, v Switzerland 29 Mar 1983

John Hewitt capped for Scotland v East Germany 12 Oct 1982, v Switzerland 16 Nov 1982, v Switzerland 29 Mar 1983

SEASON 1983/84

Date		Premier League	F-A	Att	
20 Aug	H	DUNDEE	W 3-0*	14,304	Strachan, Hewitt
03 Sep	H	ST JOHNSTONE	W 5-0	12,400	Black 2, McGhee, Stark, Miller
10 Sep	A	Motherwell	D 1-1	6,217	McGhee
17 Sep	A	Rangers	W 2-0	27,500	McGhee 2
24 Sep	H	DUNDEE UTD	L 1-2	21,100	Strachan
01 Oct	A	Hearts	W 2-0	18,200	Weir 2
08 Oct	H	ST MIRREN	W 5-0	13,300	Stark 2, McGhee, Miller, Falconer
15 Nov	A	Hibernian	L 1-2	7,000	Rougvie
22 Oct	H	CELTIC	W 3-1	22,800	McLeish, Strachan, Hewitt
29 Oct	A	Dundee	W 3-1	7,849	Strachan, Bell, Weir
05 Nov	A	St Johnstone	W 5-0	6,074	Hewitt 3, Strachan, Weir
12 Nov	H	RANGERS	W 3-0	22,800	Simpson, Hewitt, Porteous
19 Nov	H	HEARTS	W 2-0	19,800	Rougvie, Simpson
26 Nov	A	Dundee Utd	W 2-0	16,902	Strachan, Bell
03 Dec	H	MOTHERWELL	W 3-1	17,700	Strachan, Falconer, McGhee
10 Dec	A	Celtic	D 0-0	25,867	
17 Dec	H	HIBERNIAN	W 2-1*	14,000	McGhee
24 Dec	A	St Mirren	W 3-0	6,654	McLeish, McGhee, Bell
31 Dec	H	DUNDEE	W 5-2*	18,250	Strachan 2, Weir, Hewitt
07 Jan	A	Rangers	D 1-1	37,500	Hewitt
04 Feb	H	CELTIC	W 1-0	23,000	Hewitt
11 Feb	A	Motherwell	W 4-0	6,051	Strachan 2, Hewitt, Black
25 Feb	A	Hibernian	W 2-0	8,500	Black, McGhee
03 Mar	H	ST MIRREN	W 2-0	14,500	Strachan, Hewitt
31 Mar	A	Celtic	L 0-1	19,193	
02 Apr	H	HEARTS	D 1-1	16,240	Porteous
07 Apr	H	MOTHERWELL	W 2-1	15,500	Strachan, McGhee
18 Apr	H	DUNDEE UTD	W 5-1	19,562	Rougvie 2, McGhee 2, Black
21 Apr	A	St Johnstone	W 2-0	6,197	Stark, McGhee
28 Apr	A	Dundee	W 1-0	6,663	Black
30 Apr	H	ST JOHNSTONE	W 1-0	11,500	Hewitt
02 May	A	Hearts	W 1-0	14,000	McKimmie
05 May	H	HIBERNIAN	D 2-2	17,000	Porteous, Stark
07 May	A	Dundee Utd	D 0-0	7,990	
09 May	H	RANGERS	D 0-0	16,200	
12 May	A	St Mirren	L 2-3*	3,450	Stark

League Cup

24 Aug	H	RAITH ROVERS	W 9-0	9,650	Black 4, Stark 3, Hewitt, Porteous
27 Aug	A	Raith Rovers	W 3-0	3,000	Hewitt 2, Stark
31 Aug	H	MEADOWBANK	W 4-0	10,000	McGhee 2, Stark, Black
07 Sep	A	St Johnstone	W 1-0	5,100	Miller
05 Oct	H	DUNDEE	D 0-0	13,200	
26 Oct	H	ST JOHNSTONE	W 1-0	12,700	Simpson

09 Nov	A	Meadowbank	W 3-1*	2,700	Hewitt, Porteous
30 Nov	A	Dundee	W 2-1	11,019	McGhee, Bell
22 Feb	H	CELTIC	D 0-0	20,074	
10 Mar	A	Celtic	L 0-1	41,169	

Scottish Cup

13 Feb	H	KILMARNOCK	D 1-1	15,000	Weir
15 Feb	A	Kilmarnock	W 3-1	9,580	Miller, Strachan, Weir
18 Feb	A	Clyde	W 2-0	5,800	Cooper, Angus
17/Mar	H	DUNDEE UTD	D 0-0	22,000	
28 Mar	A	Dundee Utd	W 1-0	16,094	McGhee
14 Apr	N	Dundee	W 2-0	17,654	Strachan, Porteous
19 May	N	Celtic (aet)	W 2-1	58,900	Black, McGhee

ECWC

14 Sep	A	IA Akranes	W 2-1	5,500	McGhee 2
28 Sep	H	IA AKRANES	D 1-1	12,500	Strachan
19 Oct	A	Beveren	D 0-0	21,000	
02 Nov	H	BEVEREN	W 4-1	22,500	Strachan 2, Simpson, Weir
07 Mar	A	Ujpesti Dozsa	L 0-2	29,000	
21 Mar	H	UJPESTI DOZSA (aet)	W 3-0	22,800	McGhee 3
11 Apr	A	Porto	L 0-1	65,000	
25 Apr	H	PORTO	L 0-1	23,000	

European Super Cup

22 Nov	A	SV Hamburg	D 0-0	15,000	
20 Dec	H	SV HAMBURG	W 2-0	22,500	Simpson, McGhee

Friendlies

24 Jul	A	Salmrohr	L 0-2		
26 Jul	A	Schwetzingen	W 4-1	4,000	Simpson, Stark, Cowan, Bell
27 Jul	A	Luttringhausen	W 3-0	7,000	McGhee, Hewitt, Cowan
29 Jul	A	Offenbach Kickers	L 2-3		Strachan 2
30 Jul	A	Hassia Bizen	D 2-2		Simpson, Strachan
31 Jul	A	Dinamo Bucharest	L 0-2	700	
03 Aug	A	Eisbachtal	W 1-0		Hewitt
06 Aug	A	Nuremburg	D 1-1	3,500	Miller
10 Aug	A	Forfar Athletic	W 3-2*	650	Bell, Falconer
13 Aug	H	ARSENAL	L 0-1	11,700	
15 Aug	A	Ipswich Town	L 0-3	8,000	
17 Aug	A	Manchester United	D 2-2	18,042	Weir 2
28 Jan	A	Aldershot	W 4-0	3,000	Black 2, Hewitt, Weir

			Home					*Away*						*TOTALS*				
		P	W	D	L	F	A	W	D	L	F	A	Pts	W	D	L	F	A
1	ABERDEEN	36	14	3	1	46	12	11	4	3	32	9	57	25	7	4	78	21
2	Celtic	36	13	5	0	46	15	8	3	7	34	26	50	21	8	7	80	41
3	Dundee Utd	36	11	3	4	38	14	7	8	3	29	25	47	18	11	7	67	39
4	Rangers	36	7	8	3	26	18	8	4	6	27	23	42	15	12	9	53	41
5	Hearts	36	5	9	4	23	23	5	7	6	15	24	36	10	16	10	38	47
6	St Mirren	36	8	6	4	34	23	1	8	9	21	36	32	9	14	13	55	59
7	Hibernian	36	7	4	7	21	21	5	3	10	24	34	31	12	7	17	45	55
8	Dundee	36	6	1	11	28	42	5	4	9	22	32	27	11	5	20	50	74
9	St Johnstone	36	6	1	11	19	33	4	2	12	17	48	23	10	3	23	36	81
10	Motherwell	36	2	5	11	15	36	2	2	14	16	39	15	4	7	25	31	75

Attendance Records 1983/84

Highest Home Attendance	23,000	v Porto 25 Apr 1984, v Celtic 4 Feb 1984
Highest Away Attendance	65,000	v Porto 11 Apr 1984
Highest Neutral Attendance	58,900	v Celtic 19 May 1984
Lowest Home Attendance	9,650	v Raith Rovers 24 Aug 1983
Lowest Away Attendance	2,700	v Meadowbank Thistle 9 Nov 1983
Average Home Attendance	17,196	All Competitive Matches
Average Away Attendance	14,892	All Competitive Matches
Average Neutral Attendance	38,277	All Competitive Matches
Overall Average Attendance	16,732	All Competitive Matches
Overall Attendance	1,054,092	All Competitive Matches

SEASON SUMMARY	P	W	D	L	F	A
Premier League	36	25	7	4	78	21
Scottish Cup	7	5	2	0	11	3
League Cup	10	7	2	1	23	3
ECWC	8	3	2	3	10	7
European Super Cup	2	1	1	0	2	0
Friendlies	13	5	3	5	22	19
TOTAL	76	46	17	13	146	53

Home Wins	20	All Competitive Matches
Away Wins	19	All Competitive Matches
Most Wins in a row	8	All Competitive Matches
Unbeaten games in a row	27	All Competitive Matches
Most Losses in a row	2	All Competitive Matches
Clean Sheets	36	All Competitive Matches

RECORD

Premier League	Winners
Scottish Cup	Winners
League Cup	Semi-Final
ECWC	Semi-Final
European Super Cup	Winners

Debuts

Billy Stark	v Dundee 20 Aug 1983
Tommy McIntyre	v Dundee 5 Oct 1983
Stewart McKimmie	v Hibernian 17 Dec 1983
Paul Wright	v Hearts 2 Apr 1984
Ian Robertson	v St Mirren 12 May 1984

Final Appearances

Doug Rougvie	v Celtic 19 May 1984
Gordon Strachan	v Celtic 19 May 1984
Mark McGhee	v Celtic 19 May 1984

STATS OF THE SEASON

Aberdeen finished the season with a new Premier League record 57 points

The Dons continued their unbeaten sequence in the Scottish Cup that extended to 18 games

Aberdeen create a new record of consecutive matches without defeat when they remain unbeaten for four and a half months on their way to a league and cup double.

INTERNATIONAL NOTES

Jim Leighton capped for Scotland v Uruguay 21 Sep 1983, v Belgium 12 Oct 1983, v N Ireland 13 Dec 1983, v Wales 28 Feb 1984, v England 26 May 1984, v France 1 Jun 1984

Wille Miller capped for Scotland v Uruguay 21 Sep 1983, v Belgium 12 Oct 1983, v East Germany 16 Nov 1983, v Wales 28 Feb 1984, v England 26 May 1984, v France 1 Jun 1984

Alex McLeish capped for Scotland v Uruguay 21 Sep 1983, v Belgium 12 Oct 1983, v East Germany 16 Nov 1983, v N Ireland 13 Dec 1983, v Wales 28 Feb 1984, v England 26 May 1984, v France 1 Jun 1984
Neil Simpson capped for Scotland v Uruguay 21 Sep 1983, v France 1 Jun 1984

Gordon Strachan capped for Scotland v East Germany 16 Nov 1983, v N Ireland 13 Dec 1983, v England 26 May 1984, v France 1 Jun 1984

Doug Rougvie capped v N Ireland 13 Dec 1983

Peter Weir capped v N Ireland 13 Dec 1983

Mark McGhee capped for Scotland v N Ireland 13 Dec 1983, v England 26 May 1984

Bryan Gunn capped for Scotland U-21 v Yugoslavia 4 Apr 1984, v Yugoslavia 14 Mar 1984, v East Germany 15 Nov 1983

John Hewitt capped for Scotland U-21 v Yugoslavia 4 Apr 1984, Belgium 11 Oct 1983

Neale Cooper capped for Scotland U-21 v Yugoslavia 14 Mar 1984, v East Germany 15 Nov 1983, v Belgium 11 Oct 1983

Neil Simpson capped for Scotland U-21 v Yugoslavia 14 Mar 1984, v East Germany 15 Nov 1983, v Belgium 11 Oct 1983

Doug Bell capped for Scotland U-21 v Yugoslavia 14 Mar 1984

Pittodrie was the venue for the Scotland U21 clash with Yugoslavia on 14 March 1984

Aberdeen had a record six players in the Scotland team against Northern Ireland in Belfast in December 1983. It would have been seven had it not been for a rare injury to Willie Miller

SEASON 1984/85

Date		Premier League	F-A	Att	
11 Aug	H	DUNDEE	W 3-2	14,700	Black 2, Stark
18 Aug	A	St Mirren	W 2-0	5,445	Stark, Falconer
25 Aug	A	Dundee Utd	W 2-0	13,033	Black 2
01 Sep	H	HIBERNIAN	W 4-1	14,500	McKimmie, Black, Simpson, McDougall
08 Sep	A	Morton	W 3-0	5,000	Stark, Black, Falconer
15 Sep	H	RANGERS	D 0-0	23,000	
22 Sep	A	Dumbarton	W 2-0	4,500	Miller, Falconer
29 Sep	H	HEARTS	W 4-0	16,344	McDougall 2, Angus, Falconer
06 Oct	A	Celtic	L 1-2	31,418	McDougall
13 Oct	A	Dundee	W 2-1	10,990	McDougall, Stark
20 Oct	H	ST MIRREN	W 4-0	14,100	McDougall 2, Stark, Porteous
06 Nov	A	Hibernian	W 3-0	8,000	Stark, McDougall, Black
10 Nov	H	MORTON	W 3-1	14,500	Miller, Simpson, McDougall
17 Nov	A	Rangers	W 2-1	44,000	Stark, McDougall
24 Nov	H	DUMBARTON	W 1-0	13,200	McDougall
01 Dec	A	Hearts	W 2-1	10,037	Stark, Cowan
08 Dec	H	CELTIC	W 4-2	23,000	Black 2, McKimmie, McDougall
15 Dec	H	DUNDEE	D 0-0	14,000	
22 Dec	H	DUNDEE UTD	L 0-1	16,354	
29 Dec	A	St Mirren	D 2-2	6,287	McDougall 2
02 Jan	A	Dundee Utd	L 1-2	21,944	McQueen
05 Jan	H	HIBERNIAN	W 2-0	13,700	McKimmie, Weir
12 Jan	H	MORTON	W 5-0	11,000	Cooper, McDougall, Weir, Mitchell, Cowan

19 Jan	H	RANGERS	W 5-1	23,000	McDougall 3, McQueen, Black
02 Feb	A	Dumbarton	W 2-0	3,500	Black, Stark
09 Feb	H	HEARTS	D 2-2	14,700	Simpson, Weir
23 Feb	A	Celtic	L 0-2	48,834	
02 Mar	H	ST MIRREN	W 3-0	12,000	Stark, Black, Cowan
16 Mar	A	Dundee	W 4-0	9,161	Stark 2, Black, Simpson
23 Mar	A	Hibernian	W 5-0	9,000	Black 3, McQueen, Hewitt
30 Mar	H	DUNDEE UTD	W 4-2	15,600	Hewitt 2, Stark, Cowan
06 Apr	A	Rangers	W 2-1	23,437	Black, Cowan
20 Apr	H	DUMBARTON	W 4-0*	12,500	Stark, McLeish, Angus
27 Apr	H	CELTIC	D 1-1	23,000	Miller
04 May	A	Hearts	W 3-0	8,251	McDougall 3
11 May	A	Morton	W 2-1	3,600	Stark, McDougall

League Cup

22 Aug	A	Airdrie	L 1-3	5,000	Stark

Scottish Cup

30 Jan	H	ALLOA ATH	W 5-0	13,500	Stark 3, Simpson, Hewitt
16 Feb	A	Raith Rovers	W 2-1	10,000	McDougall 2
09 Mar	A	Hearts	D 1-1	23,900	Black
13 Mar	H	HEARTS	W 1-0	23,000	Stark
13 Apr	N	Dundee Utd	D 0-0	18,485	
17 Apr	N	Dundee Utd	L 1-2	10,771	Angus

European Cup

19 Sep	H	DINAMO BERLIN	W 2-1	20,000	Black 2
03 Oct	A	Dinamo Berlin (aet)	L 1-2	20,000	Angus

Friendlies

01 Aug	A	Viktoria Gogh	W 2-0	1,500	Stark, McLeish
02 Aug	A	Bayer Leverkusen	L 0-2	5,000	
03 Aug	A	1890 Berlin	L 0-1		
04 Aug	A	Stuttgart Kickers	W 1-0	2,000	Black
05 Aug	A	VFL Frohnlach	W 2-0		Hewitt 2
13 Aug	A	Leicester City	D 1-1	7,400	Black
30 Oct	H	COVENTRY CITY	W 4-2*	10,000	McDougall 2, Angus
20 Nov	A	Forfar Athletic	W 2-1	2,168	Stark, McDougall
14 Jan	A	Ismaily SC	D 2-2	11,000	McDougall 2
19 Feb	A	Queens Park	W 4-0	300	Cowan 3, Hewitt

* denotes own goal

			Home					*Away*						*TOTALS*				
		P	W	D	L	F	A	W	D	L	F	A	Pts	W	D	L	F	A
1	ABERDEEN	36	13	4	1	49	13	14	1	3	40	13	59	27	5	4	89	26
2	Celtic	36	12	3	3	43	12	10	5	3	34	18	52	22	8	6	77	30
3	Dundee Utd	36	13	2	3	47	18	7	5	6	20	15	47	20	7	9	67	33
4	Rangers	36	7	6	5	21	14	6	6	6	26	24	38	13	12	11	47	38
5	St Mirren	36	10	2	6	29	24	7	2	9	22	32	38	17	4	15	51	56
6	Dundee	36	9	3	6	25	19	6	4	8	23	31	37	15	7	14	48	50
7	Hearts	36	6	3	9	21	26	7	2	9	26	38	31	13	5	18	47	64
8	Hibernian	36	5	4	9	23	30	5	3	10	15	31	27	10	7	19	38	61
9	Dumbarton	36	4	4	10	17	29	2	3	13	12	35	19	6	7	23	29	64
10	Morton	36	3	1	14	18	44	2	1	15	11	56	12	5	2	29	29	100

Attendance Records 1984/85

Highest Home Attendance	23,000	v Rangers 15 Sep 1984, v Celtic 8 Dec 1984, v Rangers 19 Jan 1985, v Hearts SC 13 Mar 1985, v Celtic 27 Apr 1985
Highest Away Attendance	48,834	v Celtic 23 Feb 1985
Highest Neutral Attendance	18,485	v Dundee Utd 13 Apr 1985
Lowest Home Attendance	11,000	v Morton 12 January 1985
Lowest Away Attendance	3,500	v Dumbarton 2 February 1985
Average Home Attendance	16,462	All Competitive Matches
Average Away Attendance	14,794	All Competitive Matches
Average Neutral Attendance	14,628	All Competitive Matches
Overall Average Attendance	15,565	All Competitive Matches
Overall Attendance	700,431	All Competitive Matches

SEASON SUMMARY

	P	W	D	L	F	A
Premier League	36	27	5	4	89	26
Scottish Cup	6	3	2	1	10	4
League Cup	1	0	0	1	1	3
European Cup	2	1	0	1	3	3
Friendlies	10	6	2	2	18	9
TOTAL	55	37	9	9	121	45

Home Wins	16	All Competitive Matches
Away Wins	15	All Competitive Matches
Wins in a row	8	All Competitive Matches
Unbeaten games in a row	9	All Competitive Matches
Losses in a row	2	All Competitive Matches
Clean Sheets	21	All Competitive Matches

RECORD

Premier League	Winners
Scottish Cup	Semi-Final
League Cup	Second Round
European Cup	First Round

Debuts

Frank McDougall	v St Mirren 18 August 1984
Joe Miller	v Dundee Utd 22 December 1984
Brian Grant	v Airdrie 22 August 1984
Tom McQueen	v Dundee 11 August 1984

Final Appearances

Steve Cowan	v Hearts 4 May 1985
Doug Bell	v Morton 11 May 1985

STATS OF THE SEASON

Aberdeen reatined the Premier League title for the first time with a new record 59 points and a record 89 goals scored.

U-18 side win the inaugural Scottish Youth Cup defeating Celtic 5-3 at Pittodrie after being 0-3 down at one stage.

SEASON 1985/86

Date		Premier League	F-A	Att	
10 Aug	H	HIBERNIAN	W 3-0	14,846	McDougall 2, Bett
17 Aug	A	Dundee Utd	D 1-1	14,339	McKimmie
24 Aug	H	MOTHERWELL	D 1-1	14,059	McKimmie
31 Aug	A	Dundee	W 3-1	7,592	Stark 2, Simpson
07 Sep	H	HEARTS	W 3-0	12,300	Stark, Black, Wright
14 Sep	A	Celtic	L 1-2	39,450	McDougall
21 Sep	H	ST MIRREN	D 1-1	12,585	McQueen
28 Sep	A	Rangers	W 3-0	27,599	Stark, McLeish, Hewitt
05 Oct	H	CLYDEBANK	W 3-1	11,399	McKimmie, Black, McDougall
12 Oct	A	Hibernian	D 1-1	10,377	Gray
19 Oct	H	DUNDEE UTD	W 3-2	15,148	Hewitt 2, McDougall
30 Oct	A	Hearts	L 0-1	12,866	
02 Nov	H	CELTIC	W 4-1	23,000	McDougall 4
09 Nov	H	DUNDEE	W 4-1	12,600	Stark 2, McLeish, McDougall
16 Nov	A	Motherwell	D 1-1	4,960	McDougall
23 Nov	A	St Mirren	L 0-1	5,930	
10 Dec	A	Clydebank	L 1-2	2,095	Black
14 Dec	H	HIBERNIAN	W 4-0	11,819	McLeish, Angus, J Miller, Weir
21 Dec	A	Dundee Utd	L 1-2	10,085	Stark
01 Jan	A	Dundee	D 0-0	9,096	
04 Jan	H	ST MIRREN	W 3-1	11,500	Black 2, Weir
11 Jan	A	Celtic	D 1-1	31,305	J Miller
18 Jan	H	HEARTS	L 0-1	21,500	
01 Feb	A	Rangers	D 1-1	29,887	J Miller
08 Feb	H	CLYDEBANK	W 4-1	11,000	Black 3, Bett
19 Feb	H	RANGERS	W 1-0	18,700	Angus
22 Feb	A	Hibernian	W 1-0	9,500	Wright
15 Mar	A	St Mirren	D 1-1	4,448	W Miller
22 Mar	H	DUNDEE	D 0-0	13,013	
29 Mar	A	Motherwell	W 1-0	4,597	Hewitt
09 Apr	H	MOTHERWELL	W 3-2	10,300	McDougall, Bett, Weir
12 Apr	H	CELTIC	L 0-1	22,000	
16 Apr	H	DUNDEE UTD	L 0-1	8,500	
20 Apr	A	Hearts	D 1-1	19,047	Weir
26 Apr	H	RANGERS	D 1-1	17,000	Hewitt
03 May	A	Clydebank	W 6-0	2,382	McDougall 2, Weir, McMaster, Stark, Hewitt
League Cup					
21 Aug	H	AYR UTD	W 5-0	12,400	McDougall 2, Stark 2, McQueen
28 Aug	A	St Johnstone	W 2-0	5,100	Hewitt, McDougall
04 Sep	H	HEARTS	W 1-0	13,100	Black
25 Sep	A	Dundee Utd	W 1-0	12,837	Black
09 Oct	H	DUNDEE UTD	W 1-0	20,000	McDougall
27 Oct	N	Hibernian	W 3-0	40,061	Black 2, Stark
Scottish Cup					
05 Feb	H	MONTROSE	W 4-1	9,000	Stark, McLeish, W Miller, McDougall
15 Feb	A	Arbroath	W 1-0	6,017	J Miller
08 Mar	A	Dundee	D 2-2	13,188	Hewitt 2
12 Mar	H	DUNDEE (aet)	W 2-1	21,000	Black Weir
05 Apr	N	Hibernian	W 3-0	19,165	Stark, Black, J Miller
10 May	N	Hearts	W 3-0	62,841	Hewitt 2, Stark
European Cup					
18 Sep	A	IA Akranes	W 3-1	7,000	Stark, Black, Hewitt
02 Oct	H	IA AKRANES	W 4-1	14,700	Hewitt, Gray, Simpson, Falconer
23 Oct	A	Servette	D 0-0	8,000	
06 Nov	H	SERVETTE	W 1-0	19,000	McDougall

05 Mar	H	IFK GOTHENBURG	D 2-2	22,000	W Miller, Hewitt
19 Mar	A	IFK Gothenburg	D 0-0^	44,400	

Friendlies

21 Jul	A	Solothurn	W 3-0		McDougall, McQueen, Stark
24 Jul	A	Neuchatel	L 0-1	2,000	
26 Jul	A	Sion	D 0-0	2,500	
28 Jul	A	Schaffhausen	W 2-1		Hewitt, Black
30 Jul	A	Lausanne	W 6-2		Falconer 2, Irvine, McDougall, J Miller, Gray
03 Aug	A	Meadowbank Thistle	D 2-2	600	Hewitt, Bett
04 Aug	A	Inverness Caley	W 4-1	1,500	McKimmie, Stark, Hewitt, Polwarth
07 Aug	A	Dunfermline	L 0-1	5,500	
01 Dec	A	Deveronvale	W 6-0		Black 2, McDougall 2, Hewitt, Stark 16
Dec	H	BILLY McNEILL SELECT	L 1-3	16,500	McDougall
07 Jan	A	Arbroath	W 5-0	700	McMaster, Angus, McDougall, Bett, Walker

* denotes own goal
^ lost on away goals

			Home					*Away*						*TOTALS*				
		P	W	D	L	F	A	W	D	L	F	A	Pts	W	D	L	F	A
1	Celtic	36	10	6	2	27	15	10	4	4	40	23	50	20	10	6	67	38
2	Hearts	36	13	5	0	38	10	7	5	6	21	23	50	20	10	6	59	33
3	Dundee Utd	36	10	6	2	38	15	8	5	5	21	16	47	18	11	7	59	31
4	ABERDEEN	36	11	4	3	38	15	5	8	5	24	16	44	16	12	8	62	31
5	Rangers	36	10	4	4	34	18	3	5	10	19	27	35	13	9	14	53	45
6	Dundee	36	11	2	5	32	20	3	5	10	13	31	35	14	7	15	45	51
7	St Mirren	36	9	2	7	26	24	4	3	11	16	39	31	13	5	18	42	63
8	Hibernian	36	6	4	8	27	25	5	2	11	22	38	28	11	6	19	49	63
9	Motherwell	36	7	3	8	23	23	0	3	15	10	43	20	7	6	23	33	66
10	Clydebank	36	4	6	8	18	32	2	2	14	11	45	20	6	8	22	29	77

Attendance Records 1985/86

Highest Home Attendance	23,000	v Celtic 2 Nov 1985
Highest Away Attendance	44,400	v IFK Gothenburg 19 Mar 1986
Highest Neutral Attendance	62,841	v Hearts 10 May 1986
Lowest Home Attendance	8,500	v Dundee Utd 16 Apr 1986
Lowest Away Attendance	2,095	v Clydebank 10 December 1985
Average Home Attendance	15,065	All Competitive Matches
Average Away Attendance	14,084	All Competitive Matches
Average Neutral Attendance	40,689	All Competitive Matches
Overall average Attendance	16,034	All Competitive Matches
Overall Attendance	865,846	All Competitive Matches

SEASON SUMMARY	P	W	D	L	F	A
Premier League	36	16	12	8	62	31
Scottish Cup	6	5	1	0	15	4
League Cup	6	6	0	0	13	0
European Cup	6	3	3	0	10	4
Friendlies	11	6	2	3	29	11
TOTAL	65	36	18	11	129	50

Home Wins	18	All Competitive Matches
Away Wins	9	All Competitive Matches
Wins in a row	5	All Competitive Matches
Unbeaten games in a row	15	All Competitive Matches
Losses in a row	2	All Competitive Matches
Clean Sheets	22	All Competitive Matches

RECORD

Premier League	Fourth
Scottish Cup	Winners
League Cup	Winners
European Cup	Quarter-Final

Debuts

Jim Bett	v Hibernian 10 Aug 1985
Brian Irvine	v Clydebank 3 May 1986
Steve Gray	v St Johnstone LC 28 Aug 1985

Final Appearances

Eric Black	v Hearts 20 Apr 1986
Neale Cooper	v Hearts SC 10 May 1986

STATS OF THE SEASON

Aberdeen won the League Cup by keeping a clean sheet in all six ties, including the 3-0 win over Hibernian in the final

Aberdeen won both domestic cups for the first time in club history with Hampden wins over Hibernian in the League Cup and Hearts in the Scottish Cup

INTERNATIONAL NOTES

Jim Leighton capped for Scotland v Wales 10 Sep 1985, v East Germany 16 Oct 1985, v Australia 20 Nov 1985, v Australia 4 Dec 1985, v Israel 28 Jan 1986, v Denmark 4 Jun 1986, v West Germany 8 Jun 1986, v Uruguay 13 Jun 1986

Willie Miller capped for Scotland v Wales 10 Sep 1985, v East Germany 16 Oct 1985, v Australia 20 Nov 1985, v Australia 4 Dec 1985, vIsrael 28 Jan 1986, v Romania 26 Mar 1986, v England 23 Apr 1986, v Netherlands 29 Apr 1986, v Denmark 4 Jun 1986, v West Germany 8 Jun 1986, v Uruguay 13 Jun 1986

Alex McLeish capped for Scotland v Wales 10 Sep 1985, v East Germany 16 Oct 1985, v Australia 20 Nov 1985, v Australia 4 Dec 1985, v England 23 Apr 1986, v Netherlands 29 Apr 1986, v Denmark 4 Jun 1986

Jim Bett capped for Scotland v Wales 10 Sep 1985, v Australia 20 Nov 1985, v Israel 28 Jan 1986, v Netherlands 29 Apr 1986

SEASON 1986/87

Date		Premier League	F-A	Att	
09 Aug	A	Dundee Utd	L 1-2	10,910	Stark
13 Aug	H	HIBERNIAN	W 4-0	12,983	Stark, Gray, J Miller, Angus
16 Aug	H	HAMILTON	W 2-0	10,316	Stark 2
23 Aug	A	Celtic	D 1-1	46,073	J Miller
30 Aug	H	DUNDEE	W 2-0	12,486	J Miller, Hewitt
06 Sep	A	St Mirren	D 1-1	4,435	Stark
13 Sep	H	HEARTS	L 0-1	15,625	
20 Sep	A	Clydebank	W 3-1	2,766	Hewitt 2, Weir
27 Sep	A	Rangers	L 0-2	40,155	
04 Oct	H	MOTHERWELL	D 2-2	8,751	W Miller, Dodds
08 Oct	A	Falkirk	D 3-3	4,800	Stark, McLeish, Bett
11 Oct	H	DUNDEE UTD	W 2-0	14,922	Hewitt 2
18 Oct	A	Hibernian	D 1-1	9,127	Connor
25 Oct	A	Hamilton	W 1-0	3,001	Bett
01 Nov	A	Dundee	W 2-0	8,200	Porteous, Dodds
League Cup					
20 Aug	H	ALLOA ATH	W 4-0	8,052	Hewitt 2, J Miller, Connor
27 Aug	H	CLYDE	W 3-1	8,081	Stark 2, J Miller
03 Sep	H	CELTIC	L 1-1^	21,509	Connor
ECWC					
17 Sep	H	SION	W 2-1	12,312	Bett, Wright
01 Oct	A	Sion	L 0-3	11,800	
Friendlies					
22 Jul	A	Gunnilse	D 1-1		McDougall
24 Jul	A	Groheds IF	D 1-1		J Miller
27 Jul	A	Vara	W 3-0	800	Irvine, Angus, J Miller
29 Jul	A	IFK Trollhattan	W 4-0		McDougall 3, McMaster
02 Aug	H	STUTTGART	L 0-2	7,000	
05 Aug	A	Dunfermline	D 2-2	3,000	Falconer, McLeish
03 Nov	A	Inverness Caley	W 5-1	3,000	J Miller 2, Wright 2, Dodds

* denotes own goal
^ lost on pens

		Home							*TOTALS*				
	P	W	D	L	F	A	Pts	W	D	L	F	A
1	Celtic	15	11	3	1	36	8	25	36	3	1	36	8
2	Dundee Utd	16	10	5	1	30	11	25	35	5	1	30	11
3	Rangers	15	9	3	3	26	10	21	30	3	3	26	10
4	Hearts	16	7	6	3	19	12	20	27	6	3	19	12
5	Aberdeen	15	7	5	3	25	14	19	26	5	3	25	14
6	Dundee Utd	16	8	2	6	19	15	18	26	2	6	19	15
7	St Mirren	16	5	5	6	13	15	15	20	5	6	13	15
8	Falkirk	16	3	5	8	13	23	11	14	5	8	13	23
9	Motherwell	16	2	7	7	15	27	11	13	7	7	15	27
10	Hibernian	16	3	5	8	16	34	11	14	5	8	16	34
11	Clydebank	16	4	2	10	11	28	10	14	2	10	11	28
12	Hamilton	15	0	2	13	8	34	2	2	2	13	8	34

Table at 1 November 1986

Attendance Records 1986/87

Highest Home Attendance	21,509	v Celtic 3 September 1986
Highest Away Attendance	46,073	v Celtic 23 August 1986
Lowest Home Attendance	8,052	v Alloa 20 August 1986
Lowest Away Attendance	2,766	v Clydebank 20 September 1986
Average Home Attendance	12,598	All Competitive Matches up to 6 November 1986
Average Away Attendance	14,127	All Competitive Matches up to 6 November 1986
Overall Attendance	267,243	All Competitive Matches up to 6 November 1986

SEASON SUMMARY

	P	W	D	L	F	A
Premier League	15	7	5	3	25	14
League Cup	3	2	0	1	8	2
ECWC	2	1	0	1	2	4
Friendlies	7	3	3	1	16	7
TOTAL	27	13	8	6	51	27

Home Wins	7	All Competitive Matches up to 6 Nov
Away Wins	3	All Competitive Matches up to 6 Nov
Wins in a row	2	All Competitive Matches up to 6 Nov
Unbeaten games in a row	6	All Competitive Matches up to 6 Nov
Losses in a row	2	All Competitive Matches up to 6 Nov
Clean Sheets	7	All Competitive Matches up to 6 Nov

RECORD at time of departure of Alex Ferguson

Premier League	5th
Scottish Cup	Competition not started
League Cup	Fourth Round
UEFA Cup	First Round

Debuts

David Robertson	v Hamilton 16 August 1986
Davie Dodds	v Rangers 27 September 1986
Robert Connor	v Hamilton 16 August 1986

Final Appearances

Bryan Gunn	v Dundee 30 August 1986
Tommy McQueen	v St Mirren 6 September 1986
Tommy McIntyre	v Hiberian 18 October 1986

INTERNATIONAL NOTES

Jim Leighton capped for Scotland v Bulgaria 10 Sep 1986
Willie Miller capped for Scotland v Bulgaria 10 Sep 1986
Steve Gray capped for Scotland U-21 v Germany 9 Sep 1986

Head-to-Head Record Under Alex Ferguson

	Premier League			*Scottish Cup*			*League Cup*			*Europe*			*Total*			*Goals*	
	W	*L*	*D*	*W*	*L*	*D*	*W*	*L*	*D*	*W*	*L*	*D*	*W*	*L*	*D*	*F*	*A*
Dundee United	14	11	9	1	1	2	3	4	1				18	16	12	59	54
Glasgow Celtic	13	11	9	4		1	2	2	1				19	13	11	61	45
Glasgow Rangers	17	5	11	2	1		3	2					22	8	11	65	32
Dundee	22		4	3		1	2	1	3				27	1	8	79	21
Hibernian	18	2	10	2	1		2						22	3	10	79	20
St Mirren	16	6	11	1		1							17	6	12	70	34
Morton	13	9	2	0	1		2		1				15	10	3	52	27
Heart of Midlothian	13	4	4	2		1	2	1					17	5	5	48	14
Partick Thistle	9	1	6	2									11	1	6	27	14
Motherwell	11		6	1									12	0	6	45	13
Kilmarnock	8	3	1	2		1	2						12	3	2	39	13
Airdrieonians	6		2	1			1	1	1				8	1	3	32	4
St Johnstone	4						3						7	0	0	17	0
Meadowbank Thistle							5		1				5	0	1	23	3
Dumbarton	4						2						6	0	0	14	1
Hamilton Academical	2			1			2						5	0	0	13	1
Clydebank	4	1											4	1	0	17	5
Arbroath				2		1	1	1					3	1	1	12	3
Berwick Rangers							4						4	0	0	20	1
Ayr United				1			2		1				3	0	1	17	6
Raith Rovers				2			2						4	0	0	16	2
Alloa Athletic				1			1						2	0	0	9	0
Clyde				1			1						2	0	0	5	1
Falkirk			1										0	0	1	3	3
Montrose				1									1	0	0	4	1
Europe										23	12	12	23	12	12	74	46
Total	174	53	76	30	4	8	42	12	9	23	12	12	269	81	105	900	364

Under Alex Ferguson, Aberdeen played

25 Scottish clubs in competive matches

21 Different European clubs in European competition

9 Different English clubs in Friendlies or Testimonials

11 Different Highland League clubs in Friendlies or Testimonials

3 Select sides in Testimonials

5 Different Scottish clubs in Friendlies or Testimonials

30 Different European clubs in Friendly matches

1 club from Egypt in a Friendly match

TOTAL 105

Managers

	P	*W*	*D*	*L*	*F*	*A*	*% Win*
Travers, Paddy	571	269	128	174	1137	836	47.11%
Phillips, Jimmy	724	262	188	274	975	944	36.19%
Halliday, Dave	442	208	78	156	918	715	47.06%
Ferguson, Alex	435	259	100	76	865	344	59.54%
McInnes, Derek	377	202	73	102	565	382	53.58%
Turnbull, Eddie	294	141	60	93	536	377	47.96%
Shaw, Davie	197	95	24	78	429	375	48.22%
Pearson, Tommy	229	84	56	89	429	443	36.68%
Bonthrone, Jimmy	204	96	56	52	375	212	47.06%
Calderwood, Jimmy	226	94	57	75	293	266	41.59%
Miller, Willie	155	72	50	33	247	137	46.45%
Smith, Alex – Scott, Jocky	151	84	39	28	243	113	55.63%
Skovdahl, Ebbe	159	55	36	68	187	243	34.59%
Aitken, Roy	124	50	30	44	185	172	40.32%
Brown, Craig	112	37	32	43	131	131	33.04%
MacLeod, Ally	77	34	21	22	118	86	44.16%
Porterfield, Ian	88	43	32	13	116	49	48.86%
McNeill, Billy	50	31	11	8	102	46	62.00%
Paterson, Steve	68	23	13	32	82	97	33.82%
Robson, Barry	50	20	12	18	66	69	40.00%
Goodwin, Jim	43	17	7	19	66	61	39.53%
McGhee, Mark	62	17	13	32	65	99	27.42%
Glass, Stephen	40	14	6	20	51	58	35.00%
Miller, Alex	41	11	11	19	42	54	26.83%
Smith, Alex	27	8	8	11	37	35	29.63%
Ferguson, Alex – Knox, Archie	20	10	5	5	35	20	50.00%
Hegarty, Paul	20	7	2	11	28	44	35.00%
Leven, Peter	11	5	4	2	19	9	45.45%
Warnock, Neil	8	2	2	4	12	14	25.00%
irectors	4	2	2	0	8	5	50.00%
nox, Archie	3	1	1	1	6	2	33.33%
urray, George	4	2	0	2	5	6	50.00%
elin, Jimmy	1	1	0	0	3	0	100.00%
kinshaw, Keith	2	0	2	0	2	2	0.00%
erin, Paul	3	2	0	1	2	1	66.67%
s, Gardner	1	0	1	0	1	1	0.00%
A rson, Scott	1	1	0	0	1	0	100.00%
Co r, Neil / Simpson, Neil	1	0	0	1	0	5	0.00%
	5025	2259	1160	1606	8382	6453	44.96%

Up to nd including 13 July 2024